C000156699

NATIONAL CAPITALISMS, GLOBAL PRODUCTION NETWORKS

National Capitalisms, Global Production Networks

Fashioning the Value Chain in the UK, USA, and Germany

CHRISTEL LANE AND JOCELYN PROBERT

OXFORD
UNIVERSITY PRESS

OXFORD
UNIVERSITY PRESS

Great Clarendon Street, Oxford OX2 6DP

Oxford University Press is a department of the University of Oxford.
It furthers the University's objective of excellence in research, scholarship,
and education by publishing worldwide in

Oxford New York

Auckland Cape Town Dar es Salaam Hong Kong Karachi
Kuala Lumpur Madrid Melbourne Mexico City Nairobi
New Delhi Shanghai Taipei Toronto

With offices in

Argentina Austria Brazil Chile Czech Republic France Greece
Guatemala Hungary Italy Japan Poland Portugal Singapore
South Korea Switzerland Thailand Turkey Ukraine Vietnam

Oxford is a registered trade mark of Oxford University Press
in the UK and in certain other countries

Published in the United States
by Oxford University Press Inc., New York

© Christel Lane & Jocelyn Probert, 2009

The moral rights of the authors have been asserted
Database right Oxford University Press (maker)

First published 2009

All rights reserved. No part of this publication may be reproduced,
stored in a retrieval system, or transmitted, in any form or by any means,
without the prior permission in writing of Oxford University Press,
or as expressly permitted by law, or under terms agreed with the appropriate
reprographics rights organization. Enquiries concerning reproduction
outside the scope of the above should be sent to the Rights Department,
Oxford University Press, at the address above

You must not circulate this book in any other binding or cover
and you must impose the same condition on any acquirer

British Library Cataloguing in Publication Data

Data available

Library of Congress Cataloging in Publication Data

Data available

Typeset by SPI Publisher Services, Pondicherry, India
Printed in Great Britain
on acid-free paper by
the MPG Books Group

ISBN 978-0-19-921481-5

1 3 5 7 9 10 8 6 4 2

Acknowledgements

Many people on three continents have lent their time and support in the preparation of this book. Without the participation of the executives in more than one hundred companies and associations who generously shared their knowledge and insights into the various elements that make up the textile and clothing value chain—from the arcane world of quota mechanisms through the finer points of pre-production fabric checking to the management issues associated with cross-border garment production between Hong Kong and China—we would not have been able to elaborate in such detail the rich tapestry of this industry's production networks. To them we express our deep gratitude, and in particular to those who facilitated our visits to supplier countries and firms; without their assistance our task would have been immeasurably more difficult. In the latter respect we thank especially the former sourcing operation of Karstadt in Hong Kong, ITKIB (Istanbul Textile and Apparel Exporters' Association) in Turkey, and YKK in Romania.

The research was funded by the Cambridge-MIT Institute (CMI) as part of a larger project examining global value chains of several industries across our three chosen countries. In Cambridge the project was run under the auspices of the Centre for Business Research (CBR) at the University of Cambridge, where we were both based for the duration of the research. American firm interview data were collected by a team at MIT's Industrial Performance Center (IPC). To Alan Hughes, the Centre's Director, we express our appreciation for his wisdom and advice during the vicissitudes of our research, and to the administrative support team and other colleagues we extend our warm thanks for their help and interest in our work. Suzanne Berger, IPC project team leader, first sparked our interest in the clothing industry, and we must thank her and Sara Jane McCaffrey for interesting discussions and shared experiences during 2003–04.

The development of our ideas has benefited enormously from discussions with colleagues at workshops and conferences where we have presented earlier versions of parts of this book. In particular we would like to thank the participants of the workshop we held in April 2005, generously funded by CRASSH (Centre for Research in the Arts, Social Sciences and Humanities) at the University of Cambridge, and the members of the Society for the Advancement of Socio-Economics who engaged with us so enthusiastically during the annual conferences in Washington DC, Trier, Budapest, and Costa Rica.

In the actual writing of this book we have incurred more debts of gratitude. Tugce Bulut, a PhD student in the University of Cambridge, shared with us her knowledge and expertise on labour conditions in Turkey and has generously contributed to the section of Chapter 10 that deals with those issues. Jocelyn Probert wishes to thank Alan Hughes and David Connell at the CBR for their forbearance in recent months, when the book was proving more of a distraction from other work than it should have done.

Last, but by no means least, we extend our heartfelt thanks to David Lane and Miles Dodd, who have patiently borne for many months our absences, late nights, and non-availability for family life. Without their continued encouragement and intellectual and emotional support this book would not have seen the light of day.

Contents

Tables and Figures

Tables

Figures

List of Boxes

Abbreviations

AAFA	American Apparel and Footwear Association
ACFTU	All China Federation of Trade Unions
ACP	Africa, Caribbean, and Pacific countries
AGOA	Africa Growth and Opportunity Act
ASEAN	Association of South East Asian Nations
ATC	Agreement on Textiles and Clothing
ATMI	American Textile Manufacturers Institute
ATPA	Andean Trade Preferences Act
BERR	(Department of) Business Enterprise and Regulatory Reform
BSCI	Business Social Compliance Initiative
CAD	Computer aided design
CAD–CAM	Computer aided design–computer aided manufacturing
CAFTA	Central America Free Trade Agreement
CB	Caribbean Basin
CBI	Caribbean Basin Initiative
CBTPA	Caribbean Trade Partnership Act
CEC	Commission of the European Communities
CEE	Central and Eastern Europe
CEFTA	Central European Free Trade Agreement
CM	Cut and make
CME	Coordinated market economy
CMT	Cut–make–trim
CNGA	China National Garment Association
CNTAC	China National Textile & Apparel Council
CNTIC	China National Technical Import and Export Corporation
DR-CAFTA	Dominican Republic-Central America Free Trade Agreement
EBA	Everything But Arms
EFTA	European Free Trade Association
EME	Emergent market economies
EPA	Economic Partnership Agreements
EPOS	Electronic point-of-sale
FDI	Foreign direct investment
FP	Full package
FTA	Free trade agreement

GATT	Generalized Agreement on Tariffs and Trade
GCC	Global commodity chain
GPN	Global production network
GSP	Generalised System of Preferences
GVC	Global value chain
ICFTU	International Confederation of Free Trade Unions
ILO	International Labour Organization
IMF	International Monetary Fund
ITKIP	Istanbul Textile and Clothing Exporters Association
JIT	Just in time
JO-IN	Joint Initiative on Corporate Accountability and Workers' Rights
LAC	Labour arbitration committee
LC	Letters of credit
LDC	Less developed country
LLDC	Least developed country
LME	Liberal market economy
LTA	Long Term Arrangement on Cotton Textiles
MFA	Multi-Fibre Arrangements
MFN	Most Favoured Nation
MNC	Multinational company
MNE	Multinational enterprise
MOFTEC	Ministry of Foreign Trade and Economic Cooperation
MSI	Multi-stakeholder initiative
NAFTA	North America Free Trade Agreement
NGO	Non-governmental organizations
NVQ	National vocational qualification
OB	Original brand
OBM	Original brand manufacturing
OD	Original design
OECD	Organisation for Economic Cooperation and Development
OHS	Occupational health and safety
OPA	Outward Processing Arrangement
OPT	Outward processing trade
OTEXA	US Office of Textiles and Apparel
PTA	Preferential trade arrangements
RMB	Renminbi
RoO	Rules of origin
SAARC	South Asian Association for Regional Cooperation
SARS	Severe acute respiratory syndrome

SEZ	Special Economic Zone
SITC	Standard international trade classification
SIPPO	Swiss Import Promotion Programme
SME	Small- and medium-sized enterprise
SOE	State-owned enterprise
SPC	Statistical process control
T/C	Textiles and clothing
TAN	Transnational advocacy network
TCMA	Turkish Clothing Manufacturers Association
TVE	Town and village enterprise
USITC	United States International Trade Commission
USSR	Union of Soviet Socialist Republics
VET	Vocational education and training
VoC	Varieties of Capitalism
WRAP	Worldwide Responsible Apparel Production
WRC	Workers' Representative Councils
WTO	World Trade Organization

1

Introduction

This book explores the interaction between globally dispersed production networks (GPNs) and national capitalisms, and the relationship between developed and developing countries that these entail. GPNs in the clothing industry are the dense networks established by various kinds of hub firms, based in developed countries, around a large number of contract manufacturers in developing countries. The comparative capitalism literature has established that national institutional settings shape industries, company structures, and workforce capabilities in a distinctive manner, even in firms which transcend national borders (Hall and Soskice 2001; Whitley 2001, 2005). The literature on global value chains and networks, in contrast, stresses how GPNs have expanded the room for manoeuvre of western firms, affording corporate actors strategic choice beyond the confines of national institutional constraints. According to Gereffi (2005: 170), 'the competition among firms from different business systems in overseas markets tends to diminish the influence of national origins on firms behaviour.'

We suggest that although national influence remains strong, it is not invariably the dominant influence. Our study thus emphasizes the importance of conceiving of the global economy as a multi-level or -scalar entity with complex interactions among the various levels (Held et al. 1999; Dicken 2007). 'Global' in this context refers both to locations of suppliers dispersed around the globe and to international (as well as regional) institutions shaping national industries and firms. But we view these various levels not merely as geographic entities but in social institutional and 'political power' terms. Our study is based on a large-scale empirical project, utilizing material from over a hundred interviews on three continents. The hub firms in GPNs are British, German, and American.

Global production networks in the clothing industry, resulting from the fragmentation of the value chain, have now existed for several decades. Gary Gereffi's work (1994) on global commodity chains (GCC) in this industry was among the first to draw attention to the explosive growth of imports in developed countries and to show that the centre of gravity for the production and export of clothing had moved to an ever-growing array of developing countries. But the study of global value chains (GVCs/GPNs) has acquired a fresh saliency in the twenty-first century. Among the most important reasons are, first, that the manufacture of clothing has now passed almost completely from developed to developing countries, increasing the degree of polarization between western buyer firms and supplier/contractor firms in developing countries. A second reason is the change in international trade regulation introduced in January 2005 and the global transformation this has wrought in GPNs both in the run-up to and since the abolition of the Agreement on Textiles and Clothing. A third reason for a fresh look at the global clothing industry is provided by the transition of the former communist countries in CEE and China during the 1990s to market or quasi-market economies and the ensuing expansion of the contractor base this has entailed.

The value chain in the clothing industry embraces several different sets of activity, with associated roles and occupations. These steps can be separated from each other and performed in different locations, since they involve clearly identified costs, as well as different sets of capabilities and occupations. The more high value pre-production functions, as well as the post-production functions of marketing and distribution, stay mainly in developed countries. The actual manufacture of garments, in contrast, involves mainly semi-skilled sewing and assembly operations, using simple machines and requiring elementary skills. It has largely moved to developing low-wage countries. The manner of fragmenting the value chain and the distribution of its functions across different locations depends not only on available competencies and considerations of cost and speed of delivery but also on the nature of the final product.

Finally, the garments reach consumers through various retail channels. These sometimes, though not as a rule, are vertically integrated into 'manufacturing' firms, or, alternatively, may handle their own sourcing. Thus, in addition and parallel to processes of reducing vertical integration, processes of functional integration have been notable, particularly of the retailing stage of the value chain.

The main focus of this book falls on the western clothing firms which coordinate global production networks. Although nominally manufacturing firms, most of them now are principally engaged in the coordination of the fragmented segments in the value chain and the GPNs developed for this purpose. Yet most of these firms are not wholesalers because they still execute certain essential pre- and post-production functions and, in many cases, continue to command manufacturing skills and knowledge. Due to the widespread abandonment of the manufacturing function by clothing firms and the adoption of some direct sourcing by most retailers, the boundaries between types of firms have become increasingly blurred and difficult to draw. Hence an extended clarification of terms used in this study is necessary. We refer to these clothing firms as either 'manufacturers' or 'coordinating firms', using these terms as equivalents. When we distinguish western 'manufacturers' from manufacturers in developing countries, we refer to them as 'buyer' and 'supplier' firms, respectively. The latter are also referred to as 'contractors', highlighting the fact that although nominally independent (in ownership terms), they sometimes are dependent on their western buyers. 'Manufacturing' firms may be lead or hub firms in their GPN, although if they do not sell branded clothing they usually are subordinated to a big retailer who becomes the hub of the GPN. Despite the blurring of boundaries and the ambiguity of terms, in specific contexts such ambiguity should disappear.

The clothing industry encompasses many distinct product segments which entail different production methods and relations with suppliers and with retailers. One important distinction is that between making basic goods (longer repetitive runs, such as men's trousers) and fashion goods (goods subject to constant variation in fabric and style, produced in relatively short batches); another is that between women's and men's clothing. There is a very rough overlap between these two sets of distinctions as fashion products tend to be women's clothing. Our book mainly deals with women's fashion clothing. A third important distinction relates mainly to relations between 'manufacturers' on the one hand and retailers and consumers on the other, but also has implications for the construction of GPNs. This is the distinction between producers of 'private label' garments and branded 'manufacturers'. Whereas the former produce for the label of large retailers who closely specify features of design, quality, and price points of the garments to be manufactured, the latter determine all these garment features independently, in order to gain 'brand' recognition and the higher prices (brand rent) this can command. (Branded firms may be mere marketers, that is, principally engaged in marketing [Gereffi 1994], or they may be 'manufacturers', that is, they retain both pre-production functions and manufacturing experience). Our book focuses on all three groups of firms and analyses their divergent relation to retailers.

Our three-sided cross-national comparison is valuable in that it goes beyond existing studies which analyse mainly British and/or American firms and thereby also facilitates a comparison between different varieties of capitalism, namely, the 'liberal market' and the 'coordinated market' type, as conceived of by Hall and Soskice (2001). Our study compares the competitive strategies of coordinating firms in the German, British, and American clothing industries. It examines the contrasting sets of core competences these firms command and the way these have structured their organization of the value chain. We focus on their differing relationships with both clothing retailers and suppliers in low-wage countries. This comparison will make clear that both the firms and the GPNs they construct differ significantly between countries. Our contextualized approach will be able to show that embeddedness in different national institutional structures leads to divergent competitive strategies and the command of varying degrees of network power. We combine the organizational perspective usually employed by analysts of GPNs with an institutional approach, the perspective of Varieties of Capitalism scholars.

This book is not confined to the study of coordinating firms. The value chain of 'manufacturing' firms stretches beyond the industry and connects upstream with firms in the textile industry and, more crucially, downstream with clothing retailers and consumers. We trace both the connections and the conflicts they often entail. We study the strategies of clothing 'manufacturers' in global production networks, their activities within these networks, and the way they govern them. This book follows Gereffi (1994) in showing the central and growing importance of large retailers in these networks. We differ from him by making it clear that the degree of dependence on and dominance by retailers of 'manufacturing' firms varies significantly between countries. Our consideration of the interdependence between firms' core competences, their market position, and their network power makes it clear that their relationships with domestic retailers are more complex and varied than has been allowed for by Gereffi and various co-authors who have focused on the American case.

Additionally, we explore how supplier firms/contractors in developing countries experience their place in the network and the way networks are governed by western lead firms, that is, firms that control access to major resources that generate the most profitable returns (Gereffi and Memedovic 2003: 4). We seek to comprehend how flows of capital, knowledge, and power influence supplier firms and countries in both negative and positive ways. Firms are studied both in their national industry and in their regional and global contexts. Where supplier countries and firms have been studied in a more sustained way in the existing literature it is usually from a 'development' perspective focused on possibilities of upgrading. But in many studies of the clothing industry they remain shadowy actors, representing 'the periphery' (Wallerstein 1979; Gereffi 1994) in an undifferentiated manner. Supplier countries and firms are rarely studied in a sustained manner to show the consequences of the imbalance of power in favour of western firms, both for production organization and, more crucially, for the distribution of the value generated in the chain.[1] Supplier countries (and their firms) we study are China, Turkey, Romania, and Mexico, which represent a selection of the largest suppliers to both European and American buyer firms Figure 1.1 represents the various firms in GPN.

A closer look at particular networks will also show, as Applebaum (2008) makes clear, that power in some networks is gradually shifting. Appelbaum points to a small number of mainly ethnic Chinese and Korean giant transnational firms, such as Li & Fung, that act simultaneously as full-package contractors and as powerful 'middleman' agents standing between western firms and lower-tier contractors in developing countries. As such, their networks usually stretch across national borders, often using a common ethnicity as a resource for network building.

Although this book is primarily a study of firms—particularly 'manufacturing' firms (with or without actual manufacturing operations) in both developed and developing countries—it also enquires about the consequences of GPNs, particularly the unequal distribution of value and the violation of labour standards they engender. The reliance on gendered labour markets—with women as cheap, docile, and controllable labour—is a feature of GPNs in most supplier countries. We devote a chapter to the adverse consequences of GPNs for labour in developing countries and draw attention to the unwillingness/impotence of national states to ameliorate these effects. We therefore focus on the intervention by NGOs and the transnational advocacy networks (Keck and Sikkink 1998) they form, and how they attempt to fill the regulatory gap left by states. Some attention is also given to the continuing existence of sweatshops in the two western liberal market economies.

A study of company practices, including the treatment of labour, additionally has to concern itself with issues of national, regional, and international governance by state (public) and non-state (private) bodies. This requires an understanding of the multi-layered formal and informal regulatory web, which has been particularly

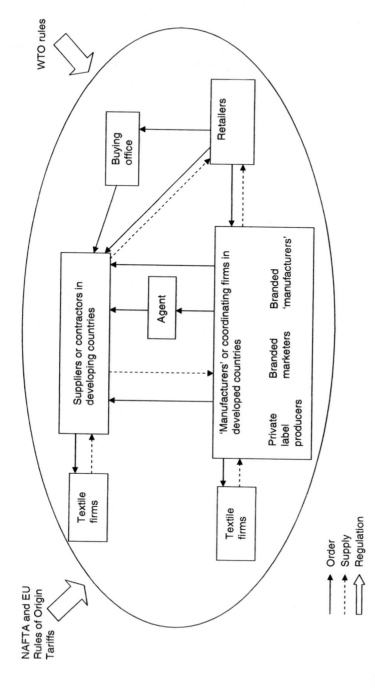

Figure 1.1. A global production network

WTO rules

NAFTA and EU
Rules of Origin
Tariffs

Buying
office

Retailers

Suppliers or contractors in
developing countries

Agent

'Manufacturers' or coordinating firms in
developed countries

Branded
'manufacturers'

Branded
marketers

Private
label
producers

Textile
firms

Textile
firms

→ Order

→ Supply

⇒ Regulation

dense and consequential in the clothing industry. The web of regulation, to which companies orient their behaviour, has been spun by national states, regional and international institutions, and private transnational advocacy networks. We highlight both the continuing role played by powerful western states in sponsoring and supporting their firms' cross-border exploitation of labour and the corresponding impotence by states in developing countries to protect labour. Particular attention is focused on where power is located in the GPN and whether and how national and international governance bodies are able to limit the power of western hub firms. This book therefore engages with international and regional trade policy and national protectionism, with labour law, and with the voluntary codes of NGOs, firms, industry associations, and, to a lesser degree, unions on labour standards and rights.

The capacity to produce and export clothing requires low investment of both capital and skill. The production and exporting of clothing has therefore dispersed across the globe, partly stimulated by trade regulation. GPNs in this industry now encompass producers on all continents. Moreover, these GPNs have experienced periodic reconfiguration in response to geopolitical developments. This study catches the dynamic aspects of networks, resulting from a high level of geographical mobility—or footlooseness—in pursuit of ever lower prices by western buyer firms. This mobility of firms in the clothing industry, which partially reflects the dynamism of economic globalization, reached a high point in the run-up to and beyond January 2005—the date when import quotas were finally abolished by the WTO. We try to capture what this radical break entails for both buyer and supplier firms and the various sourcing countries. We study the impact of low-wage suppliers on the quantity and quality of remaining employment in developed countries. This includes the disastrous consequences for employment in developing countries following the consolidation of western firms' networks, in reaction to the abolition of the Agreement on Textiles and Clothing.

The clothing industry is widely conceived of as a sunset industry, which western countries do well to surrender. Yet a study of this industry provides many valuable insights, both into industrial change in western developed countries and into our understanding of global processes and relations. An understanding of the more deeply integrated global economy of the twenty-first century is significantly enhanced by a focus on the organization and governance of global production networks, rather than merely the study of the foreign direct investment activities of multinational companies (MNCs). (Governance is defined as 'exerting power in various forms by setting parameters for products and processes, in order to extract maximum value'.) Our analysis of the global clothing industry encompasses the study of a range of pressing contemporary socio-economic and political, as well as management, issues. As Peter Dicken (2007: 249) notes, 'the clothing industry exemplifies many of the intractable issues facing today's global economy'. The issue of global sourcing and the GPNs it creates currently do not receive sufficient attention in globalization studies (with the exception of Dicken 2007), which therefore underestimate both the depth of economic global integration and the way highly asymmetric surplus extraction continues to polarize developed and developing countries. It is the functional integration and coordination of globally dispersed activities which gives current economic activity its global, rather than merely international, scope. In focusing on the role of both firms and states in constructing GPNs we adopt an actor-centred view of globalization, rather than viewing the process as purely market-driven.

A study of the industry also holds interest in relation to developed societies and their employment structures. The industry still provides a significant amount of employment in developed countries, both directly, in design and preparation for production as well as in marketing and distribution, and indirectly, in upstream (yarn and textiles) and downstream industries (distribution and retail). This employment is not only low-skill employment for the most vulnerable segments of the labour force but also encompasses more high-level technical and managerial jobs. The degree of employment upgrading achieved in the clothing industry, we shall show, differs significantly between developed countries, depending on general policies of market regulation as well as on available firm capabilities and related employee skill training.

Although the clothing industry is not commonly regarded as innovative, the close interconnection with retail has forced managers of clothing firms to adopt one significant organizational innovation—quick response production—where very brief cycles and short lead times surpass those of other industries. This industry, particularly in Germany and the USA, has also been a pioneer in outsourcing and the development of GPNs. This organizational arrangement now has become more commonplace in other industries and more disquieting in its employment consequences in western societies.

1.1. RESEARCH PERSPECTIVE

The clothing industry has been much studied by social scientists, particularly those that are American (among others by Gereffi, Korzeniewicz, and Korzeniewicz and various co-authors between 1994 and 2006; Abernathy et al. 1999; Bonacich and Appelbaum 2000; Palpacuer 2000, 2006, 2008; Collins 2003; Esbenshade 2004; Faust, Voskamp, and Wittke 2004; Palpacuer, Gibbon, and Thomsen 2004; Ross 2004; Berger 2005; Bair and Dussel Peters 2006; Doeringer and Crean 2006; Rosenberg 2006; Dicken 2007; Bair 2008). But few scholars have followed the value chain from consumers in the rich countries to producers in developing economies, while at the same time exploring the multiple interactions between global networks/processes and national capitalisms and their concerns. In our work, in-depth, empirically based accounts illustrate the above issues, as perceived and experienced by firms in buyer and supplier countries and expressed in vivid extracts from our many interviews. This book thus not only infuses life into abstract economic processes and entities but additionally contributes to a better informed understanding of poorly substantiated 'textbook' claims and generalizations about the globalization process and its impact on national capitalisms.

Economic entities are regarded as socially and institutionally embedded, as well as bringing to bear their power resources in the governance of networks. Furthermore, we view firms as being influenced by and influencing political issues and processes at both national and international level. Our study of firms, industries, and their regulators therefore applies a number of theoretical perspectives. The main preoccupation is with theories of global value chains/global production networks on the one hand and of Varieties of Capitalism/comparative capitalisms on the other. These theories will be supplemented by other, middle-level theories from management and the social sciences.

This book draws on data from 103 interviews, of which 77 were conducted in the 3 buyer countries. The data on the UK and German industry were collected by the two authors, whereas the data on American firms were collected by our project partner in the USA. The Cambridge authors conducted 51 in-depth interviews in 2003–04 with high-level managers/owners of British and German firms and associations in the textiles, clothing, and retail industries. The largest number of interviews occurred in coordinating firms, that is, clothing firms which, in the majority of cases, no longer manufacture the garments. However, our sample also includes a few firms which still fully or partially maintain in-house production.

We used the rankings of firms produced by *Klartext* (an industry publication) to identify the major players (in terms of turnover) in the German clothing industry. In the absence of equivalent listings for the UK, we consulted several leading company databases (e.g. Fame and Osiris), as well as DTI sources, general news databases, and internet materials, to compile our own list. Despite the more ad hoc nature of the UK compilation, we are confident that we identified the most important players. Written approaches and multiple follow-up telephone calls to firms yielded interviews in 11 British (a 35% success rate) and 13 German coordinating firms (43% of all firms contacted), supplemented by interviews with 4 British clothing retailers (a 56% success rate) and 3 German retailers (31% of those contacted). Access rates were much better among the textile firms (interviews in seven British and four German firms) and industry associations. All interviews were completed by December 2004, before the end of the quota system. The interviews, on average, lasted 90 minutes and were recorded and transcribed.

For the US industry, we used interview data collected during 2003 and 2004 by our collaborators on the research project informing this book—a team at the Industrial Performance Center in MIT, Boston, directed by Prof. Suzanne Berger. They conducted 26 US interviews overall, of which 8 were with coordinating firms. The latter include four of the very large and dominant US firms. Interviews in coordinating firms were supplemented by 16 interviews with textile and machinery firms, and a variety of industry associations and consulting firms that provide a broader view. The sample includes no interviews with retailers. We have supplemented the US data in two ways. First, to include more of the very large firms in our sample and to increase the overall sample to bring it into line with those of German and British firms, we collected further information on three very large American firms—VF, Jones Apparel, and Levi Strauss—and on one semi-vertically integrated retailer, The Gap, which increased the sample of coordinating firms to 12. This supplementary information was obtained by searches of the Internet for commensurate data from company annual reports and commercial industry databases. Although not as rich as the interview data, it nevertheless provides vital information on many aspects of the organization of supply chains. Second, we collected all the information on contextual industry conditions for the USA. Official statistics, company reports, and secondary sources from all three countries supplement our findings to provide the broader industry and social and political context.

Between 2004 and 2006, we followed the value chain to interview suppliers in developing countries, choosing three important (in terms of export volume) supplier countries. Turkey and Romania were chosen as important supplier countries for the EU, and particularly for Germany and the UK, while Mexico was selected as a major supplier to the US industry. The selection of China was suggested by the fact that it is the world's most important supplier country, being the largest exporter to both the European countries and the USA. In China, in 2004, we interviewed three clothing and two textile supplier firms, as well as the buying office of a large German retailer and the agent of a British firm in Hong Kong. In Turkey, in 2006, we gained access to seven textile and clothing firms, as well as to two industry associations. Finally in 2006, to include a large supplier country in CEE, we conducted 10 interviews in Romania, including clothing firms, a supplier of trim, and two industry associations. These interviews, although very difficult to arrange, proved extremely worthwhile. They provided important insights into how suppliers viewed their western buyers, particularly the differences between them, and into the often difficult circumstances in which they were placed by buyer demands. At the same time, these interviews afforded us a fascinating glimpse of the economic and political environments in which global value chains touch down. Finally Mexico, an important regional supplier to the USA, had to be studied through secondary material, such as NGO, union and consultancy reports, as well as academic secondary literature. The study of supplier firms also kindled our interest in labour standards and rights in these countries (with the exception of Romania), studied mainly from secondary sources.

Interviews were semi-structured, that is, they followed a consistent interview schedule but questions were mostly open-ended to attain qualitative data. They allowed not only lengthy responses but also departures into areas which proved highly enlightening but which, given our 'outsider' knowledge of the industry, had not been anticipated. A few questions required precise quantitative answers, useful for cross-country comparison of company characteristics and practices, such as turnover (not publicly available for the many privately owned firms in this industry) and number of supplier countries and suppliers. Altogether, this qualitative method of interviewing yielded an extremely rich database, capturing the many social, economic, and political aspects of the clothing industry.

As interviewees were guaranteed anonymity, we refer to firms only by our own internally developed codes, which combine the abbreviation of the country (UK GER or USA, for our developed countries, and CH, ROM, or T for the supplier countries) with that of the industry (C for clothing; T for textile, and R for retail) and a number arbitrarily allocated to each firm. Quotations or comments specific to a particular firm are acknowledged in this way, while more broadly voiced opinions are referenced as Interview Notes. If a firm itself has made information public, full reference to the firm is made.

1.2. CONTENTS

The chapters are organized as follows. Chapter 2 develops the theoretical frame-work which informs the study. These are chiefly the two theories of global value chains/global production networks and of comparative capitalisms. We show the shortcomings of each, as well as their complementary strengths for an under-standing of firms in this global industry. Some consideration also is given to theories of the state in the international economy, of the firm, and of gender in the labour market. We additionally develop a typology of firms, based on value chain analysis, and explore concepts central to an understanding of the clothing industry, such as 'brand' and 'fashion'. In Chapter 3, we compare the three sets of national 'manufacturing' firms, viewing them in their domestic industry environment. After a short historical exploration of recent industry development, its current place within the national economy and geographical space, and its composition in terms of firm size, we analyse firms themselves: their ownership patterns; employment and skill structures; their product and market strategies; and their export performance. Chapter 3 also briefly examines the textiles industries of the three countries and makes it clear how performance in this up-stream industry has shaped the varying fortunes of the national clothing industries. This section reveals that the close functional relation between textiles and clothing industries hides dissension between them regarding their place in global trade and their access to national states. Chapter 4 is devoted to a study of the clothing retail industry in each country, paying close attention to the shifting power relations between 'manufacturing' and retail firms. Our analysis explores the strategies retailers have adopted to cope with intensified competition and to render themselves more independent from 'middleman' national branded 'man-ufacturers'/marketers. This analysis reveals how national cultural (consumption patterns and styles) and political legacies, as well as institutional configurations, have shaped their development and current relations with 'manufacturers' in a highly divergent manner.

Moving away from the domestic context, the following chapters consider the regional, international, and global level. Chapters 5 and 6 place the clothing indus-try in its wider international context and examine the various actors and systems of regulation. Chapter 6 examines the impact of international and regional trade regulation on firms, that is, how they channel relations between western buyer firms and suppliers in developing countries. This chapter focuses particularly on the pre- and post-2005 changes in regulation and their impact on both supplier and buyer countries/firms. It additionally explores potential changes in power relations between buyer and supplier countries and the emergence of influential transnational middleman firms in some supplier countries. Having introduced the contextual conditions in which the clothing industry operates, Chapter 7 examines the production networks that German, British, and American firms have constructed in different parts of the globe, their relationships with suppliers, and the differing degrees of power they are able to wield in the network. Chapters 8 and 9 focus on supplier firms in four developing countries—Turkey and Romania (Chapter 8) and China and Mexico (Chapter 9). In Chapter 10 we examine the impact of GPNs on labour. Labour standards and rights are examined in Mexican, Turkish, and Chinese firms, as are the paradoxical effects of their introduction and monitoring by private transnational advocacy networks and public intergovernmental organizations. The Conclusion summarizes the argument and highlights the theoretical insights gained about the interaction of national institutions, international regulatory structures, global markets, and production networks.

NOTE

1. The exceptions are the recent works of Gereffi, Martinez, and Bair (2002), Bair and Dussel Peters (2006) on Mexico, and of Gibbon (2008) on Mauritius.

2

Theoretical Frameworks: The Varieties of Capitalism Approach and the Global Value Chains/Global Production Networks Framework

2.1. INTRODUCTION

Recent debate on capitalist diversity has been preoccupied with the problem of how an emphasis on institutional constraints can be reconciled with an understanding of ongoing processes of change, many of which are closely connected with processes of enhanced global integration (Streeck and Yamamura 2003; Crouch 2005; Morgan, Whitley, and Moen 2005; Sorge 2005; Streeck and Thelen 2005; Whitley 2005; Deeg and Jackson 2007; Hancké, Rhodes, and Thatcher 2007). This work has focused predominantly on change processes *internal* to political economies, particularly on processes of institutional adaptation, and much less on internationally oriented firms' changing coordination strategies. Precipitants of change are often vaguely referred to as the 'pressures of globalization'. Even when external pressures are identified (e.g. Crouch 2005; Hancké et al. 2007), the actual interaction of global actors and national institutions has not been systematically studied. The way domestic firms' global networks may affect home country institutions and the way comparative advantage is constituted have received scant attention. Equally important, relatively little attention (with the exception of Whitley 1999; Whitley 2001; and Sorge 2005) has been devoted to an examination of the reverse process of influence, namely, to what extent and how firms from different political economies shape the process of global integration.

This book analyses the way national capitalisms interact with global value chains (GVCs)/global production networks (GPNs). GPNs, in the words of Dicken (2003: 9), involve 'the fragmentation of many production processes and their geographical relocation on a global scale in ways that slice through national boundaries'. Firms extend their value chains across national borders in order to escape institutional constraints in their home countries, or to seek alternative institutional arrangements more compatible with changed strategic objectives. GPNs do not exist in an anonymous global space but remain territorially embedded, albeit in multiple locations. It therefore becomes an important research question as to how GPNs interact with specific varieties of capitalism, in both home and host countries. Hence the theory of GVCs/GPNs has to be supplemented with insights from Varieties of Capitalism (VoC) theory. As recently pointed out by Gereffi (2005: 170), 'notwithstanding the potential complementarities between institutional and organizational perspectives on the global economy, there has been virtually no dialogue between the two literatures'. This chapter seeks to promote such dialogue, by identifying not only the weaknesses of each approach but also their complementary strengths. In addition to an extended discussion of GVC/GPN theory and of the VoC approach, this chapter also undertakes an analysis of the state as an actor in both the national and international arena and concludes with a section which links the discussion of firm capabilities and strategy to the process of value chain fragmentation. The resulting integrated theoretical framework will be applied in the empirical analysis in subsequent chapters of this book.

2.2. VARIETIES OF CAPITALISM THEORY

The literature on varieties of capitalism/comparative capitalisms is now sizeable. Rather than distinguishing the various approaches from each other, we will draw out a few common features. In a second step, we will briefly outline recent refinements of key concepts and explore to what extent and how the old and the new approaches conceptualize internationalization/globalization and its impact on national capitalisms. Third, through a contrast with assumptions underlying the theory of GPNs, we suggest some criticisms of the comparative capitalism approach, as well as point to enduring strengths. Finally, we indicate how the VoC approach can extend and complement the theory of GPNs used in this book.

The work of Hall and Soskice (2001) on varieties of capitalism is firmly focused on the firm. They view firms 'as actors who seek to develop and exploit core competences for producing and distributing goods and services profitably' (ibid: 6). To do so firms engage in strategic interactions with other actors in core spheres of the national economy and seek to solve the coordination problems they encounter. Firms have to coordinate effectively with a wide range of actors in a number of spheres and develop both internal relationships with employees and external relationships. Coordination problems arise in the following areas: corporate governance; relations between management and labour within the firm; industrial relations; vocational education and training; and inter-firm relations.

The way firms solve these coordination problems is fundamentally shaped by the national institutional framework in which they are situated. Institutions both enable and constrain firms to behave in certain ways and thus shape the way such coordination problems are handled. Institutions differ systematically between societies and thus foster different firm strategies. Furthermore, sets of institutions interact with each other in a non-random way to form a distinctive national institutional configuration. The latter then creates what is variously referred to as a particular logic or rationality to which firms orient their behaviour. This approach therefore assumes that resulting types of coordination have a high degree of internal coherence. Institutions evolve in a largely path-dependent fashion, since institutional change within one domain will be constrained or amplified by the complementarities with institutions in other domains (Deeg and Jackson 2007: 153). Hence change is mainly evolutionary and occurs along predictable tracks.

The VoC approach distinguishes between discrete types of capitalism, ranging from the two polar types of Hall and Soskice (2001)—liberal market economies (LMEs) and coordinated market economies (CMEs)—to more plural typologies (Whitley 1999; Schmidt 2002; Amable 2003; Hancké et al. 2007). Such typologies outline how institutions co-vary across institutional domains. These frameworks therefore enable us to compare how institutional diversity across varieties of capitalism impacts on firms' performance and to explain national comparative advantage. According to Hall and Soskice (2001), the coordinated economy is characterized by non-market relationships, collaboration, credible commitments, and a deliberative approach to solving coordination problems. The essence of liberal-market economies, in contrast, is that relationships are competitive and arms' length and rely on formal contracting and supply-and-demand signalling. In sum, the Varieties of Capitalism approach first and foremost develops an understanding of the institutional foundations of diverse *national* patterns of coordinating the activities of firms.

More recent work in the comparative capitalisms field has further developed this theoretical framework. Following the more pronounced internationalization/globalization of economic actors during the 1990s, a number of theorists felt a greater urgency to understand change in both economic actors and institutions. The motivation has mainly been to assess whether capitalist diversity would endure or whether trends towards convergence were under way. Furthermore, recent writing has moved away from a purely national focus of research to raise searching questions about the interaction of the national and the international/global level. In this context, the impact of global forces on national varieties of capitalism is explicitly addressed in many accounts (Morgan 2001; Whitley 2001, 2005; Streeck and Yamamura 2003; Crouch 2005; Morgan et al. 2005; Sorge 2005; Streeck and Thelen 2005; Deeg and Jackson 2007; Hancké et al. 2007). More flexible conceptions of institutions, envisaging a more varied and looser complementarity between institutions and greater strategic choice for firms, have been developed by some of these authors. Institutions are no longer viewed primarily as constraining structures but as resources to be deployed by creative actors (Streeck and Thelen 2005). Linkages between institutions are analysed not merely in terms of complementarities but also as inefficiencies and tensions (Deeg and Jackson 2007: 151). Institutional change and even severe disruption of national institutional configurations now command more attention.

Concerning the *impact* of globalization on national actors, institutions, and comparative advantage, two opposed theoretical accounts may be found in the literature. On the one hand, it is held that the impact of globalization only serves to reinforce existing institutional arrangements and to intensify concentration on specific market segments, congruent with the logic of these arrangements (e.g. Whitley 1999; Hall and Soskice 2001; Sorge 2005; Hall 2007). Hall and Soskice (2001) believe in reinforcement of existing comparative advantage, because foreign direct investment (FDI) is said to flow to locations rich in co-specific assets. Even if some temporary disruption of relationships occurs, it is suggested, consultation in deliberative institutions will bring renewed coordination. Consequently, any effects of firms' global activities are assumed to be homogenous, that is, they cause further specialization in a particular productive niche, such as diversified quality or diversified mass production.

Hall and Soskice (2001) refer to the fact that internationally operating firms engage in institutional arbitrage, that is, they shift their activities abroad to secure the advantages that the institutional frameworks of host countries might provide. But oddly, they do not connect such institutional arbitrage with any disruptive effects on home institutions. Instead, they resolutely affirm their belief that firms' global activities intensify the comparative institutional advantage of firms' home base (ibid: 57). Whitley (1999) and Hall and Soskice (2001) also distinguish between how companies from different institutional environments enter global competition, holding firm to conceptions of path-dependent behaviour. Thus Hall and Soskice (2001: 30) suggest that firms from LMEs will adapt more easily to transnationalization, given 'their preference for more flexible and loose relations, both within and between firms'. In contrast, the comparative institutional advantage bestowed by home institutions in CMEs is said to make companies from this institutional environment less mobile than is commonly assumed (Hall and Soskice 2001: 56–8). Hall and Gingerich (2004: 28–9) confirm that, in the face of external shocks, holders of specific assets will oppose greater market competition and will form status- quo-supporting cross-class coalitions. In sum, although interaction between national and global influences is not ruled out, the national always asserts itself above the global, and no deviation occurs from path-dependent behaviour. In our view there is an underestimation of strategic choice on the part of firms, and an overemphasis on the rigidity of institutional and actor constellations, particularly regarding CMEs. There persists a strong tendency to view national economies as 'sealed containers', assuming a high degree of institutional and political closure and hence a large measure of integrity at national level (Hay 2005: 108).

On the other hand, a growing number of sceptics now appreciate that globalization brings interaction between diverse institutional configurations and therefore recognize that institutional reproduction is less straightforward. Change, they argue, is not only brought about by external shocks, but is often endogenous and initiated by domestic actors (Crouch 2005). These theorists realize that national actors are prone to challenge institutional arrangements seen as outmoded or to utilize gaps in coordination processes to redesign institutional arrangements. They view firms as creative actors who are not totally bound by the institutional constraints of their home environment, whether this is an LME or a CME. In common with the theory of global production networks (Dicken et al. 2001), they acknowledge the multilevel character of institutions and the fact that regulatory coverage of various institutional domains takes place at different geographical scales (Morgan et al. 2005; Deeg and Jackson 2007: 154). There also is growing awareness that national capitalisms are becoming institutionally incomplete (ibid.)

Some of these analysts strongly emphasize the great malleability of individual institutions, the loose coupling between them, and their endless adaptability to external impact and internal contestation (e.g. Crouch 2005). Others, however, view the impact of globally operating and strategically innovative firms as potentially disruptive of existing institutional arrangements and modes of coordination (e.g. Streeck and Yamamura 2003; Morgan 2005; Streeck and Thelen 2005; Deeg and Jackson 2007; Hancké et al. 2007: 11). The first authors, for example, state that 'wide-ranging institutional change nonetheless challenges the validity of existing typologies of capitalism and their emphasis on the constraining nature of national institutions' (Deeg and Jackson 2007: 154). It is also recognized that firms in CMEs no longer hesitate to liberalize factors of production and that CMEs are not immune from change. The view that neo-liberalism and global processes may undermine distinctive national institutional sub-systems has been systematized by Streeck and Thelen (2005) in a valuable typology of institutional transformation.

A related literature on the multilevel nature of economic action and institutions (Djelic and Quack 2003; Morgan et al. 2005) has paid much attention to how international regulatory frameworks impact national ones. This literature, however, remains focused mainly on institutions and less on the interaction between firms and international institutions.

2.2.1. A Critique of the VoC Approach

Despite all these revisions/refinements of the original VoC approach, a tendency still prevails to assume that national institutions retain a strong mediating influence, and international/global institutions and actors are rarely accorded direct causal influence. There often is an implicit assumption that coordination remains under the influence of only *national* institutions. Even in this more open and flexible approach study has been focused on modalities of change *within* given national capitalisms, and the external precipitants of change and their variable effects remain less understood. There is a lack of consideration particularly of global markets and how these often lowly institutionalized markets may shape the behaviour of firms. The issue of how competitive advantage of global firms is constituted, the coordination patterns adopted to this end, and the interaction of global networks with domestic institutions still need further examination. The fact that some activities of globally operating firms remain totally ungoverned has attracted the least attention. This is partly explained by the fact that, in the study of the interaction between the national and the global, the latter still receives far less analysis. A neglect particularly of the global networks of national firms, the markets they operate in, and the alternative modes of coordination these may entail leaves global influences conceptually under-specified.

When international/global firms are singled out for study, the focus has fallen mainly on multinational companies (MNCs) as agents of internationalization/globalization. In contrast, managerial behaviour in global production networks and its interaction with national and international institutions still awaits systematic study. MNCs, it is pointed out, borrow and combine practices from different national settings as well as successfully export practices from their home country (Edwards and Ferner 2004; Ferner et al. 2006), although the extent to which they do so is seen to vary between firms from different VoC/Business Systems (Whitley 2001). This literature is sensitive to the fact that firms are not necessarily unreflective carriers of domestic institutional practices but 'pick and choose' arrangements from both home and host countries according to independent criteria of what constitutes competitive advantage.

But the operation of MNCs in the global economy differs in significant ways from that of lead firms in GPNs. MNCs, through mechanisms of hierarchical internal control, retain influence over their subsidiaries and hence over the flow of ideas, practices, and information across borders. The nationally influenced templates for organizing firm behaviour are less liable to be challenged and subverted by actors originating from other varieties of capitalism. Construction of global networks of production, in contrast, constitutes a more far-reaching externalization of activities than occurs in MNCs, involving the surrender of ownership rights and the transfer of complete segments/functions in the value chain to third-party contractors. Hence important coordination problems, particularly around labour, such as firm-internal deliberation and skill training as well as industrial relations, no longer arise and important domestic institutional domains, for these firms, become redundant. Global production networks therefore constitute a more radical process of dis-embedding from the home nation, with a potentially more destructive impact on institutional coherence. This insight has hardly been considered in the comparative capitalisms literature.

When considering the specialization in a country's area of comparative advantage it is therefore ignored that, in GPNs, coordination of production processes within firms has fallen away. Furthermore, the institutions supporting specialization have been cancelled out by institutions in supplier countries. Firms in GPNs have become truncated firms, with lead firms lacking a (manufacturing) labour force, and firms in supplier countries lacking many management processes. GPNs, to reiterate, thus constitute a more severe challenge to national embeddedness of firms and hence to the central argument of VoC theory about the institutional shaping of firms.

GPNs raise a further problem for VoC theory. How can inter-firm relations be configured to create common understandings and foster commitment to joint goals when institutions in lead firms' country of origin no longer support these trans-border networks? Equally important, what mechanisms are at the disposal of lead firms to achieve control over outcomes when commitment to common values and scenarios for action cannot be assumed? How, in these circumstances, are firms able to foster exchange of information, monitoring of employees, creation of cooperation and commitment within and between firms?

Despite the above questions and criticism of the VoC/comparative capitalisms approach—in both its earlier formulation and its more recent revisions—this theoretical approach retains considerable value for a better understanding of global value chains/global production networks. A detailed consideration of how the VoC/comparative capitalisms approach can help to expand and refine the theory of GPNs is attempted once theoretical approaches in this latter field have been presented in Section 2.4. First, however, a brief outline will be provided both of the types of capitalism we apply in this study and of the spheres of coordination we think significant when analysing GPNs.

2.2.2. The VoC Approach: Types of Coordination and Institutions

Of the many typologies of national capitalisms offered in the literature, the parsimonious dichotomous typology of a Liberal and Coordinated Market Economy—LME and CME (Hall and Soskice 2001; Hall and Gingerich 2004; Hall 2007)—suffices for the three-sided comparison of the clothing industry in western developed countries we undertake in this book. Moreover, this typology is generally believed to have a good fit with the three capitalisms which are the home countries of globalizing firms in this study—Germany, the UK, and the USA (e.g. Goodin 2003: 204). Supplier countries in the clothing industry, including many emergent market economies, are too diverse to be typified in terms of the Hall and Soskice typology or even by a more pluralistic framework, such as that of Whitley (1999), Amable (2003), or Hancké et al. (2007). What they share in common, however, is the instability of their institutional arrangements which partially explains the attraction they hold for western lead firms.

Our adoption of the VoC typology does not signal an uncritical acceptance of the whole approach. In addition to some of the criticism of its rigidities already rehearsed, we see the exclusion from the framework of the state and the under-emphasis of the political dimension as a serious omission. (This now is acknowledged by Hancké et al. [2007], including by Hall [2007] himself.) In common with many other theorists, we see the state as an important system of coordination which is more or less active in all types of economy and which is deeply implicated in the very construction of national institutional architectures. But as we are concerned in this book with a multilevel analysis of economic action and its regulation we also depart from the comparative capitalisms approach of analysing the state only in relation to national actors. Instead we view the state as both a nationally and internationally oriented actor struggling to reconcile competing demands from different firms and industries. Hence a separate and more widely ranging discussion of the state is offered in Section 2.4 below.

The following national institutional complexes have shaped the organization and governance of GPNs both directly and indirectly by influencing lead firms.

1. The financial system: access to finance has shaped ownership forms and investment patterns, as well as patterns of growth among 'manufacturing' and other lead firms. These influences have created very different populations of firms in the three national clothing industries, thereby affecting available material resources for internationalizing production networks. The impact of diverse financial systems on corporate governance makes for divergent degrees of investor pressure to maintain and increase shareholder value, and thus influences distribution of value along the chain. Indeed, the rise to prominence, particularly in LMEs, of a shareholder value orientation has been connected to the very expansion of GPNs. It is understood as one mechanism allowing firms in this industry to increase value for shareholders (Palpacuer 2008). Although this explanation has considerable plausibility we modify this insight by pointing out that extraction of value in the global chain is more intensive in LMEs than in CMEs, and corresponds to the degree to which lead firms (both in 'manufacturing' and retail) are stock market listed entities.

2. The national state: as provider of infrastructure, regulator, and as champion of firms in international institutions and markets (see discussion below, in Section 2.4).

3. The system of vocational education and training (VET): this determines firms' adoption of product paradigm and market strategy and profoundly influences relations with suppliers in GPNs. Furthermore, in its function of channelling highly educated managers into or away from particular industries, the system of education has a bearing on the degree of managerial expertise available for the coordination of global networks, as well as in the area of marketing. Beyond its narrow functional impact, the system of VET also creates common understandings about the position within firms of skilled operators, and of the rights and obligations this entails. Thus the provision of skill training simultaneously creates common understandings about productive processes and commitment to the firm.

4. Inter-firm relations and cultures of contracting: these are reviewed to explore whether and to what extent distinctive national patterns of coordination— arm's length or relational—transcend national borders and also shape relations in GPNs.

5. Systems of industrial and employment relations (Whitley's 1999 authority sharing) have had mainly indirect effects. They have historically shaped the development and nature of systems of vocational education and training. Additionally, they have influenced the point in time when foreign sourcing first started. However, they are rarely exported to supplier firms in developing countries.

Although all these spheres of coordination and their parallel institutions have had some influence on how firms from different national origins form and govern their GPNs, we place a particularly strong emphasis on the system of VET—its influence on both skill formation and its capacity to integrate management and employees. We will highlight that, in GPNs, the complementarity between skill training and provision of long-term employment has been disrupted and has thus jeopardized the development of employee commitment.

Supplier countries, although mainly newly industrialized countries (including the post-communist emergent market economies [EMEs]), are highly diverse in their degree of development and in the institutional architectures they have inherited and/or newly constructed (Radocevic 2004; King and Szelenyi 2005). Although new typologies of capitalism (e.g. Hancké et al. 2007) refer to EMEs there is no unity within this bloc, and the supplier countries in the clothing industry encompass a far greater capitalist diversity. Hence any conclusions about types of institutional coordination can be drawn only at a high level of generality. For the purposes of this book it suffices to point out that in all developing countries/EMEs institutional architectures are not yet as coherent and/or as stable as in western economies. Market-shaping institutions and regulatory systems are either underdeveloped (Czaban et al. 2003: 18; Faust et al. 2004: 72; Hancké et al. 2007: 4) or, more often, weakly enforced (Collins 2003; Sum and Ngai 2005). Lack of consistent and effective regulation is particularly evident in institutions shaping employment relations within firms (ibid). Although, as is shown in Chapters 8 and 9, supplier countries also show diversity in state–economy relations, they share one commonality: in their eagerness to attract foreign capital, states—even relatively strong and interventionist states, such as the Chinese—are unable or unwilling to enforce labour legislation. They fail to compensate large segments of labour for the hardships endured in the process of increasing global integration of markets. Additionally, management education and the handling of higher-value management tasks remain underdeveloped in many, though not all, developing countries. Supplier countries in this industry thus cannot exert sustained institutional influence.

2.2.3. Global Governance, National States

In both developed and developing countries, we suggest, the state is not merely an ensemble of institutionalized practices but also has to be regarded as an actor bridging the national and the international/global domain. States in developed western countries, due to their greater power and autonomy, will be distinguished from states in developing countries, and differences in state strategies *within* each camp will additionally be highlighted. States are not viewed as unitary and cohesive entities and therefore cannot always operate in the service of an identifiable national interest (Mann 1993: 56). This stance also suggests that it does not make sense to speak, as does Gritsch (2005), of the state's engagement with capital in general, but that it is necessary to distinguish between the often conflicting interests and influences of firms/associations in different industries. Such an approach departs from VoC theory, where national states are viewed as more cohesive bodies.

Our special consideration of states and their relation to MNCs suggests that we reject the notion that states have lost all authority and have been rendered redundant by globally mobile firms. Equally, we do not support the opposite claim that the state's role in a globally more integrated economy has not been affected at all. Instead, we follow a number of authors who, albeit in different ways, see the state as merely transformed (Evans, Rueschemeyer, and Skocpol 1985; Palan and Abbott 1996; Held et al. 1999; Weiss 2003). This perspective views MNCs and states as interdependent, with firms needing the predictability only states can create and states being dependent on the revenue firms generate. At the same time one cannot ignore the fact that internationally operating firms 'prefer a world in which private enterprise is not restricted' (Evans 1985: 214). Hence we do not regard the state as a passive bystander in the international economy but as actively seeking, in varying degrees, to mould markets and institutions to support its domestic firms. It has adopted new strategies to this end. The state therefore has retained power and autonomy, albeit in reduced or significantly transformed form and with significant variation between states. This retention of a significant degree of autonomy is particularly true for developed states, whereas the manoeuvring space of national states in developing countries, we will show, has been considerably reduced (see also Evans 1985: 194–5).

Particularly useful for our study is the concept of the 'competition state', popu-larized by Cerny (2000) but more usefully elaborated by Palan and Abbott (1996). The concept of competition state and competitive strategies draws attention to the way in which traditionally domestic policy concerns are increasingly under-stood in the context of comparative international competitiveness. The notion of the competition state has two elements: (1). the pervasive belief in national competitiveness as the surest means to secure economic growth and prosperity; and (2). a change of state policies to this end from demand side to supply side measures which are held to lay the foundations for enabling firms to compete internationally. Affirming the diversity among state stances already emphasized above, Palan and Abbott stress that states have not converged towards developing the same policy responses to global competitive pressures. Instead a diversity of responses has occurred, and these are not always pursued with great efficacy (Palan and Abbott 1996: 4–5). Instead of conceiving of a homogenous competition state, these authors analyse the various competitive strategies that are available and that may be pursued singly or in combination. 'Competitive strategy' is defined as 'a set of policies that are explicitly aimed at improving the climate for business (national and/or international) and hence at enhancing the "competitive advantage" of such countries in the global economy' (Palan and Abbott 1996: 6). The following seven strategies are outlined:

1. States band together in large regional blocks;
2. They adopt the 'developmental state' model;
3. They embrace the 'social-democratic' model of selective integration into the world economy;
4. They strive to achieve hegemony;

5. They exploit their cheap and abundant labour to attract foreign capital;
6. They become tax havens and/or develop special economic zones;
7. They remain structurally impeded from joining the competitive game (Palan and Abbott 1996: 5).

Whereas strategies 1–4 are those of states in developed countries, states in developing countries are mainly confined to choosing among strategies 5–7.

Gritsch (2005) further emphasizes how national states in developed countries, particularly the G7, actively construct globalization and use their political clout in the course of competitive interaction. She seems to point to a competitive strategy which could be accommodated by Palan and Abbott's (1996) 'striving for hegemony' (strategy 4). But Gritsch spells out more clearly what is entailed for states of developed countries, enhancing the pertinence of her analysis to the concerns of this book. She draws attention to the way in which the G7 design and establish international trade agreements, organizations, and legislation that support and govern the trans-border investments and production networks constitutive of current economic globalization (Gritsch 2005: 2–3). Among the means to promote their firms' competitive advantage in the global economy she includes subsidies, manipulation of tariff classifications, and state-to-state dispute resolution (as, for example, in the WTO). G7 states influence trade and tariff policies and protect their domestic markets against unwanted foreign incursion (ibid: 3–4). Gritsch highlights the interactive and sometimes complementary quality of states' competitive strategies. She points out how they use the above instruments to gain access to other states' differentially organized factors of production to manufacture intermediate inputs or final assemblies (ibid: 8), sourcing in politically more tractable sites. This refers to the state strategy in developing countries of 'downward mobility' (strategy 5), identified by Palan and Abbott (1996). Bilateral trade agreements between developed and developing states are considered particularly open to the practice of dismantling legal and political barriers against the utilization of cheap and tractable labour. This analysis is particularly pertinent to our preoccupation with labour in GPNs, discussed in Chapter 10.

Although all these policies and instruments are indeed used by national states and regional trade blocks in the clothing industry to preserve the advantage of G7 domestic firms, it is notable that they are not invariably successful in the longer term. States may initiate these processes but will be unable to control them once they are under way. They are frequently faced with unanticipated negative consequences that defeat the original purpose of state action. Also states cannot fulfil all the demands of capital as firms in different industries (e.g. textiles and clothing) make different and often mutually opposed demands on the state. Thus although national states, particularly of western developed countries, are still powerful they are not all-powerful and often fail to obtain durable global competitive advantage for their firms. This analysis reminds us that, in many international arenas, states compete with and are occasionally out-manoeuvred by MNCs. The resources and power of MNCs, Gereffi (2005: 165) points out, can thwart the territorially based objectives of national states. Where neither states nor firms intervene, transnational advocacy networks may try and fill the gap (Keck and Sikkink 1998; Scholte 2000).

Concerning the states of the USA, UK, and Germany, their different institutional structures and political traditions significantly shape which of the above competitive strategies they pursue vis-à-vis competitors in the textile and clothing industry. Thus the American federal state, with its power fragmented and diffused over territorial and functional state levels/agencies, is highly vulnerable to political capture by industry lobbies. 'State power in the twentieth-century USA is fragmented, dispersed, and everywhere permeated by organized societal interests' (Skocpol 1985: 12). Coupled with its power in international political arenas, the American state frequently aggressively asserts the interests of domestic business in international organizations/bilateral treaties against those of foreign competitors, as well as protecting American firms domestically against foreign imports (Moon 2000: 345). The British state, in contrast, has a high degree of policy autonomy, and political lobbies are much weaker (Wood 2001: 255). Trade liberalism has been pursued more consistently. Intervention in favour of particular industries, either at home or in international forums, is relatively rare, and supportive infrastructures favouring exports or vocational education and training are underdeveloped. The German state's power also is highly fragmented but, due to the presence of countervailing powers, is less prone than the US state to capture by domestic business interests. Its liberal foreign trade policy is much less frequently distorted by selective protectionism than is the case for the US state, although interests sometimes are pursued through the EU. Like the British state, the German state eschews direct intervention in particular industries, but it instead favours facilitation and delegation to public agencies/association. Regional *Länder* states, however, may be more directive. The German federal state maintains a general legal framework, as well as following a general policy on export promotion through special credit facilities that have proven very favourable to German industry (Schmidt 2002: 166–7; Kitschelt and Streeck 2004). Comparatively high investment into the system of vocational education and training, too, comes partly from the state.

2.3. THEORY OF GLOBAL VALUE CHAINS/PRODUCTION NETWORKS

GPNs result from a strategic fragmentation of the value chain in formerly vertically integrated companies. Underlying the concept of the value chain is the simple notion of different economic activities that are required to bring a good/service from conception, through different phases of production, to final delivery to consumers, adding value at each stage. These stages, in principle, may be separated both organizationally and locationally. Such separation is based on management assumptions that, for varying reasons, some functions in the chain are better performed by external, nominally independent, contractors than within hierarchically integrated firms. The resulting distribution of functions between various independent firms in different national/international locations is captured by the notion of an international division of labour that allows producers with varying factor endowments to form cross-border networks of production.

The development of GVCs/GPNs is closely related to that of global trade. The acceleration of outsourcing and the development of GPNs during the 1980s and 1990s were facilitated by trade liberalization and particularly by an increase in intra-industry trade in intermediate goods. Feenstra (1998: 32) even referred to the rising integration of world markets and the simultaneous disintegration of production. GPNs well illustrate also the impact on western economies and their firms of exogenous political transformations, namely, the transition to market forms of organization in the countries of the former Soviet sphere of influence and in China. It is these exogenous economic and political 'shocks' that are integral to the formation and perpetuation of GPNs. Outsourcing was addition-ally stimulated and facilitated by an improvement in transport and advances in communication technology. Last, this expansion overlapped, particularly in the USA and to a lesser degree in the UK, with a process of corporatization in the clothing retail sector and the intensification of efforts to increase shareholder value (Palpacuer 2008).

Gereffi's work (1994, 1999) on global commodity chains (GCC) has laid a solid foundation for a theoretical understanding of such processes. GCCs are defined as 'sets of interorganizational networks clustered around one commodity or product, linking households, enterprises and states to one another in the global economy' (Gereffi et al. 1994: 3). (In a 2001 article with Kaplinsky, Gereffi replaces the term GCC with 'global value chain'—a term also adopted in this book.) Gereffi combines insights from Hopkins' and Wallerstein's (1977) notion of world systems and from strategic management scholars such as Porter (1990) and particularly Kogut (1984). Kogut, in an analysis of firms' global strategy, was one of the first to point out that firms make bets on certain links in the value-added chain and capture rents from placing segments of the chain in different countries (ibid: 152–3).

Gereffi envisages networks around nodes in the chain, but mainly stresses the linear nature of border-crossing chains. His focus on the value chain is neverthe-less useful as the different possible ways to slice up the chain fundamentally affect the organization, governance, and location of networks. The concept of the chain also emphasizes the sequential nature and the interconnectedness of the various elements in the value chain, as well as the fact that, despite fragmentation and spatial dispersion, these elements have to be re-integrated in an optimal way by lead firms.

The notion of the global *value* chain additionally reminds us that outsourcing is mainly about differential value extraction and, related to this, risk assumption at various points in the chain. Such effort by managers to stabilize or increase the level of value extraction in GVCs is, for Gereffi and Kaplinsky (2001), mainly focused on wage differences between developed and developing countries and the outsourcing of manufacturing operations. However, value extraction is a more dynamic process. It may be further increased by expanding the number of functions outsourced beyond manufacturing. The mode of sourcing, such as 'full package' or 'quick response', also entails a shifting of risk from the buyer to the supplier and, as such, may indirectly affect the distribution of value. Furthermore, outsourcing also takes place in *developed* countries, where savings arise less from differential wage costs and more from the realization of greater economies of scale, for example, from the outsourcing of distribution processes or various pre-assembly functions such as pattern-making or cutting. Our study of value extraction focuses not only on companies' strategic configuration of the value chain but also emphasizes the fact that value is extracted mainly from labour. This aspect, strangely, has been neglected in most studies of GVCs/GPNs. The term 'value chain' thus has several advantages. We nevertheless favour the adoption of the concept of 'network' as our primary organizational structure to draw attention to both vertical and horizontal relationships and to insert a more relational perspective into the analysis of inter-firm contracting. However, we do not think that this necessitates the surrender of the term 'value chain'; instead, we highlight its analytical utility for understanding network construction and organization.

Our adoption of the term 'global production network' is primarily influenced by two related articles by Peter Dicken and colleagues, namely, Dicken et al. (2001) and Henderson et al. (2002). They define networks as 'the nexus of interconnected functions and operations through which goods and services are produced, distributed and consumed' (Henderson et al. 2002: 445). In common with these authors, we see such networks as consisting of social processes producing both goods and services. Dicken and colleagues posit an actor-network concept which moves away from Gereffi's (1994) mainly structural account. Unlike Gereffi, Dicken and colleagues view networks as 'both social structures and ongoing processes, which are constituted, transformed and reproduced ... through asymmetric and evolving power relationships by intentional social actors' (Dicken et al. 2001: 105). Such an actor-oriented relational view of networks, revolving around differences in power resources, also forms the centre of this book. The neo-institutionalist perspective we adopt means that actors—mainly firms but also states—are shaped by the institutional environments in which they are embedded. This understanding of network also departs from Powell's (1990) conception of networks as a distinctive organizational form between hierarchy and market. We make no assumption that network relationships are always of the relational kind, that is, those in which the existence of trust eliminates opportunism.

Gereffi's (1994) most important contribution has been his focus on the governance of chains and the unequal distribution of power and authority this entails. Governance, in turn, determines how resources are allocated and flow within a chain, linking back to the unequal extraction of value. For Gereffi (various dates), GVCs are driven by large retailers and branded marketers (i.e. firms which derive value from ownership of brands but no longer themselves do any manufacturing). Hence the power struggle, which is a struggle about the extraction of the maximum possible value, occurs between such lead firms from developed countries and suppliers/contractors in developing countries.

Gereffi's conception of power mainly focuses on structural power, while actors' actual practices, particularly those crystallized in relations to network partners, are largely blended out. Hence the social foundations of power are not identified. The concept of power receives further illumination by being linked to the actor-focused relational view of networks elaborated by Dicken et al. (2001) and Henderson et al. (2002). The latter define power as 'the capacity [of a firm] to influence decisions and resource allocation—vis-à-vis other firms in the network—decisively and consistently in its own interests' (ibid: 450). While they too attribute power to actors that drive networks, they go on to enquire what makes actors powerful. Power, for Dicken et al. (2001: 93f.), derives from the control of key resources rather than merely from position in the network.

An additional contribution to the debate on network power has been made by Tokatli (2007). Like the current authors, she wishes to avoid the implication that suppliers in low-wage countries are invariably totally powerless network actors who possess no means to emancipate themselves and achieve upgrading. She points out that power is not something 'held in reserve' by the lead buyer firm and that the unequal distribution of power 'only signifies the greater degree to which one party ... may influence the conduct of others' (ibid: 68). In other words, power is not a 'zero sum' resource but may be distributed between various actors, albeit to differing degrees. Like Dicken et al. (2001), Tokatli therefore also emphasizes the fluidity and dynamism of power relationships (ibid).

These observations facilitate both a more encompassing and a more differentiating analysis of power and take better account of the complexity of relationships empirically identified in our research. They invite researchers to distinguish between the varying power resources of retailers in different social institutional environments, such as informational resources derived from close contact with consumers, as well as material resources provided by greater capital concentration and sheer market power. This more subtle approach also permits the identification of other power holders than the retailers and of the various strands of power relations in the global clothing industry. First, the power of large retailers, as we show in Chapter 4, differs considerably between countries and is affected both by state regulation/de-regulation and by the size of the domestic market, as well as by the extent to which the development of the stock market has furthered concentration in the retail sector. This approach thus allows actors from different national origins to organize their networks in a different manner and not necessarily rely solely on the exercise of power.

Second, the power that suppliers may wield depends on both their size and their level of competence, and these, too, are shaped by the institutional environment of their domestic economies, as well as by that in the buyers' country. Buyers who encourage inter-firm learning are much more likely to empower their suppliers and, sometimes, nurture future competitors. Although supplier power is still an exceptional phenomenon and relations continue to be stacked against their gain of power, shifts in the distribution of power should not be discounted a priori.

If power is purely structural then upgrading becomes impossible to achieve. Here we need to consider the position in GPNs of (largely Asian) middleman firms (agents for western firms) and the way their command of the resource of common ethnicity has, among other factors, facilitated their tremendous growth and transborder organization. Third, the power struggle occurs also between firms *within* developed countries but in different industries. Conflicts of interest between 'manufacturers' and textile producers deserve consideration. Fourth, there is the constant struggle by labour in developing countries to resist the (ownership-based) power of contractors to extract increasing effort and surplus, in order to satisfy the continuously escalating demands of western buyers for further reductions in both price and lead times.

It therefore would not be accurate to view all relationships between buyers in developed and suppliers in developing countries merely as hierarchical power relationships. As our analysis of empirical data on buyer–supplier relations shows, these differ by nationality of the buyer firm. Relational contracting may sometimes be found in long-established inter-firm relations, and often there exists a complex mix of motivations, objectives, and attitudes. Hence we do not want to reject the notion that long-established and more cooperative networks permit supplier learning and upgrading, even though this is not the modal type. Most often, however, learning occurs through demonstration effects which were not necessarily intended by the buyer and are rarely the result of targeted partner promotion. Last, following Stamm (2004: 19), we think it useful to distinguish between governance—exerting power in various forms by setting parameters for products and processes in order to extract maximum value—and mere coordination—the management of the delivery of tangible goods to the interfaces between segments of the value chain.

Gereffi's theory entails a multilevel spatial analysis of GVCs. But his highly aggregated levels—core and periphery—cannot fully capture the complexity of the diverse levels spanned by GVCs (Dicken et al. 2001), nor do the various levels receive adequate analysis. This shortcoming is mainly due to the fact that, in his eagerness to capture the arc of power represented by the chain, firms' social institutional embeddedness—in either developed or developing countries—is disregarded. Contrary to the belief of the current authors, Gereffi holds that 'the way firms do business in the global economy thus is determined to an increasing extent by their positions in global commodity chains, not their national origins' (Gereffi 1994: 433). As already noted by Whitley (1996), Gereffi therefore lacks the sociological perspective of new institutionalism that is central to the Business Systems or VoC approach.

Dicken et al. (2001) wish to consider social institutions, but as geographers, they are concerned with *geographical space*. In the absence of a notion of society it is not clear where institutions derive from and how firms and institutions interact. Henderson et al. (2002) make an explicit reference to Whitley's (1999) work and emphasize the importance of social institutions: 'inter-firm networks link societies which exhibit significant social and institutional variation ... ... in short, represent different forms of capitalism' (ibid: 441). In practice, however, they ignore the insights of Whitley and other VoC theorists in that they focus on institutions mainly as political actors that constrain firms. Institutions are not viewed as socially constituting firms and their mode of coordination with other actors. (For greater enlightenment on this we must rely on the comparative capitalisms analysis reviewed above.)

Neither Gereffi (1994) nor Dicken et al. (2001) develop a theory of the firm which is implicit in strategic value chain fragmentation and the search for new or complementary competences. The firm remains a 'black box', and issues such as motivating employees and creating commitment are not addressed. Neither the fact that the buyer firm becomes a heavily truncated and dis-embedded firm nor the impact of this on relations between buyer and supplier firm in GPNs attracts any comment. This is a particularly surprising *lacuna* in the relational approach advocated by Dicken et al. (2001). We will address this gap later in this chapter, drawing on the National Business Systems approach. While Dicken et al. (2001) and Gereffi (1994) refer to the importance of the nation state as an additional actor shaping GPNs and their changing configurations, in practice their analysis remains at the level of economic networks. (For Henderson et al. 2002, the network is even conceived of as an alternative mechanism of coordination.)

We concur with Fine and Leopold (1993) that because of multiple processes of two-way interaction in the clothing industry between production, retail, and consumption it forms a distinctive 'system of provision'. The latter therefore cannot be captured by typologies of network forms, such as the one established by Gereffi, Humphrey, and Sturgeon (2005). Their typology abstracts from a variety of industries, with different technological processes, degrees of information coding and supplier capabilities, as well as various end users. This typology, they claim, can specify and explain variation (ibid: 82). Although such a typology may be useful in other industry contexts it is not enlightening for this study. In their almost exclusive focus on the production process and technology, the authors ignore the social institutional context altogether, abandoning even the focus on international regulation found in Gereffi's earlier work. As observed by Gibbon (2008: 38), the broader objectives of different lead firms disappear from view, as does the diversity of agents along the chain. Furthermore, none of the three types elaborated—captive, modular, and relational network—fits the clothing industry very well. Their type of 'captive network', borrowed from an analysis of the auto industry, overlooks the lack of asset specificity in clothing and the ease with which both buyers and suppliers, in principle, can switch partners without incurring major costs. The additional suggestion that, with increasing movement to 'full package' production, the network is becoming 'relational' is hard to reconcile with Gereffi's earlier emphasis on asymmetric value extraction and hierarchical power relations in the chain.

Another complementary strand of work on aspects of GPNs/GVCs is the French *Filière* or Conventions theory, reviewed by Stamm (2004: 22f.) and applied by Gibbon (2008). This approach distinguishes four mechanisms by which product quality demand is coordinated among market participants:

1. Reduction of uncertainty on the basis of trust and long-term relationships or through the use of brand names and reputation;
2. Through the actions of third parties who set common standards and monitor their adherence which reduces transaction costs for buyer firms;
3. Price differences are equated with quality differences;
4. Commitment to common values and intrinsic motivation to avoid conflict.

This typology is useful insofar as it reminds us that network governance is not solely about price but that, for certain buyers, quality concerns are as high as or even higher than preoccupation with price. The above typology also counsels against viewing network governance solely in terms of the exercise of hierarchical power. Even if power asymmetry is the most prevalent feature of GPNs in this industry, other governance mechanisms, at the very least, may become uppermost for some firms in particular circumstances. Without this assumption it becomes difficult to understand how upgrading of supplier firms—an important component of Gereffi's approach—becomes feasible. We have used similar insights (not derived from Conventions theory but from VoC institutional analysis) to distinguish between strategies of buyer firms from different national origins concerning product quality. (For details, see Chapter 7.) Conventions theory also has implications for supplier firms, as captured by Gibbon (2008). Gibbon applies this theory to analyse the practices of Mauritian suppliers who have segmented the customer base into American and European buyers, each with product requirements incompatible with those of the other. Our research also discovered some segmentation practices but found that European buyers were further subdivided into German and British firms.

A last strand of theory relevant to a consideration of GPNs in the clothing industry is one that focuses on gender in the labour market and the overwhelming presence of women in clothing assembly jobs. Women are, of course, not a homogenous category either within or between societies, but have common identities ascribed to them by employers (Carr and Chen 2004). It is worth noting also that the development of export-led clothing industries has created a large number of new jobs for women and that young women often genuinely prefer the work and the limited earning capacity and independence it affords to prior agricultural work, the countryside and control by the patriarchal family (Ngai 2005). It is the low quality of these jobs, their inadequate reward, and in-built insecurity which is at issue.

As Collins (2003: 5) points out, gender ideology is central to the construction of the labour market in this industry, in that the industry depends on cheap and controllable labour. A market for gendered jobs, with low wages and gender-specific constraints and pressures, has been integral to the clothing industry in developed countries since the nineteenth century, both in home-working and, towards the end of that century, in factory production (Morokvasic et al. 1986: 406). Following the outsourcing of manufacturing operations and the building of GPNs in developing countries, such a labour regime was re-created in the developing countries. High levels of exploitation and control of female labour have reproduced the low level of wages, labour standards, and rights typical of this industry in nineteenth century America and Europe. In the global clothing industry, where female workers usually perform the large majority of assembly jobs, they share the following common features. They form a large reservoir of usually young, poorly educated female labour from predominantly rural backgrounds, usually further disadvantaged by migrant or 'informal' worker status; they are considered more pliable than men; and are less likely to join unions. However, women do not accept the hardship of jobs passively and respond to employers' high level of exploitation with low commitment to the job and frequent movement between work places. It is no exaggeration to say that this labour currently sustains the western clothing industry. The resulting harsh labour regime, as well as the global backlash against it, is analysed in Chapter 10.

Among the few scholars who explicitly explore the interaction between GPNs and national capitalisms the work of Herrigel and Wittke (2005) is notable. In their study of supplier relations of American and German auto firms, they consider the VoC thesis. But they prefer a constructivist approach to the understanding of firm strategies which, they argue, eschews institutional determinism. They conclude that, due to the turbulence and uncertainty of firms' global environment, firms from differing national origins frequently develop the same form of network governance. They thus elevate the influence of markets above that of institutions. In positing that firms act independently of national institutional effects and try to change incentives that institutions provide, they deliberately challenge some of the central tenets of VoC theory. We, too, introduce challenges to the VoC approach, but hold, in contrast to Herrigel and Wittke (2005), that it retains considerable value for the analysis of GVCs/GPNs.

2.4. GPNs AND VoC ANALYSIS: CONTRASTS AND COMPLEMENTARITIES

In this book, we regard the theory of GVC/GPN and the VoC/comparative capitalisms approach as complementary. The above discussion makes clear that we do not view firms as exercising full strategic choice completely detached from their domestic institutional environment. Firms, we will show, find it difficult to escape institutional effects and to operate in institutionally alien and incomplete environments. Furthermore, firms are not solely oriented to production but also oriented to sales. Sales markets in the clothing industry are still predominantly national, requiring coordination with national retailers. Hence this area of coordination remains influenced by national institutionalized patterns of inter-firm relations, as well as by the nature of domestic markets. The power relations established in such domestic networks, in turn, fundamentally shape the governance of the whole GPN. We therefore reject the suggestion made by Gereffi (2005) and by Herrigel and Wittke (2005) that the construction and governance of GPNs does not differ between firms from different varieties of capitalism. To the contrary, we posit that the imprint of the domestic institutional framework may also be identified in the relational aspects of GPNs. This does not amount to a claim that all firms from the same variety of capitalism behave in an identical manner. We acknowledge some diversity between firms of the same national origin, due to differences in ownership and size, as well as in product strategy and distinctive historical legacy.

At the same time we take account of the fact that, by externalizing entire stages of the value chain, lead firms become truncated firms which are only partially moulded by their domestic institutional environment. Managers have to adapt, at least to some degree, to the market for contracting, to the extremely varied institutionalized practices of many supplier countries, and to the international and regional trade rules which proliferate in the clothing industry. (For details of this last, see Chapters 5 and 6). Furthermore, the competitive advantage of lead firms is only partly constituted by their home environment and partly by constraints and opportunities flowing from regulatory regimes at other geopolitical levels.

VoC theory, which also takes account of coordination *within* firms (see Section 2.6), alerts us to the dilemmas faced by lead firms in GPNs. The theory's focus on intra-firm and inter-firm coordination problems forces us to address the following questions. How are such coordination problems addressed/solved in supra-national environments where firms face institutional incompleteness in regard to cross-border inter-firm ties and intra-firm labour relations? This also raises the serious problem of how firms maintain control over the production process when domestically utilized methods of control, such as unilateral control by top management in LMEs or joint decision-making by deliberation in CMEs, no longer apply in supplier countries with highly diverse labour regimes. Some of these problems can be solved by exporting domestic institutional resources, while other areas remain completely ungoverned. One of the focal points of this book is to explore these issues by concentrating on the relational aspects of GPNs and to point to the many tensions that arise when firms are subject to the influence of incompatible institutions.

Furthermore, the escape of lead firms from institutional constraints relating to the coordination of (shop floor) labour also creates some hollowing out of domestic institutions and undermines patterns of complementarity between institutions. This disruptive effect of globally operating firms and their trans-border networks, once it spreads to a number of industries, needs to be taken more fully into account by VoC analysis.

We therefore argue that the impact of GPNs neither acts fully to reinforce existing domestic institutional configuration, nor does it invariably disrupt them or even cancel them out. We undertake a systematic exploration in this book of the circumstances in which global firms either reinforce and even export national institutionalized practices or, alternatively, corrode national patterns of firms' coordination with other actors. Our study of lead firms in global networks of production and of the national, international, and global contexts in which they operate aims to demonstrate both the reinforcement and the disruptive effect, as well as to specify the context in which each occurs.

2.5. FIRM CAPABILITIES AND STRATEGY: IMPLICATIONS FOR THE ORGANIZATION OF THE VALUE CHAIN

Although GVC theory, drawing on Kogut (1984), takes firm competences/ capabilities and strategy as its starting point it does not have a well developed conception of the firm. For such a conception we need to turn back to VoC theory, particularly to the National Business Systems approach developed by Whitley (1999, 2001, 2005) and to some prior work on competence and strategy. Whitley, inspired by Penrose (1959), focuses prominently on the *internal* organization of the firm and on the varying capabilities developed in intra-firm relations between management and labour. If the development of GPNs is regarded as a crucial strategic move by formerly vertically integrated firms, this aspect needs further consideration. It helps us to understand the link between firm organization, competence, and strategy, on the one hand, and the way value chains are configured on the other. It further illuminates why cross-national differences are likely to emerge in value chain configuration shaped by distinctive national business systems. This framework alerts us to (but fails to confront) the problems faced by firms' managers when, in global production networks, labour is no longer under their authority and cannot be integrated through a distinctive bundle of incentives and sanctions. A closer consideration of firm competences/capabilities also draws attention to the institutional domain of vocational education and training, held in this book to be a crucial link between the national and the global spheres of firms' activities. Last, we use this theoretical approach as our starting point 1. for elaborating the stages of the value chain and their associated activities and skills and 2. depending on *how* the chain is fragmented by firms, for the identification of different types of clothing firms.

The significance of firms in capitalist economies, according to Whitley (1999: 65), 'lies in their combination of financial control over resources with employment'. Firms are 'central collective actors in the mobilization, allocation, and use of assets, especially human labour power'. They develop distinctive capabilities through the authoritative direction of employees on the basis of employment agreements (ibid: 66). Capabilities are viewed 'as sets of organizationally specific experiences, knowledges, and expertise that confer competitive advantage'. They take time to build and require employees to work together over some time in generating firm-specific knowledge. As later taken on board by VoC theory, Whitley (1999) points out that firms differ across capitalisms in the nature of the capabilities they develop and coordinate, as well as in the strategies they pursue, based on the capabilities they have cultivated. The latter form the basis of their competitive advantage.

Capabilities occur in a variety of types and the following three, based on Teece, Pisano, and Shuen (1997), are pertinent to this study: *coordinating capabilities*, which involve the development of integrative routines that gather and process information about internal and external processes and link production facilities with suppliers; *organizational learning capabilities*, which involve joint problem solving and improvement of production and related processes; and *reconfigurational capabilities*, which enable firms to transform organizational resources and skills to deal with rapidly changing markets—in other words innovative capabilities (see also Stalk, Evans, and Shulman 1992; Hamel and Prahalad 1994; Grant 1996; Teece et al. 1997). A further useful distinction Whitley introduces is between the development of competences which become integrated in administrative structures and competences that function as 'loosely coupled collections of individuals or small groups coordinated in quasi-contractual ways' (Whitley 1999: 73). In the first case, managerial, technical, and other skilled workers have to be willing to contribute their skills to firm-specific problem-solving, and managers, through authority-sharing, that is, granting discretion over work organization, have to motivate employees to do so (Whitley 2005: 236). If, in contrast, owners/top managers only share authority with other managers, the resulting organizational learning and knowledge is less likely to become sedimented in organizational routines.

Whitley here draws a contrast between employee relations in what Hall and Soskice (2001) have termed a CMEs and an LME, with organizational learning capabilities more likely to be fostered by firms in CMEs. *Organizational learning capabilities* depend not only on authority sharing between management and labour but also on the institutionalization of skill training (Quinn, Doorley, and Paquette 1991: 301; Teece et al. 1997). A system of skill training is usually supported by a developed associational system and by state facilitation of and support for such a system. Additionally, an effective skill training system requires a longer-term managerial perspective and a willingness to invest in human resources, again an institutionalized feature of CMEs. In contrast, firms in LMEs do not have a developed system of skill training for intermediate employees and rely mainly on general education. *Reconfigurational capabilities*, however, are more likely to be developed in LMEs—where transformation of resources can be accomplished in a speedy manner by acquiring firms and (by firing and) hiring employees who possess the desired novel capabilities. Although such reconfigurational capabilities are mainly connected with high-technology development, they can be relatively mundane, such as the 'quick-response' capability of some clothing firms (Richardson 1996) or frequent changes in style and fashion. *Coordinating capabilities*, found mainly at management level, appear to be less specific to a particular variety of capitalism as different coordinating mechanisms may be employed by firms in CMEs and LMEs. They are particularly important to this study because outsourcing and GPNs require careful coordination between internal and externally available competences (Teece et al. 1997: 515).

Managers' ability to command a distinctive set of skills then has to be linked to managerial strategy, in order to generate competitive advantage. Strategy is defined by Kogut (1984: 152) as the 'allocation of resources which are expected to generate excess returns over time'. While Whitley's (2001, 2005) work examines whether and how MNCs from different business systems/varieties of capitalism transfer capabilities to foreign subsidiaries, the work of Teece et al. (1997),

Kogut (1984), and Gereffi (various years) links the notions of capabilities and firm strategy to the configuration of cross-border value chains/global production networks. However, Whitley's insights about the close link between institutional environment and different sets of capabilities and his careful identification of the complementarities between different aspects of firm organization are valuable in the context of studying the fragmentation of value chains and the building of GPNs.

Managers' competitive strategy, according to Grant (1996), has to determine a firm's core and non-core capabilities. Managers have to distinguish between capabilities unique to the firm and fundamental to its competitive advantage, and those which may be externalized, acquired either through market links or in networks (Grant 1996). In other words, core activities—and the sets of assets and capabilities necessary to achieve them—are those that allow the firm to achieve its strategic goals. Consequently firms need to retain sufficient control over these activities to allow them to achieve their strategic goals (Richardson 1996: 403). This can be accomplished either through ownership or through strong control over suppliers, allowing buyer firms to effect quasi-integration of their suppliers. In practice, however, as we will show in later chapters, it is not easy to distinguish between core and non-core activities. First, not many firms in this industry possess unique/inimitable capabilities because differentiation in style is usually a short-lived advantage and, second, because changes in both market demand and technology (e.g. the shift to 'quick response' production; use of CAD technology for cutting, grading, and pattern-making) and supplier capabilities (the shift from CMT to 'full package' supply) can alter perceptions of what constitute a firm's core capabilities. Core capabilities are thus not fixed once and for all but have a dynamic character, changing with the competitive environment. This shift in what is considered core and non-core then has repercussions for both the degree of hollowing out of capabilities tolerated by lead firm and the changing distribution of value between the various nodes of the chain.

In the following subsection we present a diagram of the value chain in the clothing industry. We then derive several different types of clothing firm from the mixture of functions/capabilities required to execute the various steps in the value chain both efficiently and effectively. In Chapter 3, we link the existence of divergent types of capabilities to firms' product paradigm and market strategy. The latter, in subsequent chapters, are related to differences in network coordination and governance.

2.6. ORGANIZATION OF THE VALUE CHAIN AND FIRM TYPES

The value chain in the clothing industry embraces several different sets of activity, roles, and occupations (Figure 2.1). (The following adapts and develops ideas from Dunford 2001: 1–2.)

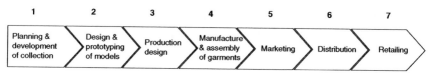

Figure 2.1. Steps in the clothing value chain

1. Development and planning of the entire collection involves several skilled activities including knowledge of market trends and of fabric availability, the integration of both into development of product lines, and the costing of the planned collection.

2. Design and prototyping of new models requires both creativity and technical aptitude in addition to understanding market demand and cost structures.

3. Production design and sample-making concerns the most cost-efficient means of producing the item, bearing in mind quality standards and fit. Decisions on manufacturing location and fabric sourcing are also brought into consideration.

4. The actual assembly of garments, or CMT (cut–make–trim), involves mainly sewing and assembly operations, using simple machines and requiring fairly elementary skills.

5. Marketing seeks to match sales channels to the quality and character of the clothes, and to achieve the broadest possible market access in a given segment.

6. Distribution entails an increasingly sophisticated logistics operation often based on computerized order tracking and inventory control systems.

7. Finally, the garments reach consumers through various retail channels.

In principle these seven steps can be separated from each other and performed in different locations, since they involve clearly identifiable costs, as well as different sets of capabilities and occupations. The manner of fragmenting the value chain and the distribution of functions across different locations depends not only on available competencies and cost considerations but also on the nature of the final product and changes in market demand, as well as in the 'supplier' base.

Our analysis leads us to identify five different types of clothing enterprise, each with its own way of organizing the clothing value chain (Table 2.1).[1] Each type, as Chapter 7 demonstrates, involves different decisions regarding the activities to be externalized through markets or within networks, as well as their geographical location.

These five types of clothing enterprise evidently differ in the capabilities and capital invested, in the resulting products and hence the markets they can enter, and consequently in the degree of autonomy and network power they develop. Whereas firm types 1–4 will be studied empirically in Chapters 3 (domestic industry context) and 7 (GPNs), firm type 5 (retailers) is covered in Chapter 4.

Table 2.1. Types of clothing firms,[a] based on different combinations of steps in the value chain[b]

	Type of firm	Steps combined	Type of product and market	Competences utilized	Costs incurred
Type 1	Branded/high fashion 'manufacturers'	Steps 1–3, 5–7	High quality brands, coordinated collections	Combines design/development competences with manufacturing and (often) retailing capability.	Very high
Type 2	Branded/high fashion marketers	Steps 1–2, 5–7	High quality brands	Combines design/development competences with marketing capability	High
Type 3	Domestic suppliers to large retailers	Same steps as type 1, but steps 1, 2, and 5 receive low emphasis	Standardized, made to order for retailers	Lower design, technical, and marketing capability than types 1 and 2	Low
Type 4	'Cut, Make and Trim' firms[c]	Step 4[d]	All types	Managerial coordination of semi-skilled operators	Medium
Type 5	Retailers, with backward integration into design and supply chain organization	Steps 1, 2, and 7	Standard clothing, full package or imported	Mainly retailing competencies, combined with some design and coordination competences	Medium

[a] Includes retailers.

[b] Steps in value chain: (1) development of collection; (2) design; (3) technical preparation for production; (4) manufacturing; (5) marketing; (6) distribution/logistics; (7) retailing.

[c] Located in developing countries or in informal sector of developed ones.

[d] If 'full package' suppliers, also buy fabric and trim.

In addition, and parallel to processes of vertical disintegration, processes of functional re-integration have been notable. In hyper-competitive markets such as those for fashion clothing, quick response to new consumer demand has become an important competitive weapon. A set of process innovations, described as 'quick response', has added timing and know-how to the old competitive weapons of either price or quality (Richardson 1996: 400; Abernathy et al. 1999). Among such innovations is the use of information technology for managing levels of stock and its replenishment and the required close coordination with suppliers, as well as for shortened production cycles on the part of the latter. There exist tensions between practices of extensive functional disintegration and the flexibility (particularly to vary capacity) it entails and more recent demands for re-integration, which call for enhanced inter-organizational commitment. As Richardson (1996) makes clear, these tensions have not been resolved in the theory of organization and strategy formation nor, we go on to show in the following empirical chapters, in firms' practices.

2.7. BRANDS, FASHION, AND CONSUMPTION

An understanding of the clothing industry, particularly of the fashion segment, must investigate the significance of brands and fashion. The rise of brands has been a key feature of consumer society. In the past, when independent traders were the norm, the latter acted as intermediaries between the product and the end user, personally guaranteeing its quality. As certain brands established their monopoly position, shopkeepers' opinion ceased to matter (Aldridge 2004: 35–6). Branded products in a mobile, urbanized impersonal society may serve as a guarantee of product quality and reliability (Wrigley and Lowe 2002). They thus promote product recognition and differentiation.

But assisting product differentiation does not exhaust the function of brands, nor does it suffice to explain the high value they can command in the market. As pointed out by sociologists of consumption and culture, a brand is a complex symbol that represents a variety of ideas and attributes (Baudrillard 1988). It serves to express individual taste and identity, thereby promoting social distinction (Bourdieu 1984).

Political economists, in contrast, point out that producers and retailers systematically establish their brands in the market, that is, they foster brand recognition and brand loyalty through packaging and advertising. Brands, by establishing a monopoly for their creators, generate disproportionate value for producers and distributors. The greatly enhanced importance of brand management to the valorization of capital and the way consumers are used to participate in the process as 'active producers of brand' are highlighted by Arvidson (2006) and Trentmann (2006). Arvidson (ibid: 83) refers to 'brand equity'. He reminds us that it not only translates into premium prices but increasingly also generates brand value directly realized on financial markets. Thus, the brand value of The Gap in the early 2000s was put at US$7.7 billion and that of Levi Strauss at US$3.3 billion (Oxfam International 2004: 49).

This anti-competitive aspect of brands and their centrality to the generation of rent for their producers—creating a less benign interpretation than that of cultural sociologists—has been highlighted particularly by Naomi Klein (2001) but also by Gereffi and Kaplinsky (2001). Corporations that nurture brands, for Klein, are both anti-competitive and exploitative. Klein, being aware that branded producers have reputational capital to protect and therefore are susceptible to public pressure, was among the most vocal advocates of holding them responsible for the low wages and labour standards in global production networks that produced branded goods for western markets. She thus fuelled the growing support for anti-sweatshop movements in both the USA and Europe, even if others had much earlier pointed to the abuse of labour in developing countries. (For further details on anti-sweatshop movements, see Chapter 10.)

Although the ascendancy of life style brands and their anti-competitive nature is undeniable, an emphasis on rent-seeking behaviour of branded firms does not have to negate brands' function of promoting genuine product differentiation on the basis of quality and reliability. The cultural and material aspects of products generally interact, and consumers are not total dupes. Product quality and utility are mostly incorporated into and promote a brand's attraction as a symbol of life style. Producers, we learnt during our interviews, are well aware of the necessity to incorporate tangible material difference into their branded products—thus designer firms in both Germany and the UK mainly used Italian rather than Chinese/Turkish fabrics. Last, as shown in Chapter 10, exploitation of producers in developing countries is not exclusive to brands but to all clothing production. It is simply the case that branded marketers, who have to rely on brand loyalty, are more vulnerable to anti-sweatshop protests than producers of private label garments.

In contrast to other industries, brands in clothing arose relatively late—during the 1980s—due to the greater difficulty of conveying varied and changing product features through packaging (Aldridge 2004). Once established, they assumed huge importance. But in the last decade or so branded marketers in the clothing industry have come up against a serious challenge. Large retailers' private label goods—which in some cases are receiving recognition as 'store brands'—are leading to a gradual blurring between 'manufacturers'/marketers' brands and store brands. The rise to prominence of 'store brands' is supported by changing consumer habits involving greater search for 'value for money' clothing and the cachet that can be derived from finding High Street and even discounter fashion that copies designer trends. This search for value manifests itself in the increasing practice of mixing expensive brands with cheap clothing, referred to as cross-shopping by hybrid consumers.

Another concept interacting in complex ways with that of *brand* is *fashion* which also shapes consumption, retail, and production of garments, and is, in turn, influenced by the latter. Both brand and fashion serve individuals' desire for expression of aesthetic taste and distinction from others. Both combine in a complex manner conformity to trends, to satisfy an urge for belonging, with desire for individualization and differentiation (Simmel 1997). At the same time both brands and fashion, in different ways, maintain/create market demand and the profits accruing both to manufacturers and, even more so, to retailers. But whereas fashion, created in a collusive manner between producer and consumer, involves constant change to overcome conformity by further differentiation and individualization, brands guarantee a constancy of highly regarded product features. In fashion clothing the ornamental function becomes more important than the functional aspect. With branded clothing, in contrast, utilitarian features such as quality and fit remain relevant. Manufacturers and retailers of fashion clothing profit from built-in qualitative obsolescence and the replacement consumption it makes necessary (Fine and Leopold 1993: 28). In contrast, brand manufacturers (while not freed from demands for fashion and image management) make their excess profit from constant reproduction of particular garment features that guarantee reliability of quality and fit and thereby may signal social superiority.

Although fashion clothing for a mass market, which is connected with rising levels of affluence even among lower classes, had already started at the end of the nineteenth century/beginning of the twentieth century (Fine and Leopold 1993; Djelic and Ainamo 2005: 48), it has recently entered a new stage. During the last decade or so, a multiplication of fashion cycles has occurred, replacing the former two main seasons with several cycles within seasons (Abernathy et al. 1999; Interview Notes 2003/04). For many retailers even these cycles have become blurred by the phased introduction of new goods throughout the season that has resulted in an increase in 'in season' purchasing and hence in the frequency of purchasing (Textile Outlook International 2005). Political economists, in contrast to cultural sociologists (e.g. Jones and Thornton 2005a), remind us that the above developments point not merely to a transformation in creative and symbolic assets, but that changes in production are centrally implicated and serve to maintain turnover and profits in an industry beset by crisis (Fine and Leopold 1993; Haupt 2002). For both producers and retailers, a turn to a much increased economy of scope— a seemingly anarchic proliferation of styles—partially overcomes the threat of falling demand.

NOTE

1. Our types differ slightly from those of Gereffi (1994) in that type 3, suppliers of retailers' own label clothing, is not singled out by Gereffi.

3

The Clothing Industry in the USA, UK, and Germany

The clothing industries in our three chosen countries, the USA, UK, and Germany, have evolved in different ways over the decades. They have distinctive character-istics that shape their ability on the one hand to compete with clothing imported from less-industrialized countries, and on the other to develop and engage with supply chains across the world. In this chapter we discuss first, how and why a process of striking economic decline has occurred; second, the structure of the industry in each country, taking into account ownership, firm size, capabil-ities, and skills, and the stance of the state towards the industry; and third, the production and market strategies of constituent firms. In Section 3.3, we assess the impact on the clothing industry of change in upstream industries, notably textiles and textile machinery, before finally drawing brief conclusions on the implications of our findings for firms' position in global and national networks. In each case, we draw comparisons between the three countries in light of the different institutional contexts in which the industry operates. This analysis of the clothing industry in its domestic context is designed to show what resources and therefore influence and power firms can mobilize, both vis-à-vis domestic retailers and in their interactions with suppliers in global production networks.

3.1. A PICTURE OF INDUSTRIAL DECLINE

The clothing industry in the USA, UK, and Germany remained important throughout the first decades after 1945, both in terms of employment and in their contribution to GDP.[1] External competitive pressures began to be felt from the early 1970s onwards. Huge discrepancies in wage levels between developed and developing countries forced developed country firms to reorganize their value chain, usually by outsourcing some or all of their production operations to lower-wage countries. (For details, see Chapter 7.) Semi-skilled jobs like sewing have almost disappeared from developed countries, and yet firms and their associations are not prepared to abandon these industries to firms in developing countries.

In all three countries, direct government intervention to save jobs has been rare and also has varied between the three countries, conditioned by their divergent political systems. In the USA, because of the high geographical concentration of the clothing industry and the impact of its decline on voters, lip service has been paid to representations of industry bodies. In Germany, in contrast, this industry has received no political support, in contrast to the huge attention devoted to decline in the Ruhr heavy industries and the heavy subsidies received (Schuessler 2008: 118, 141, 213). Lack of government support also has been the fate of the UK industry but, in contrast to the German industry, there has been no strong and activist industry association to compensate for lack of government support. All three governments, however, have utilized their strength in regional and international organizations, such as NAFTA, the EU, and the WTO, to slow the decline of the clothing industry (see Chapter 5). As this section will make clear, in recent decades they have not only lost this battle but, by fostering foreign competitors in lower-wage countries, even may have worsened the situation. Also in recent decades governments, particularly in the USA but also in Germany, have switched their support. They have been more attentive towards large firms in the retail sector—which favour market liberalization—than towards the generally weaker and often protectionist clothing industry (Schuessler 2008: 150). Where a conflict of interest between the clothing and textile industry arose, the latter has been more likely to receive government support, particularly in the USA.

Some of the early employment reduction is due to foreign sourcing, particularly in Germany and the USA where out-sourcing started well before it did in the UK. In the USA, the clothing industry experienced a 12 per cent decline in jobs between 1977 and 1982.[2] Morokvasic, Phizacklea, and Rudolph (1986) report 153,000 jobs lost in the West German clothing industry between 1973 and 1982, a 42 per cent decline, with the UK losing 129,000 jobs (−38%) over the same period; they also note that half of all clothing firms in the two countries disappeared in the decade up to 1982.

The decline in employment became precipitous in the 1990s, particularly from the mid-1990s onwards. This development can be attributed to a variety of causes, each exerting a greater or lesser degree of impact: the elimination of quota lines corresponding to the ATC phase-out plan; a reduction or elimination of tariffs on imports for selected exporting countries; the devaluation of currencies in Asia after the 1997 crisis; and, in the case of the USA, the introduction of NAFTA and the devaluation of the Mexican peso in 1994. An additional reason has been the growing concentration in the retail sector—particularly in the UK and the USA—which brought a shift in power from 'manufacturers' to retailers and hence a marked deterioration of trading terms (Gardner and Sheppard 1989; Wrigley and Lowe 2002; Doeringer and Crean 2006). According to ILO figures based on national labour force surveys (for the USA and Germany) and official estimates (for the UK), industry contraction was much more marked in the UK and the USA than in Germany. The lesser degree of recent decline in Germany must be due to the significantly earlier start of outsourcing of its firms, namely from the late 1960s onwards as well as the EU's staged lifting of quota restrictions. Any decline now is more likely a consequence of continued acute competition. The situation has been exacerbated by the declining willingness of German banks to extend credit to firms in this sector (Interview Notes 2004; Schuessler 2008)—a decisive change in the German institutional environment. Although large firms in the USA also started foreign sourcing relatively early, the USA was much slower than the EU in lifting quota restriction on sensitive products, thus causing a veritable torrent of foreign imports from January 2005. In the UK, recent decline partly reflects the late onset of foreign sourcing and partly continued intense competition from cheap imports. The contribution of the domestic industries to GDP in each of the three countries is now very low.

In the UK, ILO data chart a decline in employment of 54.2 per cent between 1995 and 2001 (Nordås 2004: 10, table 3), a trend that has accelerated during the early years of this century. Data by BERR on clothing employment reveal that the clothing industry experienced a 73 per cent plunge between 1998 and 2005 to 45,000 workers (but an even more precipitous 80% fall for enterprises with 5 or more employees, to just 29,000). Despite concerns expressed by employers in the run-up to the introduction of a national minimum wage in 1999, there is little evidence to suggest that a wage floor has influenced employment rates in the sector; rather, the greater factor has been competition from low-wage economies (Low Pay Commission 2008: 117). This interpretation is supported by the fact that the loss of jobs in the labour-intensive clothing sector over the last two decades has been far more significant than in the more capital-intensive textiles sector. The decline in turnover by firms employing five or more people, from £6.6 billion to £3.3 billion between 1998 and 2005, mirrors their loss of employment. Turnover for the clothing sector as a whole fell slightly less rapidly, from £7.6 billion to £4.0 billion. These data on enterprise numbers and employment highlight the closure or retrenchment of the UK's largest companies.

In Germany, although employment decline commenced prior to its onset in the UK, the strongest overall deterioration also occurred in the 1990s. The best available data refer to firms employing over 20 employees. The shrinkage in number of these firms (including mergers) between 1995 and 2004, from 1,296 to 880, was of the order of 62 per cent whereas the fall in employment in the same period was a somewhat slower 58 per cent (Gesamtverband Textil + Mode 2006, table 4).[3] Further declines in employment in 2005 (−5.7%) and 2006 (−2.8%), to 40,995 workers by the end of the latter year, left the German clothing industry employing broadly similar numbers of people to the UK industry. However, the reduction in turnover, from €12.0 billion to €9.2 billion, was much lower at only 23 per cent (ibid, Table 8).

In the USA, clothing industry employment declined steadily from a post-war high of 1.2 million employees around 1975 (Doeringer 2005: 26, chart 1) to 814,000 in 1995 (Nordås 2004: table 3). Thereafter the rate of job loss accelerated sharply, leaving just 279,000 employees in the industry in 2006. The overall loss of employment in the apparel industry between 1995, when NAFTA-related shifts in the industry commenced, and 2006 is thus 66 per cent; in terms of value-added, the industry's contribution to GDP declined steadily from 0.85 per cent in 1977 to 0.12 per cent (US$16.4 billion) by 2006 (all data from BEA). Domestic production of US$17.9 billion in 2005 was 13.5 per cent down on the previous year, and in volume terms 2005 was the eighth consecutive year of decline (AAFA [American

Apparel and Footwear Association] 2006). The effects of NAFTA implementation and the other developments in the global industry referred to above are said to have been significantly more severe in the USA than in the EU as a whole during the late 1990s, due to higher import penetration (Commission of the European Communities [CEC] 2003: 5). Nevertheless it could be argued that the UK industry has suffered at least as badly in more recent years.

In all three countries, but particularly in the USA, the high concentration of the clothing industry in a few regions has intensified the economic impact considerably. UK production was historically based in Yorkshire, around Dewsbury for heavy woollen garments and Bradford/Huddersfield for worsteds (Owen and Cannon Jones 2003); Lancashire for cotton; knitwear and hosiery around Leicester and Nottingham (which was also an important lace-making centre); and a heavy concentration of small firms in East London traditionally served the capital city's needs.[4] The East Midlands (particularly in Leicester but also around Nottingham) had the highest concentration of employment in textiles and clothing in 2000, with around 60,000 employees in 2,500 firms, followed by the Yorkshire and Humberside region which accounted for 14 per cent of employment; in terms of distribution of firms, London is home to one-fifth of all firms, followed by the North West (15%) and East Midlands (13%) (EMDA 2001). Germany's industry is well scattered throughout the western and southern states, but developed particular concentrations in the Bavarian district of Aschaffenburg and in the Schwabian Alps (Interview Notes 2003). In the former area, the industry reached its peak in 1972, when 396 production plants employed nearly 30,000 workers; today only 51 enterprises employing 4,194 people remain.[5] Northwest Germany in 2008 claims to be home to nearly one-quarter of the textile and clothing industry combined, with some 300 firms and 30,000 employees working across the spectrum from technical textiles through home textiles to clothing use fabrics and apparel production.[6]

In 2003 employment in the US industry was concentrated in California and North Carolina, with 48,858, and 45,018 employees respectively (Harris Info-Source undated: 11). The New York garment district in late 2002 employed a further 44,757 people in 2,661 manufacturing businesses, plus a similar number again in textile manufacturing (largely knitwear) and fashion wholesaling (Fiscal Policy Institute 2003). Job losses have fallen particularly heavily on the Carolinas and Tennessee (Kessler 2002: 91). The city of El Paso in Texas is reported to have lost more clothing manufacturing jobs in the post-NAFTA period than any other American city, as employment halved from 23,581 to 11,851 between 1993 and 2001 when jeans production moved across the border into Mexico (Spener 2002; Bair and Gereffi 2003). Decline in the New York garment district has been slightly less severe, although manufacturing employment in the sector more than halved between 1990 and 1992. New York nevertheless still accounted for almost a quarter of US manufacturing jobs in women's outerwear, including labels such as Liz Claiborne, Donna Karan, and Anne Klein, over half of which was located in Manhattan itself (Fiscal Policy Institute 2003). Even the Los Angeles (LA) garment district which was still growing until 1996, when nearly 98,000 people were employed in apparel manufacturing, had lost 45,300 jobs by 2007.[7] Overall, the centre of gravity of the US industry appears to be moving westwards as jobs disappear from the traditional southern states and even New York: proximity to production centres in Mexico and Asia, ethnic Korean networks, the emergence of LA as a design centre, and the traditional strength of the LA garment district in sports- and active-wear production all promote the relative attraction of California (Bonacich and Applebaum 2000; Esbenshade 2004).

3.2. CURRENT INDUSTRY STRUCTURES AND FIRM STRATEGIES

A comparison of the contemporary British, German, and US clothing industries shows fundamental differences in their size composition and ownership structures, as well as contrasts in firms' product strategies. We draw comparisons along the following dimensions: (1) composition in terms of firm size, employment, turnover, and ownership structure; (2) skill structures and firm capabilities; (3) product and market strategy.

3.2.1. Composition in Terms of Firm Size, Ownership and Employment

The divergences in the features listed above, we argue, are due to embeddedness in different institutional environments. Although the difference is most pronounced between Germany (a coordinated market economy (CME)) and the two liberal market economies (LMEs) of the USA and UK, we also find some contrasts between the two LMEs. Both size structure and type of ownership have been influenced by various aspects of the respective financial systems. But degree of capital concentration also is connected to the size of the home market and the degree of concentration in clothing retail.

Historically, German firms have relied for their capital on banks. Readily available bank credit and the absence of a market for corporate control have ensured both the strong presence of medium-sized firms and the preservation of private ownership—the so-called *Mittelstand*. At the present time, however, following Basel II, bank credit is less easily available, and lending to firms in the highly volatile clothing industry even is avoided in many cases (Interview Notes 2003–04; Schuessler 2008). However, as is the case for German industry in general, the clothing industry benefits from subsidized credit for investment. In the British stock market-based financial system, the large firms—until their break-up in the late 1990s—were listed. More recently, however, clothing firms have withdrawn from listing, and only a few listed companies remain. The restructuring of the industry, following the collapse of the large firms, has been facilitated by a developed private equity industry and the possibility of leveraged buy-outs, putting pressure on margins. The many small firms in the industry cannot rely on either bank credit or private equity finance. Their large share of all firms, we shall show below, is due to both the comparatively low degree of regulation around setting up a manufacturing firm, and the availability of a large pool of ethnic minority entrepreneurs. The polarized size structure of the US industry and the survival of a significant number of large and giant firms have been influenced by the presence of a well-developed stock market. The latter supported growth and industry consolidation through merger and acquisition and allowed firms to respond to market concentration in the retail sector. A consequence of this has been the further reduction of owner-managed medium-sized firms, particularly during the 2000s. The de-listing observed in the UK did not happen to a significant extent in the USA. The positive consequences of stock market financing, however, have to be balanced against the strong performance pressures on managers. The large pool of very small clothing firms in the USA has the same explanation as that advanced for the UK. The German phenomenon of widespread family ownership and management of medium-sized firms is not replicated to a significant degree in either the UK or the USA. Conversely, the large presence of ethnic minority owners of mainly very small firms in the UK and the USA finds no parallel in Germany, due to a higher degree of market regulation. These institutionally shaped differences will receive empirical substantiation in the following paragraphs.

Table 3.1 provides some figures facilitating a comparison of the structure of the three industries. The German industry achieves a higher turnover than the UK's with a significantly lower number of employees, demonstrating a clear productivity deficit by the UK industry that is acknowledged elsewhere (e.g. Euratex 1998, cited by Stengg 2001: 16, figure 7). This appears to be linked to the fact that the two industries differ significantly in their structure, in terms of firm size, and in their investment volume. Comparing the US and UK data, we find a greater degree of US employment concentration, as well as higher turnover per employee.

Table 3.1. Changing structure of the clothing industry in the USA, UK, and Germany, 2000–05

	Firms	Employees (000)	Turnover
UK[a]			
2000	5,105	103	£5,854 million
2005	3,335	40	£4,389 million
Germany[b]			
2000	549	66	€10,741 million
2004	408	45	€9,134 million
USA[c]			
2000	15,744	510	US$25,052 million
2005	10,889	243	US$16,549 million

[a] Data for firms with at least one employee.

[b] Employment in firms with at least 20 workers.

[c] Data in final column are for value added.

Source: BERR Statistics Unit, SME data; Gesamtverband textil + mode; US Census Bureau and Bureau of Economic Analysis.

In 2002, in the German industry, 560 firms with 20 or more employees achieved a turnover of €9.7 billion (VR2003: 1); by 2004, 408 firms employing 20 or more people had revenues of €9.1 billion (Gesamt Textil + Mode 2006). As pointed out above, the industry contains mainly medium-sized firms, many of which are still owner-managed. A few very large firms in the German clothing industry employ 1,000 or more employees. According to Gesamt Textil + Mode (2006), the three firms in this size category achieved average sales of €345 million, but the bulk of employment and turnover is generated by medium-sized firms with between 100 and 999 employees. Together, medium-sized firms accounted for 60 per cent of employees and 63 per cent of industry turnover in 2004. Concentration rates are high: the top six firms achieve 21 per cent of the industry's sales; meanwhile the 100 largest firms—all internationally competitive and each generating more than €25 million in annual turnover—generate close to four-fifths of the sector's annual turnover (Statistisches Bundesamt 2007: table 14.4). Euratex (2002) confirms the above-average concentration of turnover in German medium and large firms, as compared with the rest of Europe.

With the break-up of the two giant public companies, Coats Viyella and Courtauld,[8] at the end of the 1990s, the UK industry became divided between a very small number of large firms and a large number of very small firms. Due to the wide-spread prevalence of M&A, the equivalent of the medium-sized *Mittelstand* firms was absent (TCSG 2000: 11; Owen and Cannon Jones 2003: 61). This situation has worsened since as some of the bigger employers have also disappeared. A disquieting picture of UK decline therefore emerges: between the beginning of 1998 and the end of 2005 the number of clothing firms employing five or more people plunged from 3,310 to 1,330, while those with 200 or more employees shrank from 80 to just 10 firms. The total number of firms, including those with no employees (i.e. sole traders), fell more slowly, from 15,185 firms to 12,665 firms, indicating a growing tail of micro-firms. Average employment in firms with at least 5 employees halved from 44 to 22 people (BERR data, authors' calculations). Around three-quarters of clothing manufacturers are said to make an average turnover of less than £250,000 per annum (Warren 2003: 233). Thus, although the UK economy is no less stock market dominated than that of the USA, the temporally highly compressed and dramatic move to foreign sourcing in the late 1990s left UK firms with too little substance to take advantage of the stock market.

The structure of the US clothing industry differs from that of both European industries. It has a highly polarized structure. In 2003, it had a very small proportion of both giant (1,000+ employees) and of large (501–1,000 employees) firms—0.2 and 0.9 per cent of firms, respectively—counter-posed to a multitude of small firms (86.6% of firms) employing fewer than 100 employees (Harris Infosource undated: 13). Concentration in the industry occurred only in the 1990s, in response to increased concentration in the retail sector, and was facilitated by a wave of mergers and acquisitions (Collins 2003: 37). Industry data indicate that more than a dozen US apparel companies achieve an annual turnover above US$1 billion, and the so-called mega companies—VF Corp, Liz Claiborne,

Hanesbrands, Polo Ralph Lauren, and Levi Strauss—have sales of more than US$4 billion per annum. Between them the 10 largest revenue-earning companies employ over 200,000 people.[9] These giant and large firms dominate both the US industry and the global production networks to a far greater extent than in the apparently similarly polarized UK industry, because of their higher concentration of both employment and turnover. Firms in the LA garment district, in contrast, reach an average turnover of less than US$40 million per year (Interview Notes).

Evidence of ongoing restructuring in the US industry is readily apparent. Several of the larger players (as well as smaller firms) have filed for Chapter 11 bankruptcy protection. Sara Lee Corp has withdrawn from the industry entirely by spinning out its apparel division as Hanesbrands in 2006, and parts of firms or brands have been sold off to other investors (e.g. VF Corp selling its Global Intimate Apparel business to Fruit of the Loom (which itself is now owned by Berkshire Hathaway); and Liz Claiborne disposing of four brands to Li & Fung). Nowhere is the evidence of restructuring greater than at Levi Strauss which, in the process of transforming itself from a manufacturing company into a primarily third party contracting organization, slashed its US employment from 36,500 in 1994 to 16,700 in 2001 (Bair and Gereffi 2003) and 1,100 in 2007 (Company web site information).

Our own data on turnover from company web sites and interviews further amplify the above picture. Among the 14 largest German firms in the industry in 2001–02, 5 had a turnover in excess of €5 billion, 3 were between €2.5–4.9 billion, 3 between €1.8–2.4 billion, and the rest did not declare their turnover (Company web site information). The largest three UK companies in our sample, said to be among the biggest in the industry, declared turnovers that ranged from €175 to €575 million. Of the four large US companies in our sample, in 2003 two achieved a turnover of more than US$2.5 billion and two were in the US$1–2.5 billion range. Table 3.2 provides a comparison of all the firms in our sample, albeit in relative terms.

These different size structures of the three national clothing industries are indicative of the fact that, on average, firms possess divergent financial resources, which affects their ability to invest in capability development. Differing size structures are accompanied by divergent ownership profiles, which tend to further amplify the differential availability of investment capital. In Germany, total or substantial family ownership is widespread, extending even to large firms such as Triumph, Escada, Betty Barclay, and (until its takeover in 2006 by the Italian Miro Radici group) Steilmann. During interviews, several owners emphasized the fact that, beyond paying themselves a salary, all profits are reinvested. In the UK, inherited family firms are much rarer than in Germany. Nevertheless, a few of the larger British firms remain in family ownership, and a small number is quoted on the stock exchange, for example, Burberry, Alexandra, and (AIM-listed) Wensum. But the more prevalent trend since the 1990s has been a process of de-listing and frequently a break-up of formerly sizeable UK companies. These firms either have been taken into private ownership by individual large investors or equity

Table 3.2. Coordinating firm characteristics

	Firm size		Ownership[a]	Product range	Firm type[b]	Exports[c]
	Turnover[d]	Employment[e]				
UK-C-1	Very small	Small	Private	Middle	2	None
UK-C-2	Small	Large	Private equity backed	Middle	1	Low
UK-C-3	Small	Large	Family	Low-middle	2	None
UK-C-4	Small	Large	MBO	Low-middle	2	None
UK-C-5	small	Small	MBO	Low-middle	2	None
UK-C-6	Small	Medium	Listed	Low-middle	2	None
UK-C-7	Very small	Large	Family	Middle	1 + 2	Medium
UK-C-8	Very small	Medium	Family	High	1	High
UK-C-9	Small	Large	MBO	Low and middle	2	Low
UK-C-10	Large	Large	Family	Low-middle	2	None
UK-C-11	Small	Medium	Private	High	4	Yes
GER-C-1	Large	Large	Listed	High	4	High
GER-C-2	Small	Medium	Private	Middle	4	High
GER-C-3	Very large	Large	Listed	Middle	4	High
GER-C-4	Very large	Large	Family	Middle	2 + 4	High
GER-C-5	Medium	Large	Family	Middle	4	Medium
GER-C-6	Small	Medium	Family	High	1	Medium
GER-C-7	Small	Medium	Family	Low-middle	2	High
GER-C-8	Small	Medium	Family	Middle	1	Medium
GER-C-9	Very small	Medium	Family	Middle	1	Medium
GER-C-10	Medium	Large	Family	Middle	2 + 1	Medium
GER-C-11	Small	Large	Family	Middle	4	Medium
GER-C-12	Small	Large	Family	Low	4	None
GER-C-13	Small	Medium	Family	High-middle Middle; some	1	High
US-C-1	Giant	Giant	Listed	High	2 + 3	Medium
US-C-2	Small	Small	Subsidies of listed companies	Middle	2 + 3	No info
US-C-3	Small	Small	New subsidies of listed companies	Low to middle	2 + 3	Medium
US-C-4	Very large	Giant	Private equity backed	High	2 + 3	No info
US-C-5	Small	Medium	Private	Low to middle	1 + 3	No info
US-C-6	Very large	Giant	Listed	Mostly middle	2 + 3	No info
US-C-7	Very large	Very large	Listed	Full range	1 + 2 + 3	Medium
US-C-8	Small	Very large	Private	Low to middle	1 + 3	No info
Levi Strauss	Giant	Giant	Family	Full range	1 + 3	High
VF	Giant	Giant	Listed	Low and middle	1 + 2 + 3	Medium
Jones Apparel	Giant	Giant	Listed	Mostly middle	2	None

[a] Ownership: 'Family' refers to at least second generation family owner-management; MBO = management buy-out; private = first generation private ownership.

[b] Firm Type: 1 = Branded/high fashion 'manufacturer'; 2 = Branded/high fashion 'marketer'; 3 = Domestic supplier of 'own label' products to retailers; 4 = Cut-Make-Trim firm (none here).

[c] Exports: low = <10% of turnover; medium = 10–30%; high = 31–50%; very high ≥ 50%.

[d] Turnover: very small = <€50 million; small = €50–249 million; medium = €250–499 million; large = €500–999 million; very large = €1,000–2,999 million; giant = >€3,000 million.

[e] Employment: small = <100; medium = 100–499; large = 500–999; very large = 1,000–4,999; giant = >5,000. Includes staff in directly owned foreign subsidiaries.

funds, or managers have led highly leveraged buy-outs of parts of the original company. Reinvestment of profits, under this ownership arrangement, is lower as creditors and investors have to receive a share of earnings. The much lower degree of gross investment of the UK industry, as compared with the German one, is documented by the CEC (2003: 11) and also is remarked upon by a UK industry report (TCSG 2000: 7). The large US clothing firms, in contrast to the pattern in both European industries, are mostly listed companies run by professional managers. Listing has twofold consequences. On the one hand, firms can easily raise capital and achieve growth through merger and acquisition. On the other hand, however, they have to meet high performance standards and yield high dividends. US firms experience both more pressure for shareholder value and provide more managerial incentives to favour shareholders over other stakeholders than is the case in Britain (O'Sullivan 2000; Jacoby 2005). A smaller number, including Kellwood, have been de-listed and taken into private ownership. Of the four medium-sized firms in our US sample, two—US-C-2 and US-C-3—had been/were subsequently acquired by a mega firm, and a third firm expected to be acquired some time in the future (US-C-5). While no comparable figures on investment are available for the USA, a more marked annual average decline in investment, at 5.6 per cent as against only 1.2 per cent in Europe (CEC 2003: 34), is notable.

Ownership of the many smaller clothing firms in both the UK and the US industry is somewhat concentrated among ethnic minority owners. Morokvasic et al. (1986) found that in the UK ethnic minority owners and labour have been predominant since the early 1970s, with male entrepreneurs regarding setting up a business as a way out of manual labour or unemployment even if they lacked previous experience in the industry. More recently ethnic minorities have been found to constitute around 35 per cent of owners (CAPITB Trust 2001: 5) and are prominent in big cities like Leicester and in the east of London (EMDA 2001; UK-R-3). Rizvi (2007) suggests that in Leicester, where Asian entrepreneurs now dominate the industry, they have been better able than ethnic white clothing and textile businesses to withstand the pressures from cheap imports due to strong network cooperation and information sharing. Ethnic white-owned business owners (and much larger corporations), in contrast, seemed unable to reduce overheads and salary costs by cutting the incomes of family members.

In both the NY and LA garment districts of the USA, a large proportion of entrepreneurs are members of ethnic minorities, particularly of Chinese and, more recently, Korean origin (Esbenshade 2004; US-C-12). These provide potentially important links into production networks in Asia, just as the Asian business community in Leicester relies on links with Indian, Pakistani, and Bangladeshi networks. In both the USA and the UK, the existence of such entrepreneurs, often relatively new arrivals and/or first time business founders, explains the continued existence and even renewal of a large 'tail' of small and unstable firms, usually with inadequate resources for automated pre-assembly technology or marketing and wide distribution of their products (Doeringer and Crean 2006: 354, on the USA).

Conditions imposed by both upstream US textile firms and down-stream retailers cannot be fulfilled by these small firms, and their resources also are inadequate to build GPNs (ibid: 357). Such firms have survived by serving fragmented niche markets, many of which are declining (Doeringer and Crean 2006: 364), and by 'sweating' labour (Esbenshade 2004).

This development of an informal sector in the UK and the USA has been favoured by two factors in the regulation of markets not replicated in Germany. First, the absence of regulations stipulating vocational qualifications for employers has provided entrepreneurial members of ethnic minorities with an alternative avenue of social mobility (Ram et al. 2002). In both the UK and the USA the relatively low level of labour market regulation, weak unionization and, in the USA, the constant stream of new immigrants from Mexico, permit downward pressure on wages and scope for violation of labour standards. In the USA, despite anti-sweatshop initiatives/legislation by the federal Department of Labour, the state of California and the large branded firms, micro-firms in the LA and NY clothing districts routinely commit multiple violations of the Labour Standards Act (Kessler 2002: 89; Ross and Chan 2004: 117; US-C-12).

In Germany, in contrast, a higher degree of market regulation has prevented the development of such an informal sector (Donath 2004). Strict controls over immigration only allowed guest workers into the country to fill vacancies in specific industries and, until 1973, severely restricted the entry of family members (who might have constituted a flexible labour supply for the informal sector and family-owned firms) (Morokvasic 1993). The higher degree of labour market regulation also contributes to this different outcome: the wage rate extension clause, stipulating the adoption of industry-level wage rates even in non-unionized firms, is particularly pertinent. This has prevented the development of a low wage sector in this industry (Schuessler 2008: 135). In addition, legal requirements, until 2004, to produce certificates of *Meister* (Master craftsman) qualifications throughout German manufacturing industry limited the possibility for firm creation in the clothing industry even for skilled immigrant entrepreneurs. Entrepreneurs could only set up an enterprise if they were or employed a master craftsman (*Meister*) and were registered on the roll of artisans (*Handwerksrolle*) (Rath 2002: 16–17 and footnote 12). This posed an almost insurmountable hurdle to aspiring immigrant entrepreneurs.

This divergent composition of firms in terms of size and ownership— particularly the large 'tail' of small and micro-firms, frequently in ethnic minority ownership—between the USA and the UK on the one hand, and Germany on the other, is also reflected in very different employment structures. The established wisdom that loss of low-skilled jobs due to foreign sourcing is compensated for by a general upgrading of the occupational structure is not borne out by the British and US industries. Thus, whereas in the UK and the USA, white-collar staff in the managerial, technical, and supervisory categories amounted to only 20 and 22.9 per cent, respectively (AAFA 2006: 9; CAPITB Trust 2001: 16) of employees, in German firms white-collar workers amounted to a massive 45 per cent (Donath 2004).

3.2.2. Capabilities and Skill Profiles

A mapping of available skills and capabilities, based on both available statistics and interview information, will explain which product and market strategies are viable in each national industry. In each industry, capabilities and skills have been shaped by the divergent manner in which skill training has been institutionalized. Whereas in Germany, high-quality vocational education and training (VET) is provided in collaboration between employers, employees, and the state, in the USA it is left mainly to the private sector. In the UK, too, VET is mainly the task of individual firms, although periodic 'quick fix' state initiatives also take place. (Our information on the US situation is more fragmentary and necessitates a separate and less full description.)

Concerning managerial skills, two industry insiders spontaneously described British managers in the clothing industry as 'generally of very low calibre'. Levels of education and specialist expertise, with a few exceptions, appear to be significantly lower than those of their German counterparts. Graduate recruitment is problematic for the UK clothing industry as a whole (PSS 2000). According to CAPITB Trust (2001: 19), of new employees recruited each year by the industry around 0.23 per cent were graduates. The German managers we interviewed, in contrast, were mainly graduates with relevant tertiary education. However, production-related capabilities are more developed than marketing expertise (Schuessler 2008: 158).

British clothing firms are said to attach relatively less importance to design (Owen and Cannon Jones 2003) because they are generally competing on price, and their large retail customers employ their own design teams (Interview Notes 2003), sometimes engaging in 'specification buying' (e.g. UK-R-1). Additionally, available designers are not rated highly on technical competence and commercial understanding, although they score highly on creativity (TCSG 2000: 12; EMDA 2001: 29; Interview Notes 2003). Although more than 3,000 students graduate from fashion courses in the UK each year, designers and clothing brands widely report difficulties in finding new recruits with sufficient technical skills and production knowledge to transform creative ideas into workable designs (Skillfast-UK 2008). Not only is the quality of provision on design-oriented courses said to be variable, but they are also producing too many graduates for the opportunities available (Skillfast-UK 2006a). One commentator goes as far as diagnosing a crisis in the field of technical design, bemoaning the absence of a system for training and developing new recruits (Shurtleff 2003). Integrated tertiary level courses offering design, technology, manufacturing, and commercial aspects are rare (EMDA 2001: 35). Marketing expertise, due to the high degree of selling retailers' own-label clothes, has also remained underdeveloped (Interview Notes 2003).

More information is available about general skill structures. A detailed sector comparison by Steedman and Wagner (1989: 47–9) found that, at higher levels of training, more than 10 times as many German as British employees had passed vocational examinations. According to CAPITB Trust (2001: 16), technical specialists constituted a mere 4 per cent of British employees. Higher education enrolments on technical and production courses accounted for less than one tenth of total enrolments on sector-relevant programmes (Skillfast-UK 2006a). Our own impressions, too, were that there seemed to be greater numbers of—and more technically qualified—designers and technical staff in German than British firms, as might be expected given the emphasis in Germany on vocational training. Several of our UK interviewees commented on how few experienced pattern-cutters and skilled sample makers remained in the industry, and noted that even these few were reaching retirement age (e.g. UK-C-1 and UC-C-2).

Further down the hierarchy, among British supervisory staff and operatives, levels of qualification are low to non-existent and training budgets constrained. The proportion of employees in the textile, clothing, and footwear sector lacking any qualifications is, at 27 per cent, twice as large as the UK average (Skillfast-UK 2006a). Holders of NVQ levels 2, 3, and 4 qualifications are noticeably fewer than in the rest of the economy. In 2001–02, only 977 NVQ certificates were awarded at levels 1 and 2, and in clothing supervisory studies there were none at all (Owen and Cannon Jones 2003: 60). Only 56 apprentices were registered on 6 schemes in the textile and clothing industry in 2006, a tiny number attributed to lack of flexibility in rules governing the training programme. Ethnic minority workers are more likely to have no qualifications than their white counterparts in the industry and, overall, employees in lower-level occupations were the least well qualified (Skillfast-UK 2006a: 12–13). Skillfast-UK was founded in 2001 as the Skills Council for the industry, but it remains to be seen whether its activities will ameliorate the situation in the longer term. For the present it notes a widespread shortage of skilled machinists and other garment assembly operatives in all areas of the UK, as well as a shortage of experienced recruits owing to the generally poor image of the industry and the inability of many employers to provide the necessary induction and up-skilling (Skillfast-UK 2006).

The German training effort in this industry is in a different league altogether. In 2001, the ratio of trainees to total employees was 7.5 per cent, and the total number of trainees in 2000 was 2,726, of which most were fashion sewers and fashion tailors (BBI 2001–02). Although decline in manufacturing means that skilled operators are no longer sought after, technicians recruited from skilled workers, we shall show in Chapter 7, form a crucial resource for training and supervising suppliers.

In the US industry, many of the large firms were born as 'marketers' (Interview Notes 2003–04; Bair and Gereffi 2002) and never developed manufacturing skills among manual, technical, and supervisory employees. Additionally, branded marketers have largely replaced traditional manufacturers because the latter could no longer afford the large budgets for advertising and costly information technology required for 'quick response' programs (Gereffi and Memedovic 2003). Such skills are, however, still needed among the many remaining smaller manufacturing firms, and in-firm training is the predominant mode of skill formation (US Department of Labor 2004–05: 45). Public training provision for pattern makers and markers, where it is still available, is provided mainly locally by technical or trade schools and by industry associations (ibid). However, the NY Garment Industry Development Council, which was formerly concerned with helping firms upgrade training to develop the 'high end' market, has now moved away from training workers to management training (US-C-12). Many of the very small firms in the district are husband and wife outfits, plus one supervisor promoted from the shop floor without special training (ibid). In the LA area, in contrast, according to US-C-7, four local educational institutions still provide advanced technical training. More generally, the tendency among interviewees (Interview Notes 2003–04) to shift the responsibility for technical training to vendors of technology is indicative of low training effort. In contrast to the German training of CEE suppliers, US firms, which are said to frequently change suppliers, have not upgraded the skills of their Mexican suppliers (US-C-9). Furthermore, the strong recent move to full-package sourcing in any case has moved most pre-assembly preparatory functions, such as cutting and sample making, to suppliers or middleman firms in low-wage countries. We have no information on the quality of management or designers. But, given the complex sourcing and marketing strategies of the dominant large and giant US firms, we would expect a high degree of managerial professionalization, particularly in marketing and supply chain management. To sum up, the manufacturing legacy now is largely lost among large firms although manufacturing capability may still be found among some smaller firms in the clothing districts of New York and Los Angeles.

Following Whitley (2005), we pointed out in Chapter 2 that firms' capabilities are shaped by their institutional environment and permit them to follow particular strategies in pursuit of competitive advantage. These differ markedly between coordinated and liberal market economies. Whereas in the former, firms develop *organizational learning* capabilities, in the latter they enable the development of *reconfigurational* capabilities. The first are based on a collaborative effort of management and labour and facilitate the adoption of longer-term improvement in production, whereas the second are more likely to emanate from managers' initiatives and further quick adaptation to changing markets. The following section investigates how this is played out in the clothing industry.

3.2.3. Production and Market Strategies

The above structures of capabilities crucially determine both production and market strategy. Steedman and Wagner (1989: 41) not only contrast the smaller batch sizes of German firms with greater mass production by British firms but also pinpoint differences in technical design (greater complexity in Germany), as well as in fabrics and trim used (higher quality in Germany). This picture is partly confirmed by more recent sources. Thus, Euratex figures cited by EMDA

(2001: 7) show that the value of UK clothing, indicated by export prices, is less than half that of German clothing. The competitive advantage of German producers in international business rests on specialization in niche products (Groemling and Matthes 2003: 69). They cater mainly for the upper middle market, with an emphasis on quality and, in most cases, brand. BBI (2001–02: 11) identifies between 20 and 30 globally traded brands in the German industry. This market strategy depends on the presence of high skill levels at the upper end of the value chain and on a high level of control over suppliers (BBI 2001–02; Groemling and Matthes 2003). A mixed strategy of producing both branded clothing and 'private label' products for retailers is not as prevalent as among US firms. Nevertheless, there is in the German industry a small group of larger companies with this 'dual focus' strategy. Although the manufacturing function has now almost disappeared in Germany, a manufacturing tradition still is very much alive. (See also Schuessler [2008: 204] who stresses the retention of production competency and Wortmann [2005: 3] who remarks that marketers from a non-manufacturing background are very rare in Germany.)

In the UK, a very small number of firms concentrate on brands with high margins. They are counter-posed to a majority that make fairly standard clothes in the middle to low market segment. Due to the underdevelopment of technical design capabilities (Shurtleff 2003), companies are less able to compete on the good 'fit' of clothes. Abandonment of branding capability has occurred in favour of achieving the apparently greater security, but lower margins, of contract clothing production sold under the retailer's label. The close relationship to powerful domestic retailers partially relieves these clothing firms of problems of design and marketing, 'but at the cost of leaving them invisible to the consumer and with a limited capacity to innovate' (Owen and Cannon Jones 2003: 56). The TCSG (2000: 9) also comments: 'because a large part of the industry has relied on supplying "private label" garments to High Street retailers, many UK textile and clothing manufacturers have not developed high levels of marketing expertise'. Large firms that had owned both branded and contract clothing businesses, such as Coats Viyella and William Baird, seemed unable to manage the different investment and marketing strategies required and have now split up or disappeared. Several firms seem to concentrate entirely on the corporate and public sector uniforms market. If there are any innovative strategies, relying on reconfigurational capabilities, they may be found in the comparatively high 'fashion' content of British clothing, showing a considerable degree of capability and flexibility in following and realizing new fashion trends, particularly in the 'youth' market segment.

The US industry is more diverse, and a distinction between different product and market strategies has to be adopted. There are nevertheless some generalizations to be made and contrasts to draw with European counterparts. Due to the much larger market size and the overwhelming influence on the industry of giant retailers, there is a much stronger emphasis than in the UK, and more so Germany, on relatively long runs of standardized clothing in the 'lower-to-moderate price' segment of the market for items such as jeans, T-shirts, jogging suits, and men's clothing more generally. The huge volume of production of, for example, jeans is expressed in the following facts: of the 10 largest jeans-producing supplier factories in one region of Mexico, the largest factory made 480,000 pairs per week, and the smallest 135,000 pairs (Bair and Gereffi 2002: 1895); one giant company in our sample (US-C-6) made 30,000 units per week of one style for large retailers. However, since 2001 more emphasis has been put on shorter runs for 'quick turn' fashion products in women's wear (US-C-1), and runs for up-scale garments would also be much shorter. But even these two categories, due to market size, would involve larger runs than are commissioned by European firms. Although there are many branded marketers in the US industry, the huge buying power of retailers has forced most of them to operate a dual strategy of serving both the 'private label' and the 'branded product' market, as well as producing for diverse price segments. One large company, for example, catered both for very large runs of low-price and relatively small runs of high-quality garments (US-C-1), and even the smaller firms have followed this practice (Interview Notes 2003–04). In this, they differ markedly from UK firms, whose managers felt unable to combine the two strategies.

Several of the US branded marketers had not created and grown their brands but had acquired them (e.g. US-C-6, US-C-4) and are also very active in-licensors. Most large companies are multi-brand firms, with a portfolio of both own and licensed brands: VF Corporation, for example, owns 34 brands, including licences. These portfolios are frequently reshaped through acquisitions and disposals, as the histories of the big firms demonstrate. These facts point to a complex-ity of sourcing and marketing activities that requires high levels of managerial skill in both private label and brand specialisms. This strategy differs markedly from that of most German branded 'manufacturers' which mostly specialize in one brand (usually developed in-house) or very few brands and only one price segment—generally the 'middle to high' segment. Large American firms thus compensate for their lack of capabilities in manufacturing through innov-ative market-oriented initiatives and, as will be shown in Chapter 7, innovative sourcing strategies. But strategies are different in the many small firms in the two US garment districts of NY and LA. Except for a small group of high-end producers of niche products and collections, they mainly act as suppliers to the larger coordinating firms and retailers, mostly for replenishment and for shorter runs that require 'quick turn' and flexibility (Palpacuer 2002; Doeringer 2005).

The divergent production paradigms and market strategies followed by firms in the three national economies, in turn, shape the export performance of their clothing enterprises. German firms achieve the relatively high export ratio of 32 per cent (VR 2003), with some firms, for example, GER-C-1 achieving a significantly higher share. Efforts to export intensified with stagnation in the domestic market and, between 1995 and 2001, firms achieved export growth of 6 per cent per annum. In international comparative terms, the rate of export growth exceeded that of the UK, USA, and even Italy (Groemling and Matthes 2003: 77). Since 2002 export performance has been more volatile (Gesamt

Textil + Mode 2006: table 10). An analysis by Euratex (2002: 86) suggests that Germany's share of EU sales to non-EU countries rose from 12.4 per cent in 1996 to 19.1 per cent in 2000, making it one of the EU's most successful exporters. Destinations are mainly the neighbouring West European countries, but CEE countries and particularly Russia have seen a steep increase from a low base (VR 2003). The USA accounts for only 3 per cent of German clothing exports. Comparatively high export performance by German firms is boosted also by the strong orientation to export of the industry association and by government subsidized credit for exporting to industry more generally (Kitschelt and Streeck 2004: 6).

British exports, with a ratio of 17 per cent in 2000 (Trends Business Research, cited by EMDA 2001: 21), stood at only half the German level. Euratex (2002: 105–6) notes that UK trade with non-EU countries remains below the EU average, while the share of sales directed to other EU countries, at 25.7 per cent, was approximately 10 percentage points below the EU average. This pattern is consistent with the orientation of most large firms to focus on domestic retailers. The majority of large firms we interviewed do no exporting at all, nor do they intend to do so. Even at the higher-quality end, export ratios are relatively low or non-existent. Exceptions are brands such as Paul Smith and Burberry, and firms making medium- to highly priced men's suits, such as BMB and Berwin & Berwin. This comparatively weak performance by firms is not compensated by the availability of support from either the industry association or the state. The general remarks on the stance of the British state towards industry by Schmidt (2002: 153), that 'having been left to sink or swim on its own, British industry sank more often than not', is also applicable to the clothing industry.

Many of the US brands, particularly those in the jeans and sportswear segments, boast a reasonably large share of sales in international markets but for the most part these are not goods exported from domestic production plants. In proportion to the overall volume of production, the US industry performs less well in export markets than its German counterpart (Groemling and Matthes 2003: 77). In 2005, garment exports from the USA including cut parts (for making up in Central American or Caribbean Basin plants) amounted to just US$4.5 billion, a drop of 3.4 per cent from the previous year that continued the trend exhibited since 1998. Exports to the EU and Japan rose by 18–20 per cent in 2005, but from a low base to just US$292 million and US$280 million, respectively (AAFA 2006). One of the giant companies among the interviewees noted frankly that 'international expansion is not our strong suit'; it had recently acquired a European clothing firm to boost its international sales turnover (US-C-1).

Many clothing firms try to stem declining sales by forward integration into retail, also referred to as semi-verticalization. (Full vertical integration, following the Zara model, was rare, due to the large-scale abandonment of in-house manufacturing.) Verticalization, particularly for branded 'manufacturers', permits them to counteract their growing dependence on and domination by the big retailers.

The thinking behind this strategy was well articulated by a German clothing firm:

Retail outlets we want to push on, first of all to be more independent from market developments, with [independent] retailers closing down and the problem that we are not located in some important cities any more.... Secondly, we gain experience in retail ... gain retail knowledge. And thirdly, of course, to have a share of controlled distribution that we can always rely on ... [Fourthly], we also consider retail business ... especially in big cities or capitals ... as marketing investment. (GER-C-5)

Verticalization is, however, a difficult and risky step to undertake as it requires both ample investment capital and new skills, and the certainty of success is hard to predict. Consequently, 'manufacturers' mostly undertake it very gradually, opening retail outlets first in their home country and gradually adding 'flagship' stores in foreign capitals.

Semi-verticalization, to gain control over the market, however, was gaining ground among branded firms, albeit not in all three countries. In Germany, forward integration into retail was becoming fairly common, with most of our interviewees among branded 'manufacturers' practising it to some degree. German firms have changed their strategy in recent years, if in a very gradual manner, as forward integration is regarded as a high-risk strategy (Interview Notes 2003; SIPPO 2006). BTE (Bundesverband des Deutschen Textileinzelhandels) (2006) reports that producers own 828 shops, and additionally utilize a very large number of contractually diverse tie-ups with independents to sell their brand (ibid: 75). Among our interviewees, an up-market designer brand already distributes the majority of its sales—53 per cent—in this way through its own stores and 12 per cent through franchise shops (GER-C-1), many of them abroad. Another company, with 25 owned retail outlets in Germany and parts of Europe that generate 8–10 per cent of total sales, articulated this strategy as follows:

We have always been a supplier ... we have to think more retail-based, and our strategy is to become a semi-verticalized company ... we have retail stores which are also operated by us, we have done that for the last ten years ... [but at that time it was more accident than strategy]. Our strategy is to go parallel, to work still with ... independent customers, but at the same time, be able to do our own retail businesses more professionally. And so we call this strategy semi-vertical strategy. (GER-C-5)

This company intends to increase sales from its own retail business to 20 per cent within five years. A much smaller company had recently paired up with two other clothing firms in the region to open shops selling the complementary brands of the three firms (GER-C-9). A particularly successful implementation of this strategy has been accomplished by Gerry Weber which, in its own words, is transforming itself 'from a wholesale business into an international lifestyle corporation'.[10] It now has 102 stores in Germany and abroad, either operated by the company or by franchise partners. It raised retail sales to €30 million in 2005, representing 8 per cent of total sales.

In the UK, a prominent designer retailer/wholesaler has long been organizing the whole value chain but only a relatively small proportion of all sales—20 per cent in 2003—came from direct selling through its own shops, both in the UK and abroad (UK-C11). Otherwise, forward integration into retail has been relatively rare, due to the fact that few clothing firms have their own brands but are instead tightly linked to the big multiples, such as M&S.

In the USA, many of the large clothing firms have a whole stable of brands. But they nevertheless find forward integration into retail problematic, as the firm is not closely associated with any one brand in the perception of consumers. Thus, US-C-1 deemed itself not sufficiently high-end to pursue a verticalization strategy, and US-C-6, a branded marketer with a large stable of unrelated brands, commented that the company had not formed around a brand image and therefore could not open a store on Fifth Avenue: 'so we can't leverage prestige and life style'. However, the businesses more closely related with a particular brand, such as Calvin Klein, Ralph Lauren, and Donna Karan, do, of course, have their own stores and are semi-verticalized. Ralph Lauren, for example, is said to sell 50 per cent of its merchandise in the firm's own stores (US-C-6). Levi Strauss, too, had 67 retail and outlet stores in 2005, of which 24 were in the North American region and the rest in Europe and Asia Pacific (Company web site 2006), and Jones Apparel Group have a total of 402 speciality shops, located both in the USA and abroad (Hoover's Company Records 2005).

Meanwhile retailers in all three countries are increasingly developing their own sourcing operations, thus cutting out 'middleman' coordinating firms, particularly those without a brand. Chapter 4 discusses in some detail the structure of the retail sector in the three countries and the strategies retailers adopt vis-à-vis the coordinating firms. This chapter continues with an overview of upstream industries that have a strong impact on the clothing industry, since these can be important shapers of the competitive ability of clothing firms.

3.3. UPSTREAM INDUSTRIES: TEXTILES AND TEXTILE MACHINERY

The clothing and textile (for apparel) industries are mutually dependent, each relying on the other for both innovatory stimulation and commercial inputs. A large proportion of clothing firms' costs lies in fabric and trim, and both appearance/quality and the length of the production cycle of garments are determined by the fabric input. Hence geographical proximity or co-location to a vibrant textile industry is of high importance to the clothing industry. Although fabric suppliers do not necessarily have to be domestically located, such co-location can provide a large comparative advantage, as the cases of Italy, Turkey, and China demonstrate. Conversely, the textile industry is highly dependent on a thriving domestic clothing industry, both for ideas on new developments and, more so, for orders. Although a high textile export ratio can partially compensate for the absence of a large domestic market, it cannot wholly make up for it. Such interdependence, however, does not always translate into common interests, particularly since the beginning of outsourcing of clothing production processes. This has become abundantly clear in often diametrically opposed government lobbying.

Both the clothing and the textile industry, in turn, benefit from proximity to an advanced industry for textile machinery. Close contact between customers and machinery manufacturers encourages the search for technological solutions relevant to clothing design and/or manufacture and gives access to early knowledge of new technological developments on either side. Hence the social consequences of a thriving or declining clothing industry in terms of employment creation or destruction are magnified, as neither the textile (for clothing) nor the textile machinery industry survives the demise of the domestic clothing industry in the longer term. Recognition of mutual dependence has led to some migration to low-wage countries also of textile and some machinery companies to the main foreign manufacturing sites of national clothing firms, albeit to varying degrees and with divergent rates of success. Investment costs in the textile industry are high, with an individual workstation costing €150,000 (GER-C-14), and companies therefore find it problematic to be as mobile as clothing ones. The case for mobility also is not as compelling as for clothing firms, since wage costs in this highly automated industry constitute only a small part of overall costs—15 per cent in the case of the German industry (GER-C-14).

The end of the MFA/ATC in 2005 has influenced the textile industry as much as the clothing industry although the impact of liberalization has differed between the EU and the USA. Several German interviewees predicted that 2005 would constitute a greater challenge for the USA than for Germany, as the US textile industry has tended to maintain a focus on basic product lines, for which Asian competition is much stronger. German producers, because they are concentrated in higher value textile segments, did not fear 2005 (survey by GesamtTextil, cited by GER-T-6; also GER-T-5) and, within the EU, they advocate a liberal trade strategy (GER-T-1). Additionally, the almost complete absence in the EU of tariffs on yarn enables spinners to import cheaper inputs—an option not open to their US competitors where considerable tariffs remain in place. 'European spinners are more ready for 2005 and globalization than US ones' (GER-T-6). ATMI, the association of southern US textile producers, has engaged in strong lobbying of successive US governments to restrain competition from China (US-T-3), but with only limited success. Duties on textile imports, particularly woollen fabrics, are high (US-T-4), with tariff peaks of 25 per cent on some fabrics and 13.2 per cent on yarns. Although we received no comments from UK respondents on the anticipated impact on the industry of quota removal, it seemed likely that the remaining producers of high-quality woollen fabrics had little need to fear the end of the quota system.

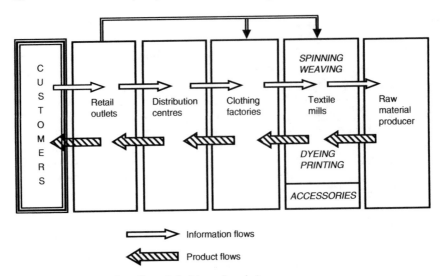

Figure 3.1. Integrated textile and clothing value chain

This interdependence of the textile and clothing industries, which is explored below, is, of course, mediated by the size, compositional character, and competitiveness of each national textile industry. The following sections mainly cover the apparel-use segment of the textile industry, including knits and hosiery, and largely disregard discussion of the household, medical, and technical textiles segments. Figure 3.1 shows the value chain of the textile industry and how it relates to upstream and down-stream industries.

3.3.1. The UK Textile Industry

The recent history of the British textile industry is one of precipitous decline and the 'clinging on' of only a handful of producing firms in a few sub-segments. This decline is evident in the structure of the industry itself and its dwindling population of firms, as well as in its supporting institutions and in the demise of a textile machinery industry.

The decline of the UK textile industry, albeit from a high base, started significantly earlier than that in the other two economies—from the 1970s onwards—and thus predates that of the UK clothing industry. As a retail respondent informed us: 'The UK fabric industry went a generation ago' (UK-R-1). As in many UK industries, but magnified by the structure of demand from domestic retailers, there was a focus on commodity products (UK-T-6) and upgrading to higher value products did not occur (Rigby 1996). 'This country was cheap and cheerful, sold through the multiples, and that industry has just virtually gone' (UK-T-3). Additionally, the early demise of the textile machinery industry prevented innovatory stimuli, and the poor provision of technical training and low wages also took their toll (UK-T-2; UK-T-6; Pye 2002). The calibre of people in the industry also is indicted. 'People are parochial... they didn't globalize, they did not move with the time... the industry didn't attract the best and the brightest' (UK-T-2), or 'When you [the industry] get left behind [in terms of wage levels], you have to attract what you can attract' (UK-T-5). Perhaps one result of this attitude is the lack of UK participation in EU textile research initiatives.

Decline accelerated in the 1990s, as British clothing firms began to relocate production to lower wage countries, and is expressed in the following figures which differ significantly between sources. By 2000, the UK textiles industry was significantly more concentrated than was the case in other countries, with the five largest companies accounting for over half of sales, compared with 30 per cent in the USA and 20 per cent in Germany (Eurostat, cited in EMDA 2001: 23). In 2002, the industry had around 5,000 firms, employed between 98,000 (UK-T-6) and 121,000 people (Annual Employment Survey, cited in Labour Market Trends) and had a production value of £5,102 million (Office of National Statistics data, provided by UK-T-6). Of the 5,000 or so firms in the industry, 64 per cent had fewer than 10 employees and very low annual turnover, and only 5 per cent had more than 100 employees (Annual Employment Survey, cited in Labour Market Trends). By 2005, the most recent year for which data are available, ONS Labour Market Trends statistics identified just 88,000 jobs remaining in the textiles industry—7,000 fewer than the year before. Pye (2002: 25) states that only 5.1 per cent of firms in 2001 had a turnover of more than £5 million, while 45 per cent achieved less than £100,000. Only a minority of firms are still producing, and the majority are simply merchants importing wool or fabric from the Far East or Turkey (UK-T-5; UK-T-6), thereby further undermining the viability of indigenous textile producers. Some are 'manufacturers without a loom' (UK-T-3), merely coordinating the production process. The number of firms producing fabric now is very low (UK-T-3), and yarn spinners—both for synthetic and woollen yarn—have almost disappeared from the UK (UK-T-3; UK-T-4). For those producers still remaining in the industry, the financial environment has become very hostile (UK-T-1). Pye (2002: 23), not surprisingly, considers the textile industry to be in a worse state than the clothing industry. Reflecting historical strengths, the East Midlands region dominates UK activity in the hosiery and knitted fabrics segments (EMDA 2001).

Industry decline has been particularly heavy in the production of cotton textiles and synthetics. Although the creation of lyocell (trademarked as tencel) as a new man-made fibre, in what used to be the Courtaulds Research Laboratory in Coventry, was one bright spot for the industry (UK-T-6), the break-up of Courtaulds put commercialization first into Dutch and then, in 2004, into Austrian ownership. (Production continues at the original Grimsby site.) In more traditional areas of strength, a small segment producing woollen fabrics (estimated to constitute 10% of the whole industry) survives and is a successful exporter. Firms in this segment either are small niche producers of high-value fabrics mainly for exports or, if selling domestically, often outsource the production process (e.g. UK-T-3) or supplement their own production with fabrics imported from lower-wage countries. But even in this industry segment the infrastructure is eroding, with only a handful of vertically integrated producers surviving (UK-T-2), as well as some commission weavers. The woollen industry now has only a handful of large firms (UK-T-3; UK-T-6). Few firms have more than 200 employees, and the average firm employs 50–60 people (UK-T-6), with one successful 'manufacturer without a loom' getting by with only 47 employees (UK-T-3). None of the main inputs into production—raw material, yarn, textile machinery—is produced domestically on a significant scale (UK-T-3), and firms seeking skilled labour have to develop it in-house (UK-T-2). Even the more successful firms are struggling to achieve a turnover which keeps pace with rising overheads (UK-T-2). Their competitors now are in continental Europe (UK-T-2 and UK-T-3). 'Our competition? Who else is there in the UK? Virtually nobody operating in the UK market now' (UK-T-3).

Nevertheless, firms in the woollen segment generally are high exporters—their fabrics (top end worsteds) are too expensive for domestic retailers (UK-T-2; UK-T-6). It must be this segment which supported the industry's high export ratio of 50 per cent in 1996 (DTI). But the export volume is low (worth £3.5 billion in 2001; BCIA Report 2001–02: 14) and has declined in unit value between 1998 and 2000 (Stengg 2001). Those producing 'middle market' quality fabrics also export to countries in CEE, to suppliers of UK clothing firms, and they still have to contend with the market power and demanding conditions of big UK retailers. Referring to the power of big retailers, one respondent remarked: 'You just have to roll with the punches . . . because you can see twenty or thirty people who can supply what you are supplying . . . So that's the reality and you have to accept it' (UK-T-3).

One way for textile producers to survive is to co-locate with the suppliers to the domestic clothing firms. As foreign sourcing by coordinating firms in the clothing industry started only in the late 1990s, most textile firms were already too weak to find the substantial investment capital required. There exist no data on FDI in the textile industry, but information from various respondents suggests it has been insignificant in the UK industry (e.g. UK-T-1). Another survival strategy is to cultivate technical textiles or another niche strategy. EMDA (2001) notes that what little activity there has been in technical textiles is located in the North West. Citing Euratex data, EMDA also suggests that the UK in 2000 was the second largest producer of technical textiles (16%) in Europe behind Germany (17%), but some subsequent deterioration of this position seems likely. Companies in our sample that claimed a more technical orientation to their apparel textiles were more likely to be producing for the protective clothing sector than for mainstream clothing use (e.g. stretch fabrics and active-wear fabrics). In general, reorientation towards niche strategies was not particularly prevalent in our sample nor, we believe, in the industry as a whole, since such a shift requires both large investment and the availability of skilled labour.

3.3.2. The German Textile Industry

The German industry was one of the strongest in Europe until the early 1990s (Rigby 1996), but has also suffered significant declines in employment and output since 1996. Whereas German clothing firms once bought German textiles, they now tend to buy from Turkey and South Korea (where fabric is cheaper) and from Italy (where it is more stylish) (GER-C-14). But, in contrast to both the UK and US industries, the German industry is noted for its successful restructuring away from fabrics for general apparel and into technical textiles (including textiles for sportswear and underwear). This segment now constitutes 40 per cent of total production value (GER-T-4). It makes Germany the world's leading producer (*Financial Times*, 16 April 2002), ensuring the textile industry's future (GER-T-4). This conversion has been aided by the high level of technical training, as well as by the availability of investment capital that is indispensable for such conversion (GER-T-1). The German state has not been protectionist like the US state. There is available some state support for innovation, manifested in support for an important industry research institute. The Institute of Textile Technology and Process Engineering Denkendorf receives mixed funding (from *Laender* and federal states, firms, the EU, and foundations), and its 250 mainly scientific staff do research, mainly in collaboration with and partly financed by firms, in technical textiles. 'Smart' textiles and textiles for protective clothing directly benefit the clothing industry (Interview Notes 2003).

The remaining 60 per cent of the industry is divided between clothing and home textiles (GER-T-1). Although in severe trouble, the decline of the clothing fabric segment has been neither as serious as in the UK, nor as precipitous as in the USA. There remain a number of very strong firms in fabric and trim, with a large export volume. But most firms have moved out of the volume market into niche markets (Rigby 1996) where there is no competition from producers in low-wage countries. 'We can't compete with China at the low end, but we are still very competitive up-market' (GER-T-3; also GER-T-6), or 'we cannot trade on low costs but on technical excellence and speed of delivery' (GER-T-5). The most successful companies are those which are highly vertically integrated, as they are able to react most quickly to orders (GER-T-4). The industry is highly automated, and still contains a number of yarn spinners. It is supported by a strong textile machinery industry which exports all over the world (GER-T-4).

In 2004 the industry's 880 remaining firms employing more than 20 people—down from nearly 1,200 in 1990—were largely small- and medium-sized enterprises (SMEs) but also included a very few large firms. The composition of the industry in 2004 shows 6 firms employing over 1,000 people, but 70 per cent of firms employed fewer than 100 workers; turnover, however, is largely concentrated (56%) in the hands of firms employing between 100 and 499 workers (Gesamt Textil + Mode 2006). The largest firm in our sample—(GER-T-5), a global producer and supplier with around 25 per cent of the global market in its speciality, had well over 20,000 employees, of whom around 40 per cent are still in Germany. The large companies are often structured as holding companies, containing a number of firms that are active in complementary segments in a loose federation under one financial roof. Employment in the industry in 2004 was around 95,000, compared with over 150,000 in 1995, a decline of 37 per cent. The industry is evenly divided between private and publicly owned firms, but even in the latter there still persists substantial family ownership (GER-T-4).

Firms in Germany consistently accounted for around 70 per cent of OPT between the EU-12 and CEE in 1988–97, with the Netherlands (especially in the early years of this period), Italy, and France together making up a further 20 per cent. Hence large volumes of fabric were being exported temporarily to neighbouring countries.

The industry adapted better than its US and UK counterparts in terms of restructuring and moving up-market. German firms also had greater foresight than their UK counterparts in that they followed clothing producers into CEE, particularly after the transformation in the 1990s. They are currently looking towards China, sometimes to serve the Chinese market and not just German clothing firms' suppliers (GER-T-1; GER-T-7). But they have not been as quick as US firms in this respect, reflecting perhaps the lower dependence on Chinese clothing suppliers by German coordinating firms.

3.3.3. The US Textile Industry

The US industry has been much larger than its UK counterpart and experienced significant decline much later. This may be explained partly by firms' greater size, investment capital, and more developed strategic initiatives, such as co-location with clothing firms in Mexico and China, and partly as a consequence of stronger state protection behind tariff walls. The presence of a strong upstream source of (state-subsidized) raw cotton has played a key role in the ability of some segments of the textile industry to compete. The capacity of lobby groups, ranging from cotton farmers through to textile producers and clothing manufacturers, to wring concessions for the industry out of Congress has been legendary (Rivoli 2005), though their power is waning as retailers and consumer groups argue for cheaper retail prices. As the industry declines, some of these industry associations are dissolving (e.g. the American Textile Manufacturers Association [ATMI] and the American Yarn Spinners Association [AYSA]) or merging to stay alive. Apparel absorbed 36 per cent—the largest share—of total textile production in 2002 (ATMI 2005). Textile machinery production is not thriving (GER-T-4; US-T-6; US-T-8) since customers have moved out of the USA. But even before that began to happen European, particularly German and Swiss, machines were being imported (GER-T-3).

In 2001, 40 per cent of apparel-use cotton needed by the clothing industry was sourced in the USA (US-T-4). The US cotton-producing industry has a long history and over the years has become highly organized. In the process, it has come to play an important role in shaping much of the US cotton textile industry. The fibre it produces, particularly for denim, has a good reputation and exports are said to be high. Indeed, China is now an important purchaser—cotton was America's ninth largest export to China in 2003 (Rivoli 2005) (see also Chapter 9, on China). US cotton production is, however, heavily subsidized by the federal government, at an average rate of 19 cents per pound between 1980 and 2002. A recently enacted US farm bill is said to provide around 12,000 large-scale cotton farmers with an estimated US$1 billion a year in subsidies for the next five years (Williams 2008). Moreover, since (cheaper) foreign cotton imports are highly restricted in order to aid US cotton farmers, the federal government also provides subsidies to cotton textile producers to purchase US cotton (Rivoli 2005). Domestic cotton and denim fabric manufacturers thus enjoy an important price advantage over foreign producers.

As the previous paragraph implies, there are divisions between various segments of the industry in terms of production focus and trade political interests. Texan cotton farmers' production subsidies do not suit the interests of textile producers in North and South Carolina, who prefer to source more cheaply elsewhere—hence the need for purchasing subsidies. Clothing firms have been frustrated by the lack of innovation in fabric production and high domestic prices that protection of the textile industry via free trade agreements has engendered. The US textile industry comprises producers of cotton, synthetic, and woollen textiles yet despite—or perhaps because of—the way the industry is organized fabric made from man-made fibres now forms the largest part—around 65 per cent—of all fabrics used. Although the USA was the largest supplier of synthetics in the world during the 1980s (Berger 1989), the bulk is now produced outside the USA (Lynch 2002/IPC notes). Woollen textiles, mainly produced by medium-sized mills in the North, are not very important in the industry in proportional terms (US-T-4). One such firm (US-T-2), once among the best in the USA, had ceased production of its camel hair fabric when we visited.

The production strategy of the textiles industry has long been one of 'long-run production of standard goods for the mass market, with the use of inexpensive fibres and machinery' (Berger 1989: 297). As in the UK, many firms no longer rely wholly on their own production of fabrics but supplement it with imported and therefore cheaper fabrics which they convert (US-T-7). The high level of tariffs imposed on fabric and yarn imports (plus important additional limitations on cotton and wool imports), however, has limited the extent to which textiles are brought in from non-NAFTA or CAFTA countries; free trade agreements also facilitate exports to beneficiary countries under 'yarn forward' arrangements (see also Chapter 5 on free trade agreements).

OTEXA data show that between 1995 and 2007 imports of textile fabrics increased only 30 per cent to US$5.5 billion, with China taking over from Canada as the largest source only in 2005.[11] Export data from the same source show faster growth of 50 per cent between 1995 and 2005 with Mexico and Canada the principal destinations of US fabrics. These two countries take over half of US fabric exports, with CAFTA signatories accounting for a further 22 per cent in 2005. China and Hong Kong together imported US$470 million of US fabrics, equivalent to 5.8 per cent of exports (although this represented a 23% increase for China), whereas the AGOA countries accounted for a tiny US$27 million of exports. As for yarn exports, CAFTA nations took nearly 40 per cent—indeed, Honduras alone accounted for 26 per cent—with Canada and Mexico ranking second and third with 22 and 16 per cent, respectively.

Despite the high degree of state protection, the textiles industry is suffering severe decline. Gradual industry decline from a high base—there were 832,000 employees in 1981 (AAFA 2004: 7)—ensued during the 1980s. This was due to the relocation of clothing firms and their greater use of Asian fabrics, but was also influenced by low innovation compared with Europe (GER-T-4). Precipitous decline started only in 1998. The year 2001 was a particularly bad year for the industry—the worst since World War II, with 124 plants closing, half of them in North and South Carolina. Between 1997 and 2007, the National Council of Textile Organizations recorded 578 textile plants closures,[12] and 200,000 jobs disappeared (BEA data).[13] Figure 3.2 shows the geographic spread of the closures during this period.

By the end of the 1990s some firms had relocated to Mexico, in some cases investing on a very large scale (it costs around US$30 million to set up a modern textile mill, according to US-T-3). A number had also engaged in risky forward integration into making clothes (US-T-1). But in the face of currency re-valuations by East Asian economies, and confronted with competition from Mexican textile mills, US firms found themselves overstretched (US-T-2) and began to go bankrupt in large numbers. Among those filing for Chapter 11 protection were Burlington Industries and Cone Mills (both now acquired by

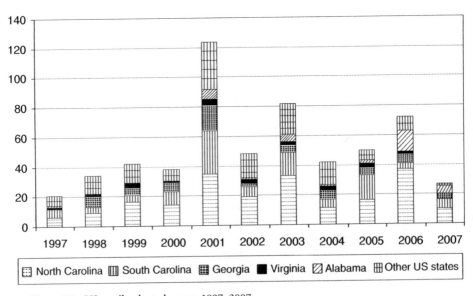

Figure 3.2. US textile plant closures, 1997–2007

Source: National council of textile organizations, www.ncto.org

the US International Textile Group), Guilford, Galey & Lord, and Dan River, all of which had attempted full package supply from Mexico (Bair and Dussel Peters 2006: 214). 'Investments in Mexico have been a disaster', because of an unreliable infrastructure and the high expense of substituting US for Mexican staff' (US-T-1). The Caribbean Basin Initiative has also had a negative longer term effect, with competition coming not from indigenous firms but from East Asian, particularly Korean, inward investors.

By 2005 only 218,000 employees remained employed in American textile mills, down from 492,000 in 1990, of whom around 80 per cent of them dedicated to production activity (AAFA 2006), down from 720,000 in 1990. Since 1997 textile sales have dropped by 30 per cent and production by 25 per cent (US-T-3). 'I knew it was the sunset [of the textile industry], but the end came cataclysmically, like someone pulled a plug' (US-T-4). Thus the US industry appears to be in deep trouble, despite the frequent state support it has received. Nevertheless, the US industry still has a lot more substance left than its UK counterpart.

The decline of the domestic clothing industry in each of the three countries and intensifying global competition in fabric for apparel have taken their toll on all three textiles industries. While the UK fabric industry, except for a small woollen segment, was already in terminal decline before the middle of the 1990s, the US and the German industries, for somewhat different reasons, have suffered significant decline only during the last decade or so. Apparel-use textiles continue to constitute a significant proportion of the industry in the USA and, due to the strategy of standardized mass production, will lose further ground in years to come. In contrast, the rump of the German textile industry will prove more resilient: significant restructuring into technical textiles on the one hand, and into higher-tech niche products on the other, will secure its future, albeit on a reduced scale. The survival of a competitive textile machinery industry in Germany, but not in either of the other two economies, offers a further boost to this outcome. However, the absence in all three countries of a vibrant textile (for apparel) industry, in the longer run, will shift global competitive advantage further in the direction of countries which can exploit the advantages of co-location.

3.4. CONCLUSION

The discussion of the three national clothing industries has indicated that each country contains a very distinctive population of firms. They clearly bear the imprint of their respective institutional frameworks, particularly of the system of vocational education and training, but also of the financial system and the state's role in the economy. They possess differing capabilities and seek competitive advantage in different market niches and at different geographical levels. Organizational learning capabilities, which involve joint problem-solving and improvement of production and related processes, are well developed in German firms, whereas in US and UK firms they are much less prominent. This, in turn, has shaped the product strategy adopted. Whereas in Britain there is a dominance of firms supplying domestic retailers with 'private label' clothing, German firms are predominantly branded 'manufacturers', that is, they are still informed by a manufacturing tradition and retain in-house most functions preparatory to production. US firms are both branded marketers—but less rooted in a manufacturing culture than German firms—and providers of 'private label' products to retailers. But differences between the firms from the two LMEs—the UK and USA—are also notable, with decline in both the clothing and the textile industry more advanced in the UK. It is difficult to pin down the origins of these divergences. But it seems likely that the lack of investment in human resources and brand creation is due to the lower calibre of British management, as well as to the later onset of outsourcing, influenced by the dominance of Marks & Spencer. The very different size of the British domestic market, permitting a lower degree of capital concentration and corporatization than in the USA, may be a further contributing factor. Additionally, the absence of strong industry lobbies and the completely hands-off stance of the British state towards textiles and clothing have meant that decline has been allowed to proceed unchecked. We also highlighted some diversity *within* national firm populations, but commonality among firms engaged in global sourcing (which excludes the many small and micro-firms in this industry) has been more evident than diversity. Moreover, diversity in the industry is diminishing, in the face of striking industry consolidation, particularly in the USA.

We have shown that the clothing industry in all three countries has suffered severe decline, in tandem with the upstream textiles industries. But clothing firms, we have suggested in Chapter 2, operate not merely at the domestic level but also at international and global levels. In subsequent chapters, we explore how the different national profiles of the clothing industry shape their relations to other actors in the value chain, particularly retailers (Chapter 4) and contractors in low-wage countries (Chapter 7). We will show how clothing firms' diverse sets of resources—employee capabilities and market strategies, financial resources, and investment patterns, state support in the international sphere and the benefits of sheer size—shape the degree of influence and power they can wield in both their domestic market and in global production networks. Deployment of these resources is, however, further mediated by national, institutionally shaped traditions in the sphere of inter-firm relations with customers and suppliers, that is, the different degree to which market-type relationships are moderated by a more relational style of contracting in the two varieties of capitalism.

NOTES

1. In the UK and US employment accounted for a significantly larger proportion of manufacturing employment than in Germany.
2. See http://www.bea.gov/industry/gdpbyind_data.htm

3. Earlier data do not include statistics for East German states.
4. The East London industry probably started with immigrant Jewish tailors, and since then has seen many successive waves of immigrants. A high concentration of Ugandan Asians settled in Leicester in the 1970s, having been offered jobs by a Marks & Spencer sock retailer (Interview Notes 2004); more recently Somali refugees have become involved in the Leicester clothing industry.
5. See http://www.agv-bekleidung-aschaffenburg.de/verband/historie.htm
6. See http://www.textil-bekleidung.de/Brancheninfos/Ueberblick/brancheninfos.htm
7. California Employment Development Department (http://www.calmis.ca.gov/file/indhist/la$haw.xls).
8. They employed 42,000 and over 20,000 people, respectively, before their break-up in 1998–99.
9. Data from Osiris, authors' calculations.
10. Gerry Weber press release 2006, downloaded on 10 September 2007 from www.gerryweber-ag.de/en/presse/pdf/pr171_060220_Gw_PM_bilanz
11. See http://otexa.ita.doc.gov/msrpoint.htm
12. See http:/www. ncto.org/
13. See http://www.bea.gov/industry/gdpbyind_data.htm

4

Fashion Retail

4.1. INTRODUCTION

Retailers, Gereffi wrote in 1994, have become very powerful actors in the clothing value chain, dominating producers. But Gereffi has focused primarily on the chain, rather than singling out retailers for systematic scrutiny. Thus, we still do not fully understand when and why power passed from producers to retailers, how retailers utilize their dominance in the chain, and whether this imbalance of power may be found in all western clothing industries. This chapter provides an in-depth investigation of these and related questions. We recognize that a study of retail needs to take into account consumption but will be equally concerned to show the somewhat neglected connection between retail and production. Following Fine and Leopold (1993: 25), we view the fashion industry as consisting of interconnected chains of provision linking production, distribution, marketing, and consumption.

Retail, in the same way as production, is shaped by its national institutional environment, as well as by cultural values expressed through consumption. Different national state competition policy and regulation of distribution, embodying divergent, historically grown political traditions, as well as national values vis-à-vis consumption, are considered particularly important (Haupt 2002; Brewer and Trentmann 2006). The varying financial systems which have shaped the growth and size of retail enterprises, as well as their differential capacity for self-organization and market coordination, are also relevant for an understanding of the structure of the retail sector. Hence this chapter analyses not only the organization of clothing retail but also accounts for the varying national institutions and values which have shaped patterns of distribution according to divergent rhythms and sometimes in entirely different directions. This approach demonstrates that the notion of capitalist diversity is useful also for understanding an important service sector industry. It serves to reveal that the forms taken by American (consumption and) retail, widely considered to have provided the model for the organization of retail in all advanced economies (Gereffi 1994; Crewe and Lowe 1996; Wrigley and Lowe 2002) are, in fact, in many ways distinctive, particularly in comparison with the continental European model (De Grazia 1998). However, some convergence also will be noted.

The clothing retail sector is not uniform. It is highly internally differentiated within societies by size, organization, and product/market and sourcing strategy, as well as differing substantially between societies. We focus mainly on retailers of fashion (mostly women's outer wear) and fashion basics (e.g. fashion jeans and T-shirts), rather than basic clothes (e.g. socks, most underwear, standard jeans, and T-shirts) and hence mainly on women's, rather than men's and children's, clothing.

It is now widely accepted that, from about the 1970s onwards, and particularly during the 1980s, large retailers became the most powerful actors in the chain who dealt with any crises of profitability by exacting new or higher contributions from 'manufacturers' and suppliers. To understand their rise to supremacy necessitates a study of fundamental transformations in the retail sector during the last 25 or so years. Causes of change have ranged from the entry of new domestic and foreign retail actors and the increased internal competition and pressure on margins, to the transformation in sourcing opportunities and available technology. Responses of retail firms have included processes of concentration, new market and sourcing strategies, verticalization, and more internationalization. An understanding of these interacting changes requires, first, a broad outline for each national retail sector of its recent historical development and structural composition, and second, a detailed analysis of the many recent strategic and structural transformations.

4.2. HISTORICAL DEVELOPMENT OF THE RETAIL SECTOR: STRATEGIC AND STRUCTURAL CHANGE

The following outlines of both the evolution and final structures of the retail sector in the three countries dwell on the developments which eventually relegated manufacturers to a subordinate position in the value chain and elevated retailers to a position of considerable power.

Major innovations in the distribution of clothing developed from the end of the nineteenth century (Jefferys 1954; Ritter and Kocka 1982; Fine and Leopold 2002; De Grazia 1998), although the full establishment of mass retailing, particularly in women's clothing, did not come until after World War II (Doeringer and Crean 2006: 360). Independents came under increased competitive pressure from the 1930s onwards, but accelerated decline occurred only in the post–World War II period and, in Germany, only in recent decades. At first, independents came under pressure from the emergence of multiples of clothing specialists and variety stores which, through specialization and ensuing economies of scale, were able to offer more varied, more fashionable, and significantly cheaper merchandise. Another competitive challenge for independents arose when, in tandem with suburbanization, shopping malls/shopping centres developed, particularly in the USA.

More recently, from the early 1990s onwards, actors with a new retail concept and locational strategy have risen to prominence—discount stores. Their comparatively lower costs and prices, together with the new openness of consumers to mixing cheap fashion basics with branded clothing, fuelled their expansion.

The emergence of these different forms of retail outlets created an over-provision of shopping area and goods which resulted in intense competition in domestic markets. Declining proportional spending added to the pressure on retailers. While most of the above developments occurred in all three economies, both their timing and the intensity of resulting competition varied between them, due to nationally specific consumption values/styles and institutions, as well as industry structure.

4.2.1. In Germany

The traditional German politics of protecting the *Mittelstand* of small independent owners, supported by new social and political forces since WWII, has survived right into the current time, albeit with some erosion during the last two decades. This policy stance comprises both public policy intervention and practical support in terms of grants/preferential loans and training (Shaw 1983: 108–10). These were further supported and reinforced by another German political economy tradition, namely, an entrenched tendency for coordination by market actors. These policies prompted a number of initiatives, restricting competition, of which five stand out: (1) legal limitation of business expansion, by inhibiting the establishment of a system of multiples (*Mehrbesitzverbot*) (De Grazia 1998: 72); (2) a restriction on the discounting of goods; (3) a zoning system for retail location; (4) a highly restrictive regulation of shop opening times; and (5) the self-organization of independents into purchasing associations (*Verbundsystem*). The existence of a clothing manufacturing sector, also organized on the *Mittlelstand* principle and dedicated to the production paradigm of comparatively small series of quality goods, further reinforced the survival of independents.

The restriction of multiples has been highly consequential in retarding consolidation and concentration (De Grazia 1998: 74). Although this regulation is no longer enforced, it explains the low incidence of German-owned multiples and the competitive scope afforded to foreign ones, such as Zara and H&M. The second anti-competition policy, which restricts the number of clearance sales and limits the proportion of stock which may be marked down (Bickerton 1999: 111), prevents the undercutting of prices of smaller retailers by larger ones. The severe restriction of opening hours, since 1956, is part of the same anticompetitive trend. This legislation confined opening hours only to day-time hours (until 6 p.m.) and week days. It received strong support not only from organized independents but also from the unions and the churches (De Grazia 1998: 80). A first substantial relaxation of this law came in 1996 (Retail Intelligence 2000*b*), and a further possibility for the extension of shopping hours was introduced in 2000, albeit with differential enforcement at the *Laender* level. Thus, since 2000, excepting only the proscription of Sunday shopping, the opening hours have not differed significantly from those in Britain.

The 1968 land use and building plan (*Baunutzungsordnung*) of the federal government includes a zoning system for retail location. This legislation, which was further extended in 1977 and 1990, makes planning a collaborative undertaking between local authority and *Land*, within the framework of a federal land use and building plan. It stipulates a three-tier hierarchy of retail centres, based on shopping floor space, type of outlet, and number of people within a catchment area (Shaw 1983: 119–21; Rudolph, Potz, and Bahn 2005). By keeping stores with a very large floor area out of city centres and surrounding inner suburbs, it has sheltered both department stores and independents from the competition of super- and hypermarkets. Moreover, it has prevented the 'over-storing' characteristic of the USA. Additionally, a 1977 federal ruling prohibited developments outside city centres. But this tight regulation has recently been relaxed (Retail Intelligence 2000*b*: 101), and a rapid proliferation of out-of-town, large-scale complexes has occurred (Shaw 1983: 111). New shopping centres, developed much later than in the UK and the USA, have become strong rivals since the 1990s (Bloecker and Wortmann 2005). Although they have expanded the available shopping area, the latter remains smaller than in other countries (BTE 2006: 26–7). In contrast to American urban landscapes, central locations still remain the key shopping areas.

Last, the self-organization of independents into purchasing associations goes a long way to explain how they managed to persist. The biggest association today, KATAG, dates the origins of buying associations in textiles to the early 1920s, when a small group of retailers recognized that the bundling of purchasing power in a buying association increases economic success (KATAG 2007). Buying associations, which operate in the mid-to-upper price segment, buy directly, or through agents, from abroad (SIPPO 2006: 72), and their buying strategy is not dissimilar to that of multiples. In addition to collective purchasing, they also provide centralized marketing and logistics services (ibid). Although buying associations in clothing have lost some importance and are much less prominent than in food retail, it would be wrong to rate them as unimportant, as does Wortmann (2003). Despite some crisis in this area in recent years, buying associations remain crucial for independents' survival. According to SIPPO (2006: 72), 55 per cent of independents are still members of buying associations.

Although the absence in the recent past of a developed stock market has not prevented consolidation in the sector, it has obviated the M&A frenzy witnessed in the USA. Hence there exists a comparatively low degree of concentration. Last, the continuing but declining influence of unions and of the system of VET have raised costs and depressed profit margins for German retailers (Interview Notes 2003), retarding investment and innovation (Retail Intelligence 2000*b*).

The lack of serious electoral challenge of this restrictive regulatory environment, which has constrained choice, may be partly explained by support from strong pressure groups and partly by a historically evolved distinctive German consumption style (De Grazia 1998; Haupt 2002; Trentmann 2006). Both these historians/social scientists and contemporary market analysts note a strong current among consumers that welcomes a restrained, low-profile retail sector, abjuring hedonism. General statistical indicators of more ascetic consumption norms and practices support this interpretation. Spending on clothes and shoes has shown continual relative decline since 1988 (BTE 2006: 89f.). There exists a relatively low amount of per capita spending on clothing, with Germany coming only in eleventh place in Europe (Retail Intelligence 2000b: 40), paralleled by a generally high savings ratio in excess of those in most other European countries (ibid: 36). As one retail executive told us: 'Germans have enough money. The Germans are rich, but they don't spend it, they save it' (R-GER-3).

German purchasers of clothing are additionally portrayed as particularly demanding—the opposite of consumption dupes—insisting on good product quality at extremely low prices (BTE 2006). They thereby are sustaining the production paradigm of 'diversified quality production' (Streeck 1992). Shoppers are reputed to be among the best informed about prices in Europe (Retail Intelligence 2000b: 103), and price is held to be of more concern than among UK shoppers. 'But also the price is a little bit more problematic here in Germany due to the tough competition... whereas in the UK, price is not an issue' (GER-C-5). Many people correspond to the new 'hybrid consumer' in that they combine both brand awareness and bargain-hunting, but in different types of shops (Retail Intelligence 2000b: 108; Barth and Hartmann 2003: 61; SIPPO 2006: 51f.).

Both the above institutional environment and the cultural values sedimented in consumption style have shaped the structure and composition of the German clothing retail sector. Mass consumption developed somewhat later than in the two Anglo-Saxon countries (De Grazia 1998), and the structure of the sector has been more polarized. On the one hand, small independents are still a significant, albeit declining presence; on the other hand, large department store chains, mail order firms, supermarkets, and discounters, together with foreign multiples, now threaten the continued survival of independents. But retail concentration remains well below that in both the UK and the USA, and retailers' power vis-à-vis manufacturers is less pronounced. Additionally, the late development of the stock market has retarded corporatization, seen as typical for the US and UK sectors (Wrigley and Lowe 2002).

Thus retail development in Germany has long been very distinctive. Even the heightened American influence after WWII, following the 'European Recovery Program' mission and the flooding in of American capital, did not fundamentally undermine the traditional structural pattern in clothing retail (De Grazia 1998: 79). When, from the late 1980s onwards and particularly during the last decade, the traditional consumption orientation became undermined by a young generation's taste for cheaper and faster fashion, coinciding with a firmer embrace of economic liberalism, the structural conservatism in the retail sector also began to unravel. From the 1990s onwards, a gradual trend towards convergence to the Anglo-American patterns has been discernible.

Independents are not the only retail segment affected by the intensifying market competition, but other retail channels have felt the pressures, too. Department stores, seeing their share of the clothing market reduce since the 1970s (Barth and

Hartmann 2003: 62), have responded with mergers. The originally large number of different regional and local stores gave way first, to four major stores and then, in 1993, to two very large firms, Kaufhof and Karstadt, plus a few medium-sized, more up-market, and local stores. In 2004, the share of department stores of the clothing market stood at 12 per cent (SIPPO 2006: 70)—a considerably higher share than in the UK and the USA, due to the lesser development of multiples. Thus despite serious difficulties in the department store sector, they remain important actors in terms of turnover, market share ranking, and popularity among consumers (BTE 2006). They thus continue to sustain German branded 'manufacturers'. Nevertheless, their market share has been declining, and this trend is likely to be progressive.

The retail segment of clothing specialist multiples in German ownership, as pointed out above, has remained underdeveloped due to now obsolete legislation protecting independents. Among established German multiples, only the upper-middle market Peek and Cloppenburg (P&C) and the middle-market C&A stand out. C&A, which only sells its own labels and has a large number of subsidiaries, is the most successful clothing multiple in Germany, with a market share of 8.2 per cent (BTE 2006: 166).[1] Another established multiple with a large share of the German market is Esprit, which is now under majority Hong Kong ownership.

Home shopping is an above average avenue for fashion sales in Germany (Myers 2006: 8)—a likely consequence of the highly restricted shop opening hours in the past. The mail order sector is highly concentrated. Three very large firms—Otto, Quelle, and Neckermann (the latter two are part of the Karstadt Quelle Group), dominate the mail order market. Otto is considered the leading global player in this market (Retail Intelligence 2000b: 140), as well as having the second largest market share in Germany. Pure internet sellers so far have only a very small proportion of the trade (BTE 2006: 74).

The discounting retail segment, first introduced in the grocery sector in 1962, seems to be an indigenous development rather than an imitation of US practice. In Germany, the downward movement in prices could not express itself in special offers (which were prohibited) but instead resulted in an early and full embrace of the discount principle—that is, permanently low prices across a range of merchandise (Barth and Hartmann 2003: 59). The continuous and, since the 1990s, accelerating growth of discounters, has affected all other forms of retail negatively (ibid: 59, 64; SIPPO 2006). (See figures in Table 4.1.) Their high degree of popularity makes it difficult to present German consumers any longer as interested only in quality goods.

Discounters are divided into the specialized clothing discounters and the food super/hyper markets, selling low-price clothing in their large stores. Specialized clothing discounters often belong to larger groups, such as Metro or Tengelmann, showing incursions from the highly developed food retail sector into the less developed clothing retail sector. They keep down costs by employing the same sourcing and operating principles as their UK and US counterparts, including the use of low-pay untrained employees (Bloecker and Wortmann 2005: 95).

The clothing discounters have a very large share of the market—12 per cent in 2004 (SIPPO 2006: 71)—equalling that of department stores and exceeding the market share of British discounters (Euromonitor International 2007*b*). The five largest now have a place among the 20 largest German clothing retailers (BTE 2006: 163). All have a very large number of outlets (>500), some also outside Germany (ibid). The largest food stores selling clothes had a market share in 2004 of 7 per cent (SIPPO 2006: 71). They mainly sell basic clothing, particularly for children, but increasingly also fashion basics and sports clothes. Although important new competitors, they have not yet reached the huge market shares of some British and American supermarket chains.

Foreign-owned clothing retailers have also made significant inroads into the German market. They owe their popularity to the fact that their backwards integration into manufacturing enables 'quick response' selling of constantly changing fashion clothing at relatively low prices (BTE 2006: 168; SIPPO 2006: 65). These stores now dominate the best shopping areas, except for Germany's largest cities (ibid). Among them, Spanish Zara (a joint venture with Otto) and, more so, Swedish Hennes and Mauritz (H&M) stand out.

Table 4.1 sums up the structure and competitive landscape of clothing retail in Germany, and also shows recent gains/losses in market share.

In contrast to the German manufacturing sector, 'Germany's retail sector is by no means the efficient, customer-oriented industry one might expect it to be' (Retail Intelligence 2000*b*: 7). Insufficient investment has been made in stores, management, and IT. Clothing retailers are believed to be well behind major rivals in the UK in terms of efficiency, innovation, and profitability (ibid). German retail is certainly more fragmented than its UK counterpart, with no channel dominating the retail scene. Competition remains very intense and margins much lower than those enjoyed by British retailers, partly as a consequence of higher wages (Interview Notes 2003). Hence performance is not primarily shaped by managerial capabilities but more by institutional constraints.

Although the organization of German retail has shown some signs of convergence towards the Anglo-American pattern in terms of kinds of retail outlets

Table 4.1. Clothing retail channels by market share, Germany, 2000–04, in %

	2000 (%)	2004 (%)
Independents	28	25
Clothing multiples	28	20
Department/variety stores	13	12
Super- and hypermarkets	5	7
Textile discounters	3	12
Sports shops	3	3
Mail order	14	15
Other (factory outlets and Tschibo)	9	9

Source: SIPPO (2006): 69f.

developed, there still remain many distinctive features of a CME. Enduring distinctiveness is evident in the persistence of independents and retail buying groups, as well as in a different consumption style. The rational consumer, less swayed by fashion and more interested in comfort and fitness for purpose—the antithesis of the consumer prevalent in postmodern analyses—forms the largest group among German consumers (BTE 2006).

But it is clear that the German *Sonderweg* is under threat. In the face of changing consumption habits and the rise to prominence of new competitors, attempts at organizing the market now constitute a rearguard action. They stave off, but cannot indefinitely postpone, the gradual convergence of the German to the Anglo-Saxon pattern of retail organization. The decline of independents from 60 per cent in the 1960s to 25 per cent in the 2004 (Bloecker and Wortmann 2005: 93; SIPPO 2006: 54) illustrates one important aspect of change.

4.2.2. In the USA

In the USA, in contrast to Germany, both the institutional environment and the consumption values and style have been very conducive to the development of an early mass market in clothing (Jefferys 1954; Haupt 2002) and a compatible retail sector. The latter is both comparatively highly concentrated and largely corporatized. In addition to the large size of the home market, both state policy and the nature of the financial system have facilitated this development, as has the relatively low influence of unions. Consequently independent stores, although enduring in significant numbers until the early 1950s (Wrigley and Lowe 2002; Aldridge 2004: 35), had in fact already lost the battle with big business in the late 1930s (Cohen 2003). Not only did independents not receive significant government support, but a very liberal state policy on both opening hours and land-use planning systematically favoured big business from the late 1940s onwards. Thus, opening hours have been far more liberal than in both Germany and the UK—by the 1960s, shops were open until 21.30 on six nights a week (Cohen 2003: 265). Low restrictions on land use encouraged large-scale suburban mall development and out-of-town hyper markets from the late 1940s onwards (Cohen 2003). Expansion of retailers through M&A and gradual increases in capital concentration, in reaction to the above spatial and temporal changes of the sector, were facilitated by the existence of an active capital market. The financial system also encouraged an early and strong evolution of a credit economy, fuelling expansion of consumer demand. Relatively low wages for service workers, tolerated by largely powerless unions, additionally sustained the expansion strategies. In addition to institutional factors, consumption patterns contributed to this pattern of change. A highly developed consumerism and distinctive consumption orientations evolved comparatively early as a result of a confluence of economic, social, political, and institutional factors.

In the USA, in contrast to Europe, consumption attained a more central position in the self-understanding of citizens. Indeed, consumption became very closely entwined with what it means to be an American citizen. It was during the 1930s, particularly during the peak years of the New Deal (1933–36), that the groundwork was laid in both ideology and policy for the establishment of the notion of the 'consumer citizen' (Cohen 1998; De Grazia 1998; McGovern 1998). This notion well expresses both the influence of a consolidating LME and a commensurate political ideology. At this time, the notion of social citizenship became equated with the entitlement to a decent social standard of living for all (Cohen 1998; De Grazia 1998), to be achieved through an expansion of production and consumption, rather than the development of a redistributive welfare system. The gains of this, it was believed, would benefit both capital and labour (Cohen 1998). 'American people, fitfully but firmly, came to equate the consumer with the citizen, a consumer standard of living with democracy, and the full participation in such an economy of spending...with being an American' (McGovern 1998: 37).

Consumerism became more deeply entrenched during the 1950s and 1960s, through the introduction of three new business developments: the creation of the 'credit economy'; the evolution of a new retail format; and the rise to prominence of marketing and advertising. The explosion of consumer credit— the value of credit increased 11-fold between 1895 and 1960—kept the mass consumption economy afloat (Cohen 2003: 123). The promotion of shopping malls as the new 'village green', offering fun and entertainment for the whole family, established shopping as a prime leisure pastime (ibid). The 'discovery' by the marketing profession of the concept of market segmentation, that is, the practice of breaking down an undifferentiated consumer mass into individual market segments distinguished by age, household type, income, and lifestyle, to fuel consumer differentiation and increase market share, became highly consequential in both social and economic terms (Gardner and Sheppard 1989; Cohen 2003: 295).

The almost unimpeded advance of consumerism and a strong retail sector in American society were facilitated both by the political legitimation it received and by the liberal economic policy, erecting few regulatory hurdles to the development of retail. Furthermore, the absence, after the New Deal, of strong economic downturns provided the context in which consumer citizens could freely develop.

The US clothing market today is complex and highly diffuse, with extensive differentiation according to ethnicity/sizing and climatic condition. But a relatively high degree of homogeneity in style nevertheless prevails, achieved both by production and by marketing method. There prevails a strong emphasis on casual clothing, such as jeans, T-shirts, and sweat shirts. Congruent with this, the youth market is highly developed and the high-quality end of the market for more mature customers is less developed. There are, however, several luxury brands traded globally, such as Ralph Lauren, Calvin Klein, and Donna Karan.

From the late 1940s onwards—after the building of a US-wide road network and large-scale suburbanization and co-incident with the ideological push of the concept of 'consumer citizen'—the development of shopping malls was to prove very consequential for the transformation of the retail landscape (Abernathy et al. 1999: 42). The suburban share of total metropolitan retail trade rose from 31 per cent in 1948 to almost 60 per cent by 1961 (Cohen 2003: 257). At this time department and speciality stores, partly in response to mall development, established a national network of branches (ibid: 273). A significant expansion in clothing multiples occurred which, by the early 1980s, had a share of 40 per cent of all clothes retailing (Wrigley and Lowe 2002: 23)—a share somewhat lower than in the UK around the same time (ibid). So-called mega chains with more than 100 branches constituted a significant proportion among multiples. A drastic increase in shopping mall floor area led to a creation of overcapacity (Abernathy et al. 1999: 46). The USA industry also developed a strong mail order channel, due to the relatively large and highly dispersed rural population.

In addition to specialized clothing chains, the highly concentrated department store sector has remained a significant retail industry actor. Among department stores, a small number of so-called mega stores came into existence: Federated Department Stores, May, Dillard's, and Proffitt's (Abernathy et al. 1999: 48). By 2002, the four largest chains accounted for about two-thirds of department store sales (Doeringer and Crean 2006: 360). By 2005, further consolidation had occurred, with acquisition of May by Federated Department Stores (Dow Jones Newswires 2005).

The 1980s and 1990s saw the emergence of mass merchandisers or discounters, including warehouse clubs, variety stores, and hyper markets which have added clothing to the goods sold. By 1990 both Wal-Mart and K-Mart surpassed Sears as the largest retailer in terms of sales (Gereffi 1994). Discounters buy in huge quantities and price their goods for a mass market (Doeringer and Crean 2006: 358). They deal mainly in fashion basics and basics, but most recently Wal-Mart and J. C. Penney have also introduced store-brand versions of national brands, such as Levi Strauss Signature jeans in Wal-Mart. These features mean that discounters have had a very negative impact on all other retailers, but particularly on department stores (*Economist* 2003: 89). During the 1990s, mass merchandisers have enjoyed a 5-fold increase in sales, whereas department stores have achieved only negligible growth (Singhal, Agrawal, and Singh 2004: 124).

In the USA, as in the UK, capital concentration now is high in this sector, but the US market is more fragmented, with no clear market leaders (Euromonitor International 2007a). Nevertheless, from the 1980s, retailers were able to take the dominant position in the value chain and impose price and other conditions on USA and foreign producers and marketers. Their dominance was facilitated by their huge purchasing power and their technologically mediated closeness to consumer demand, and it was spurred on by both intense competition and pressures from investors. Although many producers also consolidated and grew in size since the 1980s, they do not rival retailers in economic strength and have not attained countervailing power.

4.2.3. In the UK

In the UK, both the early evolution of a mass market and the subsequent falling behind developments in the USA were shaped by historical contingencies and institutional influences, as well as by interaction with consumption patterns. Although the UK industry developed along the trajectory of an LME, it nevertheless became distinguished from the USA by some distinctive features in its early evolution. As in the USA, a liberal regulatory stance fostered strong competition (Howe 2003; Trentmann 2006) and, in comparative European terms, a less prescriptive planning system (Howe 2003). Together with a lack of protection for independents, this led to an early consolidation of the retail sector and a comparatively high level of standardization of clothing. There were no restrictions hampering the creation of chain stores (De Grazia 1989). The abolition of resale price maintenance in 1964 allowed larger-scale businesses to out-compete smaller independents on price (Howe 2003: 163). Although the 1950 Shops Act regulated opening hours, these were not as restrictive as in Germany. When, by the mid-1980s, these regulations were widely flouted, opening hours became almost completely deregulated. Building restrictions, too, were haphazard and not as systematically enforced as in Germany.

However, the development of the welfare state after World War II obviated the development of a pure market mentality in the area of distribution and prevented the evolution of the 'consumer citizen'. As in the USA, consolidation was facilitated by the stock market. But in contrast to the USA, both government liberalism and consumer prosperity were more fitful, with World War II and post-war austerity constituting a particularly sharp break which had been absent in the USA. In contrast to the situation in Germany, restriction of consumption had been less prolonged and austerity less deep. After war-time restrictions up to the early 1950s, the regulatory environment again became quite relaxed, and retail development continued its unencumbered course (De Grazia 1989; Howe 2003). In the UK, unlike in the USA, historically quite a strong producer influence prevailed in consumption movements (the cooperative movement) (Trentmann 2006), but in contrast to German developments this did not raise either quality standards or wages.

As in the USA, a fairly persistent free market orientation has favoured a strong consumerism which, in turn, has shaped both the size of the retail sector and the nature of the products sold. Per capita consumption of clothes in UK is high in comparative European terms. Per capita spending in 2006 was €1,117.2, compared to €829.4 in Germany (Euromonitor International 2007*b*).

In the UK, a process of retail consolidation was facilitated even before WWII by several influences: the early development of a large working class; urbanization; standardized factory production, particularly of men's clothing; and a relatively liberal regulatory environment. Growth in homogeneity of social behaviour and taste between different parts of country came in the inter-war years (Jefferys 1954: 316). The UK experienced a comparatively early emergence and consolidation of multiples, that is, chains of specialist (and variety) clothing stores. Multiples sold indifferent quality cheaply (Jefferys 1954: 297). Concern with quality clothing became confined to a small sector of particular department stores.

The first variety store, entering the UK from the USA in 1909, was Woolworth, to be followed a few decades later by British Home Stores, Littlewoods, and Marks & Spencer (Howe 2003: 156). Multiples selling women's outer wear developed only from the 1930s (Jefferys 1954: 342, 351). By that time, clothing multiples had acquired sufficient weight in the retail sector to make a negative impact on the small independents. The latter did not have the capital for good locations or for buying the range of stock increasingly demanded by fashionable consumers (Jefferys 1954: 335). By the end of the 1980s, the multiples controlled 80 per cent of the market (Gardner and Sheppard 1989: 26).

Department stores which had developed in the last decades of the nineteenth century (Jefferys 1954: 326–7) experienced a strong process of concentration in the inter-war years. But, given the importance of the multiples and the lack of thorough-going consolidation, they did not gain the same size and power as their US counterparts. UK retailers, with a few notable exceptions, have been less successful at the designer end. The most expensive London shopping locations, such as Bond Street, are dominated by foreign brands, among them many US brands. The qualitative aspects of consumer demand and the structure of the retail sector together shaped and were shaped by the evolution of the manufacturing sector, discussed in the previous chapter.

Mail order clothing businesses, so important in Germany and the USA, have had and still have a relatively low share of the market for women's wear in the UK and are rarely mentioned as serious market competitors (Howe 2003: 164). However, internet shopping has gained greatly in popularity, with the UK said to be among the leaders in Europe (Euromonitor International 2007*b*: 1).

Development of large shopping centres in the UK came almost a decade later than in the USA, from the late 1950s onwards, and initially they were built in city centres on 'brown field' sites. Large-scale, mainly out-of-town shopping centres— the equivalent of the American malls—developed much later in the UK, from the late 1970s onwards, and were substantially based on the US model of a mall (Gardner and Sheppard 1989: 102f.). The mega centres came only in the middle 1980s and early 1990s (Wrigley and Lowe 2002: 340–1), and their style— excepting only the US-inspired Metro Centre—was generally more British influenced (Gardner and Sheppard 1989: 109). However, since 1997 a reaction has set in against out-of-town shopping centres (Euromonitor International 2007*b*: 23).

The emergence in the 1990s of specialized clothing discounters and the sale of clothing lines by super- and hypermarkets lagged behind comparable US developments (Wrigley and Lowe 2002: 76). Discounters also emerged later than in both the USA and Germany. Both their buying patterns and operating modes differ little from those in the other two societies. But it is notable that there is a higher fashion content in the merchandise of both supermarkets and discounters, and the employment of freelance designers is greater than is found in either the USA or Germany. This has facilitated the promotion of strong store brands (UK-R-4; on Asda's George label, retained by Wal-Mart). Both types of discounter established themselves very quickly. Their prices are well below those of the High Street chains, with Tesco and Matalan being priced at roughly half their level and Asda and Primark below half (Singhal et al. 2004: 130). There therefore exists both strong rivalry within the low-cost market and intense competitive pressure on the High Street stores. In 2007 Primark—which has greatly increased the fashion content of its clothes—was in the lead with a market share of 8.9 per cent in terms of volume. The supermarket Tesco had edged up to second place with 8.6 per cent, while Asda took third place with 7.5 per cent. On the High Street, only Marks & Spencer sell a greater volume, coming in at 11.4 per cent (*Guardian* 2007: 41). The inroads made on the sales of traditional High Street chains is illustrated by the following figures: the value (cheap) clothing market, now worth an estimated £8.5 billion, accounts for 25 per cent of the clothes bought in the UK and was set to outperform the clothing market as a whole in 2007 (*Guardian* 2007: 5).

In addition, multiples and department stores have come under pressure from recently arrived foreign fashion chains, particularly Spanish Zara (Inditex Group) and Swedish H&M. Their strength, in addition to relatively low prices, has been their superior ability to produce 'fast fashion' and achieve constant renewal of goods on offer, due to their control over the whole supply chain. Recent distribution of market share is indicated by Table 4.2.

In sum, clothing retail in the UK is both highly concentrated and very efficiently organized. The degree of concentration is indicated by the fact that the top five players in the UK take 45 per cent of the market, as compared with 26 per cent in Germany (Mintel 2005, cited by Myers 2006: 8). Retailing has become one of the pivotal and dynamic sectors of the economy (Wrigley and Lowe 2002: 23–4). In terms of sector sales, the UK leads the rest of Europe by a long way, despite Germany's much larger population (Mintel 2005, cited by Myers 2006: 8, figure 1). This makes them the dominant actor in the value chain, especially as both concentration and efficiency are absent among 'manufacturers'. Fierce competition between the different players, as well as investor pressures, force retailers to extract the highest possible value in their dealings with producers. In the UK, however, no single operator holds the buying power of their giant corporate US counterparts. Corporatization, although initially as advanced as in the USA, has been partly unravelling in the UK. As one interviewee commented: 'We are not

Table 4.2. Clothing retail channels by market share, UK, 2003, in %

Specialist clothing multiples and variety stores	38
Department stores	9
Clothing discounters	10
Supermarkets	8
Independents	8

Source: Keynote 2004, cited by Oxborrow 2005: 2.

a fashionable area to invest in. Retail generally is terrible. They [investors] are either investing in the really fix-quick people, or they are not investing at all' (UK-R-2).

To conclude, British retail has experienced its own indigenous early development and only much later, and with considerable delay, came to copy some developments in the USA, such as mall design for the early large-scale out-of-town shopping centres, super- and hypermarkets, discount stores, and marketing practices (Wrigley and Lowe 2002: 44; Singhal et al. 2004: 130). But development and structural characteristics of UK retail nevertheless place it closer to its counterparts in the US liberal market economy than to its European neighbour Germany—a CME.

4.3. PRODUCT AND MARKET STRATEGY

In addition to the development and structure of the retail sectors, product and market strategy also have diverged in significant ways, due to societal differences in consumption styles and domestic manufacturing traditions. As elaborated in Chapter 3, the British and American strategy since the 1980s has been diversified mass production oriented towards the lower middle market. The German paradigm, distinguished by an emphasis on quality and fit, is akin to diversified quality production (Streeck 1992; Hollingsworth and Boyer 1997) and caters more for the middle and upper middle market. A further distinguishing feature between the three paradigms is the greater orientation in the USA and the UK towards the 'young fashion' market. Whereas in the USA the orientation is towards 'fashionable classics', updated by variation in colour (Salmon and Cmar 1987: 102; Ross 2004), in the UK a focus on constantly changing fashion is particularly pronounced. British 'young fashion' is said to be less standardized than US fashion: 'The Americans generally make much more basic products, and there are much higher numbers' (UK-R-2). In a survey of 10 developed countries, British consumers were among the top 5 most interested in fashion (Textile Outlook International 2005: 181). In Germany, in contrast, a more restrained design is oriented to demand for more classical garments (Heidenreich 1990: 175), and there exists a greater focus on the 30–60 age group and on larger sizes (Interview Notes 2003; Myers 2006: 9). The differing product and market strategies of retailers in the three countries are summarized in Figure 4.1.

In both the USA and Germany, brands occupy a central position in the market. German retailers acquire brands mainly from their originators, German branded 'manufacturers'. US retailers, in contrast, deal with some of the clothing giants who have acquired or in-licensed a whole stable of different brands, a strategy fostered by investors. In the UK, however, despite the abundance of designer talent, multiples' private label products or 'store brands' seem to have crowded out branded marketers of significant size. (The main exception to this is Burberry, turned into a highly lucrative branded marketer by a succession of American

	Germany	UK	US
Product strategy	Diversified quality mass production for mid–upper-market	Mass production for lower–mid-market	Mass production for lower–mid-market
Dominant age group	30–60 age group	Young fashion	Young fashion
Fashion style	Classical fashion	High fashion	Fashionable classics
Brand strategy	Brands of German 'manufacturers'	Retailers' private labels/store brands	Brands of US 'marketers'/ store brands
Key retail channels	Independents, department stores, discounters	Multiples, discounters	Department stores, discounters
Retailer position	Fragmentation; less efficient; hold relatively less power in the value chain	Highly concentrated and efficient; dominate value chain	Highly concentrated; efficient; dominance in the value chain

Figure 4.1. Retailers' product and market strategies

CEOs.) In all three societies foreign brands, particularly in the luxury class, are now sold by up-market department stores or in brands' own outlets.

Product strategy also differs, however, between the different types of retailers within countries. Thus, the multiples tend to be much more fashion oriented than department stores and, more so, discounters. Department stores have multiple product strategies, selling recognized national and international brands, their own store brands and fashion basics and basic clothing. Discounters fall at the other end of the continuum, with a relative small range of products, sold in greater volume. This diversity in product strategy, it will be shown in subsequent sections, leads to different strategies concerning business organization and particularly sourcing.

4.4. INTENSIFYING COMPETITION AND RISING CONCENTRATION

In all three industries, despite varying sector structures and product paradigms, from the 1980s onwards a number of new retail actors entered the market for fashion retail and greatly sharpened competition. The format of the discounters posed a particularly severe challenge. In the face of the continual expansion of retail floor space and of stagnating or declining demand, competition became intense in all three industries, although the nature and degree of competition and the challenges posed differed between the three societies.

In the USA, due to the continuous expansion of malls and retail floor space, overcapacity was a particularly severe problem (Abernathy et al. 1999: 46;

Economist 2003: 90). In Germany, in contrast, a severe and a more prolonged reduction in demand, representing consumer reaction to the depressed economic situation during the last decade or so (SIPPO 2006), created a particularly unforgiving retail environment (Myers 2006). The consequences of what BTE (2006: 165) describe as ruinous competition have been price increases below inflation, generating stagnant or even reduced turnover (BTE 2006; SIPPO 2006), and some of the slimmest profit margins in Europe. In the USA demand merely stagnated (Singhal et al. 2004: 127), and in the UK it even remained comparatively buoyant (Textile Outlook International 2005). In the UK overall absolute expenditure on clothing and footwear rose between 2003 and 2006 and per capita spending in 2006 was the highest in Europe (Euromonitor International 2007b: table 1.43). Fierce competition made it impossible to raise prices in all three countries. Instead, the cost savings made from sourcing in low-wage countries benefited consumers (Singhal et al. 2004: 126). The pressures felt by retailers were increasingly passed on to manufacturers and suppliers, leading to a downward spiral in sourcing prices (Palpacuer et al. 2004). In sum, 'increasing product proliferation, retail overcapacity, falling relative per capita expenditure on apparel and constant pressure to provide lower prices to consumers created an unforgiving competitive environment for retailers' (Abernathy et al. 1999: 47). In Germany and in the US business failure of long established retailers occurred, resulting in a 'dizzying shake-up of ownership' (Bonacich and Applebaum 2000: 84f.), while in the UK the take-over of M&S was narrowly averted. From the 1980s onwards, retailers reacted to intensified competition with a whole raft of measures, to be reviewed below, starting with increasing consolidation and capital concentration.

4.4.1. In the USA

As the above comparison has shown, sectoral competition was intense and the ensuing crisis sharp. During the 1980s retailers therefore reacted with radical consolidation, particularly in the department store sector but also among clothing speciality stores. By 2002 the four largest department store chains accounted for about two-thirds of department store sales, up from 29 per cent in 1972, and the corresponding figure for women's speciality shops in the same period is 30 per cent, up from 11 per cent (Doeringer and Crean 2006: 360). By 2005 further consolidation had occurred. Given the dominance of the stock market, consolidation was accompanied by corporatization, and retailers began to experience the pressures for shareholder value. Tokatli and Eldener (2004: 179) attribute corporatization to the need for capital which outsourcing on a large scale required. However, developments in the UK and, more so, Germany do not support this claim.

In 2000 the five largest clothing retailers, in order of size, were Wal-Mart, J. C. Penney, Federated Department Stores, Gap, and Target (Ross 2004: 131). In the same year, the 10 largest had a market share of 71.8 per cent (ibid). The purchasing power of a speciality chain, such as The Gap, is indicated by its turnover figure which, in 2005, was US\$16.3 billion (Datamonitor Company Profiles, 22 October 2005). US 'manufacturers' see this consolidation process and the increased bargaining power it brings as a strong threat: 'Due to consolidation among customers [retail stores] of Jones Apparel, the bargaining power of the customers would increase thereby putting pressure on the company pricing structure' (Dow Jones Newswires 2005).

From the 1980s retailers' increased size and their commensurate purchasing power has led to a reversal of dominance within the clothing value chain. Large manufacturers, who until this time had called the tune, now faced a loss of control to the mega stores and the speciality multiples (US-C-6; Ross 2004: 128f; Doeringer and Crean 2006: 360). Their purchasing power was magnified by the fact that, in contrast to their British counterparts, most also centralized their buying offices (Doeringer and Crean 2006: 372). This dominance is even more pronounced among the new mass retailers of fashion basic goods. Wal-Mart alone now controls almost 30 per cent of the apparel market (Petrovic and Hamilton 2005), selling US\$33 billion worth of clothing in 2000 (Ross 2004: 128), giving it unrivalled power over producers. The new power of retailers is not only economically founded but also has a parallel in politics. The Retail Industry Trade Action Coalition has emerged as the new pay master and the most influential lobbying group in Washington, pushing aside the once powerful manufacturing interest groups in the textile and clothing industry (Rivoli 2005: 136).

4.4.2. In the UK

Although concentration in the UK had already started in the 1930s (Jefferys 1954), the really significant change came in the post–World War II period and particularly since the mid-1970s. During this period, 'retailing was transformed... into an industry increasingly dominated by big capital in the form of large corporations' (Wrigley and Lowe 2002). It was also during the 1970s that manufacturers had to cede their dominant position in the value chain to retailers (ibid; Gardner and Sheppard 1989).

Nevertheless, as malls had not proliferated in the same way as in the USA, competition during the 1980s has not been as fierce and concentration has not increased to quite the same extent. It affected mainly the already sizeable multiples in the middle market segment, while concentration in the department store sector in recent decades has not paralleled that in the USA. Nevertheless, in European comparative terms, concentration in the British clothing retail sector is very advanced. Concentration is the highest in Europe and much higher than that in Germany. As in the USA, it has been accompanied by corporatization (Wrigley and Lowe 2002), with stock market listing more common than among large continental European retailers (Palpacuer et al. 2004). 'British retailing is uniquely the province of big business' (Wrigley and Lowe 2002). This shift in power is also reflected in retailers' profitability as compared with 'manufacturers' and is ascribed to the control of the market by a few very large retailers (ibid).

However, since the 1980s several big de-mergers have occurred, particularly the break-up of the Burton Group in the late 1990s, and stock market listing is no longer so sought after.

In 2003, specialist multiples and variety stores dominated with a 38 per cent share of the market for clothing. According to Mintel 2005, cited by Myers (2006), the top five players have a market share of 45 per cent, against a share of 26 per cent in Germany. The biggest British retailers have a sales volume 8 to 10 times greater than that of even the biggest British clothing firms. The high level of buyer concentration, contrasting with a low level of seller concentration, indicates a huge imbalance of power and a consequently large negative impact on sellers' margins (Warren 2003: 233). This is expressed by one retail respondent in the following terms: 'Because in the UK the dominant people were the retailers, who are far bigger than just about any of the suppliers...they are the ones who say "jump!" ' (UK-R-3). The power held over manufacturers by Marks & Spencer in particular has been legendary, and during the last few years Arcadia too has used its growing muscle to depress clothing firms' prices.

4.4.3. In Germany

In Germany the process of concentration in clothing retail proceeded more slowly and did not assume the same extreme degree as in the UK and the USA (Myers 2006: 7). This is due to the fact that, historically, protective legislation preserved the independent sector for a much longer time (see Section 4.1) while simultaneously preventing the development of the multiple clothing specialists which became so dominant in the UK. The only sizeable clothing specialist multiples are C&A, Peek & Cloppenburg, and Esprit, with the first registered in the Netherlands and the last in Hong Kong. What concentration has occurred was thus mainly in the department store and the mail order sectors. In the former, two giants, Karstadt and Kaufhof, became dominant following a series of mergers in the 1980s and 1990s. In the latter, two giant firms—Otto and Quelle—have a virtual monopoly. Thus in Germany the top five players have a market share of 26 per cent, as against 45 per cent in the UK (Mintel 2005 Data, cited by Myers 2006). Although concentration is less advanced in Germany, it is nevertheless considerable, and mergers have left 'manufacturers' with much less choice concerning domestic customers.

The lesser degree of concentration among retailers and the predominance of medium-sized branded 'manufacturers' among clothing firms means that the former do not wield the same power as, nor enjoy the superior profits of, their Anglo-American counterparts. According to one of our retail informants, until the late 1990s the situation regarding margins was exactly the opposite: 'and the producing group, they were really profitable—if you look at the share of the total line, you can see it was between 15 and 18 per cent of the price were profit. But on the retail side... it was only 0.7–2.5 per cent' (GER-R-3). In sum, in Germany the same radical shift in power relations has not occurred, and relations between clothing firms (mainly branded) and big retailers have remained more collaborative, according to one of our department store interviewees (GER-R-2) and confirmed by Wortmann (2005).

Relatively low concentration within the clothing retail sector is, however, paralleled by considerable ownership concentration in German retail capital more generally, showing the typical German pattern of cross shareholding. Both Karstadt and Kaufhof are, in turn, part of giant groups. The Karstadt Quelle Group owns the second- and third-largest mail order firms (Quelle and Neckermann) and, in 2005, had a turnover of €4,424 million (BTE 2006: 164). Kaufhof is part of the Metro Group, a company that has a big stake in the food retail sector and, in 2005, had a turnover of €3,245 million (BTE 2006: 164). Both the food retailers Metro Group and Tengelmann Group also own clothing discounters, Adler and KiK, respectively. The acquisition of Kaufhof by Metro Group has been highly consequential in that it enabled the department store to modernize its concept and make substantial investments to refurbish its stores. It also is perceived as having become more aggressive vis-à-vis competitors (GER-R-3). Concentration in Germany does not necessarily equal corporatization, due to the historically low development of the stock market and the persistence of private ownership of even very large companies. Both Kaufhof and Karstadt have only a minority of their shares listed (Retail Intelligence 2000*b*: 4).

In all three countries concentration occurred largely within sub-sectors and, because of an early evolution of a multiplicity of retail channels, the sector overall is considered fragmented.

4.5. NEW RETAIL STRATEGIES I: THE DEVELOPMENT OF STORE BRANDS AND DIRECT SOURCING

Power is not merely a function of size but also depends on the adoption of strategies securing greater independence from national 'middle-men' clothing firms. Two new developments, which assured retailers of both the growing control of their markets and the greater appropriation of value in the chain, gained ground from the 1980s onwards. The first was the increasing development of 'private label' clothing or 'store brands' exclusive to a particular retailer. The second, partly precipitated by the first, was the engagement in direct sourcing, that is, the establishment of their own foreign sourcing offices and the cutting out of national 'middle-men' producers. The reversal of power relations to which the two strategies strongly contributed is well summarized by Abernathy et al. (1999): The big retailers 'are using their buying power to pull goods through the supply chain, on behalf of the consumer so that the production "push" system of the 1980s has given way to a "demand pull" system of the 1990s'.

Although several retailers had long sold only 'own label' clothing (e.g. British Marks & Spencer and Next, German C&A, and American The Gap), for most retailers these strategies fundamentally changed business models and the sourcing risks incurred. While an emphasis on store brands was first adopted by some multiples and department stores in the 1980s, by the 2000s several low-cost retailers had begun to imitate this strategy. Some discounters and supermarkets even signed up top designers to create a small collection for their store and, in the process, acquired brand status for some of their products, though at middle rather than top level. Consumers, it was pointed out above, were not averse to the embrace of discounter 'brands', buying them either exclusively or mixing them with top brands. This widely reported blurring between brands and store brands naturally exerted pressure on branded 'manufacturers' and marketers who had long been able to extract premium prices for their branded clothing. Such pressure was strongest for middle-level branded marketers whose quality levels and snob value do not exceed those of store brands to a significant degree.

Retailers' enhanced independence and move to dominance in the value chain allow them to lay down the terms of sourcing. They do not merely determine the final price and delivery date but save further costs by transferring various functions and risks to suppliers. However, backward integration has not been a costless change of strategy as it has required large investments in design and sourcing capabilities. Such a change could not be accomplished overnight but was initiated as a gradual process.

4.5.1. In the USA

In the USA in-house product design and creation of private label clothes, although starting in the 1970s (Doeringer and Crean 2006: 360), achieved significant growth only in the 1980s (Abernathy et al. 1999: 43; Gereffi 1999: 46). By 1998, private-label merchandise accounted for 32 per cent of the sales of women's clothing (Bonacich and Applebaum 2000: 100). By the mid-2000s, according to Gereffi (2005), private label goods encompassed about one-third of all clothing retail sales. There is, however, a very uneven distribution between various types of retailers, with the department store Macy having up to 50 per cent of house brands in some product categories, the speciality store The Limited 70 per cent (Salmon and Cmar 1987) and Wal-Mart and Target between 80 and 90 per cent (Applebaum 2008: 71). Abernathy et al. (1999: 43) point to the pressure exerted on blue jeans producers such as VF (holders of the Wrangler brand) and Levi Strauss by such store brands as Penney's Arizona line and Sears' Canyon River Blue line (ibid). More recently, Levi Strauss felt compelled to provide mass discounters—Target and Wal-Mart—with a low price store brand still carrying their name, Levi Strauss Signature (Singhal et al. 2004: 124)—a high risk strategy.

Direct sourcing is said to have started in the 1970s (Gereffi 1999: 61; Interview Notes 2004). Discounters such as J. C. Penney and K-Mart took the lead, working through their Asian buying offices (ibid), but for most retailers this was initially at a low level. By the mid-90s, however, direct sourcing had affected 50 per cent of all retailers' merchandise (Gereffi and Memedovic 2003: 7). This, however, must be very unevenly distributed among the different categories as department stores still depend to a high degree on offering brands. Most US retailers (the exceptions are the The Gap and The Limited) buy through intermediaries, such as AMC (for Target) and Mast (for The Limited) (Gibbon 2008: 34) and Hong Kong TAL for J. C. Penney (Applebaum 2008: 73–4). (See also Chapter 6 on the intermediaries.) Use of agents who take over most aspects of sourcing denote an arm's length relationship with suppliers, typical of an LME.

Given that all sizeable 'manufacturing' firms supply to the large retailers and, in many segments, do not have a large export volume, the power of US retailers over them has become legendary. According to one interviewee 'power relationships have *totally* shifted, even for the hot lines' (US-C-6). Because big retailers have immense buying power even major vendors have found these demands hard to resist (Salmon and Cmar 1987: 101). They not only exert strong pressure on prices and margins but also impose demanding conditions which smaller firms cannot handle (US-C-3). Concerning prices, Wal-Mart—referred to as the 'evil empire' by one respondent (US-C-5)—has a policy of 'one plus', which obliges suppliers to make an improvement in either price or quality every year (US-C-7). Several respondents made it clear that, in order to operate concessions or 'stores in stores' within department stores, they have to carry all the risks. They have to guarantee retailers high and difficult-to-achieve margins (US-C-3; US-C-6) and fulfil a host of onerous requirements for the presentation of clothes. Federated Department Stores routinely impose a range of requirements relating to ticketing, coding, packing, and shipping of goods and to billing and accounting procedures. Non-fulfilment of the conditions stipulated incurs financial penalties (Abernathy et al. 1999: 79; Bonacich and Applebaum 2000: 94; Doeringer and Crean 2006: 355). Most acrimony surrounds retailers' demands for 'charge-backs', that is, the cost of any unsold garments is demanded back from the supplier, even if the store had ordered what was perceived to be 'unrealistic volume' (US-C-5). This practice, according to another respondent (US-C-6), almost amounts to providing retailers with a 'revenue stream'. A British high-end 'manufacturer' described the situation in very similar terms: 'American retailers are so demanding. They want four seasons, they want the best price, they want charge-backs, they want advertising' (UK-C-11). Another British retailer additionally described the low quality of retailer–supplier relationships: 'The Americans…might order huge quantities, but in terms of the whole collaboration, it's just not there…they are so price-driven that they turn in and out of factories that much quicker…they don't appear to have relationships in the same way we do' (UK-R-2).

4.5.2. In the UK

In the UK, according to Howe (2003: 166–7), the shift in power from the manufacturer to the retailer already occurred in the 1970s and was not merely brought about by the move to direct sourcing. He implicates additionally the abolition of resale price maintenance and of building controls and the closeness to the consumer gained by the use of information technology. The latter, however, was not in common use in the 1970s and, as other authors have emphasized, this occurred only from the 1980s onwards.

The picture concerning the adoption of 'private label' clothing and direct sourcing is very uneven. Although the multiples nearly all sell exclusively own label clothing and Marks & Spencer have done so for many decades, they do not necessarily all complement this strategy with direct sourcing from low-wage countries. Several big retailers still buy a significant proportion of their clothes from British middle-men 'manufacturers'. In the late 1990s, Arcadia sourced one-third of clothing sold in the UK, River Island and New Look both 50 per cent, and Debenhams, a department store, 60 per cent (Bickerton 1999: 84). According to Oxborrow (2005), however, these proportions have decreased in more recent years. For UK-R-2, a department store chain, 'own label' garments represented around 60 per cent of non-concessionaire business.

Many retailers use British 'middleman' firms to gain supply from low-wage countries. Of the two largest High Street clothing multiples, Marks & Spencer and Next, only the latter has long combined own label goods with direct sourcing. Marks & Spencer, in contrast, was well known for maintaining its 'buy British' strategy until the late 1990s. Although by 2004 ninety per cent of clothes were sourced abroad (Marks and Spencer 2004: 2), a large proportion was still sourced via British middle-men firms. In 2003, M&S still had a comparatively low proportion of direct sourcing from low-wage countries—15 per cent (Interview Notes 2003). However, during subsequent years, after the retailer had come under severe market pressure, the proportion of its direct souring has gradually risen (Marks and Spencer 2004: 9). In 2006, it finally opened sourcing offices in Shanghai and Hong Kong, and in 2006–07 directly sourced 28 per cent of clothing and home products (Marks and Spencer 2007: 13). According to Palpacuer et al. (2004: 418), only 4 out of 11 UK retailers they interviewed, as compared with 7 out of 11 Scandinavian ones, had overseas manufacturers as the main sourcing channel. Although major UK retailers had adopted policies to increase direct sourcing, intermediaries still played a major role in their sourcing networks (ibid). However, two large retailers, interviewed in 2003, started direct foreign sourcing much earlier, well before many clothing 'manufacturers' (UK-R-2; UK-R-3). 'So, yes, we certainly as retailers...went global far more quickly than the manufacturers—already in 1979' (UK-R-3), and they established a sourcing office in HK at that early time, too. 'I set up an import operation so we could start to go direct, so we could start to take the cost out of the supply chain, so we could start to establish economies of scale (UK-R-3). But these two respondents seem to represent a minority of British retailers.

According to Palpacuer et al. (2004), UK retailers have adopted the main supply chain management doctrines: they try to reduce the size of network; set highly detailed and demanding standards for core suppliers; engage in intensive monitoring of supplier performance; show high levels of inter-organizational integration with core suppliers; and use formal procedures. Close integration is indicated by the fact that they buy around 60 per cent from their top 20 suppliers (ibid: 419, Table 6). Concerning the quality of relations with suppliers, 9 out of the 11 retailers they interviewed describe the relationship as a partnership. However, subsequent remarks do not bear out the partnership model. Thus, only three cite mutual obligation/volume stability and only one mentions trust and loyalty (Palpacuer et al. 2004: 421, table 9).

Our own interviews show that, on the hand, UK retailers tend to have longer-term relations with suppliers than their US counterparts and do not impose the same high and sometimes punitive demands. Charge-backs, for example, are unknown (UK-C-5). One department store respondent reported long-term relations with most suppliers, of 10 to 15 years (UK-R-2). 'We don't do the closing factories overnight because we have chosen not to deal in that country anymore. So that's our long-standing relationship I think our supply base tends to like' (UK-R-2). On the other hand, relations with suppliers nevertheless fall well short of genuine partnership relations. The same respondent regretfully confided that the lack of open costing was based on lack of mutual trust: 'Historically [this company] have always held back, to their interest, and likewise suppliers know that they need to hold back because we will stitch them up' (ibid). A supply chain manager at a large group of multiples commented in similar terms: 'the intention is for longer-term partnerships, not here today, gone tomorrow sort of thing... and some of the suppliers have been with us a long, long time' (UK-R-3). But the same respondent also commented that 'retailers are much bigger than their... individual suppliers. They are the ones who say "jump"; they are the ones who say we want to do this, that and the next thing'. He also reported on a new strategy of de-risking, that is, shifting all the risk for product on to the supplier, adopted by the Group's chief executive. When we asked about the impact of this on relationships the answer was 'there is that risk [of upsetting a good relationship with a supplier], in which case we would try and establish relationships with other suppliers'. 'You must not be beholden to each other [i.e. the retailer to the supplier]'. Although US Wal-Mart is usually singled out in the literature for demanding yearly discounts from suppliers, it is clear that a demand for discounts has also been adopted by some UK retailers (e.g. UK-R-2; UK-R-3).

In comparison to US retailers, UK retailers appear to have less advanced sourcing practices, as well as a lesser degree of independent capacity in the areas of product development and design. However, in recent years, the use of high-profile, freelance product developers/designers has become prominent, not only by multiples and department stores but also by supermarkets. Thus although British retailers, like their American counterparts, have become the most powerful actor in the supply chain, as a group they do not appear to have gained the same degree of independence from clothing firms and, hence power, as have their US counterparts.

4.5.3. In Germany

The strategy to increase margins through 'private label' sales has progressed significantly (Volksbanken, Raiffeisenbanken 2003; Faust 2005). Thus, among our respondents from department store chains and clothing specialists in 2003, in one case 55 per cent of garments were 'own label', of which 38 per cent were direct imports (GER-R-1); in a second case, the corresponding figures were 70 per cent and 35–40 per cent for import business (GER-R-3); while a third respondent— representing a slightly more up-market and much smaller clothing multiple— cited 40 per cent 'own label' and 40 per cent direct imports (GER-R-2).

Bloecker and Wortmann (2005: 103–5) rightly point out that sourcing behaviour differs according to retail segment. Discounters buy in very large volume from mainly Asian countries and, with the exception of NKD, use German 'middlemen' suppliers with their own bureaus in Asia. Traditional retailers have a more mixed strategy of buying from German middle-men suppliers and from Asian ones. Both the large department store chains have long maintained their own sourcing offices in Hong Kong. These are sizeable and expertly staffed operations which explore the markets, make contact with and check out potential suppliers of both fabric and finished products, undertake quality control, but do not do the buying themselves (Interview Notes 2003).

Concerning relationships of traditional retailers with suppliers in CEE countries, Bloecker and Wortmann (2005: 101) note that they tend to be cooperative. Our interviews, too, established the impression that long, as well as cooperative, relationships were fairly common and that the power difference between retailers and suppliers was not as routinely exploited as in the other two countries. Thus the supply chain manager of one clothing specialist (GER-R-2) commented: 'we are not so quick to change, or change too often because for us the quality is very important, it's a little bit risky to change sometimes' or 'A long-term relationship is a partnership, I think it is the best way to work together. . . . If they have a little problem, we still buy or keep, try to do the best . . . We help each other'. He then amplified: 'But also if the supplier is not so powerful, we still want to have a partnership. We don't want to push them too much, because next season we also want to buy there . . . So I think it is always, you have to see both sides. And so also for these suppliers there should be a partnership' (GER-R-2). Another department store supply chain manager expressed similar sentiments: 'it does not always make sense to jump from one supplier to another supplier because they are 50 per cent cheaper than it was with supplier A. I think you have to be reliable, very reliable, then you have more advantages' (GER-R-1). Another illustration of the lesser power of the retailers vis-à-vis brands is that big branded 'manufacturers' try to tell retailers at which periods of the year discounted brands may be sold (GER-R-2). He was trying, our interviewee amplified, to 'keep the market more silent [calm]'—a very German sort of endeavour. However, the big department store chain Kaufhof, since becoming part of Metro, is seen to have become a little more aggressive on pricing, leading some 'manufacturers' to avoid selling to them (e.g. GER-C-11).

Thus in all three countries the twin strategies of developing 'own label' clothing and engaging in direct sourcing, both connected with improving margins, further increased the autonomy and hence the power of retailers in the value chain. These strategies led as well to an increased blurring of the distinction between clothing producers without in-house manufacturing and retailers who have moved into product development, design, and direct sourcing.

4.6. NEW RETAIL STRATEGIES II: CHANGIN MARKET STRATEGIES

Notwithstanding the distinctions between national product strategies outlined in Section 4.1, more recent changes in marketing and markets have also introduced common challenges. From the 1970s onwards and particularly during the 1980s, a change in market strategy occurred which has had an impact on clothing production and retail in all three societies, albeit to differing degrees. Problems of declining market share, as well as the emergence of a more affluent and leisured population, are said to have prompted a re-orientation in strategy away from mass to segmented markets. Although this strategy originated in the USA (Cohen 2003), where mass markets had been the most pronounced, it was soon also embraced in the UK, with the 'discovery, at first, of a distinctive "youth" market and further age and lifestyle segmentation from the early 1980s onwards' (Gardner and Sheppard 1989: 79). Market segmentation, growing product differentiation, and proliferation has also affected German retailers, even if the embrace of marketing was more hesitant and, due to a lesser emphasis on mass production during the previous decades, brought less dramatic change. This change in strategy was initiated by retailers and the expanding marketing profession, partly in response to increasing social and lifestyle differentiation. Nevertheless mass production, for example of jeans, endured into the 1990s and only gave way to a shift to more diversified mass production with smaller runs per model in the 2000s, particularly in fashion clothing (Rosenberg 2005). This latter model was avidly embraced by consumers and, because of intense sectoral competition, was subsequently driven to greater and greater extremes, as will be explored in Section 4.8 on the turn to fast fashion.

The pressures of product proliferation are particularly severe for retailers trying to serve the whole market and thus dealing with a huge number of stock-keeping units, as is the case for many department stores. For the rest of the sector the pressures were to some degree alleviated, though not eliminated, by greater differentiation into retail formats addressing only particular market segments— in terms of age, socio-economic status, and/or life-style. Thus, to illustrate with examples from the UK market, the recently emerged discounters appeal particularly to the highly price-conscious 16–26 age group, while multiples like Top Shop (Arcadia) try to capture members of the same age group who are willing to spend a little more for higher fashion value. Chains such as Karen Millen promote a fashionable and highly distinctive style aimed at a better-off and slightly older age group. But, as several authors have pointed out (e.g. Textile Outlook International 2005; BTE 2006), in all three societies such clear market segmentation (and with it the profession of marketing) is now being undermined by the increased blurring of lines between target groups and the emergence of hybrid shoppers who practise cross-buying.

The notion of market segmentation according to different social target groups originated in the USA where, to stimulate demand, it had already been articulated by the late 1950s. But it became an undisputed marketing rule only in the 1970s (Cohen 2003: 295–6). Cohen speaks of 're-conceptualising of mass markets as discrete communities of consumers with distinctive needs, wants, and product preferences' (ibid: 298). Segmentation crucially was supported not only by advertising and marketing but also by transformation towards more flexible production, with smaller runs, from the1960s (Cohen 2003: 306). Mass production gave way to batch production (ibid). This not only increased demand but also had a serious downside for retailers, in that it greatly complicated the ordering and selling process. As shown by Abernathy et al. (1999: 45, 46, figure 3.2), between the late 1970s and the 1990s, diversification of products and hence in the number of stock-keeping units, has grown in every apparel category, including such fashion basics as men's shirts. The requirement to match the retailer's product mix to the tastes, sizes, and incomes of its targeted customers became a major undertaking. Mistakes in such matching or simple inability to predict rapidly changing trends would result in very adverse effects on profits. Up to the 1980s the risk entailed was borne by retailers. But as they gained in power vis-à-vis manufacturers, they increasingly sought to shift this risk onto manufacturers and suppliers.

In the UK, as detailed by Gardner and Sheppard (1989), market segmentation was embraced only a little later than in the USA. A 'youth and teenage' market first emerged in the 1960s (Benson 1994). While the development of the new 'retail culture' was partially arrested during the economically difficult 1970s, it greatly accelerated during the more free-spending 1980s, and market segmentation by lifestyle further progressed' (Gardner and Sheppard 1989: 81–2). This is also confirmed by Wrigley and Lowe (2002: 25), who point not only to the de-massification of markets but also to retailers' growing sophistication at orchestrating them. In the UK, too, product proliferation has become a major issue, and the coping strategy of increased discount selling—cut-price sales have multiplied in recent decades—has been eroding margins and image (Textile Outlook International 2005: 174). As in the USA, the clear transfer of power from manufacturers to retailers from the 1970s onwards (Gardner and Sheppard 1989; Howe 2003) was utilized by retailers, albeit somewhat less aggressively, to shift some of the risks entailed by product proliferation and growing market instability onto manufacturers who, in the UK, do not possess any powers of resistance at all.

In the literature on German retail, this process of product segmentation and proliferation is not explicitly addressed, but some of our interviewees on the manufacturing side spoke of the problems of product proliferation. Whether this indicates a less dramatic change in product paradigm—due to a less pronounced pre-existing massification of markets or a less enthusiastic and more hesitant

embrace of marketing—is difficult to determine. It is clear, however, that use
of one mechanism to deal with the overstocking often associated with product
proliferation—frequent sales—is precluded by the strict German legal regulation
of discounted selling (see Section 4.1). The strategy of risk shifting to the 'manufacturers' noted in both the USA and, somewhat less, the UK also appears less
prevalent in Germany.

4.7. NEW RETAIL STRATEGIES III: VERTICAL INTEGRATION

Another new strategy, designed to gain more control over the market and reduce
lead times as well as appropriate a higher share of value generated, is vertical
(backward) integration or verticalization, that is, either executing all or most
of the steps in the value chain in-house or assuming tight control over the
manufacturing process. Full adoption of the model thus necessitates not only
in-house manufacturing of clothes but also own production of textiles. Verticalization started from the 1990s onward and, in the USA, was pioneered by
firms, such as The Limited (Richardson 1996). It reached greater perfection in
Europe, where Swedish Hennes & Mauritz and Spanish Zara/Inditex adopted this
strategy and consequently achieved strong market dominance in many European
countries. They thereby provided the New Vertical model which decisively reshaped the competitive landscape, as well as the discourse on organization and
strategy among firms. Zara was fully vertically integrated from the beginning.
Followers tried to achieve this status by either backward integration of retailers
into manufacturing—a relatively rare occurrence—or direct sourcing of all their
apparel in very close integration with foreign suppliers—a more frequent strategy
exemplified, for example, by American The Gap or European Benetton.

A second variant is that of 'manufacturers' integrating forward into retail—
a growing phenomenon. In the latter case, we are dealing only with semi-
verticalization as these clothing firms no longer execute manufacturing in-house,
nor do they produce their own textiles. As these new retailers are not fully vertically integrated, 'quick response' selling still eludes them, and they mainly gain
greater market control. A detailed consideration of such 'semi-verticalization' by
'manufacturers' is provided in Chapter 3.

Vertical re-integration is, of course, closely related to and, indeed, has been
prompted by the introduction of the 'fast response' strategy by retailers.

4.8. FAST RESPONSE FASHION AND 'JUST-IN-TIME' RETAILING

The introduction from the 1980s onwards of fast fashion and 'just-in-time' (JIT)
retailing is said to have dramatically transformed both retailing and manufacturing (Abernathy et al. 1999 on the USA; Appelbaum, Bonacich, and Quan 2005: 7;

Myers 2006: 7, on Europe). The acceleration of the fashion cycle, driven both by the competitive struggle within the sector and by consumer demand (Corcoran 2004), entails a huge reduction of lead times, more product churning (frequent stock rotation). It results in JIT or lean retailing. Lean retailing, prompted by the losses suffered from overstocking and mark-downs, means ordering by the retailer in smaller batches as and when the goods are required on the sales floor. This practice thus shifts the stock-carrying risk from the retailer to the manufacturer and preserves retailer capital (Ross 2004: 137). Both lean retailing and fast fashion are vitally dependent on the development of new retailing technology, particularly electronic point-of-sale (EPOS) technology. The information technology revolution in the retail sector 'has led to a tremendous shift in bargaining power within the channel—away from manufacturers and suppliers to lean retailers' (Corcoran 2004: 54). Lean retailing, according to Abernathy et al. (1999), has four building blocks: bar codes; a set of enabling computer technologies; the modern distribution centre; and the promulgation of standards across firms. Thus, lead times have been drastically reduced. In some instances, this has resulted in the cutting of the 'total time to market' from 46 weeks to only 9 weeks which, in turn, has entailed a reduction in production times from 12 to 4 weeks and shipping from 6 to 1 week (Singhal et al. 2004: 130, 175). Corcoran (2004) speaks of a reduction of turnaround time by manufacturers from 6 to 3 months. Many retailers have increased stock turns from 4 to 12 times a year (ibid).

Lean retailing, however, is difficult to achieve because it requires huge investment in technology for ordering, logistics, and supply chain management more generally, as well as a high degree of vertical integration or geographical proximity to suppliers. Lean production and very short fashion cycles are best achieved by vertically integrated retailers with complete or strong control over production, such as Zara and Hennes & Mauritz. Alternatively, it needs close cooperation between retailer and manufacturer—the case of The Gap. Globalization of the supply chain and the frequent move between suppliers and countries, mostly in search of lower production costs, are not conducive to the achievement of lean production. Short lead times additionally require close proximity or, ideally, co-location between clothing and fabric producers and a move from the CMT method of sourcing to that of Full Package sourcing. (For details on the latter, see Chapter 7.) Full-package production capability has not yet been achieved by all sourcing countries and suppliers. Many retailers maintain suppliers in a range of locations, of whom only some can satisfy the requirements of lean production. Hence a strong tension exists between JIT sourcing and globalization of production networks. It is evident that lean retailing, in many cases, is more of an ideal or at least a very problematic reality than a widely achieved goal.

JIT sourcing is pursued only by some segments of clothing retail. Thus, at one end of the continuum are the clothing specialist multiples, devoted to fast turn selling and almost continuous sourcing, and at the other end, the discounters who source only a few times per year and then buy in great bulk. In between the two are department stores which stock a very wide range of merchandise and are not at the forefront of fashion. Department stores tend to be more fashion followers, rather than leaders. In the words of one of our British retail interviewees:

'We are not a fashion setter, we are very much a fashion follower; so you'll have a new trend, and you might go into New Look, Zara...and see it is very much of the moment. We develop that into a commercial look, and wait until...it's really commercial for the High Street, rather than just the odd fashion buffs' (UK-R-2)

Many of our interviewees in all three countries referred in a wistful way to Zara's achievements in this respect, but simultaneously expressed a resigned recognition that firms without in-house manufacturing could not achieve the short production cycles of Zara. Thus an American executive of a large clothing firm, US-C-1, commented as follows: 'The king of speed is Zara. Everybody wants the short cycle, speed-to-market Zara model, but unless you control your mills the way Zara does, quick turn is nearly impossible....Zara has it all in one box: from design to fabric to assembly to transportation'. Both Zara and H&M are known for their ability to design, produce, and deliver new styles to stores within 3 weeks (Corcoran 2004). Not surprisingly, Zara has a much higher profit margin than ordinary retailers: its net margin in 2001 was reported as 10.5 per cent (Ascoly 2003).

US retailers have been the pioneers in lean retailing, with Wal-Mart at the forefront. It adopted an efficient, highly centralized EPOS-driven system as early as the late 1970s (Abernathy et al. 1999: 49). Consumer demand 'pulled' in the orders. American suppliers gained access to Wal-Mart's information system and could schedule their production accordingly (ibid: 50). Other technologically advanced retailers were K-Mart and J. C. Penney. The latter, for example, has a dynamic routing system, enabling it to coordinate several suppliers' deliveries to save on trucking costs (Corcoran 2004). Department stores developed this capability later as the high number of stock keeping units made it much harder to achieve such coordination. Federated Department Stores changed policy in the 1990s when it started centralized buying and adopted electronic links with suppliers (Abernathy et al. 1999: 52). Federated Stores and many other retailers have a number of significant money penalties for manufacturers/suppliers who do not adhere to their ticketing/bar-coding standards of goods delivered ready for sales—a fact bitterly complained about in some of the American interviews. Among clothing multiples, The Gap is singled out for its advanced use of electronic systems and innovative software (Corcoran 2004).

But despite this technological superiority of many US retailers, other factors work against their consistent achievement of fast supply for JIT retailing. Close geographical proximity to suppliers has become more elusive, as Mexican and Caribbean Basin countries cannot satisfy US buyers' demand for 'fast fashion' (Birnbaum 2004: 25). Many retailers have abandoned their Mexican suppliers in favour of Chinese ones, attracted by Chinese superiority in terms of price, 'full-package' capability and general efficiency (ibid; US-C-6).

UK retailers, too, have had to cope with the changed pace of fashion, adopting various measures and, in several cases, also developing a system of electronic 'just-in-time ordering' from suppliers.

'The whole technology—we call it digital supply chain, other people call it e-sourcing...—but the technology that's available to us now makes collaboration with our suppliers easier, so that we are working in real time with our suppliers, we're not sending paper work, it all goes through the web' (UK-R-2)

But this particular retailer did not practise open costings, that is, working as if they were in the same company. Both Corcoran (2004) and Oxborrow (2005) single out the low-cost retailer New Look as having a particularly efficient system. This enables the firm to speedily repeat 'best sellers' within 36 hours, cut its lead time and turn over its entire stock within 6 weeks. This technological system, allied to a good management system, allows New Look to gain on stock turn what it loses on gross margin. Its retention of a significant proportion of British suppliers also has facilitated quick turnarounds and replenishment. Marks & Spencer, too, have partly moved in the direction of fast fashion. The 2005 Annual Report speaks of 'more regular buying phases to enable faster product delivery. We now buy less, more frequently'. Per Una, in particular, is a 'short-lead, fashion-led offer, following key trends' (Marks & Spencer 2005: 7), while the Classical range still adheres to a 'slow-response' model (*Guardian Weekend* 12 August 2006). Department stores, due to their greater product range, cannot follow this trend to the same degree. For them, longer lead times but with flexible times for final specification [of colours or style details] has been a satisfactory way to organize orders. Thus, delaying for as long as possible the final decision on important product parameters has been an important tactic used to remain 'fashionable', though rarely fashion leaders (UK-R-2 and UK-R-3).

In Germany, the entry into the market of foreign New Verticals also brought recognition that adoption of the 'fast turn' model was necessary and entailed technological upgrading by 'manufacturers', as well as retailers (Schuessler 2008: 127). Tight, electronically based integration between retail and manufacturing, enabling lean retailing, is said to be well developed in food retail, having started in the 1980s (Wortmann 2003: 9). But, with the above exception, there is little mention of it in the literature on clothing retail, nor was it mentioned by our department store interviewees. However, given the ownership links between the clothing retailers and large food retailers it seems highly likely that elements of this system have been transferred to the clothing retail segment. Also several of our 'manufacturer' interviewees remarked on more modest tactics to produce collections at much increased frequency: 'We have six main seasons...and then, in between, we have monthly "Season Express" programmes' (GER-C-5); another 'manufacturer' spoke of topping up the main seasons with 'flash programmes' (GER-C-9). On the other hand, interviewees from the department store sector did not have 'fast fashion' as a strong concern but were more preoccupied with flexibility of sourcing, similar to the UK department store respondents. Thus the retailer might place a large initial order of fashion basics, but have them delivered only in smaller batches as and when each batch is sold (GER-R-1). German suppliers of branded clothes choose their own assortment of clothes going into the shops and change it if some items do not sell well (ibid).

4.9. INTERNATIONALIZATION OF OWNERSHIP AND MARKETS

Internationalization of retailers may refer to either their sourcing arrangements or their ownership structures and sales operations. It is the latter which is the topic of this section, whereas Section 4.5 has dealt with the internationalization of sourcing. Sales may be internationalized as a mode of expansion or as an attempt to compensate for fierce domestic competition and erosion of margins (Barth and Hartmann 2003: 67). In retail, it mainly takes the form of foreign direct investment (FDI). Both outward and inward FDI of retailers will be covered. A consideration of inward FDI examines the fortunes of inward investors in different economic and cultural contexts and underlines their contribution to an ever fiercer domestic competition.

Internationalization of retailers through FDI, according to some authors, is said to have become a prominent development. Bloecker and Wortmann (2005) note a high degree of internationalization by German retailers, and Wrigley and Lowe (2002), with reference to the UK and the USA, even speak of the 'emergence of global empires'. In our view such a view is too indiscriminate and only very partially tenable. First, if either outward or inward FDI in retail is compared with that in manufacturing, it is relatively insignificant. Second, a view of 'global retailing empires' does not sufficiently distinguish between clothing and food retail and fails to note that the degree of internationalization has been much lower in the former than the latter. Third, these and other authors, for example, Myers (2006), also over-generalize from a small proportion of international retailers to the whole sector and do not make the distinction between inward and outward investment. While outward investment has been relatively insignificant for German, UK, and US retailers, inward investment by foreign retailers into all three countries has been growing in recent years. Bloecker and Wortmann (2005) and Wrigley and Lowe (2002) further fail to note that most internationalization for European firms means Europeanization, with German and British retailers failing to penetrate US and Japanese markets to a significant degree. Furthermore, north-west European companies do not enter southern Europe, although the reverse trend does not hold. US retailers have also achieved only limited success with entry into Europe, although retailers of high-margin branded designer clothes form the exception to this rule. Indeed, with a few notable exceptions internationalization in clothing, as opposed to food retail, has been greatly retarded by differing national consumption styles and regulatory environments. The lack of entry into the American market, we were told by several German interviewees, is additionally due to high US import tariffs on clothing, which make entry infeasible for all but the luxury brands. (For further detail on tariffs, see Chapter 5.)

4.9.1. Germany

International expansion by German retailers has been driven by fierce competition and the resulting very low profit margins. Internationalization thus has been necessary for survival. 'As far as the markets are concerned, we are aware of the fact that major growth cannot be achieved any more in Germany' (GER-C-5). While German food retailers have managed to expand abroad in a significant way, clothing retailers have made only modest advances. When internationalization is measured in terms of the number of countries in which firms are present, German firms do not figure significantly among international European clothing retailers (Myers 2006: 9). Hence, the number of foreign companies operating successfully in the German market has been larger than the number of German companies operating abroad (Barth and Hartmann 2003: 67). However, German clothing retailers (e.g. Karstadt, Peek & Cloppenburg; Tom Taylor and S. Oliver) have had some limited success in their internationalization strategies (*Der Spiegel* 2008: 92), with Peek & Cloppenburg, for example, having 12 foreign branches (BTE 2006: 167). Esprit, which is only partly German owned, has been the most successful in gaining footholds abroad. Retail FDI has been mostly into neighbouring northern European countries and, more recently, into CEE and Russia (*Der Spiegel* 2008: 92), showing the importance of cultural affinity. Southern Europe, in contrast, and to a large extent US and UK markets, have been less targeted. Internationalization has been higher, however, among luxury brands such as Boss and Escada. Thus although German women's clothing has enjoyed significant success in terms of exports by branded 'manufacturers', the degree of outward FDI by retailers has not been striking and reflects the weakness of the fragmented German clothing retail sector.

When we turn to inward investment by foreign retailers, internationalization is more pronounced. Although we have not found comparative statistics, our impression is that it is more developed than either in the UK or in the USA. As the largest and richest market for clothing in Europe, inward retailer investors from both Europe and the USA have been trying to gain a foothold in Germany. But, as will be shown, success has been very mixed. This has been due to the fact that, on the one hand, it is an intensely competitive and difficult market with high (wage) costs, low profits, and big regulatory hurdles, and, on the other, cultural differences, particularly for Anglo-American investors. Among successful foreign retailers are Benetton, Mango, Zara, French Mulliez, and above all Swedish Hennes & Mauritz. This last now outclasses German clothing specialist retailers both in terms of the number of shops and turnover. Thus, H&M in 2004 recorded a turnover of €1,965 million and had 288 branches (BTE 2006: 164). By comparison, P&C (both branches), the best-performing German clothing specialist, achieved a turnover of €1,700 million in 104 branches (BTE 2006: 66). Zara, present in Germany since 1999, has not been a run-away success in comparative terms, with a turnover of only €161 million and 33 outlets (BTE 2006: 80). It is notable that nearly all the successful inward investors serve the lower to mid-market, whereas P&C and the two big German department stores serve the middle to upper market (SIPPO 2006). Thus, in the burgeoning fashionable youth market where German-owned retailers have not kept up, they have been replaced by foreign ones.

When we turn to Anglo-American retailer investors into Germany the story is somewhat different. Germany, according to Bickerton (1999: 110) and Retail Intelligence (2000*b*: 5), is Europe's toughest retail market. Planning and property laws are very complex and vary between localities. The cost of retail staff is almost double that elsewhere in Europe (Bickerton 1999: 110), resulting in comparatively low margins (Retail Intelligence 2000*b*: 5). The hurdles presented by these circumstances to UK and US investors will be explored in the following sub-sections.

4.9.2. The UK

When internationalization (outward FDI) is measured by the number of countries in which firms are present, British clothing retailers, like their German counterparts, do not figure significantly among international European retailers (Howe 2003: 166; Myers 2006: 9). Two of the biggest retailers, Marks & Spencer and Arcadia, come well towards the bottom of the ranking order in outward investment (Myers 2006: 9). Arcadia has preferred to take the less risky road of opening concessions, many of which are in the Middle and Far East (Interview Notes 2003). Attempts to internationalize by British clothing retailers have been beset with problems and the eventual necessity to withdraw investment (Bickerton 1999: 21). Most of the UK lower- to mid-market players, such as Next, River Island, Monsoon, Oasis, French Connection, and New Look have had poor success in exporting their retail format into continental Europe because they failed to do their homework on cultural differences in terms of style, sizing, and colour (Bickerton 1999: 21). Marks & Spencer, too, experienced only very limited success before its withdrawal in 2000 from all overseas markets, except Hong Kong. Its attempt to establish itself in Germany is portrayed as a high profile failure, as they made no concession to the local market (Bickerton 1999: 22). Internationalization has been higher, however, among luxury and upper middle brands such as Burberry, whereas Paul Smith has internationalized through reliance on concessions and mainly to Japan (Interview Notes 2003).

Historically, inward investment into the UK retail sector has been low (Howe 2003: 165). Retail Intelligence (2000*a*: 243) explains this by reference to the fact that the UK industry is very competitive, setting high barriers to entry. Moreover, rents for prime city positions are comparatively high. But in recent decades this picture has begun to change, with both low- to mid-players and high-end retailers having established themselves during the 1990s and 2000s. Among mid-market players, Zara and Hennes & Mauritz have been highly successful and The Gap and Japanese Uniqlo moderately so, whereas at the top end both American and Italian designer firms have crowded out British retailers in prime sites such as Bond Street (Wrigley and Lowe 2002). Yet, overall, the level of inward investment remains modest compared with the relatively high proportion in industry (Howe 2003).

4.9.3. The USA

Among American retailers, who do not face the handicap of high tariffs for their exports to Europe, a few of the luxury brands and some jeans specialists have had notable success. Among luxury brands, Calvin Klein, Tommy Hilfiger, and Donna Karan are well known in Europe. Among middle-level brands, a number selling jeans and casual wear more generally have established themselves in European markets. But their sales volume remains relatively small. Thus, The Gap—the speciality chain with the biggest market share in the USA—manages only 5.4 per cent of total sales in Europe and a further 3.6 per cent in Asia (Datamonitor 2005). While The Gap enjoys limited success in the UK, it did not flourish in the German market. At the lowest end Wal-Mart has done badly in Germany, with only 8 outlets in 2004–05 (SIPPO 2006: 80) and a low popularity rating among German consumers (BTE 2006). As many authors have observed, attempts to internationalize by both British and US clothing retailers have been beset with problems and have eventually necessitated withdrawal of investment (Bickerton 1999: 21). Divergent consumption styles, particularly in Germany, no doubt have also contributed.

Concerning inward investment, high US tariff walls largely keep out foreign retailers, except at the luxury end. Among the 13 retailers with the highest market share in the 2000s, only one mid-market foreign chain was included—Swedish Hennes & Mauritz. Although its market share was relatively low, it beat the two big department store chains, Federated and May (Euromonitor International 2007*a*).

To sum up, internationalization in the clothing retail sector is underdeveloped compared with that in the clothing industry, in terms of both inward and outward FDI. The volume of outward FDI by German, UK, and US retailers has been modest, and no 'global empires' are discernible. Both cultural and real economic barriers are still formidable. It is slightly more justifiable to speak of internationalization if inward investment into the three countries is considered, but even here only a few foreign retailers have overcome the barriers and have become European, rather than international players. Although US retailers have made inroads at the luxury end of casual wear, it is premature to claim that they have conquered European markets. An evaluation, particularly of the level of outward FDI of retailers in all three countries, leads to the conclusion that a paradox exists of enduringly national selling, but highly globalized sourcing.

4.10. CONCLUSIONS

Our comparison of the clothing retail industries of Germany, the USA, and the UK has viewed the sector as part of the clothing value chain or, in the terms of Fine and Leopold (1993) as part of a distinctive system of provision, stressing the interconnection with both production and consumption. We have placed particular emphasis on the connection with production and have explored when and why the retail sector assumed the position of dominance in the value chain it now holds. We dated this shift in power to the 1970s (in the UK) and 1980s (in the USA) and pointed to the various factors which had contributed to it. In addition to the much higher turnover of retailers, their use of information and communication technology had secured them a much closer connection to the end user, helping them to trade more efficiently and cheaper. Last, and by no means least, they had made themselves increasingly independent from domestic producers, by developing store brands and engaging in direct sourcing.

In contrast to much earlier writing on this sector, our comparative study demonstrates that power relations in the value chain vary between Germany on the one hand, and the USA and the UK on the other. Power differences are much less pronounced in the German industry and contracting relations less adversarial. We elaborate the contrasts between the three industries by applying the Varieties of Capitalism approach, but supplement it with an emphasis on both the size and nature of home market, as well as on varying culturally and historically shaped consumption patterns. Societal institutions with strong shaping influence have been state policies on competition and the divergent stances towards SME owners they embody; the financial system which either stimulates or retards concentration trends; and the interaction between dominant production paradigm and consumption style. This last feature, shaped by and reinforcing both the material aspects of the structures of production and retail, has also been moulded by divergent social and political traditions. These have led to different social interpretations and political uses of consumption. The latter run to a large extent along CME and LME lines.

It is particularly notable that in the UK an extremely weak manufacturing sector is counter-posed to a thriving retail sector, while in Germany the reverse pattern holds—a finding which lends some support to the VoC approach. However, the success of German food retailing and of the clothing discount and mail order sectors makes arguments about differing degrees of managerial competence suspect. The lagging of the German retail sector may be largely explained as a consequence of protectionism and the resulting lack of consolidation. But it is also connected with much higher wage and social payments, generally held to be much less sustainable in the service than in the manufacturing sector. In the USA, large and giant firms in retail and 'manufacturing' seem, at first sight, more evenly balanced. But the much larger turnover volumes of retailers, together with their greater closeness to the consumer through the use of sophisticated information and coordination systems, have in fact created a very strong imbalance of power. This imbalance also appears to be more fully exploited in the USA.

This general conclusion must, however, be complemented by findings which stress both differences within the LME category and some divergences within each society. First, the British retail sector, often derided as a copy of the American one, has some distinctive historically evolved features connected with different consumption styles and markets. Although both retail sectors thrive on the consolidation and concentration that liberal markets, a relatively high degree of standardization of goods and the strength of the stock market have afforded them, there nevertheless remain subtle differences between them. First, as already mentioned above, relationships with suppliers seem more constant and somewhat less adversarial in the UK than those in the USA. Whereas in the US complexity of sourcing arises mainly from regional and ethnic differences in a large market, in the UK complexity results from a markedly stronger focus on fashion and constant changes therein. However, being weak at the luxury/designer end of the market, British clothing retail has been less internationalized than its US counterpart.

Additionally, there are important differences within national retail sectors between traditional retailers and the discount sector. This is particularly critical in Germany and is leading to the erosion of the more traditional segment, particularly of independents. It is this internal gulf and the competitive pressures it exerts which have brought about some pressures/tendencies towards convergence in German retail towards the LME type. The discount sector, which is both large and well accepted by consumers, is organized on very similar patterns to those in the USA and the UK, including the use of low-wage labour. Moreover, its manner of sourcing—largely full-package sourcing from Asian suppliers—does not bode well for the German 'manufacturing' industry. Also the regulatory environment has changed considerably in recent decades, with little spatial and temporal restriction on the expansion of new retail formats. A further impetus towards convergence has come from consumers. German consumers fully embraced the discount principle. Also among young people in particular, transnational preferences for casual fashion basics and more frequent fashion changes—not the traditional strength of German 'manufacturers'—have gained a lot of ground. Although The Gap, Wal-Mart, and Marks & Spencer have not yet achieved wide acceptance among German consumers, many barriers to their acceptance now have been lowered.

NOTE

1. It is difficult to establish whether C&A is a German company. While its private owners are German and one of the two head offices is in Germany, it has long been registered in the Netherlands. Given that sector insiders and most scholars regard it as German, we will work on this assumption too.

5

Global and Regional Institutions and the Regulation of Trade

Trade regulations and the global and regional institutions within which they are framed have distinctively shaped the textile and clothing industry for almost 50 years. In addition to multiple tariff regimes and preferential trading arrangements (PTAs) addressing various groups of countries, onerous rules of origin (RoO), and a global web of quantitative restrictions have distorted the free movement of textile articles from developing countries to industrialized countries. While the aim of such regulation was to shelter the textile and clothing industries of the developed world from unrestricted competition in order to protect the jobs of un-skilled or semi-skilled workers in those countries, employment has nevertheless declined dramatically. The unintended result of protectionist trade regulation has been the dispersion of clothing production around the world, as the hierarchy of low-wage supplier countries in the developing world has shifted in response to the various mechanisms regulating trade.[1] Important new economic actors have emerged to coordinate increasingly complex cross-border supply chains.

In this chapter we review, first, the quantitative restrictions imposed by the Multi-Fibre Arrangements (MFA) and the Agreement on Textiles and Clothing (ATC), its successor under the Generalized Agreement on Tariffs and Trade (GATT) and the World Trade Organization (WTO), until their expiry on 31 December 2004; second, the principal agreements on preferential access that govern tariff rates between the USA or the EU on the one hand and their T/C trading partners on the other; and, third, the highly complex pattern of rules of origin that shape the flow of component parts along the various stages of the clothing value chain.

5.1. THE MULTI-FIBRE ARRANGEMENTS (1974–94) AND THE AGREEMENT ON TEXTILES AND CLOTHING (1995–2004)

Trade distortion in the textile and clothing industry occurs via quantitative restrictions on imports (quotas) and/or via import duties (tariffs). In view of the bilateral nature of quotas and the differing extent of their restrictiveness across producing countries, trade in the textile and clothing industry has for nearly half a century satisfied neither core tenet of the international trading system: transparency and non-discrimination (Mayer 2004). Yet protectionism by developed countries has inadvertently had the effect of encouraging trade partners to upgrade their own industries (Rivoli 2005), allowing them to compete ever better against manufacturers in the USA and Europe.

The use of quantitative restrictions on textiles and clothing imports dates back to the late 1950s when developed countries first became exercised by the pressure put on their domestic industries by developing countries, which were then beginning to acquire comparative advantages in this area. Japan, at that time still a developing country, introduced 'voluntary' restraints on exports of cotton goods to the USA in 1955, but the unintended consequence was a sharp increase in US cotton imports from other countries newly entering the industry, such as Hong Kong, Portugal, Egypt, and India (Krishna and Tan 1997; Rivoli 2005). The UK imposed similar 'voluntary' restrictions in 1959 on producers based in Hong Kong, India, and Pakistan (Hoekman and Kostecki 1995). The Short Term Arrangement on Cotton Textiles signed in 1961 by North American and European countries became the Long Term Arrangement on Cotton Textiles (LTA) in 1962, but its consequence was a sharp increase in imports to these industrialized nations, this time of man-made fibre products, as developing country exporters switched from cotton garments to items made of the new fabrics. As quickly as one protective barrier went up, ways around it were found. Lasting initially for five years, the LTA was extended twice while powerful lobbies within the major importing countries sought to formalize quantitative restrictions on textile and clothing trade, by negotiating multilateral exemptions from GATT non-discrimination rules. In 1974 the LTA was revised as the MFA, a four-year agreement covering woollen and man-made fabrics and clothing products in addition to the cotton goods already restricted. Signatories to the MFA were the USA, Canada, Japan, the EU, Norway, Finland, Sweden, Austria, and Switzerland[2] (François, McDonald, and Nordström 1997). In this way the T/C industry became the only major manufacturing sector not to operate under GATT rules (Hoekman and Kostecki 1995; Nordås 2004; ILO 2005; Dicken 2007).

Although originally intended as a 'temporary' protective measure the MFA was extended five times, each round becoming more restrictive as a wider range of products and countries were encompassed (Krishna and Tan 1997; Appelbaum et al. 2005; Dicken 2007). Country coverage extended to include newly emerging suppliers such as Bangladesh and the Maldives (Krishna and Tan 1997); meanwhile some developing countries (such as Nepal) emerged as clothing producers almost entirely due to efforts to circumvent the MFA's restrictions (Dicken 2007). The MFA provided for the imposition of quotas by each importing country on individual lines of clothing at a high level of detail, either by bilateral agreement or unilaterally if a surge of imports caused or threatened market disruption. It also restricted the annual rates of export expansion allowed on a country-by-country basis to on average just 6 per cent. It was pressure from developing countries to improve market access for their manufactured goods that ultimately played the key role in linking textile and clothing trade back into the GATT (achieved by establishing an implicit link with EU and US demands to liberalize international trade in services). Curiously, the protests of consumer organizations over the higher prices for clothing caused by the quota system were barely heard (Hoekman and Kostecki 1995).

Years of complex negotiations finally led at the end of the Uruguay Round of multilateral trade talks to the replacement of the MFA by the Agreement on Textiles and Clothing (ATC), a 10-year plan commencing in 1995 to phase out the quota system in four stages and to bring textiles and clothing trade into line with regular World Trade Organization rules. The four phases of the ATC eliminated quotas on 16 per cent of total import volumes in 1995 (based on import volumes in 1990), a further 17 per cent in 1998, 18 per cent in 2002, and the remaining 49 per cent in 2005. Progressively more rapid growth rates on residual quotas were also introduced in each of the first three phases (by 16%, 25%, and 27%, respectively), in an attempt to ensure that the clothing industries of importing countries were subject to increasing competition (Hoekman and Kostecki 1995). Each importing country was able to choose which products to integrate under WTO rules at each phase, as long as items in each of the four categories (yarn, fabrics, made-up textile products, and clothing) were encompassed (François et al. 1997).

The ATC also provided a special 'transitional safeguard' mechanism to protect member countries from import surges of products not under quota, if an importing country could show that there was a substantial increase in imports from a specific exporting country and that the importing country's domestic industry was suffering, or risked suffering, serious damage. The USA invoked the special safeguard on 24 occasions in 1996 alone, although only twice in 1997 and once in 1998 (WTO undated).

From 1 January 2005, all textile and clothing trade was scheduled to take place under normal WTO rules. Anxiety over the effect of unrestricted exports from China, however, had led the USA to negotiate a special provision—the so-called China safeguard—to China's Protocol of Accession to the WTO in 2001. This allowed the imposition of new quotas on Chinese textiles and clothing products that caused or threatened to cause market disruption for three years beyond the end of the ATC. Other WTO members, including the EU, Mexico, and Turkey, also put in place mechanisms to introduce short-term restrictions on specific imports from China, in the case of market disruption. Concerned at the potential risk of externally imposed sanctions, the Chinese government voluntarily announced the imposition of export duties on certain textile and clothing products as a means of restraining production and export (Appelbaum et al. 2005).

In 2003 the USA had already implemented controls on five categories of exports from China, of which three had been liberalized under the ATC agreement only the year before (Mayer 2004). Both the USA and the EU had re-imposed controls on various categories of Chinese textiles and clothing by mid-2005, following significant surges in quota-free imports in the early months of that year. For the USA this involved safeguard quotas on 22 categories of Chinese textiles and clothing lasting until the end of 2008. The EU chose to come to a political settlement[3] with the Chinese authorities, rather than use WTO safeguard rules, to re-introduce quantitative restrictions on the 10 categories deemed to be the most sensitive for the EU market, with the intention of achieving fully liberalized trade by the end of 2007. However, concerns over new perceived threats from the start of 2008 this time led the EU and Chinese authorities to institute monitoring arrangements for the year, via export licences and permits on eight categories of product. Meanwhile the Chinese authorities on their side had in July 2007 reduced to 11 per cent the tax rebates available to clothing exporters, as part of a package of measures to restrain its escalating trade surplus with the USA (Just-Style 2007). It should be noted that, despite the intentions of the EU measures, in practice the China restrictions for mid-2005 until end 2007 were able to provide only marginal relief to EU producers since the permitted annual uplift in quotas (up to a maximum of 12.5%, depending on the product line) was faster than the 4 per cent annual growth seen in EU consumption (Brocklehurst and Anson 2007).

An increase in the use of anti-dumping measures against China and other low-cost producers such as Vietnam is seen as a distinct possibility for the future, thus replacing quotas with a different form of non-tariff barrier.[4] UNCTAD (2005) notes that the EU had already been active in initiating anti-dumping investigations in the 1990s, bringing 64 actions (57 against developing countries) in the textile sector alone during the period 1994–2001. Egypt, India, Indonesia, and Pakistan, for example, which were all targets of investigation, saw the volume of their imports of cotton fabrics into the EU reduced significantly in the mid-1990s.

5.1.1. Clothing Quotas in Practice

Since not all the lines covered by the MFA were actually restricted by importing countries (ILO 1996), it is perhaps unsurprising that the EU, Canada, and USA each left those with the most impact until late in the liberalization process. After the third phase elimination of restrictions in 2002, the EU continued to maintain 167 quotas and Canada retained 239 quotas. But the USA back-loaded a far greater proportion of the liberalization effort than either the EU or Canada, keeping 701 quotas in force until the bitter end (Mayer 2004; SOMO 2004). China benefited from the third stage of ATC liberalization once it had joined the WTO in 2001; although Vietnam joined only in 2007, it had benefited from quota-free access to the EU—though not the USA—since 2004. As of 2001, the EU maintained import quotas against 14 countries under the ATC and, under bilateral agreements, against a further 9 countries that were not members of the WTO (including, at that stage, both China and Vietnam). However, these quota-limited countries accounted for only 30 per cent by value of total EU textiles and clothing imports; the remaining 70 per cent was imported from countries not subject to any quota restriction, including the

USA, Canada, CEE, Mediterranean rim countries, ACP (Africa, Caribbean, and Pacific) countries, and all of the least developed countries (such as Bangladesh) (Stengg 2001).

The MFA quota system was highly complex, requiring both importing and exporting firms to maintain close watch over quota utilization rates. Once the quota limit was reached, for example, on the number of pairs of cotton trousers imported into the USA from Bangladesh in any given year, importers had to seek additional sources of supply from other countries. 'Quota-hopping' could thus become a significant issue for supplier countries, although in practice relatively few (mainly Asian) countries and products were 'constrained' by quotas[5]—and the products involved were naturally the quota eliminations deferred until the later stages of ATC liberalization. Complicating the matter further for exporting countries was the fact that MFA categories were not standardized across all importing signatories to the MFA, nor were the same product lines necessarily subject to quota by all importers. Bilateral negotiations, which could take place annually, also resulted in significant variation in the quota growth rates for different countries and products (Appelbaum et al. 2005). The administrative burden for both importers and exporters of keeping up to date on utilization rates and on changing rules was thus significant.

The mechanism for agreeing levels at which new quotas were imposed was usually based on average trade levels for the previous three years (Interview Notes 2003). This meant that those countries first subject to quotas in the early 1970s— such as India and Hong Kong—had relatively small quota limits compared with countries subsequently brought under the MFA regime, which quickly inhibited their ability to expand. The solution of East Asian suppliers, such as Hong Kong, was to invest in other countries especially in, but not limited to, the Asian region that were (initially) either not subject to quota at all or had low quota utilization rates. Esquel Corp. of Hong Kong, for example, shifted production to mainland China in the late 1970s when it could no longer obtain quota for cotton shirt exports to the USA; when US quotas on China tightened, it moved production to Malaysia, then again to Sri Lanka, Mauritius, and the Maldives (Rivoli 2005). We examine in greater detail such shifts in manufacturing investment and capacity as a response to trade distortion in the following chapter.

As Krishna and Tan (1997) illustrate, using World Bank data on exports to the USA for 1981–89, the number of product categories subject to quota varied not only by exporting country but also over time. Hence, both Hong Kong and Korea exhibited high quota utilization rates of 94–99 per cent throughout the period, and at the same time saw the number of product lines subject to quota increase from around 20 to around 30. Meanwhile the USA imposed no MFA quotas on apparel from Indonesia until it reached a threshold presence in 1982, but the number of categories subject to restraint then increased rapidly from 2 to 18 in 1985 and to 20 by 1989 as export levels rose. A similar picture emerges for Bangladesh, which first experienced quota restrictions to the USA in 1986. On the other hand when quotas on particular categories were under-utilized they could be dropped, as was the case for India: although 31 product lines were subject to restraint in 1981 the quota utilization rate was below 70 per cent; quotas on the under-utilized categories were eventually replaced with less restrictive consultative arrangements, and the overall utilization rate on the remaining six lines shot up to 98 per cent in 1983; thereafter the number of categories subject to restraint gradually increased once more as Indian manufacturers diversified production into new lines of clothing.

Since quotas were export-administered, their distribution within any given supplier country was left to the authorities (e.g. the trade ministry) of that country. Each evolved its own way of allocating quotas among exporters, usually based on past trade volumes and with some quota held back ('free' quota) for allocation to new companies or to those wanting more on a first-come-first-served basis (Krishna and Tan 1997; Interview Notes 2003). Quota trading took place in such countries as China, Hong Kong, and Macao, as well as in South Korea, India, and Pakistan, although the degree of transferability permitted varied by country. 'Free' quota was not normally transferable (Krishna and Tan 1997) although some governments appeared to do little to prevent trading happening (Interview Notes 2003).

Because quota was effectively a 'right to export', it developed a value of its own and in some countries was traded almost like a commodity. Hong Kong allowed relatively unrestricted trading on either a temporary or permanent basis (Krishna and Tan 1997). Hence established firms that had been allocated quota on their historical trading record could sell their unused 'rights' on an annual basis (Interview Notes 2003), thereby earning a comfortable rent. Other countries either regulated the transfer (e.g. South Korea) or required permanent transfer (e.g. India, Pakistan, and Bangladesh) (Krishna and Tan 1997). In practice, most countries operated some kind of quota trading system, the main exception being China, which ran annual auctions.[6] There was nothing to prevent traders who bought quota at auction from selling it on, although firms that purchased in this way could end up paying a higher price (Interview Notes 2003). Firms that lacked sufficient quota to utilize their full production capacity saw their costs increase since they had to purchase additional rights if they were selling into the EU or North American markets.

An exporter in possession of quota was obliged to obtain an export licence for each shipment of goods, which would be then be swapped for an import licence in the EU or USA. Without this document, the importer could not bring the product into the country. This could mean that there were times towards the end of a year when a valid export licence had been issued but the import licence was not available because the quota category was exhausted, the exporting country having failed to manage the quota supply properly (Interview Notes 2003). Nor was it necessarily predictable that quota would be available when western importers needed it. In 2003 certain quotas for China and India were fully utilized, yet importers would certainly have brought in more goods if shipments had been allowed. Similarly in 1999–2000, when beaded embroidered dresses were particularly fashionable, India's quota on this product line was exhausted by August, even though importers had already placed orders for the Christmas season for shipment in October (ibid).

For many intermediaries operating within the system—local agents, traders, and buying offices, as well as principals—quotas offered plenty of lucrative possibilities (IFM and partners 2004). Mayer's (2004) analysis of US imports of newly liberalized clothing categories from Greater China (mainland China, Hong Kong, Macao, and Taiwan) in 2002, after the third stage of ATC quota eliminations, reveals a far sharper decline in the unit value of items imported into the USA directly from the mainland than was seen for garments from the rest of the area. In all probability at least part of the drop in unit price can be explained by the removal of middlemen in Hong Kong, Macao, and Taiwan from the supply chain. This underlines the extent to which international trade regulations provided opportunities for intermediaries who understood the complexities and functioning of the quota system. Unit prices dropped again when quotas were fully removed since the *raison d'être* of many small agents disappeared.

The price of quota in any exporting country depended on such variables as the time of year, fashions, and the utilization rate of a particular quota line, hence would change daily and could add considerably to the cost of goods. In China, for example, quota on Category 5 (knitwear) garments for the EU at one stage reached US$8–10 per garment, but in late 2003 was trading at US$5–6 per garment (Interview Notes 2003). In 2001 the most expensive US quota premiums were for men's/boys trousers, which at times approached US$3 per piece (Gibbon 2002). However, since many exporting countries also imposed penalties on firms for non-use of an export licence by reducing future allocations (Krishna and Tan 1997), towards the end of the year it was sometimes possible for importers to induce their suppliers to reduce the price of their offering.

The bigger importing firms wielded greater clout over suppliers in terms of ensuring quota availability. Any contract would be subject to the provision of an export licence and would also detail how much the quota cost. Since the quota premium was agreed at the time of contract rather than at the time of shipment, this required the exporter to take a forward position on the price it would pay for quota. It was common practice for importers to ask during negotiations whether the supplier firm had had to pay for its quota; in theory, if the answer was no (because it was obtained under a 'free' allocation) the current cost of quota would not be included (Krishna and Tan 1997). In practice, supplier firms would usually charge the importers some kind of market rate for the right to use their quota, even if those firms had been given it as a free allocation or had paid only a small administrative charge for it. In this respect, exporters with a strong reputation had the upper hand over importers keen to source from specific suppliers (Interview Notes 2003). Although the bulk of the quota rents accrued was captured by the exporting countries (the government and/or individual firms and agencies), there was scope for powerful importing firms to extract some of that rent through price negotiation.

Paradoxically, the highly restrictive MFA/ATC system did not prevent developing countries from gaining significant market share. However, the quantitative restrictions imposed did inhibit export expansion by the most efficient developing country producers and encouraged the dispersion of textile and clothing production to countries that were not constrained in the same way (as indicated in the Esquel example given above). When export capacity in the latter countries built up to the point that their exports, too, faced constraints, production activity moved again to other places hitherto unaffected by quotas. A clothing industry was thus enabled to develop in relatively uncompetitive countries which enjoyed free(r) market access to MFA importer countries. In addition to relocation of some production to non-MFA affected countries, manufacturers might seek to evade the MFA by resorting to illegal acts (such as sewing in false labels of origin) or by switching to the production of other garments when quota ceilings in their main area of expertise were reached (Dicken 2007). The example of Hong Kong is notable for the way in which its firms changed the sorts of garments they produced: to obtain full economic advantage from the territory's limited quota, they ceased low value-added production (which shifted to southern China) and instead attempted to fill all quota with higher value clothing such as technical garments (e.g. sportswear) that required higher value fabric (Interview Notes 2003). Producer countries not subject to MFA quotas were also likely to specialize in the clothing lines that commanded the highest quota premiums (Gibbon 2002), although these could vary from year to year. In this way, western countries helped to foster future competitors.

Much has been written about the welfare consequences of the MFA, in terms of the added costs to importing and exporting countries and consideration of the allocation of quota rents generated (see, for example, Krishna and Tan 1997). The broad assumption was that removal of the quota regime would result in more efficient resource allocation and lower consumer prices, but that individual supplier countries would experience the benefits of free(r) trade unevenly (Mayer 2004). To some extent this has been the case, as discussed in the next chapter, although the re-imposition by the USA and the EU of restrictions on some Chinese clothing categories has delayed the complete reconfiguration of supplier nations. But, because developing countries with a less efficient clothing industry (than China, especially) knew that they would be unable to compete on price, and would therefore see the transfer of production to more competitive locations and a consequent deterioration in their clothing exports, they felt threatened by the phasing out of the ATC (Appelbaum et al. 2005). Their rearguard—ultimately unsuccessful—action in favour of renewal of the quota system stood in contrast to the more general view that the lifting of quota restrictions should be regarded as favourable for world trade. Of particular concern to labour movement advocates was the possibility that the elimination of quota restraints would threaten gains made against sweatshop labour (see Chapter 10 for a discussion of this topic), by allowing predatory importers to source unlimited products from countries with little worker protection.

5.2. TARIFFS AND PREFERENTIAL ACCESS

Operating alongside—and continuing beyond the elimination of—the MFA/ATC quotas is a highly complex network of tariffs which also affect the allocation of production by importers: WTO rules governing clothing and textile trade place no obligation on importing countries to reduce tariffs, hence it cannot be said that the removal of the MFA/ATC's quantitative restrictions opens the way for completely free trade. Developed nations will continue to extract partial protection for their textile and clothing industries via tariffs, offsetting some of the pressures of quota elimination, but this time within the framework of international trade regulations.

Tariff regimes have gained in importance and visibility since the ending of quotas, although tariff levels applied to clothing products are regarded as less onerous than quotas.[7] Applied tariffs on textiles and clothing nevertheless remain relatively high compared with the manufacturing sector as a whole (Table 5.1), although orders of magnitude vary between developed and developing countries on the one hand and between the USA and the European Union on the other. Hence in 2004 the USA was applying so-called peak tariffs (of more than 15%) on one-fifth of all clothing lines compared with 4.2 per cent for manufactures as a whole, whereas the European Union imposed no such peak tariffs on either textiles or clothing (Mayer 2004). Although EU average applied tariffs on textiles

Table 5.1. Applied tariffs on manufactures, textiles, and clothing

	Manufactures		Textiles		Clothing	
	Simple averages	Share of tariff lines over 15%	Simple averages	Share of tariff lines over 15%	Simple averages	Share of tariff lines over 15%
Developed countries						
European union (2002)	1.3	0.6	2.8	0.0	3.8	0.0
USA (2004)	3.3	4.2	6.9	4.4	10.3	20.6
Developing countries						
China (2004)	9.7	15.1	11.4	11.4	17.0	86.7
Mexico (2003)	18.5	51.3	21.5	87.4	34.3	98.2
Romania (2001)[a]	10.7	22.1	14.9	41.6	21.9	63.6
Korea (2003)	7.8	0.4	9.5	0.0	12.5	0.0
Taiwan (2003)	5.7	3.4	8.8	3.4	11.9	14.3
Turkey (2003)	1.7	0.6	2.9	0.0	5.4	0.0

[a] Romania's tariff rates were harmonized with EU rates on its accession in 2007.

Source: adapted from Mayer 2004, based on UNCTAD and World Bank, World Integrated Trade Solution database.

were twice the average tariff levied on manufactured goods as a whole and on clothing were nearly three times the rate, again they were lower than the equivalent average applied tariffs in the USA. In general developed countries apply far more swingeing tariffs on clothing than on textile imports. Meanwhile many developing countries protect their domestic industries by applying punitively high tariffs on imports of both textiles and clothing, as shown in Table 5.1.

The lack of breakthrough in the Doha Round of trade negotiations suggests that progress on reducing tariff protection in textiles and clothing by developed and developing countries alike remains some way off. But this situation suits the least developed countries (LLDCs) since their nearly completely unrestricted access to EU markets, and unrestricted access for some LLDCs to the US market, means they retain a meaningful margin of preference over the tariffs levied on developing countries' exports to western countries.[8]

Over and above the issue of tariffs per se is the problem of tariff escalation, which occurs when duties are imposed at higher levels on semi-processed and processed products than on unprocessed or raw materials. Escalation impedes the technological upgrading of raw or unprocessed materials by producing countries, by discouraging diversification into downstream stages of processing before sub-sequent export. Although developed and developing countries alike apply tariff escalation, there is marked variation between them with respect to the products involved (e.g. cotton, man-made filaments, man-made staple fibres, or garments) and the degree of processing at which escalation occurs. Data from Mayer (2004) indicate that the EU in 2002 used escalation as a protective measure to a much lesser degree than the USA did in 2004. Neither the USA nor the EU, however, imposed as draconian escalation rates as did most of the big developing country textile and clothing importers.

Tariffs on clothing products can vary along several dimensions, of which the type of fabric used in their construction is the most significant. The US tariff regime is both more complicated than that of the European Union and contains wider differences in applicable rates. (Rivoli [2005] also notes the extreme detail with which the Harmonized Tariff Schedules specify items of clothing, and convincingly concludes that they were probably written for the benefit of clothing manufacturers in the USA that lobbied successfully for additional protection.) The EU's Market Access database of comprehensive duty rates for imports into other countries indicated that in January 2008 imports to the USA of men's/boys' overcoats containing more than 36 per cent wool or fine animal hair attracted duties of 27.7 per cent, compared with just 4.4 per cent on the same garments made of man-made fibres and containing specific percentages of down.[9] Other product lines show similarly wide variations, based on the fabric used. In contrast to the highly complex US regime, the entire EU tariff structure was simplified in 2004. Maximum tariffs were cut to 12 per cent on clothing and other made-up articles, 8 per cent on fabrics, 4 per cent on yarns, and a 0 rate on fibres. On any clothing item where the tariff was already below 12 per cent, the rate remained unchanged.[10] In addition the EU makes no distinction between suits on the one hand, and jackets, trousers (and skirts) imported as individual items on the other—which the USA does, with attendant differences in tariff rates (Interview Notes 2003).

In sum, therefore, tariffs remain an impediment to the free flow of international trade in textiles and clothing but more active political lobbying by interest groups in the USA has created a structure of tariffs that is more complicated to navigate and that levies duties at much higher levels than is the case in the EU. Not only does this affect the ability of German and UK (and other European) clothing companies to export their brands to the USA, but at an institutional level it also betrays a significantly different political approach to developing and less-developed countries. The US champions free trade as long as its domestic interests are not threatened. The following discussions on preferential tariffs and rules of origin reveal how much more aggressively the USA shapes its interactions with trade partners.

5.2.1. Preferential Tariff and Trade Agreements

The tariff levels shown in Table 5.1 do not apply uniformly to all exporting countries, because of the widespread use of preferential access agreements. Tariff preferences are the classical instrument to assist industrialization and diversification in developing countries, by promoting export earnings. The basic programme is the Generalized System of Preferences (GSP), operated since 1971 as a waiver from GATT anti-discrimination rules to allow developed nations to grant unilateral trade preferences to all developing countries.[11] No discrimination among developing countries is allowed, except in favour of least developed countries.

The EU GSP is considerably more generous with respect to textile and clothing products than the US scheme, since quantitative limitations on all products from whatever sector were abolished in 1995; instead, the EU varies its tariff preferences according to the sensitivity of the product on the EU market and confers a 20 per cent reduction of duties from the Most Favoured Nation (MFN) rate on textiles for most countries. The only two countries deemed to have 'graduated' from the EU GSP, on the grounds of their dominant share in GSP imports to the EU (and only since 2006), are India with respect to textiles, and China for both textiles and clothing (Scheffer 2006). Countries meeting so-called GSP+ requirements on good governance, by ratifying international conventions on labour, environmental, and other standards, are able to ship their products duty-free to the EU. Sri Lanka is one beneficiary of this arrangement.

In contrast the US GSP bars any product made of wool, cotton, man-made fibres, and certain other fibres from receiving preferential treatment,[12] which means that very few textiles and clothing items can enter the USA under this scheme. Instead textile and clothing imports into the USA from most developing countries are subject to full MFN tariff rates (UNCTAD 2005), including those from all the main textile and clothing producers in Asia (until Malaysia signed a free trade agreement in 2006). The USA does operate some special (unilateral) preference programmes for particular groups of countries, as described in Box 5.1, in addition to a growing list of bilateral trade agreements (i.e. which require the counter-parties to open their markets to American goods in return for having access to the US market), but only the Africa Growth and Opportunity Act (AGOA) is truly liberal in its application.

As well as being more generous with its GSP—in 2004 EU imports of all products under GSP amounted to €40 billion, compared with €22 billion of imports under the US GSP (European Commission 2005)—the EU also has special schemes that cover a wider range of LDCs and LLDCs (less and least developed countries) than the US's unilateral programmes. With a sharp increase in notification of preferential trade agreements to the WTO since 1995, the World Bank estimates that roughly one-third of all world trade now takes place at preferential rates (Cadot et al. 2006).

Trade regimes offering privileged access to the USA and EU fall into two broad categories:

1. Free trade agreements (FTA), which are reciprocal agreements between partner countries to open their markets to each other, such as the North American Free Trade Agreement (NAFTA). Chapter 9 discusses the effect of NAFTA on the Mexican textile and clothing industry. The USA has signed FTAs with several individual countries including Israel (1985), Jordan (2000); Malaysia (2006); and Morocco (2004);

2. Preferential trade arrangements (PTA), which are non-reciprocal and are usually between developed and developing countries. They may be applicable to a wide range of countries under the GSP, or to a specific region or grouping of developing countries such as the EU's Lomé Conventions with 77 African, Caribbean, and Pacific (ACP) countries (replaced in 2000 by the Cotonou Agreement) and the USA's AGOA.

Box 5.1 outlines the main PTAs in force with the EU and the USA.

Box 5.1. Significant free trade and preferential trade agreements

The USA has in place the following significant free trade agreements:

The North America Free Trade Agreement (NAFTA) eliminated quotas and tariffs on textile and clothing trade with Mexico in 1994, in general as long as clothing is produced using North American fabrics and yarns. This rule is known as 'triple transformation', since each step from yarn to fabric to clothing must be carried out within the NAFTA area.

The Central America Free Trade Agreement (CAFTA), signed in 2004, covers Costa Rica, El Salvador, Guatemala, Honduras, Nicaragua, and the Dominican Republic, although in 2008 Costa Rica had yet to implement it. CAFTA includes the same 'yarn forward' provisions for clothing exports to the USA as those found under NAFTA, that is, they are less restrictive than the fabric requirements for exports from other Caribbean countries.

US preferential trade agreements include:

The Caribbean Basin Initiative launched in 1983 and expanded under the 2002 Caribbean Trade Partnership Act (CBTPA). Nineteen countries are beneficiaries under this programme (as well as Costa Rica, until it implements CAFTA). To qualify for tariff- and

(*cont.*)

Box 5.1. (*Continued*)

duty-free access to the USA an item of clothing has to be fabricated in a beneficiary country from US-made fabric and yarn, and the dyeing and finishing of the cloth and the cutting of the fabric also has to take place in the USA; if US sewing thread were used to construct the garment, fabric cutting could be done in the Caribbean (Rivoli 2005).

The Andean Trade Preferences Act (ATPA) covers Bolivia, Columbia, Ecuador, and Peru, and has since 1991 reduced or eliminated import duties by allowing duty- and quota-free imports to the USA of clothing made from US fabrics or of certain specialized fabrics (e.g. alpaca and llama). Expanded in 2002 (and with a name change to Andean Trade Promotion and Drug Eradication Act), the programme aims to combat drug trafficking by encouraging legitimate trade in other products. Clothing items assembled in the Andean region from US fabric or fabric components have unlimited access to the US market.

The African Growth and Opportunity Act (AGOA), signed in 2000, ran initially until 2004, and was then extended until 2015. As of 2007 it covered 40 African countries, of which 27 are eligible for preferential treatment on textiles and clothing. The principal economic impact of the Act was to give oil and oil products exports to the US duty-free status (UNCTAD 2005) but, unlike the US's other preferential agreements, clothing producers in the eligible countries enjoy a special 'third-country fabric' rule.

The following preferential access arrangements are applied by the European Union:

The Euro-Mediterranean Association Agreements replaced cooperation agreements with partner countries in place since the 1970s.[13] Signed by the different partners at various times between 1998 and 2004, they provide for a free-trade area between the EU and Mediterranean countries to be implemented in full by 2010. The partner countries are Algeria, Egypt, Israel, Jordan, Lebanon, Morocco, the Palestinian Authority (interim agreement only), Syria, and Tunisia. The EU concluded first generation association agreements with its other Mediterranean partner, Turkey, in the 1960s and as a result entered into a Customs Union in 1996. Combined with the Pan-European zone (created in 1997 by agreements between the EU and European Free Trade Association (EFTA) members—Iceland, Liechtenstein, Norway, and Switzerland—and extended in 1999 to Turkey), the Pan-Euro-Med zone creates a free trade area covering 42 countries.

The Cotonou Agreement in 2000 replaced the African, Caribbean and Pacific (ACP) Agreement, which itself superseded the Lomé Convention. Like the Lomé Convention and the ACP, the Cotonou Agreement was a non-reciprocal preferential trade arrangement when signed in 2000 that allowed quota- and duty-free access to EU markets for most ACP goods. WTO rules required the renegotiation and transformation of the Cotonou Agreement into Economic Partnership Agreements, beginning in 2008.

The Everything But Arms (EBA) initiative has provided special arrangements since 2001 for 49 LLDCs, of which 34 are sub-Saharan, by eliminating tariffs on all imports from these countries into the EU except for arms and ammunition (and, temporarily, sugar and bananas), providing rules of origin are met. Where inputs to the finished products are sourced from third countries, 'sufficient' processing must take place within the beneficiary country or, cumulatively, within particular regional groupings of countries.[14]

The EU's relationship with the Cotonou Agreement countries, however, is undergoing change, driven by a challenge from a number of developing countries to the EU's right under WTO rules to exclude them from the same privileged access to EU markets that LLDCs receive. However, the WTO's anti-discrimination rules do allow regional groups of countries to liberalize trade among themselves without giving the same privileges to outsiders (*Economist* 2008). Since 2005, therefore, the EU has been negotiating so-called Economic Partnership Agreements (EPA) with regional groupings of the 77 ACP countries, which will be reciprocal rather than dependent in nature while still allowing some protections for the 39 least developed countries. The new arrangements were due to come into force on 1 January 2008, and although agreements had been concluded with five regional groups by the end of 2007, only one full EPA had been signed covering the Caribbean countries.

Preferential tariff rates are tied to conditions concerning the origin of inputs to the finished product, the so-called Rules of Origin (as discussed in the following section). Cotton T-shirt imports to the USA, for example, attract a tariff of 17.4 per cent unless they meet the requirements for preferential treatment under one of the trade agreements noted above, including conforming to the rules of origin on fabric and yarn; unless the T-shirts came from Jordan in which case a tariff rate of only 10.9 per cent is imposed, or from Israel for which the tariff rate is zero (Rivoli 2005). Because not all trade between preferential partners qualifies in terms of the criteria on processing, the degree of utilization of a scheme not only varies between beneficiary countries but may be far below the maximum potential. Rates of take-up also vary depending on the scheme, with Mediterranean countries making greater use of access under the Pan-Euro-Med agreement than under the (less beneficial for them) EU GSP. Approximately 62 per cent of textile imports into the EU were eligible for full or partial duty rebates in 2005, for example, but less than two-thirds of eligible imports were actually granted preferential access, accounting for approximately 39 per cent of all EU imports (Scheffer 2006). Comparing this performance with that of the USA, AAFA (2006) notes that the share of clothing imports from PTA beneficiary countries actually fell in 2005 to 24.7 per cent of all US clothing imports from 26.2 per cent the year before, partly because of the removal of quotas but also due to restrictive provisions underpinning the PTAs, which led to lower utilization rates.

The variation in applicable tariff rates between schemes, as well as the countries to which they apply, thus gives rise to substantial differences in treatment for exports arriving in either the USA or the EU from any given developing country. The competitive price advantage, amounting to perhaps 5–10 per cent, that is conferred over non-member countries (Mayer 2004) means that preferential treatment available via one particular scheme can exercise an important role over sourcing decisions. Hence the regional trade agreements applicable to Eastern and Central European countries (prior to their accession to the EU in 2004 or 2007) and Turkey have allowed these countries to achieve far greater growth in exports to the EU than they do with the USA, with which no such preferential arrangements are in force. Similarly, Mexico performs much better in exporting to the USA under the North America Free Trade Agreement than it is able to achieve in the EU. (Proximity to the EU and to the USA, respectively, conferring rapid replenishment opportunities, additionally account for some of the differential performance, as well as the strategic preferences of firms to concentrate on familiar markets.) The EU applies effective tariff rates of zero on textile and clothing imports from Bangladesh under its GSP rules for LLDCs, whereas Bangladesh's exports to the USA are treated under Most Favoured Nation rules and hence attract average tariffs of 6 per cent on textiles and 11.6 per cent on clothing (Mayer 2004). The differential impact on trade flows of preferential tariffs is evident from the fact that Bangladesh saw its import share of clothing to the EU remain constant in the early 2000s despite the challenge from more efficient producers such as China, but experienced a decline in its share of US imports in the same period.

And yet, as Nathan Associates Inc. (2002) demonstrate, the market position of preferential suppliers to the USA (e.g. under NAFTA, AGOA, or CBI) has nevertheless depended on the competitive shield for Mexico and other such countries provided by MFA quota constraints—which apply to more than half of clothing exports from Asian countries (especially China) to the USA. As of 2003, China had captured a share of just 14 per cent of US clothing imports compared with up to an 80 per cent share of other industrialized countries' imports (Rivoli 2005). The extent to which quotas protected Mexico's share of the US market, especially for the particularly sensitive product lines liberalized in the final stage of the ATC, became fully apparent immediately following full quota removal in 2005. As discussed in greater detail in the next chapter, and despite the re-imposition of quotas under safeguard rules, China's share of the US market leapfrogged Mexico's with ease.

Turkey's position vis-à-vis the EU is anomalous. Its preference agreement, dating back to the early 1970s when preferences were tied to rules of origin, is based on 'free circulation' (Interview Notes 2003). Hence a single transformation only (e.g. from yarn to fabric or from fabric to sewn garments) is required for products made in Turkey, unlike the double transformation normally required under EU preferential origin rules (Scheffer 2006). Once goods have been customs cleared and all duties and taxes paid they can move freely between Turkey and the EU on a particular document. Twenty-five years later, in 1996, full customs union between Turkey and the EU came into force. For a long period of time Turkey was able to promote a domestic integrated textile and clothing industry because it could combine free trade with the EU with high tariff barriers for imports from third countries—although its other advantages in terms of capital base, a very strong factor endowment, and proximity, as detailed in Chapter 8, were crucial factors. Cumulation agreements (described below) further enhance the position of Turkey's textile industry within the Pan-European zone.

5.2.2. Rules of Origin

Rules of origin (RoO) determine how much of a product's value-added has to occur in a beneficiary country to qualify for unrestricted market access, both in terms of the origin of imported materials and in terms of the minimum local value content of exports. They have grown in importance with the spread of preferential trade agreements, since it is the originating status of imported materials that underpins differentiation between beneficiary and non-beneficiary exporting countries (Mayer 2004; Cadot et al. 2006): often, though not always, they are regionally based.

RoO may be designed to promote the trade and development of a signatory developing country or group of countries, with the explicit intention of avoiding giving benefits to non-targeted countries (Krishna 2006)—for example by preventing the use of fabrics from Asian developing countries in the manufacture of garments by a Caribbean country that will have preferential access to the USA. But they may also be highly contentious since, as Rivoli (2005) reveals, lobbying by interested parties within a developed country/region to introduce high RoO hurdles can lead to the emasculation of the benefits supposedly introduced through a PTA. Moreover there are frequent changes to the rules, for example, that govern whether the collar of a garment counts as a component or as trim, or where the fabric of a T-shirt can be dyed and finished in order to meet the transformation requirements. And, for the USA at least, the details of those rules for the same product vary significantly from one preferential scheme to another (ibid: 118–19), leading to potentially great confusion among importers and global suppliers.

Hence detailed technicalities turn RoO into protectionist instruments of trade policy by their ability to offset tariff liberalization benefits. They create tariff-like burdens on imported intermediates. At the same time they affect the price of domestically produced intermediates, since developing country clothing producers must use regionally sourced materials to qualify the finished garments for preferential tariff treatment, even if these inputs are more expensive than imported materials (Estevadeoral and Suominen 2006). In other words, RoO can be just as trade distorting as quotas used to be. They also shape the structure of the industry in exporting countries by promoting vertical integration more or less strongly, with a bias towards CMT operations and enterprises, for example, when little choice is given over fabric sources (Gibbon 2002). A further impact of RoO is evident in the degree of product specialization induced in the structure of the industry: firms operating in countries with preferential access arrangements tend to concentrate on producing lines that would otherwise attract the highest duties in the importing country.

Clearly, then, the design of the preferential trading arrangement determines the extent to which regional production networks will develop (Cadot et al. 2006). Incentives for producers to use local intermediates are greater where the rules are more restrictive (Mayer 2004). Stringent rules can foster the emergence of inefficient cross-border supply chains, or simply impede their smooth operation (Cadot et al. 2006). Restrictive rules prevent developing country manufacturers from using third country intermediates, whereas less restrictive terms confer originating status on intermediates from third country members of the same PTA, or allow regional cumulation of origin, or even allow global sourcing of components as long as the garment is fully assembled in the beneficiary country (Mayer 2004). In particular, triple transformation requirements—generally speaking the transformation of raw materials into yarn, yarn into fabric, and fabric into assembled products (Scheffer 2006)—act essentially as a 100 per cent local content rule of origin. Thus the rules governing NAFTA and the CBI discourage producers in Mexico and the Caribbean countries from sourcing yarns and fabrics from Asia or Latin American countries, while also dissuading CBI/CAFTA nations from developing their own textiles industry (Abernathy, Volpe, and Weil 2006).

Estevadeoral and Suominen (2006) point to three different ways that RoO can be made more stringent: via lists of processing operations deemed insufficient to confer origin (e.g. cutting of fabric, and various important non-manufacturing processes such as pattern-making, grading, and marker-making; Scheffer 2006); via prohibitions on duty clawback (i.e. preventing refunds of tariffs paid on non-originating inputs used in the final product); and by introducing complexity into certification requirements. But if restrictions are drawn too tightly, producers are likely to ignore the preferential regime altogether and choose instead to ship under MFN rules: if they can use lower-cost intermediate inputs from elsewhere they can cut their finished-good prices and hence increase imports into the target market, thereby completely circumventing the purpose for the restrictive RoO (Krishna 2006).

An important concept within RoO is that of cumulation, which refers to the system of allowing substantial transformations to be carried out in different countries included within a PTA. In other words, cumulation is generally seen as introducing some degree of leniency into the RoO, by spreading the requirements for double or triple transformation across more than one country. However there has to be a substantial transformation (e.g. garment assembly) in the final country, and usually the fabric utilized has to have already obtained preferential origin. So-called tolerance rules allow the use of a limited amount (usually 8–10% by weight or value, depending on the PTA) of non-qualifying inputs, but here again there is scope for complexity. In the EU case garment producers can use metal buttons and zips without restriction, but items such as sewing thread and garment labels count towards the maximum limit, and non-qualifying linings and interlinings cannot be used at all—creating an important barrier for countries that lack a proper textile industry and representing a significant benefit for EU lining and interlining manufacturers (Scheffer 2006). Some complicated products such as bras, which require a very broad range of inputs, can fall foul of the tolerance rule because the value of the tiny amount of lace used represents more than 10 per cent of the garment's value, leading to loss of preferential status (ibid). The USA has similarly tricky rules determining preferential status for bra imports, as Rivoli (2005: 118–19) describes: free access is allowed only if at least 75 per cent of the value of the fabric used in the components of the bra is sourced in the USA. This led to a 'debate over which parts of the brassiere "count" toward the 75 per cent ... and was finally negotiated to include cups, sides, wings, and backs but to exclude straps, bows and labels'.

As with other aspects of RoO, cumulation also has varying levels. Despite operating double transformation rules for most textile products, the EU goes quite some way to offset them via rather broad cumulation options covering many different countries (Scheffer 2006). The most basic form, bilateral cumulation, allows one partner to use inputs originating in the other partner—as is the case for outward processing activity (see the following section). This type of RoO can generate an exclusively CMT-type industrial structure in the producing countries (Gibbon 2002). Diagonal cumulation (and the closely related regional cumulation), on the other hand, allows cumulation between third countries that have free trade agreements containing identical origin rules and provisions for cumulation. The Pan-Euro-Mediterranean agreement, for example, allows materials with originating status in any one of the 42 signatories to be added to products originating in any of the other countries, as long as there are bilateral agreements between each of the countries involved. So a garment produced in Morocco from fabric made in Lithuania and lace made in Switzerland can be brought duty-free into the EU. Crucially, once the necessary bilateral agreements were implemented between Turkey and Morocco and Turkey and Tunisia in 2005, cumulation between the EU, Turkey, and Morocco/Tunisia could begin, opening the way towards much more extensive use of Turkish fabric. This was particularly important for UK importers, who had hitherto been paying duty on finished garments made in Morocco of Turkish fabric (Interview Notes 2003).[15] Similarly, South Asian countries benefit from SAARC cumulation as do Southeast Asian countries under ASEAN cumulation (arising from the EBA initiative) for access to EU markets, and the clothing industries in Bangladesh and Cambodia, respectively, appear to be prospering as a result (Scheffer 2006). Both diagonal and regional cumulation foster the development of an industrial structure that encompasses full package supply as well as CMT operations, despite the high barriers to entry to full package manufacturing (Gibbon 2002). The most generous cumulation rule, full cumulation, allows the use of any materials from any third country as long as processing takes place entirely within the beneficiary country/area. In the developed world the European Economic Area, encompassing the European Union, Iceland, Lichtenstein, and Norway, operates full cumulation.

AGOA includes a temporary proviso allowing sub-Saharan Africa LLDCs to use third country fabrics in the clothing they export duty-free to the USA—a crucial provision, given the limited local availability of good quality fabrics—and thus is also an example of full cumulation. Developing country signatories, though, have to achieve double transformation within diagonal cumulation rules (meaning clothing producers must use cloth from eligible African countries or from the USA if their exports are to gain duty-free access). However, in practice AGOA preferences are fiendishly complicated—by design, it is suggested (Interview Notes 2003). Among the potential beneficiary countries only Lesotho has substantially increased its US exports, by 30 per cent per annum since the mid-1990s (Mayer 2004; Cadot et al. 2006) once The Gap, Wal-Mart, Levi Strauss, and other companies began sourcing there. (See also Box 6.3 in the next chapter for a fuller discussion of Lesotho's clothing industry.) Of the 40 African countries covered by the Act—several LLDCs are completely excluded on political grounds—only 23 are given preferential treatment on textiles and clothing. These industries together account for only a small proportion of US imports under AGOA, the bulk of which is accounted for by oil and oil products (84% in 2001) (Gibbon 2002). As developing countries, neither Mauritius nor South Africa qualifies for the less restrictive

RoO status enjoyed by countries such as Lesotho, and both have seen their market share of US imports stagnate (Mayer 2004). Gibbon (2002), however, points out that the textile and clothing industries in both Mauritius and South Africa were traditionally oriented towards domestic or EU markets, whereas production in Lesotho has been built up specifically with the US market in mind. One impact of AGOA rules of origin has been the substantial uptake of Southeast Asian and Chinese fabrics in the beneficiary countries, with 85 per cent of US imports based on non-origination fabrics (Scheffer 2006); a second is foreign direct investment in some of these countries. But, as Scheffer points out (2006: 18), this suggests trade diversion from Asia to Africa in terms of origin and from the EU to the USA in terms of destination, while the temporary nature of the AGOA regime begs the question of how sustainable is the nature of the industrialization taking place.

As the example of African countries demonstrates, RoO may help to predispose supplier firms in a given developing country to focus on one particular developed country customer or another. Bangladesh's clothing exports qualify for duty-free access to the EU only if local or EU raw materials are used. Its denim weaving capacity in 2003 was insufficient to meet the demands of local jeans producers, which had to pay duty on imports into the EU of garments made from third-country fabric (Abernathy et al. 2006). But by 2006 nearly four-fifths of the EU's imports from Bangladesh met the RoO, in part because of the boom in domestic raw material investments that the requirements stimulated, and the EU accounted for three-quarters of the country's entire clothing exports (Just-Style 2007*b*). Denim production capacity nearly quadrupled to meet demand, from around 40 million m^2 in 2005 to 160 million m^2 by the end of 2007 (Arvind Mills 2007).

Side deals to trade agreements in order to protect domestic producers can often end up undermining their competitive position. Rivoli (2005) highlights the detrimental effects for American yarn producers of the 'yarn forward' requirements contained in CBTPA: they are discouraged both from exporting yarn to the Caribbean and from moving production to more cost-efficient locations. The powerful American Textile Manufacturers Institute (ATMI), representing fabric producers, has generally not been supportive of legislation promoting offshore fabric production unless it was clearly in the interests of members. Competing interests among the various textile and clothing industry lobby groups have created higher costs for each other: the success of lobbying efforts by the American Yarn Spinners Association, for example, to get tariffs imposed on imported yarn raised the prices of the best yarns wanted by ATMI members. Constant lobbying of trade policymakers for new or different provisions within a trade agreement, or the agreement's extension or removal, generates additional regulatory risk for clothing producers by the climate of uncertainty created. In 2002 the condition for clothing made in the Caribbean to receive preferential market access was suddenly extended from use of American-made fabric to fabric that was not only made but also dyed and finished in the USA, as a quid pro quo for a one-vote majority in Congress for the President on his fast-track trade negotiation authority. The immediate effects were plain to see: investments in new printing technology for dyeing and finishing in Honduras were abruptly halted and work transferred to printing presses started up in South Carolina (Rivoli 2005: 158).

5.2.3. Production-Sharing Arrangements

Trade policy regulating another type of preferential access, so-called production sharing arrangements, has been used extensively by both the USA and the EU to protect their domestic textile industries. It involves (normally) a developed country unilaterally providing benefits to neighbouring countries for a specific period of time (Nathan Associates Inc. 2002). The economic effects of these arrangements are similar to those of rules of origin (Cadot et al. 2006). Initially an early step in the globalization of value chains made in response to MFA quotas, since quota restrictions applied only to finished goods, 'outward processing' has permitted developed country importers to ship ready-cut fabric to a nearby developing country for sewing and then re-import the partially processed items for finishing and packaging. The disadvantage for the developing country is that the practice discourages the development of an indigenous textile industry.

In the USA this practice was encouraged by Special Tariff Item 807 (now clause 9802), which allowed outward processing companies to pay duties only on the value added overseas. These concessions encouraged the establishment of *maquiladora* garment assembly plants along the Mexican side of the US border and in other areas of the Caribbean. By the late 1970s the value of US textiles flowing each year to Puerto Rico, Costa Rica, Mexico, and other Caribbean and Latin American countries was in excess of US$ 400 million (Cavanagh 1981). Clause 807A, which is an amended version of the original clause, gives even more preferential access (via lower tariff rates and virtually unrestricted quantities) to US firms' imports of assembled garments if the fabric is not just cut in the USA, but also made there (Bair and Gereffi 2002). Garments processed in 807/807A countries from non-US fabrics are subject to much higher tariff rates, effectively eliminating the advantage of production in a lower-cost location.

In the EU the equivalent arrangement to 807/807A is known as Outward Processing Trade (OPT). Again, fabric or ready-cut fabric may be temporarily exported to another customs area for further processing and the finished garments re-imported into an EU country. As with the USA, garments made of non-EU fabrics attract considerably higher tariffs. German firms were the first to start using CEE countries for processing activities in the 1970s, and the practice has been regulated within the EU since 1982 (Bair and Gereffi 2002). OPT mitigated the impact of MFA-like arrangements with Romania, Poland, Bulgaria, Hungary, and Czechoslovakia in the late 1980s, enabling the rehabilitation of the industry there. Quotas were abolished when Association Agreements with various CEE countries that created free trade areas came into force in 1991–93 (Yoruk 2001; Interview Notes 2003), which were joined later by the Baltic States and other countries including Ukraine and Moldova. Since then, OPT no longer has any meaning in customs duty terms although the term remains in widespread use.

In the mid-1990s a high proportion of EU clothing imports came in under OPT rules, especially to Germany and, to a lesser extent, Italy and France. Germany consistently accounted for around 70 per cent of OPT activity among the EU-12 countries whereas, as Chapter 3 has noted, the practice was practically unknown among British firms until the late 1990s. OPT trade has also accounted for an important share of exports from CEE countries, especially in their early transition years. (See Chapter 8 for a discussion of the role of OPT in Romania's clothing industry.)

Finally, RoO encourage the cross-border shipments of raw materials and garments at various stages of production, sometimes multiple times for a single garment. This creates a complex burden both for the customs agencies attempting to determine where the majority of the transformation work was carried out, and for the importers in documenting their sourcing activities. (In much the same way, the MFA in its time created an entire bureaucracy within both the importing and exporting countries to administer the rules governing quotas [Rivoli 2005].) When RoO documentation demands to achieve duty-free access become too great, importers may prefer to pay the tariffs—particularly if highly priced local materials must also be used to confer originating status (Cadot et al. 2006). Widespread use of Outward Processing Trade between the EU and CEE countries continued in the 1990s despite the latter group's' duty-free access to European markets because the cost of proving origin reportedly exceeded the duty payable using OPT provisions (Krishna 2006).

5.3. CONCLUSION

Although one level of trade distortion has disappeared with the ending of quotas and the textile and clothing industry is now back within the WTO system, trade distorting policies by developed country governments remain widespread, in the form of preferential tariff regimes and carefully crafted rules-of-origin provisions. Nevertheless, in parallel with the elimination of quota protection, there is evidence to suggest that overall import duties are falling. While the EU has worked to simplify its tariff system via the 2004 revisions, US duties remain both high in absolute terms and very complex. Whereas eligibility for reduced duty or duty-free access to EU markets under various preferential trade/GSP arrangements has expanded (from just 28% of all EU T/C imports in 1994 to nearly half in 1999 [Stengg 2001] and to over 60% in 2005 [Scheffer 2006]) especially following expansion of the Pan-Euro-Med zone, the same cannot be said for the US market. Aside from AGOA, which is—temporarily—important to clothing exporters in a small number of individual African countries and is in any case insignificant in terms of its overall impact on the US market (less than 3% of imports), the USA mostly offers easier access only to countries where its own textile and/or clothing companies are likely to have business interests.

Protectionist activity has also introduced tensions between different interest groups within the US textile and clothing industries. Tariffs and rules of origin that protect the domestic textile industry by and large prevent domestic clothing firms from sourcing cheaper and more fashionable fabrics from competitive foreign (mostly Asian) producers. Restrictions on using these suppliers have made it more difficult, rather than less, to keep clothing manufacturing in the USA (Rivoli 2005). The elimination of quotas has eroded the advantage for producers (e.g. Mexico and the Caribbean Basin countries) with preferential access to developed country markets over those without (primarily the efficient Asian nations), and clearly revealed the extent to which quotas insulated the less well endowed or organized producers. Since 2005 US importers have been opting to disregard RoO requirements on higher-cost regional intermediates and forego the preferential access duties levied on products from Central American and Caribbean nations, particularly with regard to clothing lines carrying average tariff rates or lower (Nathan Associates Inc. 2002), in favour of lower-cost Asian sources.

Overall, the thrust of EU trade policy in textiles and clothing vis-à-vis developing countries and LLDCs since the mid-1990s appears to be more developmental and less restrictive in nature—thereby to some extent helping to foster foreign competitors—than is the case with US policy. Free trade advocates in the USA appear to be no match at all for vested interests in this industry. The US textile and clothing regime applied quotas under the MFA/ATC against many more countries, including many LLDCs, than did the EU, it maintains far fewer preferential trade relations, and its trade tariffs are high. According to Stengg (2001), this had the effect of diverting to the more open EU market products that would otherwise have been exported to the USA. But despite these efforts it is clear that western countries have failed comprehensively to save either their textile or their clothing industry, since imports continue to increase their share of the market in both the EU and the USA irrespective of the barriers mounted against them.

Continuing our examination of the international environment for the textile and clothing industry, the following chapter will examine how the various trade policies discussed here shape the rise of so-called vertical trade and the use of 'triangle manufacturing'. It will also discuss in greater detail the issue alluded to briefly above: the question of which countries have benefited from and which have been disadvantaged by the elimination of quantitative restrictions or changes in tariff regimes governing textile and clothing trade.

NOTES

1. Developing countries also protected their own industries from imports, by instituting high import duties and/or a variety of other non-tariff barriers (Stengg 2001; Mayer 2004).
2. Finland, Austria, and Sweden were members of the EU not at the time. Sweden withdrew from the MFA in 1991, having liberalized its T/C regime, but accession

to the EU in 1995 brought the re-imposition of quotas; neither Japan nor Switzerland imposed MFA quotas, but their signatures to the Arrangement indicated their readiness to do so if circumstances required it.

3. See http://ec.europa.eu/trade/issues/sectoral/industry/textile/index_en.htm for details.

4. 'Anti-dumping' refers to the practice of one party—under WTO rules—levying a duty on a product that is dumped (i.e. sold at a 'less than normal value', in other words at a lower price in an export market than in the domestic market) and which causes or threatens to cause material injury to an established industry in the plaintiff country. The threat of an anti-dumping action is seen to be an effective way of discouraging imports from a given country, because the likelihood of such action being taken is widely regarded as unpredictable (*Just-Style* 2007a).

5. In the USA a quota was defined as 'constraining' if the fill rate reached 85–90%; in the EU constrained quotas were 95% full (Nathan Associates Inc. 2002). Textile suppliers were rarely constrained by quotas, in contrast to clothing suppliers.

6. There was one main auction per annum plus subsidiary auctions that restricted participation to particular types of company (Interview Notes 2003). Note 12 in the chapter on China (Chapter 9) gives more detail on Chinese quota allocation processes.

7. Nathan Associates Inc. (2002) compares average US clothing tariffs of 17% with the 40% or more tariff equivalent of quotas (tariffs that would produce the same restrictive effect as quotas) that China and other East Asian exporters face.

8. One Doha proposal, which would give Asian LLDC clothing producers such as Cambodia and Bangladesh the same unrestricted access to the USA as AGOA beneficiary countries, is—unsurprisingly—meeting opposition from African countries whose textile and clothing exports to the USA would come under threat. The breakdown of the Doha round has created big losers further upstream, particularly with respect to cotton subsidies which the USA had promised to cut as part of the Doha round. Instead, African cotton farmers must compete against approximately 12,000 large-scale US cotton farmers who are estimated under the latest US farm bill to receive US$1 billion in subsidies per year for five years (Williams 2008).

9. See http://mkaccdb.eu.int/ to examine the EU's Market Access database.

10. Prior to 1995 most garments attracted tariffs of either 13 or 14%. Although the aim was to reduce tariffs by one-third in 2004, which would bring clothing tariffs down to 8–9%, it was decided that the overall reduction should be by one-third. Hence if the tariff on an item is brought down to 0 this is a 100% reduction, allowing tariffs on other items to fall by significantly less (Interview Notes 2003).

11. See http://ec.europa.eu/trade/issues/global/gsp/gspguide.htm

12. See http://www.ustr.gov/Trade_Development/Preference_Programs/GSP/Section_Index.html for details.

13. See http://ec.europa.eu/ external_relations/euromed/med_ass_agreemnts.htm

14. See http://ec.europa.eu/trade/issues/global/gsp/eba/ug.htm for details.

15. They had been able to get some relief under Outward Processing Relief, but nevertheless had to pay some duties.

6

Shifting Global Networks and the
Development of a New International
Hierarchy of Firms and Supplier Countries

The regulatory regimes described in the previous chapter have undoubtedly
shaped global trade in textiles and clothing, underpinning the changing division of labour between developed and developing countries. But the policies of
developing country governments also help to explain how some countries have
experienced rapid development of an export-oriented clothing industry from the
1980s onwards, whereas in other countries the industry remains far more vulnerable to shifts in global dynamics. Navigating between both international trade
regimes and industrial development policies to exploit the best global production
opportunities is an important group of new economic actors that began to emerge
in the 1980s: supply chain specialist firms, often of East Asian origin. A few of these
have metamorphosed from earlier commission-based agency or buying business
activity into broadly based transnational giants, although the more common
model combines global reach with a more narrowly focused product range.

Throughout the 1970s world clothing production revolved around the textile
industry. Multinational manufacturers of synthetic fabrics invested in plants in
countries where the low cost, mass production of relatively standardized garments
was likely to occur—particularly in Asia—and later these countries established
their own independent textile mills. This was a largely supply-driven model for
garment production and distribution (ILO 1996). But, as described in Chapters 3
and 4, in the 1980s design-oriented branded clothing firms and powerful retail
chains replaced textile and clothing entrepreneurs as the major movers in the
industry and separated, if incompletely, ownership of garment production from
ownership of upstream and downstream functions. Despite the efforts of North
American and European states to shape and use international trade agreements
to protect their domestic industries, the market share for clothing exports from
developing country producers nearly doubled between the early 1970s and the
mid-1990s, to around 60 per cent (ILO 1996). By 2007 developing countries
accounted for about 85 per cent of all clothing imported into the USA. Developed country buyers selected foreign suppliers on the basis of criteria such as
cost, quality, speed, and reliability, and in the process promoted industrialization
in developing countries. But at the same time buyer firms introduced—even
encouraged—competition between developing countries for contracts.

Bair and Gereffi (2002) note that the first major shift in textile and clothing production, from North America and Europe to Japan, began in the 1950s (and led to the first imposition of volume import controls, as discussed in the previous chapter), followed by displacement in the 1970s and 1980s from Japan to its near Asian neighbours. Three successive waves of economic activity established Asia as the key region of clothing exporters (Mayer 2004). In the first wave the newly industrializing economies of Hong Kong, South Korea, and Taiwan built enormously successful clothing industries based on full package production capability (Gereffi 1999). As labour costs increased beyond competitive levels, firms scaled back domestic production and invested in the neighbouring countries of Indonesia, Malaysia, Thailand, and the Philippines, constituting the second wave. As these countries in turn achieved important positions as world clothing exporters they too began to suffer labour shortages and wage increases, and some of them, again with Korean, Taiwanese, and Hong Kong firms, shifted their attention to less expensive locations such as Vietnam, Pakistan, and Bangladesh, which thus became the third wave of Asian suppliers.

In the supplier countries that proved unable to develop a viable clothing industry through their own resource endowments, it is the foreign investors who have captured most of the economic and skill-based benefits. These countries are highly vulnerable to changes in the international hierarchy of supplier nations, yet may also be heavily reliant on the clothing industry for economic growth, job creation, and export activity.[1] In 2003 clothing accounted for more than 70 per cent of total merchandise exports from Cambodia, Haiti, the Northern Mariana Islands, Bangladesh, and Macao; several other countries relied on the industry for 50 per cent or more of export earnings (UNCTAD 2005).

In this chapter we discuss first sub-regional economic activity and the use of so-called triangle manufacturing in Asia as a response to the quota system, a practice that explains the emergence of the new economic actors, the industry's transnational firms. We then move to an examination of shifts in sourcing patterns by the USA and Europe, and conclude the chapter with an analysis of the countries that could be regarded as 'winners' and 'losers' in the international hierarchy as the industry consolidates in the post-quota era.

6.1. INTRA-REGIONAL NETWORKS AND THE EMERGENCE OF TRIANGLE MANUFACTURING

In the previous chapter we discussed the USA's 807/807A/clause 9802 production sharing programme and the EU's OPT arrangements, both of which promoted the development of intra-regional production networks through the shifting of production to nearby low-cost countries. In the EU's case, countries in CEE, Turkey, and North Africa—notably Tunisia and Morocco—performed the low-cost garment assembly activity (see for example Chapter 8 on Turkey and Romania), while Caribbean and Latin American countries fulfilled an equivalent role for the USA (as described in Chapter 9 on Mexico). In a parallel development involving third-country markets, Hong Kong's outward processing arrangements (OPA) with China (for which see the section in Chapter 9 on China) played a crucially important role in the continued growth of Hong Kong firms' exports to developed countries. This represented one embodiment of another type of intra-regional network. It involved not simply bilateral trading between a developed country firm and a developing country/region's suppliers but encompassed a third economic actor between the buyer and supplier: the specialist firm capable of handling the complexities of cross-border trade and dispersed manufacturing, as discussed below. Even where no formal processing agreements are in place, the out-sourcing of garment assembly activity to a third country by a developing country supplier has become an important feature of international trade in the industry. The ensuing networks, known as 'triangle manufacturing', became increasingly important with the shift towards buyer-driven supply chains (Gereffi 1997, 1999; Bair and Gereffi 2002). Factories used in triangle manufacturing networks might be wholly owned subsidiaries, joint ventures, or independent contractors. Finished garments are shipped directly to the overseas buyer, under the quotas (until the end of the MFA/ATC) or tariff arrangements of the producing country.

Triangle manufacturing first emerged as a strategy in the 1970s primarily in response to quota constraints, when export limits for particular clothing categories destined for (usually) the US or EU markets were reached, although unfavourable supply side factors such as labour shortages and high land prices, in addition to rising wage costs, accelerated the process (Gereffi 1999). Hence dispersion of garment assembly activity became almost synonymous with internationalization of production. Having attained full package production skills, a segment of the clothing manufacturers in Hong Kong, Korea, and Taiwan proceeded to upgrade their manufacturing capabilities in the home country to specialize in higher value-added production activities, while simultaneously developing international trade/production networks in order to retain orders from their long-established customers for lower value-added garments. Hence all or part of a buyer's order might be placed with offshore factories in lower-wage countries, primarily in Asian countries such as China, Indonesia, and Vietnam (Bair and Gereffi 2002) but later also in Caribbean countries and sub-Saharan Africa (Adhikari and Yamamoto 2007). This strategy enabled the more resourceful and better-organized suppliers to remain competitive despite their high cost locations and complex international trade regulation designed to protect US and EU markets from the inflow of imported clothing.

The global contract manufacturing model developed by these East Asian firms differs entirely from the industry model found in other developing countries where full package production is less well understood. In South Africa, for example, the industry is regulated and protected in such a way that firms have been unable to develop manufacturing systems capable of functioning efficiently in lower wage areas (Gibbon 2002, 2008). The domestic institutional framework of the supplier country thus has a profound impact on the industry's ability to evolve competitively. The underlying characteristic of the East Asian model, according to Gibbon, is its portability. One of his informants refers to it as a 'caravan': a business that can survive without government subsidies purely by exploiting whatever endowments (e.g. quota availability or preferential access) are available in any given environment. Key requisites are adaptability to low local skill levels, high volume orders (enabling workers to learn how to produce efficiently), and political skills to navigate through quota restrictions and/or PTA requirements. The demands of private label US retailers dovetail particularly well with this model, whereas the generally much shorter-run orders of European firms are less suited to the characteristics underpinning the portability concept. The speed and efficiency with which the organizers of the network are able to coordinate the supply chain—handling electronic orders from buyers, and planning and tracking production—represent a more enduring form of competitive advantage than simply chasing the lowest cost labour (UNCTAD 2005).

6.1.1. Organization of Triangle Manufacturing/Global Contracting Networks

These firm-centred networks are both socially and historically embedded (Gereffi 1999; Dicken and Hassler 2000). They may also have a strong regional dimension. The countries to which Hong Kong firms began shifting production in the 1960s and 1970s all had strong ethnic, linguistic, and cultural ties with Hong Kong, facilitating cooperative working arrangements with or without direct investment. A further major opportunity for East Asian firms came when the mainland Chinese economy began to open up. Dicken and Hassler (2000) describe the tight linkages created between the headquarters of Taiwanese firms, which organize regional production networks and have close working relationships with ethnic Chinese clothing factories in Indonesia, and the buying offices of primarily US retailers and brand-name firms. The vast majority of the orders placed in Indonesia by the Taiwanese headquarters come either from the buyer in the USA or from the buyer's representative offices in Hong Kong or Singapore; there is no direct contact between the buyer and the manufacturers in Indonesia; and the finished goods are shipped directly to the USA from Indonesia. From the perspective of the Taiwanese firm, its entire production network can be organized cost-effectively from a single office, where specialized human resources are concentrated and marketing operations centralized. Control over these sometimes far-flung production networks is achieved by staffing the senior positions in each factory with managers of the same nationality as the headquarters firm (Dicken and Hassler 2000; Interview Notes 2004).

But foreign investment by Asian firms even takes place in countries without any linguistic and familial ties. Korean and Taiwanese manufacturers flocked to the Central American and Caribbean region in the 1990s, and to Mexico after NAFTA was implemented, to take advantage of preferential access from there to the important US market. Lesotho similarly became an important location in

Africa for Taiwanese jeans producers from the late 1990s because of AGOA—a later phase of development than that described by Gibbon (2002): a cluster of small and medium-sized Taiwanese clothing firms was attracted to an area of South Africa in the 1980s by low labour costs, financial assistance from the Taiwanese government, and the South African government's regional development programme. These SMEs served the domestic market, and in the early 1990s were joined by a few larger Taiwanese firms that owned quota. They engaged in export-oriented production, using South African regulations that allowed duty-free imports of yarns, fibres, and fabrics for use in exported clothing. Hence these firms were readily able to make up garments for orders placed by US retailers and importers in Taiwan using fabrics sourced from Asia rather than from South Africa's indigenous textile industry.

6.2. NEW ECONOMIC ACTORS

Full package suppliers from Hong Kong, Korea, and Taiwan that master the organizational skills necessary to manage the entire production chain as well as meet volume, quality, and reliability requirements are able to play a more important role vis-à-vis retailers and branded marketers than those with less-developed capabilities. Over time they develop into experienced and professional service suppliers with respect to fabrics procurement, clothing design, quality control, logistics arrangements, sales and marketing, and the complexities of international trade rules and regulations. Coordinating these types of activity raises the status of the network organizers from that of mere supplier to the US or EU buyers, to that of 'middleman' in a regional division of labour between the higher-cost coordinating countries and the lower wage countries performing the labour-intensive activity (Bair and Gereffi 2002). As such the position of US or European coordinating firms is challenged, since the overseas buying offices of US and European retailers and branded marketers are able to communicate directly with lynchpin East Asian firms for their needs.

Many East Asian firms have established regional production networks, and a smaller number have become significant global players. But leaving aside differences in geographical spread a distinction can be made between two types of actors in the distributed clothing supply chain. The first is essentially a highly sophisticated version of the long-established agency role, described by Fung, Fung, and Wind (2007: 8) as 'network orchestrators', comprising firms that work with third-party factories rather than owning their own production facilities. The second is referred to as the 'giant transnational contractor' (Appelbaum 2008), which does own factories (but which may supplement their capacity with production in third-party facilities).

'Network orchestrators' have become the most highly sophisticated practitioners of supply chain management in the industry. The business of the network orchestrator is to identify and negotiate with suppliers, procure fabric and other inputs, handle quality control (Gibbon 2008), and manage all the logistics associated with getting the products from the factory floor to the buyer's warehouse—and sometimes directly to the retailer's shelves. They not only disperse manufacturing processes across the world but also achieve flexible sourcing by creating relationships with hundreds of factories: they select a combination of suppliers for each customer order that best meets the specifications (Fung et al. 2007). Customization of the supply chain in this way means that a repeat order from the same customer a few weeks later would command a different supply chain because supplier capacity may have changed in the intervening period; similarly a repeat order requiring a shorter delivery date would also use different factories since some suppliers are better able than others to respond rapidly. The purpose is to create the best package for the customer rather than merely the cheapest (Brettschneider 2006). These firms organize not only the work flow and the flow of physical materials but also flows of information and flows of funds between the different elements of the chain, including fabric mills, factories, logistics companies, and the importers themselves. Crucially, they shorten the buying cycle, stripping out both time and cost from the supply chain. The distribution and logistics elements are areas where costs can more easily be stripped out than by attempting to further squeeze pure production costs. Successfully managed, the complete supply chain is said to be not only more efficient but also more cost effective for the customer, even taking into account freight and handling costs for raw materials and goods—an important skill in an industry where deflationary pressures are intense.

Among the network orchestrators are Li & Fung of Hong Kong (profiled in Box 6.1), Newtimes Group, and Linmark Group.[2] The privately owned Newtimes Group was founded in 1971, with offices in Hong Kong and Taiwan, as an exporter of sundry goods from the Greater China region to Central and South America. Later it became a buying agent for US apparel manufacturers. Over the last decade it has transformed itself into a network of offices and quality assurance hubs across Asia and the Indian subcontinent 'dedicated to managing clients' product development and supply chain outside their own boundaries'.[3] Linmark, which was founded in Taiwan but is currently Singaporean owned and listed in Hong Kong, describes itself in broadly similar fashion, as a 'fast growing one-stop global sourcing and supply chain management solutions provider'.[4] It, too, operates through a network of offices in Asia and the Indian subcontinent. Its revenues derive in approximately equal shares from the USA, Europe, and the southern hemisphere, a diversification away from North America achieved in part through acquisition. More suited to the large-scale orders of major retail chains and branded apparel firms of the USA than the much smaller order sizes placed for the fragmented European markets, it is not surprising that network orchestrators historically have tended to focus more closely on the American market. Important European-oriented buying organizations providing some of the services offered by network orchestrators, notably Inchcape Buying Services and KarstadtQuelle International Services, have been acquired by Li & Fung as a means of broadening their customer base.

Box 6.1. Li & Fung Group[5]

Originating in 1906 in southern China, Li & Fung is today a global company. Its Hong Kong-listed export trading arm turned over US$11.85 billion in 2007 and employed over 13,000 people in more than 80 offices and 40 countries.[6] Ten years earlier, its revenue had been a mere US$1.7 billion and its workforce spread across 35 offices in 20 countries. Soft goods comprise 69 per cent of turnover, of which an important though undisclosed share is clothing. Historically strongly oriented to the US market, which accounts for around 70 per cent of turnover, the acquisition in 2006 of KarstadtQuelle International Services increased European revenue from around 20 to 26 per cent. No other region generates more than 4 per cent of turnover. China is the source of 48 per cent of goods (including non-clothing items) supplied. Growth is achieved both organically and through acquisition.

Li & Fung acts both as agent and as principal, in the latter case managing customers' entire production programmes. Adopting what it calls a 'capital-light' strategy, it owns no manufacturing facilities, no processing facilities, and no production equipment. Instead it has relationships with around 7,500 specialized suppliers and manufacturers across the globe, leveraging their assets and brokering its own knowledge. By taking 30–70 per cent of a manufacturer's capacity over the long term, Li & Fung is able to maintain bargaining power and receive priority attention while not allowing the supplier to become overly dependent; where necessary the company can also leverage its supplier network to achieve better prices on fabrics and other inputs than a manufacturer with more limited purchasing power can achieve. It has invested heavily in sophisticated information technology, on which coordination of the supplier network and the interface with customers depends and which is an important source of competitive advantage.

Transformation into a global sourcing company began nearly 30 years after the second generation Fung family had re-established the company in 1949 in Hong Kong. It functioned as a simple commission-based intermediary matching buyers and sellers of clothing, toys, and other merchandise until the mid-1970s. By this time the growing power of both retailers and producers had reduced agency margins from over 10 per cent to just 3 per cent since major buyers were able to deal directly with the relatively limited number of manufacturers in Hong Kong. When the US-educated third generation Fung brothers joined the company they began to position Li & Fung as a regional sourcing agent, establishing offices in Taiwan, Korea, and Singapore. Expertise gained in the buying and selling of quotas for clothing exports to the USA brought with it relationships with hundreds of suppliers and manufacturers and an understanding of local production strengths (e.g. synthetics in Taiwan and cottons in Hong Kong). This enabled the firm to provide customers with a coordinated regional sourcing network and region-wide manufacturing information.

The opening of China in the early 1980s—when Hong Kong re-positioned itself as a coordinator for less expensive production on the mainland—marked the start of the next stage: managing and delivering manufacturing programmes for clients (mainly from the USA) based on no more than the buyer's sketches and general indications of look, colours, and quantities. Value-added work—researching yarns, matching colours to dye swatches, developing samples, contracting for all the inputs and materials, and planning and working with factories—took place in Hong Kong. Production was subcontracted at first only to factories in China. Once the challenge of managing dispersed manufacturing in China was mastered, the geographical scope of sourcing broadened in search of new and better

(cont.)

Box 6.1. (*Continued*)

sources of supply, including quota availability. The purchase in 1995 of Inchcape Buying Services,[7] which had offices in India, Pakistan, Bangladesh, and Sri Lanka, accelerated the process of geographical dispersion; in addition it extended the company's European customer base, and reduced dependence on the US market. Sourcing offices opened in 1996–97 in Egypt and Tunisia further support expansion of the European business. It now has a widely dispersed network of manufacturing relationships that the company refers to as its 'borderless manufacturing' model.

Recently Li & Fung has begun to acquire in-house proprietary brand management and marketing capabilities, primarily in the USA, through the purchase in 2007 of the Regatta group and four brands from the Liz Claiborne group.

Dispersal of supply chain activities across different locations demands highly sophisticated use of modern logistics and information technology. It is the investment in and utilization of these management information systems that creates competitive advantages that are hard to replicate. Acting as principal for customers, Li & Fung handles every aspect of the supply chain associated with a production programme, from research on consumer demand, through production development and planning, all the functions associated with manufacturing, distribution, and logistics management, to sales and customer service. According to Fung et al. (2007) the company manages steps in the supply chain in parallel rather than in sequence to shorten the delivery cycle—but this requires flexibility and a deep knowledge of the capabilities of individual suppliers. Decisions on where to produce an order to give the customer the most advantageous solution in terms of quality and cost advantages demands both careful analysis of the value chain and regional coordination. Yarn might be bought from one country but woven and dyed in a second; the best trim and accessories might be available from a foreign-invested factory in a third country; and the choice of final manufacturer would depend on information on labour costs and skills as well as current export or market access constraints. Production could even be split between several factories to ensure on-time delivery on the customer's shelves, yet garments must look as though they have all been produced in the same place. Finally, the network orchestrator business model cannot operate successfully without strict quality assurance: factory evaluations, lab testing, on-site production monitoring, and multiple inspections.

With the accumulation of all these skills and knowledge of the factory base as well as a steady process of backward and forward integration into design and merchandising activity and brand management, these firms represent a real challenge to western coordinating firms' relationships with retailers. Li & Fung, again, is indicative of the way that client relationships may evolve: the company is now responsible, under licence, for the design, manufacture, and marketing in the USA of men's tops for various Levi Strauss labels (Abernathy et al. 2006), including both the flagship Red Label and the mass market Signature brands.

The second group of firms, known as 'giant transnational contractors' (Appelbaum 2008), differs from the network orchestrators in that they are deeply implicated in both the manufacturing process and the coordination of the global supply chain. Here, direct ownership of factories is seen as a source of advantage. Taiwanese-owned Nien Hsing Textiles, which is said to be the world's largest jeans manufacturer, is one such firm. Brief profiles of Nien Hsing and a few similar firms are given in Box 6.2. A non-East-Asian example is MAS Holdings, the Sri Lanka-based lingerie specialist which operates 39 facilities in 8 countries and supplies such retailers as Marks & Spencer and Victoria's Secret, Nike, and Adidas. Unlike Li & Fung and the other network orchestrators, which rely on third-party sourcing, these 'giant transnational contractors' have established wholly owned production subsidiaries in various countries—often supplemented with other factory relationships—to satisfy the needs of major customers. Their ability to establish close ties with giant retailers and manage far-flung manufacturing locations through the use of technology lifts them out of competition with smaller, less globalized players. In an increasingly commoditized industry, these firms have acquired a position in the value chain far more akin in terms of power to the giant retailers than to simple suppliers. In some cases the transnational contractors are integrated fabric and garment producers, with fabric mills co-located with key clothing factories; sometimes they even backward integrate into raw material production as Hong Kong shirt-maker Esquel has done with its cotton-growing farms. Since fabric procurement is an important factor cost, and the time required to source fabric is additionally a key element in garment lead times, fabric availability at relatively low prices affords considerable competitive advantage. Building on a proprietary manufacturing presence these contractors have the opportunity to add further value to customer relationships by seeking new ways to upgrade the services they offer, often around fabric and new product development. TAL Apparel, for example, styles itself as an 'innofacturer' for its innovations and capabilities in new material development—crease-free shirting, pucker-free seam technology, stain resistance, etc.

Box 6.2. Giant contractor profiles

Nien Hsing Textile Co[8] is a vertically integrated firm based in Taiwan that produces denim fabrics and makes jeans for major American brands including Calvin Klein, Tommy Hilfiger, The Gap, and DKNY as well as private labels for Wal-Mart, Target, and J. C. Penney. Founded in 1988 and listed in 1992, the Nien Hsing Textile group invested in Nicaragua in 1993, Mexico in 1997, and Lesotho in 2002, with additional investments in Nicaragua and Mexico over the years. In Lesotho, for example, it operates one textile factory (under the name Formosa Textiles) and three apparel factories (under the names C&Y Garments, Global Garments, and Nien Hsing). Since 2000, following acquisition of a Taiwanese casual garment producer, it manufactures casual wear in Vietnam, Cambodia, and Nicaragua, primarily for mass market American retailers. Employing around 33,000 workers worldwide, its fabric mills in Taiwan, Mexico, and Lesotho and garment factories in Nicaragua, Mexico, and Lesotho provide the internal manufacturing flexibility to maximize use of US

Box 6.2. (*Continued*)   (*cont.*)

PTAs and satisfy the quick response demands of American buyers. Nien Hsing is now the world's largest specialized integrated denim fabric and clothing producer.

Boolim,[9] a sportswear, casual wear, and knitwear producer headquartered in Seoul, South Korea is a supplier to Nike and other American branded clothing firms. It operates a global sourcing business based on partnerships with factories throughout Asia and Central America, as well as in Korea. Representative offices in Vietnam and Indonesia facilitate order placing and the management of relationships.

The Hong Kong owned shirt-maker *Esquel*[10] is fully integrated: growing cotton, spinning yarn, weaving it into fabric, and manufacturing the final garment for branded marketers and retailers. It boasts of strong product development capabilities and a research centre that develops new technologies (e.g. pucker-free seams, crease-resistant fabric) for the benefit of clients. The China-based textile operations supply Esquel's clothing factories in mainland China, Hong Kong, Malaysia, Mauritius, Sri Lanka (where there are four sewing plants operating under the name Polytex Garment), and Vietnam as well as the factories of other shirt producers. In Mauritius, where it is one of the largest Hong Kong investors, it uses its market power with US importers to ensure not only that its fabrics are specified for use in the Esquel Mauritius sewing plant but also that it is the 'nominated supplier' for other apparel factories in Mauritius (Gibbon 2008).

TAL Apparel,[11] another Hong Kong company, meanwhile, claims to make one in six of all dress shirts costing over US$ 50 sold in the USA (Tsang 2007). Production of shirts, blouses, trousers, and other outerwear items takes place in its factories across the Asian region, in Hong Kong, Macao, mainland China, Taiwan, Thailand, Indonesia, Malaysia, and Vietnam. Like other suppliers to the American market TAL no longer appears to manufacture in Mexico but since 1988 has owned spinning and weaving operations in the USA, acquired from Burlington Industries, producing greige fabric for its own use (e.g. in Mexico under NAFTA rules) and for sale to other clothing producers. Distinguishing TAL from other OEM contractors is the close relationship developed with retail customers based on coordination of the supply chain with their product development on the one hand and their marketing/sales operations on the other. Integrated technologies such as electronic data interchange, purchase orders, order status tracking, and point of sales allow TAL to collaborate with key clients such as J. C. Penney on synchronizing supply and demand, benefiting J. C. Penney by reducing inventory and time-to-market and itself by locking in its customer base (Koudal and Long 2005).

One of our interviewee firms, *CH-1*, established in Hong Kong in 1960, first built a factory in China 25 years ago for exports to non-quota countries such as Japan. Only in the 1990s did it begin using Hong Kong/China OPA for exports to western countries to learn to work with US and European firms. Now with factories in China, Cambodia, Bangladesh, and Hong Kong, *CH-1* is able to cater to different price points for different customers: supermarket customers' orders may be directed to its production facilities in Bangladesh or Cambodia, for example, while medium to high price level clients could have their orders filled in the Guangdong factories. Its spinning operations supply cotton yarn to its textile operations in China for onward supply to the garment factories.

With the exception of the network orchestrators, which rely on 'virtual' manufacturing facilities, foreign direct investment (FDI) has played an important role in the development of triangle manufacturing. Indeed, the foreign-owned affiliates of producers dominate the exports of some developing countries (UNCTAD

2005). Dicken and Hassler (2000), for example, find that clothing exports from Indonesia are organized in large part by foreign-owned firms operating within global production networks. Hong Kong firms, as is evident in the examples of transnational contractors above but is also true of many other much smaller firms, have been active investors around Asia. Taiwanese and Korean firms established production plants in the Caribbean and sub-Saharan Africa, as well as in such Asian countries as Bangladesh and Vietnam, in an effort to produce cost-effectively. But even relatively minor participants in the global textile and clothing industry such as Sri Lankan and Mauritian firms have side-stepped quota restrictions by establishing factories in the Maldives and Madagascar, respectively (Adhikari and Yamamoto 2007).

Countries with only a short history of clothing production, such as Cambodia and Lesotho, attracted direct investments in the 1990s because their exports were relatively unconstrained by quotas and they had available a large pool of inexpensive labour. Supplier countries heavily implicated in CMT operations are currently experiencing labour readjustment through the closure of smaller sites, sometimes compensated for by the opening of much larger, more cost-efficient facilities. In Cambodia, for example, clothing factories employing over 5,000 workers are said to represent the fastest-growing category—although they remain relatively few in number—while the share of those employing fewer than 1,000 workers is declining (Sajhou 2005).

The East Asian model of investment, requiring very low sunk costs and taking the form of large plants producing large runs of a narrow range of products, is particularly well suited to rapid changes in circumstance since dependence on skilled workers is minimal. Moreover the 'portability' of the caravan model means that a supplier's factory in, for example, Central America will essentially look the same and function in the same way as its factory in Africa or Southeast Asia. Where necessary, a small number of experienced machinists could be shipped in from another low cost location (e.g. from China or Bangladesh to Lesotho) in order to meet production deadlines. Designed to optimize the economies of scale found in producing for the American mass market, the model also minimizes the risks that confront suppliers faced with US retailers' 'ruthless pursuit' of flexibility (Gibbon 2008: 36).

The ubiquity of the portable investment model can be gleaned from historical accounts of firms' locations. Hong Kong-based Luen Thai, which describes itself as 'one of the leading apparel manufacturing and supply chain services providers worldwide',[12] currently has manufacturing and logistics facilities in China, the Philippines, Cambodia, Saipan, Guam, Vietnam, and Korea, but ceased manufacturing in Mexico. TAL has also ceased operations in Mexico and Esquel has closed down factories in the Philippines and Jamaica. Tristate, another Hong Kong-listed firm with factories throughout Asia, has withdrawn from manufacturing in Taiwan and Macau. And the Korean multinational Yupoong closed down its production activity in the Dominican Republic in 2007.

To sum up this section: triangle manufacturing has become an important means of organizing the production function within the clothing value chain.

Moreover, the most efficient proponents—mostly East Asian firms—have shown that it is possible to extract value from this segment of the supply chain in ways that western clothing firms appear to be unwilling or incapable of achieving. The 'caravan' approach (Gibbon 2002) is one such means, with whatever consequences for the local labour force and the domestic economy if the details of preferential trade agreements shift in favour of other locations. But the second important outcome of the global dispersion of the manufacturing function, combined with the shift in dynamics between western clothing firms and retailers (in favour of the latter), is the emergence of very large and increasingly powerful supplier firms. These new economic actors redress the power asymmetry typically found between retailers and suppliers (Appelbaum 2008) and, as they assume more and more functions and attain higher skills that gradually become lost to the buying firm, may even begin to hold the upper hand in the relationship particularly with respect to price negotiation. As for the smaller buyers, they are clearly in a weak position vis-à-vis these very large suppliers and in consequence may find themselves shut out of the best manufacturing locations, which could be held captive by the large contractors or network orchestrators by virtue of ownership or partner relationships. Finally, for the smaller indigenous manufacturing suppliers in industrializing countries mastery of the requirements for exporting as well as the basic disciplines of efficiency and reliability is necessary if they are to become noticed by agents, trading houses, and network orchestrators and integrated into the global supply chain.

The next section will discuss how the ending of the quota system and the implementation of preferential trade agreements is driving the process of investment and disinvestment—and hence the hierarchy of supplier nations—as buyers on the one hand consolidate their supplier lists and the suppliers on the other seek to develop the most flexible and cost-effective locations.

6.3. EFFECTS OF CHANGING TRADE REGULATION ON SOURCING PATTERNS

While economic development and industrial upgrading in developing countries account for some of the shifts in sourcing patterns for US and EU clothing importers, the trade distorting effects of both quota restrictions and preferential access agreements have been significant. More than 140 countries produce textiles and clothing for export, primarily destined for the US and EU markets (UNCTAD 2005). The US Office of Textiles and Apparel (OTEXA) database, for example, lists 198 countries that export clothing to the USA. Before regulation of international trade in the clothing industry was brought into the WTO, finding new locations where clothing could be produced with no, or little, quota constraint was seen as one of the few ways in which exporters could expand their share of prized western markets (Dicken and Hassler 2000). Hence there is a strong argument to be made that globalization of the clothing industry occurred as a reaction to trade barriers rather than in response to the open markets stance (Rivoli 2005) routinely proclaimed by the USA in particular.

Because of the vagaries of the quota system and/or PTAs some countries (e.g. those in the Caribbean region and African countries such as Lesotho) produce for export almost exclusively to a single country or region, which exposes them to risks of regulatory change or the loss of market share to more competitive producers (e.g. China). The elimination of quotas has undoubtedly encouraged importing firms to begin streamlining supplier networks after years of diversification to avoid quota restrictions (Interview Notes 2003–04; Sajhou 2005). As the advantage for countries with preferential tariff treatment is eroded, greater competition between clothing-producing countries ensues (UNCTAD 2005). Meanwhile the signing of new PTAs and shifting rules of origin that act as sometimes important non-tariff barriers will constrain the activities of manufacturers in countries with existing 'free' or preferential trade agreements. It seems likely therefore that changes in the international hierarchy of supplier nations will continue to occur at the margin, even after the safeguard quotas imposed on China since the end of the MFA/ATC have reached an end.

The distorting effects on international trade of MFA quotas certainly played an important role in diffusing supply chain activity, but so did domestic government policy in shaping the industry that developed. In the 1980s the Indonesian state took an active role in moulding markets and institutions to support development of its indigenous textile and clothing industry, beginning by abolishing import substitution policies that had previously heavily protected domestic yarn and fabric production (Dicken and Hassler 2000). International sourcing of more competitive inputs combined with relaxed foreign investment regulations to enable non-Indonesian ownership of export-oriented businesses encouraged a flood of new foreign investment. Foremost were highly productive Korean firms that invested upstream in the textile industry as well as in clothing production, but powerful ethnic Chinese Indonesian firms were still able to enter into and participate in regional supply chains.[13] The emergence of a clothing industry in Cambodia during the mid-1990s similarly relied on relatively permissive foreign investment laws and an open trade regime, as well as an absence of quota restraints. It has been claimed (Bargawi 2005), not entirely credibly, that low wages played only a secondary role in attracting clothing producers and buyers to Cambodia. Since over 90 per cent of Cambodian garment producing firms are foreign owned, primarily by investors from Hong Kong, Korea, China, and Taiwan, and a relatively high proportion of output occurs in clothing categories on which the USA has imposed safeguards for Chinese exports, the industry remains vulnerable to migration elsewhere. Bangladeshi state policy during the 1990s and early 2000s, in contrast, was to favour domestic investment and discourage FDI by requiring foreign investors in the clothing industry to make parallel investments in a backward linkage industry, with the aim of retaining quota allocations largely for the benefit of domestic firms. The result is that Hong Kong, Korean, and Taiwanese investors play a much more limited role in Bangladesh's clothing industry than is the case elsewhere.[14] Despite heavy protection of the domestic textile industry against imported yarns and fabrics, Bangladeshi clothing firms proved able to compete successfully in world markets for basic standardized items due to other domestic policies, including the introduction in the 1980s of a bonded warehouse system and the use of back-to-back letters of credit (World Bank 2006*b*).[15]

With the ending of quotas, the selection of countries from which to source is more directly influenced by clothing industry attributes combined with backward linkages. Preferential tariffs may affect some choices, by facilitating market access for some countries (especially the least developed nations) and restricting it for others (generally, more advanced developing economies), but they do not drive footloose behaviour in the way that quotas did. As in the pre-2005 days, the post-MFA world requires supplier country firms to be competitive with regard to cost, reliability, quality, and productivity—and, increasingly, to meet acceptable labour standards. But a far more crucial consideration in the current environment is proximity to an efficient textile industry, a factor that had been of only secondary importance in the quota-dominated years (Sajhou 2005). (Indeed, Abernathy et al. 2006 suggest that concerns in the USA over the impact of quota elimination were at least as strong in the textile industry as they were in the clothing industry.) Either actual or virtual integration between textile and garment production via national or international partnerships is necessary to enable supply chain efficiencies and quick response manufacturing, and to be able to compete in the rapidly growing full package segment of the market. The ability of the Dominican Republic (Schrank 2004) and Honduras (Sajhou 2005) with respect to the USA, and Turkey with respect to the EU market, to compete relatively strongly in the post-MFA world is closely associated to their capabilities in full package production. Moreover the continuing use of OPT has allowed buyer companies to continue to influence the fabrics chosen by producer firms in Europe (Yoruk 2001; Interview Notes)[16] and in Central American countries.

6.3.1. Impact on Less-Developed Nations

The least developed countries have typically been unable to develop diversified clothing industries. Instead they focus on the production of low-quality or commodity items such as T-shirts and underwear, often driven by the vagaries of the quota system. Some countries have been led historically also to concentrate on producing for a particular final market, or else individual factories within a country produced particular lines of quota-constrained clothing rather than others (Gibbon 2002). Hence, network organizers become accustomed to serve customers in one specific market from a different set of factories or countries than those used to fulfil orders from another market. Most clothing exports from Sub-Saharan African countries are destined for the USA, where they qualify for preferential access under AGOA, but their share of the US market is only about 2–3 per cent and three-quarters of exports are concentrated in just two categories: plain knit shirts and trousers.

As the profile of the Lesotho garment industry described in Box 6.3 indicates, the majority of exporting factories in Lesotho are owned and managed by East Asian (primarily Taiwanese) nationals, and several belong to at least partially globalized firms. According to Gibbon (2002) the rapid growth in the industry, which began in late 1999 when AGOA was nearing approval, occurred because jeans could be sourced from there more cheaply than from Mexico based on differences in wage rates (lower in Lesotho) and the preferential tariffs Sub-Saharan Africa would then enjoy. As noted earlier in this chapter, some of the largest firms investing in Lesotho, including Nien Hsing and Carry Wealth (a Hong Kong listed firm) already operated factories in Central America to supply the US market. With their relationships with US suppliers already in place, it was a relatively simple matter to route orders from headquarters to Lesotho rather than to their Central American factories.

Box 6.3. The textile and clothing industry in Lesotho

The experience of Lesotho, a landlocked country in southern Africa whose export-oriented garment industry is overwhelmingly foreign-owned, illustrates how government policy, multilateral trade regulations, preferential trade agreements and rules of origin, and currency exchange rates shape a country's industry and its position in the hierarchy of supplier nations. Lesotho's clothing exports to the USA grew at about 30 per cent per annum from the mid-1990s (Cadot et al. 2006: 2) and it has become the largest single user of the provisions of the Africa Growth and Opportunity Act (AGOA), accounting for over a quarter of total Sub-Saharan African garment exports to the USA (Bennett 2006). The country's attractions for foreign investors include its relative political stability, a reasonably well-educated and productive workforce, a liberal and non-discriminatory export and investment promotion policy, some degree of preferential access to both the US and EU markets, and access to the supporting infrastructure of South Africa's textile and clothing industry (OECD 2005). Together these factors created the conditions for a flourishing clothing industry, which became the country's main source of economic growth and employment. In 2004 around 70 per cent of employees in the industry were producing T-shirts and other knitted garments, and the remainder were making jeans. Some 98 per cent of the 26 million pairs of jeans produced in Lesotho each year are made for famous retailers and brands in the US market, including The Gap, Jones Apparel, Levi Strauss, Ralph Lauren, Wal-Mart, and Sears (Bennett 2006)—and, under AGOA provisions, escape the 17 per cent duty on denim trousers that would otherwise be payable (Laing 2001).[17] The industry is thus both highly specialized and highly focused on a particular geographic customer.

The first foreign investors were South African manufacturers who in the early 1980s were avoiding anti-apartheid sanctions (Gibbon 2002; UNCTAD 2005). Taiwanese investments arrived from 1987 onwards to produce clothing in CMT facilities for exports to the USA under the Generalized System of Preferences tariff regime. Europe was not a target market for these investors, not least because Lesotho did not satisfy the rules of origin on backward local integration into textile production necessary to benefit from duty- and quota-free access to the EU under the Lomé Convention.[18] Significant further US-oriented investment took place when AGOA came into effect in 2000: more than half of plants that were operating in 2002 had opened since 1999 and the vast majority were Taiwanese

(cont.)

Box 6.3. (*Continued*)

owned (UNCTAD 2005). Early Taiwanese investors in Lesotho included China Garment Manufacturers (CGM) and Nien Hsing (under the name C&Y), both of which became dominant players. CGM's second jeans factory, opened in 2000, increased its production capacity by 40 per cent (INSAT 2005); by 2005 Nien Hsing was operating three denim apparel plants. Both firms backward integrated into denim fabric manufacturing in preparation for AGOA, which requires the use of locally produced inputs. Nien Hsing's Lesotho plant, Formosa Textiles, imports ginned cotton from other African countries including Benin, Malawi, Mozambique, Tanzania, and Zambia, and supplies its denim fabric both to its own Lesotho plants and to other denim products manufacturers in Botswana, Kenya, Madagascar, Mauritius, and South Africa (Bennett 2006). CGM acquired a denim fabric mill near Durban in South Africa in 2000 to produce primarily for its Lesotho jeans operations, but closed the plant down in 2007 (Ryberg 2008).

Between 1999 and 2004 employment in Lesotho's export-oriented CMT activity ballooned from under 10,000 full-time workers to about 50,000, making the industry the country's largest employer by far, with important additional indirect employment in packaging, freight transportation, etc. By 2005, however, the number of directly employed operatives had plunged to 35,000 after seven factories producing knitted garments shut down, although employment in the denim clothing factories apparently remained stable. Bennett (2006) attributes the industry's difficulties to: the strength of the local currency/weakness of the US dollar (the rate shifted from 11.44 loti to the dollar in January 2002 to 5.58 loti in December 2004); diversion of garment procurement from Lesotho to Pakistan, India, and other countries following the end of quota restrictions on those countries' exports to the USA (and consequent loss of price advantage for Lesotho); erosion of Lesotho's zero-rated duty advantage as industrial tariffs worldwide decline; and the absence of crucial (for AGOA preferences) backward linkages into knit fabric manufacturing that had been achieved in denim manufacturing.

But when quota restrictions on other countries' exports to the USA (and EU) were lifted at the end of 2004, AGOA countries—South Africa, Mauritius, Kenya, and Swaziland, as well as Lesotho—experienced not only loss of market share but also absolute declines in their exports to the USA (Gibbon 2008). In contrast, export trade with EU markets under the preferential access arrangements of the ACP/Cotonou agreements has historically been concentrated on Mauritius and Madagascar, and neither country appeared by 2006 to have experienced a profound and lasting decline in their industry (Gibbon 2008: table 6.1). On the contrary, Madagascar experienced strong growth in 2006, suggesting it may even have captured trade from other countries.

Changes to the tariff regime for any given supplier country can have a dramatic effect on its attractiveness as a garment producer for a particular market, as data for Vietnam demonstrate. From a mere trickle of imports worth less than US$50 million in 2001, the value of Vietnamese-made clothing brought into the USA jumped to nearly US$900 million in 2002 and trebled again to more than US$2.7 billion in 2005 as punitively high import duties were reduced to 'normal' levels. Vietnamese imports to the EU, in contrast, already benefited from preferential

Table 6.1. Top 20 countries supplying clothing to the US market (US$ value), selected years

1990	1995	2000	2005	2007
Hong Kong	Hong Kong	Mexico	China	China
China	China	China	Mexico	Mexico
Taiwan	Mexico	Hong Kong	Hong Kong	Vietnam
Korea	Taiwan	Dominican Rep.	India	Indonesia
Philippines	Dominican Rep.	Honduras	Indonesia	India
Italy	Korea	Korea	Vietnam	Bangladesh
Dominican Rep.	Philippines	Bangladesh	Honduras	Honduras
Indonesia	Indonesia	Taiwan	Bangladesh	Cambodia
Singapore	India	Indonesia	Dominican Rep.	Hong Kong
India	Bangladesh	Philippines	Philippines	Thailand
Mexico	Thailand	Thailand	Guatemala	Philippines
Malaysia	Italy	India	Thailand	Sri Lanka
Thailand	Sri Lanka	Canada	Cambodia	Pakistan
Bangladesh	Honduras	El Salvador	Sri Lanka	El Salvador
Sri Lanka	Canada	Guatemala	El Salvador	Guatemala
Macau	Costa Rica	Sri Lanka	Italy	Italy
Costa Rica	Macau	Italy	Canada	Jordan
Turkey	Guatemala	Macau	Pakistan	Dominican Rep.
Jamaica	Malaysia	Turkey	Macau	Macau
Pakistan	Turkey	Pakistan	Korea	Nicaragua

Source: OTEXA, authors' calculations.

tariff rates and hence saw no WTO-related surge. Indeed, in 2002 and 2003 Vietnamese clothing imports into the EU actually declined slightly, perhaps because production capacity was diverted to fulfil American orders.

6.3.2. Supplier Hierarchies in the USA and EU

Table 6.1, showing the principal clothing suppliers to the US market in recent years, indicates how the sourcing patterns of US buyers have changed since 1990, influenced by quota restrictions and preferential trade agreements. The importance of Hong Kong has declined noticeably with the ending of the MFA/ATC, as has that of Macau as an OPA location, while China is now firmly established in the top rank with a market share of over 30 per cent. Imports to the USA up to the 1980s had come mainly from China, but the introduction of NAFTA in 1993 together with the Mexican peso devaluation in 1994–95 led to regionalization of the outsourcing system. Mexican firms thus became the preferred sourcing partners, rising from 11th place in the principal supplier rankings in 1990 to third in 1995, and in 1996 surpassing China as the largest exporter of garments to the USA. The implementation of NAFTA—which also explains Canada's appearance in the rankings in the mid-1990s—also changed the terms of sourcing. (See Chapter 9 for a detailed discussion of the effect of NAFTA on the Mexican textile and clothing industry.) But when quota elimination left Mexico in direct competition with China in 2005, even the continuing market access advantages of NAFTA were insufficient to offset its production inefficiencies. By 2007 Mexico's share of the US market had declined to just 6.2 per cent from over 14 per cent in 2000.

After the Caribbean Basin Initiative (CBI) in the early 1980s, preferential access to the US market also was granted to Caribbean and Central American countries for garment assembly, but the 'yarn forward' requirements of the Caribbean Basin Trade Partnership Act introduced in 2002 left these countries vulnerable to competitive Asian countries for clothing lines that did not require rapid replenishment. By the time the DR-CAFTA agreement was officially signed in May 2004, putting these countries on an almost equal footing with Mexico, they were already suffering turbulence associated with the elimination of quotas (Sajhou 2005). The combined share of DR-CAFTA nations has thus shrunk from 15.7 per cent in 2000 to 11.7 per cent in 2007. Vietnam rapidly became an important supplier almost from a standing start when it joined the WTO in 2002, jumping from 61st place in 2001 to 21st in 2002, before reaching 3rd place in 2007 behind China and Mexico. Bangladesh, Cambodia, and Indonesia have also achieved high rates of growth in their imports into the USA. The presence of Jordan in the list of top 20 suppliers since 2004 is entirely due to the 2002 implementation of a free trade agreement with the USA, although it accounts for a minuscule 0.2 per cent of all clothing imports. Finally, Italy is the only EU country to appear within the main US supplier rankings. Turkey's imports into the USA grew steadily through the 1990s but peaked in 2003 at US$1.3 billion and have halved since then.

As for shifts among suppliers into EU markets, during the 1990s a noticeable trend was the increased weight of CEE countries as European firms—especially in Germany and to an increasing extent in Italy—expanded their outward processing activities as it became easier to access production facilities in those countries. Hence, between 1993 and 1998 Germany's imports from CEE countries rose from 17 to 23 per cent and Mediterranean countries (including Turkey), which had historically been one of the first areas to which European clothing industries began delocalizing production, also increased their share from 23 to 26 per cent (Baldone, Sdogati, and Tajoli 2000). This growth came largely at the expense of Asian countries (comprising China, East Asia, Southeast Asia, and the Indian subcontinent): imports from this region fell from 44 to 37 per cent (ibid.).

If we consider individual country suppliers of clothing (SITC 84) to the entire EU-15 region there has been great consistency at the head of the rankings, with China and Turkey always ranked first and second for well over a decade, as Table 6.2 indicates. Both, as discussed in Chapters 9 and 8 respectively, enjoy a range of competitive advantages including, as far as Turkey is concerned, full customs union with the EU since 1996. However, whereas Turkey's share of extra-EU-15 imports has expanded only slowly, from 11.3 per cent in 1995 to 13.1 per cent in 2007, China had by 2007 captured one-third of the market compared with 13.8 per cent in 1995. The major leap in China's share occurred, as anticipated, in 2005, when imports surged by €5.5 billion—leading to the imposition of

Table 6.2. Top 20 countries supplying clothing to the EU-15 region (Euro value), selected years

1995	2000	2004	2005	2006	2007
China	China	China	China	China	China
Turkey	Turkey	Turkey	Turkey	Turkey	Turkey
Hong Kong	Hong Kong	Romania	India	Bangladesh	Bangladesh
India	Romania	Bangladesh	Bangladesh	India	India
Tunisia	Tunisia	India	Romania	Romania	Romania
Morocco	Bangladesh	Tunisia	Tunisia	Hong Kong	Tunisia
Poland	India	Morocco	Morocco	Tunisia	Morocco
Romania	Morocco	Hong Kong	Hong Kong	Morocco	Hong Kong
Bangladesh	Poland	Indonesia	Indonesia	Indonesia	Indonesia
Indonesia	Indonesia	Poland	Bulgaria	Bulgaria	Vietnam
Hungary	Hungary	Pakistan	Pakistan	Pakistan	Pakistan
Pakistan	Thailand	Bulgaria	Poland	Thailand	Bulgaria
Thailand	Korea	Thailand	Thailand	Vietnam	Sri Lanka
Malaysia	Pakistan	Sri Lanka	Sri Lanka	Sri Lanka	Poland
USA	Sri Lanka	Hungary	Hungary	Poland	Thailand
Korea	Bulgaria	Czech Rep.	Vietnam	Hungary	Hungary
Czech Rep.	Vietnam	Vietnam	Switzerland	Malaysia	Switzerland
Slovenia	Malaysia	Korea	Malaysia	Switzerland	Malaysia
Mauritius	Mauritius	Switzerland	Czech Rep.	Czech Rep.	Czech Rep.
Sri Lanka	Macau	Malaysia	Cambodia	Cambodia	Cambodia

Source: Eurostat, authors' calculations.

new controls, as described elsewhere—for a jump from a 22.2 per cent share to 30 per cent. Bangladesh has been the other big winner: with the benefit of preferential access to the EU its market share more than doubled between 1995 and 2007. Imports by the EU-15 from North African countries, especially Tunisia and Morocco, peaked in the early 2000s in both absolute value and share terms. As for CEE countries, the most important suppliers—Romania, Bulgaria, Poland, the Czech Republic, and Hungary—likewise saw their share peak in the early 2000s at around 15 per cent.

Finally, whereas in 2005 many countries lost ground to China as buyers switched their sources in the new post-MFA/ATC era, the following year several Asian countries, including Bangladesh, Vietnam, and Sri Lanka, achieved much higher growth rates into the EU-15, particularly of bras, dresses, blouses, and trousers, than did China. Vietnam's EU imports topped €1 billion for the first time in 2006, a jump of nearly 50 per cent from the previous year, and volume growth was nearly 150 per cent (and much greater still for the quota-constrained categories) (Brocklehurst and Anson 2007). Although the high growth rates seen in 2006 by these other Asian countries were not sustained in 2007, buyers are expected to retain supplier relationships with Vietnamese producers once restraints on Chinese imports are finally removed (*Just-Style* 2007c).

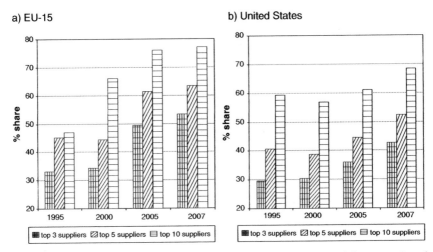

Figure 6.1. Concentration rates among suppliers to EU-15 countries and the USA, selected years

Source: (a) EU-15: Eurostat, authors' calculations; (b) USA: OTEXA, authors' calculations.

The picture painted above also holds for the broader EU-27 group of countries, with China, Turkey, Bangladesh, and India firmly in place as the principal suppliers, and Tunisia and Morocco the only other non-Asian suppliers in the top 10 rankings. A number of other East European states, including Croatia and Ukraine, appear in the next tier as West European buyers search for suppliers within easy reach of their markets that are now more cost-competitive than the recent entrants to the EU bloc. Since Germany and the UK are the largest importers of textiles and clothing within the EU, with shares of 23 and 19 per cent, respectively, in 2005 (Gambini 2007), their actions are likely to be driving the shifts just described.

Examining the concentration rates among supplier countries to the EU-15 and the USA (Figure 6.1), it is clear that in both cases the biggest suppliers have become progressively more important but that the capture of market share over the last decade is considerably more pronounced in the EU-15 than it is in the USA. Also noticeable is that the US imported slightly less from its 10 largest supplier countries at the turn of the century than it had done in 1995, suggesting active engagement in the search for different sourcing locations to take advantage of quota allocations. Even in 2005, as sourcing networks reorganized in the wake of quota elimination, the concentration rate among the top 10 suppliers to the USA was only slightly higher than in 1995.

Finally, it is important to note that the preceding discussion of US and EU sourcing patterns focuses on aggregate data. For individual products (e.g. denim jeans for men) or categories of clothing (e.g. women's dresses) there may be considerable variations from the aggregate, depending on the fashion content of the garment in question (since this is strongly correlated with levels of replenishment), specialization of production and design, and historic capabilities in highly skilled sewing details (Abernathy et al. 2006). The principal suppliers of jeans to the US market are highly concentrated in Central America, plus (in 2006) Bangladesh and Lesotho, with Mexico alone taking 44 per cent of the market by volume and 49 per cent in value terms. Costa Rica was the second biggest supplier in volume terms, with a share of just 5.4 per cent. Bangladesh and Lesotho are suppliers of relatively low cost jeans, whereas Hong Kong and China—both relatively far down the list in volume terms—appear to focus on more fashionable styles given the high unit cost of the jeans they export to the USA. Guatemala appears by 2006 to have repositioned itself as a fashion supplier of jeans, compared with the analysis conducted by Abernathy et al. (2006) for the 2003 year. Looking at the EU market Bangladesh was the primary volume source in 2007, thanks to low wages and its preferential market access arrangements with the EU, but its unit prices are relatively low compared with imports from Mediterranean countries including Tunisia and Turkey (fifth and fourth placed, respectively, in the volume rankings). Unlike the USA, the EU has no dominant jeans supplier in either volume or value terms, although imports from China had risen to second place by 2007 from 12th in 2003, despite disruption caused by temporary import restraints on this product line.

6.4. CONCLUSION

Countries that faced the elimination of MFA/ATC quotas in 2005 with trepidation were typically those that competed on labour costs alone, had a limited product range, and were heavily reliant on a single market—either the USA or the EU (Appelbaum et al. 2005). The clothing industry in these least developed countries generally achieved relatively low productivity and efficiency rates, produced lower quality goods, and were trapped at the bottom of the value chain doing simple cutmake assembly work. Lacking either backward linkages to an indigenous textile industry or forward linkages to end customers, firms were unlikely ever to satisfy demand for quick response manufacturing, particularly given the poor infrastructure of the country. Although some countries, for example Bangladesh and Nepal, achieved the indigenization of their clothing industries via investments by local entrepreneurs, other countries remain highly dependent on foreign investment. The riskiness of this strategy in a famously footloose industry becomes apparent when foreign investors withdraw—whether because the country's quotas were the most attractive characteristic and this became irrelevant in 2005, or because the preferential trading agreements of other countries are more favourable. Small island nations and land-locked countries burdened by supply-side constraints (e.g. insufficient labour, expensive inputs, and poor infrastructure) are typically at risk (Adhikari and Yamamoto 2007). A second source of concern is the potentially negative impact on workers' rights and codes of conduct if production were to be more concentrated in China, where labour exploitation is regarded as widespread (see Chapter 10).

And yet, not all the countries estimated to be at risk have in fact lost out. The Sri Lankan, Cambodian, and Bangladeshi garment industries, which are the biggest contributors to exports and employment in those countries, have survived surprisingly well the removal of quotas. Some observers attribute this success primarily to the temporary 'safeguards' imposed by the USA and EU on imports from Chinese producers (*Just-Style* 2007*b*), although others have questioned the actual impact of the safeguards on EU imports from China (Brocklehurst and Anson 2007). Indeed, the Bangladesh knitwear sector achieved an impressive 31 per cent growth in exports in 2005, and in the previously quota-restricted US market it has performed extremely well in the 2005–07 period. This suggests that quotas had restrained exports from Bangladesh more than had been presumed in the pessimistic forecasts made before January 2005 (World Bank 2006*b*).

Consolidation of the supplier base by western clothing firms is an additional, related concern at the firm level. The removal of quotas is encouraging firms to reduce the number of factories with which they work, as well as the number of countries they source from. Liz Claiborne, for example, expects to cut its manufacturing base from 300 factories in 40 countries to 120 factories in 15–20 countries over the next few years (Clark and Tucker 2006). The suppliers that remain on the list will assume greater responsibilities for functions currently still conducted in the USA, including colour approval and even final sample approval. Other observers suggest an even more dramatic streamlining of supplier lists is in progress: some American customers are said to have reduced the number of suppliers from over 1,000 to just 200. This process of consolidation points to the prospect of substantial consolidation in the industry, with an increasing likelihood of smaller manufacturers partnering with larger firms to avoid the cost pressures placed on them by more powerful customers (Ho 2007). But at the same time the transfer of additional functions from, typically, US customers to bigger manufacturing suppliers will require closer, probably more collaborative, relationships than have typically been found hitherto (Clark and Tucker 2006). While evidence does exist of European firms reducing their supplier base (e.g. GER-C-5), the phenomenon of consolidation appears far more marked among US firms.

From the perspective of supplier countries, proximity to an important market can over the medium to longer term prove to be a double-edged sword. On the one hand a supplier country should be in a strong position to benefit from increasingly important quick turn and replenishment activity, particularly if fabric procurement is both rapid and at acceptable cost, as Turkey but to a lesser extent Mexico achieved. But on the other hand, as the experience of Mexico and several Central American states has shown, there are strong risks attached to heavy dependence on a single market, either because of fluctuations in demand owing to economic downturn or because buyers/importers become so exacting that it becomes impossible for firms to operate profitably. The more diversified customer base developed by Asian countries including China, Vietnam, Cambodia, India, and Bangladesh at least offers the opportunity to balance the demands of different customers.

What, then, are the possibilities for supplier countries to retain their place in the international hierarchy of clothing suppliers to the developed world? The Cambodian government with the help of the ILO and the World Bank is emphasizing social responsibility as a strategy to protect its clothing industry against the migration risk, by promoting and demonstrating a firm commitment to high labour standards (Sajhou 2005). Western buyers including The Gap, Nike, and H&M are reported to be supporters of this initiative. An alternative strategy at the individual firm level is that followed by the Sri Lankan lingerie producer MAS: it is emphasizing environmentally friendly development by building what it describes as the world's first carbon-neutral clothing factory which, among other initiatives, relies on hydro- and solar-power for its energy requirements (*Economist* 31 May 2008). Built at the instigation of Marks & Spencer, the factory is not only an experiment in eco-branding but also represents a means for a supplier in a relatively expensive location to carve out a particular high value-added niche in an otherwise crowded industry.

More generally, the removal of quotas has thrown into sharper relief differences in the economic infrastructure of supplier countries. Tariffs remain in place and can exercise a powerful influence over sourcing patterns while potentially affording considerable advantages to beneficiary countries. But preferential market access alone has clearly been shown to be an insufficient advantage in a quota-free world. Mexico, for example, has largely shown itself unable to compete with China on full package supply to the US market: almost every factory that attempted this strategy was forced to abandon it (Bair and Dussel Peters 2006).[19] Hence in-country upgrading of managerial and organizational skills has emerged as an important factor in the shifting international hierarchy of the clothing industry. The reduction of non-labour costs, including the streamlining of customs procedures and other administrative tasks, is a potentially powerful investment incentive for domestic and foreign entrepreneurs alike. And, with lead times increasingly important due to retailers' replenishment requirements, proximity to a competitive textile industry represents a significant advantage for clothing producers since it reduces the procurement costs of fabric. Also crucial are efficient transportation and logistics facilities, since inputs and finished garments are useless unless they can reach their destinations in timely fashion.

NOTES

1. A key differentiating factor between clothing producers in industrialized nations and those in developing countries is that the former primarily serve their national markets and perhaps other countries within their regional grouping whereas developing country producers are overwhelmingly dependent on export markets because their domestic markets are generally small (due to low purchasing power) and poorly organized.

2. American and European buying groups fall very loosely into this category, but the networks they build operate differently since they are constructed around neither ethnic nor linguistic commonalities. Examples include New York-based AMC, which is now owned by and focused on supply to the Target group although it previously also served Marshall Fields and other US retailers, and the US company Mast Industries which was bought in 1978 by the Limited Brands group (owner, *inter alia*, of the Victoria's Secret lingerie business). Approximately one-third of Mast Industries' turnover of over US$1 billion derives from non-Limited Brands sourcing activity, according to an investor briefing by Limited Brands executives in November 2007. It has over 400 factory relationships, many in Asia (where nearly two-thirds of its 950 staff are located) and an apparently decreasing number in Central America and Africa. German-based KATAG is Europe's largest fashion buying group, serving 380 independent or regional retailers. Its revenues of €665 million in 2007 are well below the €1 billion generated in the 1960s, when Germany's independent retail sector was stronger (see also Chapter 4), but the existence of such buying groups has been an important factor in the survival of the independent sector.

3. See http://www.newtimesgroup.com
4. See http://www.linmark.com/index_f.html
5. This section draws principally on De Meyer et al. (2005) and Magretta (1998), in addition to the company website http://www.lifunggroup.com/heritage/heritage04.htm
6. In 1985 the retail arm, comprising the Asian operations of Toys 'R' USA and Circle K, was hived off as a separate company.
7. Inchcape was a *hong*, a British-owned trading company based in Hong Kong with business interests in other colonies or former colonies.
8. See http://www.nht.com.tw/en/nh.php
9. See http://www.boolim.com
10. See http://www.esquel.com
11. See http://www1.talgroup.com/en/index.html
12. See http://www.luenthai.com
13. Between the mid-1980s, when 60% of clothing exports flowed to the USA and 15% to the EU, and the mid-1990s, when exports were split 20/30/10% between the USA, the EU, and Japan, the Indonesian industry also underwent a marked shift in foreign trade structure, driven by the tightening of US quotas. Here we see an example of accelerating clothing exports from an individual developing country prompting the manipulative use by a developed nation state of trade regimes in order to protect powerful lobby group interests.
14. They are not entirely absent, however. Two joint ventures with the Korean firms Daewoo and Youngone Corp are credited with enabling the rapid development of the Bangladeshi garment industry in the early 1980s. An estimated 15% of firms, mostly located in the Dhaka export processing zone, have some foreign equity.
15. Back-to-back letters of credit (LC) enable a firm to use the overseas buyer's LC to open a second LC with its local bank to cover the cost of importing the necessary inputs to complete the order.
16. Yoruk (2001) goes on to point out that most big CEE firms leverage the knowledge they have gained of European fabric suppliers while working for European buyers to source similar fabrics for use in their own brand-name production.
17. A portion of Lesotho's tiny EU exports is said to comprise merchandise for The Gap's store chain there.

18. In contrast to the Lesotho case Mauritius did have some textile knitting mills to supply local industry and hence became the principal sub-Saharan African exporter to the EU under the ACP (Gibbon 2008).
19. Worse, several American textile firms that established mills in Mexico to facilitate upstream linkages and shorten production cycles went bankrupt, including Burlington, Guilford, and Cone Mills.

7

The Global Production Networks of US, UK, and German Firms

This chapter surveys the factors that have given rise to foreign sourcing and analyses the divergent manner in which national institutional environments, as well as international regulatory bodies, have shaped the coordination and governance of global production networks (GPNs). We show how, in building GPNs, firms' various strategic concerns, particularly cost reduction, flexibility (in terms of capacity variation), and management of the extremely volatile competitive environment, have interacted with both domestic and global institutional opportunities and constraints, to result in a complex web of influences. Among institutional influences in the home countries of firms, it was shown in Chapter 3, those moulding employee capabilities and therefore product paradigm are of particular importance. The nationally diverse capabilities and resources of domestic retail customers, we have shown in Chapter 4, additionally exert a strong influence on power relations in the GPN.

The clothing industry is a highly labour-intensive industry in which wages for relatively lowly skilled workers account for a significant share of the production costs. With intensification of competitive pressures from low-wage countries (see Figure 7.1), the manufacturing function has relocated to lower-wage countries all over the globe. Additionally, some pre-production functions, as well as quality control and distribution, have become candidates for outsourcing, particularly among companies in the USA. At the same time, from the 1990s onwards, the new pressure from retailers for fast-response supply has prompted some efforts at re-integration of the value chain. Most coordinating firms are finding the conflicting pressures of disintegration and re-integration through ownership or increased control over suppliers a huge challenge, both in terms of organizational and locational choices. They find it difficult to combine flexibility of supply with the deepened commitment quick response retailing entails. (A discussion of 'manufacturers'' attempts to achieve forward integration into retail is provided in Chapter 3.)

The diagram of the clothing industry value chain (see Figure 2.1) shows the various segments which can, in principle, be outsourced to independent suppliers. In addition to considerations around labour costs and market volatility, the geographical focus and control of global production networks (GPNs) have been shaped by the cost and availability of quota (until January 2005), tariffs (see Chapter 5), and the location of fabric producers. As fabric is the largest component

Figure 7.1. Garment industry costs per working minute in different countries (in Euros), 2003

of final product cost and influences the garment's quality and fashion value, as well as determining lead time, proximity of good fabric producers to garment assemblers (suppliers) is a very important determinant of the way in which GPNs are constructed. Co-location of fabric producers and assemblers has acquired enhanced importance since the introduction of 'fast fashion' and 'lean retailing' (see Chapter 4). Cost calculations interact in complex ways with considerations around quality, punctuality of delivery, and lead time reduction. Finally, the capability of suppliers, particularly their ability to produce 'full package' fast-fashion products, completes the complex mix of requirements which determine the overall sourcing strategy and locational choices of buyer firms.

Bearing in mind these influences, this section first considers the general sourcing strategies of US, UK, and German coordinating firms and then explores the nature of supplier relationships along a number of important, largely qualitative dimensions. Drawing on both survey information and our own qualitative data, our analysis of GPNs affords an unprecedented insight into the reasoning behind strategy. Additionally, and more important, our theoretical focus on the relational aspect of GPNs entails an analysis of the quality of relations with suppliers. This includes such aspects as selection and control, length of relationship and degree of commitment and reciprocity, as well as the imbalance of power between coordinating firms and their suppliers. The resulting configurations are not static. The elimination of quota (for details, see Chapter 6), together with more incremental developments in both developing countries and domestic clothing markets, also necessitate a brief exploration of recent changes in general strategy.

In the fashion industry, buyer–supplier interaction is not concerned with standardized goods and highly codified information. Garments, particularly in the fashion segment, are continually changing in both form and appearance. Thus, although this is a low-tech industry, the interchange between buyer and supplier cannot be described by the term 'modular', borrowed, for example, by Faust et al. (2004), from writing on value chain governance in the electronics industry. The competences externalized by coordinating firms may be described as fairly standard. In principle, they facilitate the easy substitution of one supplier by another. But suppliers nevertheless have complementary capabilities. The quantitative coordination of output volume and the qualitative coordination of product features, all under intense time pressure, could not take place purely through market links. They require a degree of cooperation. But as mutual commitment between buyers and suppliers is not high in this industry, technical coordination requirements and quality of buyer–supplier relationships stand in constant tension.

Supplier relations thus are subject to contradictory pressures and hence are informed by an incongruous mixture of attitudes and expectations on the part of coordinating firms. On the one hand, there is the need for close coordination to develop acceptable product and process standards and to cultivate longer term and cooperative relations. But on the other hand, coordinating firms constantly endeavour to hold or preferably reduce the level of product cost—compelled by the relentless pressure for price reduction from retailers, especially for firms in the competitive lower to middle market segments. Therefore in many ways a purely transactional mode of contracting is practised, with little acceptance of mutual obligation. While this paradoxical make-up was identified *within* many relationships, we also found differences in weight given to each element *between* different coordinating firms and countries of origin, depending on product strategy. The supplier responses to buyer firms' demands for commitment, without guaranteeing reciprocity, are explored in Chapters 8 and 9.

7.1. TYPES OF STRATEGIES AND MODES OF SOURCING

To understand the sourcing strategies of coordinating firms and the nature of resulting GPNs, we briefly consider two of their basic elements: 1. the varying combinations of in-house and third-party manufacturing, either domestically or off-shore and 2. the mode of third-party contracting, with each mode implying not only different cost structures and lead times but also variation in the degree of control over the final product and in the nature of the supplier relationship.

Three basic variants of the make-or-buy decision may be utilized by coordinating firms. They are practised in either pure or dominant form or, more often, in some combination:

a. Retaining production in the home country, either in self-owned production facilities or by engaging in domestic outsourcing;
b. Retaining the manufacturing function in fully or partially owned production facilities, through FDI/joint ventures in lower wage countries;
c. Manufacturing to order by third-party contractors, with or without an agent as intermediary, predominantly in low-wage countries.

When we examine the mode of third-party sourcing, at least three important distinctions have to be made.

i. Cut–make–trim (CMT)—this mode leaves the buying of fabric and trim in the hands of the coordinating firm, together with other pre-assembly operations such as producing sample products and managing the technical aspects of constructing the garment. (Very often this mode entails only the 'cut and make' [CM] functions or even the mere assembly of pre-cut parts, but we will nevertheless use the term CMT.) In Europe, it is often described as outward processing trade (OPT) in the context of overseas sourcing, in reference to its (now defunct) implications for customs duty. In the USA, the reference is to 'production sharing' or *maquiladora* production, to indicate that mere assembly is entailed. The disadvantage of the CMT mode for coordinating firms is that it requires them to make substantial pre-manufacturing investment in the buying of fabric and trim, as well as lengthening the total lead time. On the positive side, it affords coordinating firms a greater input in determining the look, quality, and fit of the product. This mode is therefore most common among branded firms with a manufacturing legacy or 'branded manufacturers'. It relieves the supplier of considerable investment risk, but also deprives him of opportunities to master all the elements of the manufacturing process. It thus diminishes his control, as well as his opportunity to develop experience and skills. Firms in low-wage countries are left as mere assemblers who mainly supply labour and coordinate the labour process. In other words, upgrading of supplier capabilities is not fostered. However, if this strategy is combined with extensive training efforts by the buyer firm such as occurs, for example, in relations between German buyers and Turkish or Romanian supplier firms, notable cases of upgrading nevertheless take place. (Examples are Mavi Jeans and Sarar in Turkey, and J&R Enterprises Group in Romania.)

ii. Full package (FP) is a loose term indicating the assumption of a variety of manufacturing and buying functions by the supplier. But at a crucial minimum, it means that the coordinating company no longer buys the fabric and trim, although it may retain a greater or lesser degree of influence over its purchasing. The fabric is paid for by and goes directly to the supplier, cutting out one level of mediation and thus reducing lead time, as well as lowering coordinating firms' investment costs. It is thus prominently associated with the adoption of the 'quick turn' model in retailing and the demands on clothing firms entailed by this development. It is popular among pure marketers that lack any manufacturing experience. Additional functions taken over by 'full package' suppliers may include development and distribution functions, as well as such pre-production functions as grading and pattern making. Full-package sourcing thus may turn western 'manufacturers' into mere marketers or sometimes wholesalers. The 'full package' mode, where fabric is bought as close as possible to the manufacturing process, favours those countries in the international division of labour which have both viable textile and garment-assembly industries. As the spread of full-package sourcing has been significantly influenced by the growing demand of retailers for 'fast response' fashion, a trend towards a stronger adoption of this mode has been notable in all three countries (Adler 2003; Interview Notes 2003–04). This has introduced significant shifts in order flows between supplier countries and has brought about a reconfiguration of GPNs. It is facilitated and further amplified by the end of the WTO-imposed quota system, as well as by the growing capabilities and financial resources among the larger supplier firms.

iii. Full service sourcing—direct buying of the finished product without any or with greatly reduced prior input by the western firm—is currently used by coordinating firms mainly for very basic garments or for 'filler' items in collections, often as accessories to products designed and developed in house. It is, however, a prevalent strategy among large retailers. This strategy presumes a high level of competence and know-how among suppliers and facilitates their transformation into 'own brand' producers.

Our interviews made evident that firms mostly carefully deliberate on the several options outlined above, weighing up the gains of a particular strategy against losses entailed. They relate make-or-buy decisions and the mode of sourcing to their available resources and to their strategic goals. But we also found some cases where firms simply continued practices they were familiar and comfortable with, such as continuing in-house production because they were loath to relinquish full control.

Although a good deal of commonality exists in the way UK, German, and US coordinating firms utilize and combine these two elements of strategy—make-or-buy at home or off-shore and mode of sourcing—the following account predominantly highlights the more interesting contrasts. These differences, it must be reiterated, are primarily differences between 'manufacturers' of own-brand garments, branded marketers, and suppliers of domestic retailers' 'private label' garments. Thus, for example, up-market designer firms have a different strategy from that of firms producing solely 'private label' garments for large retailers. However, certain types were more likely to be found in a particular national industry, influenced by the domestic institutional environment. Diversity within a given variety of capitalism also was found around the decision to off-shore. In all three countries, there was a very small minority of manufacturers who, for ethical reasons, continued to manufacture at home. Lack of off-shoring may additionally indicate a lack of financial and organizational resources, as is the case with many of the smaller firms in the US industry (Bonacich and Applebaum 2000).

7.2. SOURCING STRATEGIES OF GERMAN COORDINATING FIRMS

German firms already began to abandon strategy a. (production in fully owned or third-party manufacturing in Germany) from the late 1960s/early1970s onwards (Froebel, Heinrichs, and Kreye 1980; Heidenreich 1990). (Many firms had practised domestic outsourcing during the 1960s and 1970s. They used the so-called *Zwischenmeister* [very small production units led by a qualified craftsman], often located in the economically less buoyant and hence less expensive border regions of Germany which enjoyed some government subsidies [Interview Notes 2003; Morokvasic et al. 1986].) According to Froebel et al. (1980: 111), 70 per cent of firms in the clothing industry in 1974–75 were already involved in production abroad. But it is vital to view this figure with some caution. Very few manufacturers outsourced all their production, preferring instead a mixed strategy. Most, in fact, pursued relocation of production to low-wage countries hesitantly and as a very gradual process (Interview Notes 2003; Schuessler 2008). During the 1960s increased rationalization of domestic production, in the form of more centralized and more efficient factories, was tried to stave off relocation of manufacturing (Morokvasic et al. 1986; Schuessler 2008: 138, 140).

This early withdrawal of manufacturing from Germany was negotiated with, and not opposed by, the then *Textil and Bekleidung* (Textiles and Clothing) union. There was insufficient demand among their members for these relatively low-skilled and low-paid jobs, and relocation at least saved higher level jobs. Thus foreign sourcing at that time did not occur primarily in search of lower wages but to escape a tight labour market (Heidenreich 1990: 199). Off-shoring additionally was supported by the German state in the form of the German Development Society (*Deutsche Entwicklungsgesellschaft*), which viewed both FDI and outsourcing as development aid (Froebel et al. 1980: 167f.). From the 1970s onwards, however, rising wages and social costs became more of an issue. Since 1974 German governments have advocated the surrender of low-tech industries in favour of higher-tech production (Schuessler 2008: 148). Moreover, retailers strongly favour a more liberal foreign trade regime, and German governments found this preference more consonant with their own policy stance. In competition for state support by different fractions of capital, the clothing industry usually lost out.

Hence the demise of clothing manufacturing in Germany did not occur in the 1970s and 1980s but in a long drawn-out process of gradual attrition (see Chapter 3). In the early 1980s, domestic in-house production still amounted to 62.8 per cent (Adler and Breitenacher 1984, cited by Heidenreich 1990: 197). By 1993, 31.5 per cent of all production still occurred in Germany, most of it (25.6%) in-house (Adler 2004: 35, table 11). The majority of firms in our sample, too, had withdrawn from Germany very gradually, and most sought to maintain a mixed strategy of domestic production and outsourcing for a long time. Some firms were in the process of relinquishing their last fully owned domestic operations in the early years of the twenty-first century. This gradual and negotiated withdrawal ensured that the impact on domestic production and employees was not as drastic as it was in the UK and, to a slightly lesser degree, in the USA.

Three firms (one a fully vertically integrated textile and clothing manufacturer [GER-C-12]) either maintained a fully owned, exclusively domestic production facility or continued to produce a small part (16–18%) of output in that way (GER-C-11). This strategy was informed by sentiments of social obligation to their locality. A third firm was contemplating closure of its remaining relatively large German factory at the time of our visit and since then has executed this plan (GER-C-10). Additionally, a relatively large multinational firm continues to manufacture in fully owned subsidiaries spread over three continents and retains a small, somewhat symbolic, amount of production at its original German site (GER-C-4). Such regional rootedness and feeling of responsibility to the traditional production locality were seen as fairly typical on the part of *Mittelstand* clothing firms. (See also Schuessler 2008: 11.)

The one firm which still manufactured 100 per cent in Germany and in-house (GER-C-12) was able to remain viable through a combination of strategies and circumstances. The family enterprise had low outgoings: it had an extremely lean management team and relied only on internally generated profits; it practised a dual market strategy of flexible small batch production for niche customers (e.g. supplying a sports club with a special logo T-shirt at short notice) and selling larger batches in its own retail units in rural areas, akin to factory outlets; the firm advertised heavily on television, capitalizing on its exceptional status as a firm and production site loyal to Germany; and, being in a very remote rural area, the firm still was able to recruit lower-level employees. According to Schuessler (2008: 207), this firm was viewed by other enterprises as an incomprehensible exception and not as a role model.

Residual manufacturing capacity in Germany is dedicated to the handling of last-minute and special tasks, and to core manufacturing for the preparation and support of foreign production (Adler 2004). Small workshops for the preparation of sample garments remain relatively common. Domestic sourcing for short runs and re-orders in Germany is said to be infrequent, presumably due to the absence of an informal sector and a segmented labour market, and instead occurs mainly in neighbouring CEE countries (Donath 2004). However, a few of our German respondents mentioned replenishment and repair activity in the home country (BBI Interview 2003; GER-C-11).Data from a larger interview sample in 2002 (Adler 2003: 74, table 1) estimated the proportion of turnover from in-house domestically produced garments to be 17 per cent. But this estimate seems rather high. The industry association, the BBI, put the proportion as low as 5 per cent for the same year (BBI Interview 2003), and this lower estimate was confirmed by industry experts in 2007 (Schuessler 2008: 121)—leaving Germany with the lowest domestic production volume of the three countries in this study.

Strategy (b), setting up fully owned or joint venture (a rare choice) manufacturing facilities in lower wage countries, had been adopted by only a small minority of the German firms interviewed. There was no firm adhering solely, and only one dominantly, to this strategy. This result concurs with Adler's (2003) findings. It is also confirmed by the industry association, which attributes the lack of popularity of this strategy to the poor experience German firms had when they invested in Portugal in the late 1950s (GER-C-14). Where some FDI had occurred, Central and Eastern European countries had been the main destinations. The strategy of manufacturing in fully owned subsidiaries is motivated either by a reluctance to relinquish control or by a wish to utilize the substantial machine park of the formerly sizeable German facilities that had been closed down. The foreign facility was sometimes viewed as a competence centre, utilized to train third-party suppliers and to work out a cost-efficient 'best practice' for suppliers to follow. On the debit side, this strategy was widely seen to seriously restrict flexibility of geographical movement and of response to new fashion trends, as well as entailing maintenance and employment costs during periods of lull in the fashion and production cycles. In other words, even German 'manufacturers' regarded a fully owned production facility as a mere cost or even liability—a stance which is difficult to square with the emphasis on manufacturing strength identified by Varieties of Capitalism theory in coordinated market economies.

Strategy (c), use of third-party suppliers in lower-wage countries, is by far the most frequently used by German firms. This strategy was evident not only in our own sample but has been identified also by another more quantitative study (Adler 2003). The popularity of the foreign sourcing option rests on the following reasons. It offers a high degree of flexibility and sufficient, even if not complete, control as well as a low tie-up of capital. (However, contracting for German firms was not necessarily a cheap alternative as, due to their interest in high-quality production facilities, investment was always involved.) Flexibility mostly refers to the freedom to move from one supplier or country to another, as well as to the ability to vary production capacity. Because German firms have, on average, much higher turnover than their UK counterparts and also retain less in-house production in foreign subsidiaries, they have significantly larger supplier networks—up to 100 very big suppliers and many additional speciality ones in the case of one of the largest firms. In comparison with the larger US clothing firms, however, neither turnover nor number of suppliers are very big. (For details, see Table 7.1 in this chapter.)

Concerning the mode of third-party contracting by German coordinating firms, CMT (also referred to as outward processing (OPT) or as *Lohnveredelung*) has been by far their most prevalent strategy, and one that has gained in importance since the end of the 1980s (Adler 2003: 74, table 1). The ratio of OPT to national production in Germany grew from 13 per cent in 1989 to 29 per cent in 1996 (Baldone et al. 2000), and in 1998 Germany had by far the largest share in terms of value of outward processed clothing among major European countries (Dunford and Greco 2005). As this involves coordinating firms in the buying of fabric and trim, the making of sample garments and in the specification of the more technical aspects of garment manufacturing, it gives them control over the appearance, fit, and quality of the garment. This is a course of action congruent with the possession of manufacturing competence and an emphasis on all-round quality and branding. But it also is a strategy that entails a longer lead time and a higher investment risk. The degree of power asymmetry which may be entailed in a 'cut and make' relationship is vividly indicated by Tokatli (2007: 81) in her analysis of the relationship between the then German Hugo Boss and Turkish Sarar: 'Thus Hugo Boss exerted pricing control; ... dictated the specifications of suits; decided when and how these suits were manufactured; and ... exerted asymmetric information control with regard to research, design, sales and marketing issues'. Yet, given the traditional skilled craftsmanship of German firms and the extensive training efforts expended by them, this strategy by no means excluded upgrading by suppliers to 'own brand' manufacturing. (See, for example, the case of Mavi Jeans outlined in Chapter 8 on Turkey, as well as the case of Sarar in Tokatli 2007.)

In distant second place have come both the 'full package' and the 'full-service' strategies (Adler 2003: 74, table 1). Our own data broadly confirm Adler's findings. One large German firm (GER-C-2) was unique among our interviewees in using the FP mode exclusively. This firm, which had become a successful retailer, had always operated as a wholesaler and its CEO for a long time had worked in the USA. Another very large 'manufacturer', Gerry Weber (not among our interviewees), has been successful at forward integration into retail and is also a strong 'full package' user. The FP strategy seems to be destined for further increase in future, as sourcing in the Far East increases. Whether resorting to FP supply will entail some surrender of control over garment quality and appearance will depend on the degree of involvement that firms manage to retain in the selection (rather than buying) of fabric and trim. Another strong pressure towards full package sourcing, the turn to 'fast fashion', was less evident in the German than the UK and US clothing firms although it was not totally absent.

Our data also indicate that 'full package' was significantly more important than the 'direct buying' or 'full service' mode where the firm imports clothing without providing prototypes. This model, if used at all, was only to supplement the main strategy in a small way. Our finding is also supported by Schuessler (2008: 181), who interviewed an entirely different set of German 'manufacturers' in 2007. Our findings additionally show that German firms are less likely than UK and US firms to use agents to source either fabric or garments. An explanation for this may be their stronger capital base, as compared with their UK counterparts, and a stronger manufacturing legacy than is found among US firms. Schuessler (2008: 225), who confirms the lack of use of agents among German firms, plausibly attributes this phenomenon to firms' quest for retaining control.

This overview of the sourcing strategies of German firms still shows the imprint of the German variety of capitalism, particularly in the enduringly strong concentration on the CMT mode and the relatively low incidence of full-package and -service sourcing. But the surrender of ownership control and in-house manufacturing and the preparedness, at intervals, to move between countries in search of lower wages are more consistent with a liberal-market approach. It shows the victory of independent business strategy over habitual ways of conducting business.

7.3. SOURCING STRATEGIES OF UK COORDINATING FIRMS

In the UK, systematic studies of make-or-buy decisions by coordinating firms and associated strategies about location and mode of sourcing are not available. We therefore rely mainly on our interviews and on statistics from the trade association to present an account. In contrast to German firms, outsourcing of manufacturing to low-wage countries started very late, from the mid-1990s onwards (BATC 2003). During our interviews in 2003, the last vestiges of domestic in-house production were being/had just been surrendered, and we found not one firm making a substantial share of clothing in-house. The withdrawal from manufacturing in the UK thus occurred within a remarkably short period of time and in a comparatively rapid manner. It therefore exerted a very negative impact on employment, particularly in the regions where there had been high concentrations of the industry. The conflictual manner of withdrawal of manufacturing from the UK was very evident, for example, when Burberry closed its last factory in a deprived part of Wales in 2007. Although job losses were relatively small, union representatives joined with MPs and pop stars to stage a demonstration of protest which made the national news (*Guardian* 31 March 2007: 9). Hence strategy (a). (retaining manufacturing domestically in either fully owned or third-party facilities) was as underdeveloped in our British as our German sample of firms. The only firm still fully manufacturing in-house was a knitwear producer of higher-end products where automated machinery is more important than labour. Another large firm with a long record of family ownership and a sense of responsibility to the locality had closed most sites only in 2002 and still held on to one small operation. Its owner justified these decisions in the following terms: 'you can't abandon everything overnight ... it's not all about chasing the dollar' (UK-C-3). Unfortunately, this firm—holding on to a strategy incompatible with an LME environment—has since ceased to trade.

But this picture of the end of domestic production is a partial one. Industry sources reminded us that domestic manufacturing is by no means uncommon in the UK. It continues among the smaller, mostly ethnic minority-owned firms in the informal sector, to which we gained no access. This sector has a long history in the UK, starting with Russian and Polish Jewish immigrants to the East End of London in the late nineteenth century. The sector was revived in the 1970s when fresh waves of immigration from the Commonwealth supplied both new small entrepreneurs and new workers (Morokvasic et al. 1986: 408, 411). Firms in this sector often have several tiers of their own suppliers and use home work (Warren 2003). Pay at or even below the minimum wage, plus few social payments, sustains this practice (UK-R-3; KFAT et al. 2000; Warren 2003; Williams 2005). But it is not clear which part of the market these firms are now supplying. Oxborrow (2005) points out that the UK has become unimportant as a provider of quick/flexible and fashionable clothing, although several retailers still acquire a significant proportion of their clothes domestically (see Chapter 4, on retail). The prevalence of this informal sector, and the late surrender of the 'Buy British' policy by Marks & Spencer, are two reasons why strategy a) continued so much longer in the UK. Thus the following remark by Berger (2005: 43) does not at all apply when considering the historical take-up of outsourcing in the UK: 'Less dependent on relationships in their home country for vital assets, more confident about using the market to buy the necessary resources, companies from liberal market economies are primed for the world of fragmentation and outsourcing'.

FDI in lower-wage countries (strategy b) in order to retain an in-house sewing facility was more prevalent than in the German sample. It was found to be the dominant strategy mainly among the larger firms that supply exclusively to Marks & Spencer. The rationale for this course of action is best expressed in the words of one of these firms: 'If we didn't own the factories I'd be sitting here and I'd be worried ... Otherwise what value do I add if I am going to a third party? I am only a middleman, so why doesn't the customer [Marks & Spencer] go direct?' (UK-C-10). Paradoxically a large retailer, while understanding the motives of Marks & Spencer suppliers, expressed this view on ownership: 'the big bit in the middle [of the value chain], manufacturing, nobody's actually very interested in owning that anymore' (UK-R-1). The positive side of ownership was deemed to be the retention of greater control, for example, retaining flexibility in response to sudden changes in demand, and never having the fear of being relegated to the end of the queue in favour of a customer with a bigger order. When asked about the negative aspects of ownership, namely, being tied to a location where wage levels could rise, two respondents declared their preparedness to move again: 'Closing things down is a core skill, unfortunately' (UK-C-4). These two UK firms thus displayed an incongruous mixture of ownership commitment and a very loose attachment to their factories, viewing them effectively like contractors.

Strategy (c), outsourcing to independent third-party suppliers in lower-wage countries, was favoured by a majority of UK firms as either the dominant or a supplementary strategy. In contrast to the situation in German and US firms, the number of each firm's third-party contractors was much smaller, ranging from only one supplier to at most 10. There also was a greater tendency than among German firms to use agents, particularly in the Far East, because the greater shortage of capital and human resources had not allowed the same degree of professionalization of supply chain management. The reasons for choosing outsourcing, although largely similar to those given by German firms, also differed subtly in regarding manufacturing as an unnecessary evil. Some firms simply did not want the organizational burden of having in-house manufacturing: 'I am not in the business of trying to run offshore manufacturing. It's hard enough trying to sell, you know' (UK-C-6) or '[We] don't have the overheads, the warehousing, the headaches, the staffing' (UK-C-1). Others welcomed the flexibility this mode implied, such as being able to accommodate a sudden increase in capacity (UK-C-4).

General statistics indicate a comparatively low use of outward processing (or CMT) by UK firms: OPT of clothing in 1998, to the value of €444 million, was small compared with Germany's €3,196 million (Dunford and Greco 2005). As Baldone et al. (2000) note, it is the strong currency countries that made greater use of OPT relative to their domestic production than weaker currency nations. Firms in our sample that used mainly third-party contractors utilized a mixture of CMT and full package (FP), with somewhat higher recourse to FP than among German firms. Several firms still in the CMT mode indicated that they wished to move towards FP in the future. The reasons for the growing popularity of this mode were varied, but the fact that it reduced the necessity of longer term capital investment weighed heavily (e.g. UK-C-9). Where clothing firms are supplying to a dominant retailer, the choice of fabrics in any case has never been fully their responsibility but one they have shared with the large retailer customer. According to Baden and Velia (2002: 66),the UK also has relied quite strongly on direct import.

To sum up, the late development of outsourcing in the UK was connected with both a lowly regulated labour market segmented by gender and ethnicity and a paternalistic attitude vis-à-vis domestic suppliers by the dominant UK retailer, Marks & Spencer. The two dominant sourcing strategies of UK firms were also shaped by domestic institutional influences and market demands. Whereas suppliers to Marks & Spencer felt compelled to invest in their own production facilities to retain the control their exclusive customer required, most other firms retained relatively low indirect control over the final product—consistent with diversified mass production of 'private label' clothing for low- to middle-market domestic retailer customers. Retention of own manufacturing in foreign subsidiaries was not allied to an ownership mentality but was combined with a distant, market-type relationship compatible with an LME institutional environment. Additionally, the influence of the UK financial system was evident in the fact that coordinating firms—excepting the big Marks & Spencer suppliers—were relatively small and lowly endowed with both financial resources and managerial capacity.

7.4. SOURCING STRATEGIES OF US COORDINATING FIRMS

In the USA, as in Germany, outsourcing began, according to most sources, from the 1970s onwards. However Liz Claiborne, widely seen as the pioneer of foreign sourcing, only started down this route in the *late* 1970s. Hence a significant move to off-shoring only got under way during the 1980s, significantly later than in Germany. According to our interviews and to secondary accounts, it was not the same gradual process as in Germany. Instead, abandonment of domestic manufacturing by large firms accelerated greatly during the 1990s, probably due to the back-loading of compliance with the stipulations of the WTO's Agreement on Textiles and Clothing for important categories of garments. Thus in the USA, though somewhat less than in the UK, there occurred a more concentrated and rushed withdrawal from domestic manufacturing. This caused disruption and hardship in the regions where textiles and clothing had been concentrated. (For details, see Chapter 3.) In contrast to the situation in the UK, it provoked a backlash by voters and pressure on the government to intervene by their Congressmen.

US firms, particularly branded marketers without a manufacturing tradition, have also abandoned strategy (a), manufacturing domestically. 'Manufacturers', however, similar to German companies, have closed their own plants very gradually, many only in the 2000s. Thus Levi Strauss, the oldest blue jeans producer, for example, and a family firm with a social conscience (Esbenshade 2004: 23), had long resisted closure of domestic plants but felt compelled to close its last North

American plants by 2004 (Hoovers 28 September 2005). The domestic share of US apparel consumption (dollar basis) was 10.7 per cent in 2005, down from 16.2 per cent in 2003 (AAFA 2006: 2).

There is one medium-sized LA firm in the US sample (US-C-8)—remarkably similar to the one vertically integrated German firm—which for social reasons still manufactured domestically in-house and used this as a prime marketing point. The firm managed to maintain this strategy of vertical integration, despite its low-end products (T-shirts) and without resorting to sweatshop methods, through being highly responsive to consumer demand. However, as is the case for its German counterpart, distribution to final consumers is a problem. (This firm has since been acquired by a publicly traded investment company.) The remaining three medium-sized firms (one of which has now been acquired by a very large firm) still did 20, 30–40, and 90 per cent, respectively of their sourcing domestically, in the Los Angeles garment district. US-C-2 believed that simple styles of CMT jeans were done most economically in the USA, as well as achieving quickest time to store. The other two smaller firms (US-C-3 and US-C-5) and three of the larger firms (US-C-1; US-C-4; US-C-6) also did some residual or 'quick turn' sourcing domestically.

As in the UK, however, a myriad small clothing firms still exist, particularly in the LA and New York clothing districts, which continue to manufacture in the USA. These firms do not appear in our sample. Among the firms retaining their sourcing networks in the USA, according to a study of the Los Angeles Clothing District (Bonacich and Applebaum 2000), small- and medium-sized firms are particularly prominent, and many of them also are predominantly 'private label' producers. Ninety per cent of firms in Los Angeles simply do not have sufficient scale to off-shore, as Mexican supplier companies are not interested in producing small runs of fashion garments (ibid: 70). Nor do such firms have the resources to establish and maintain far-flung GPNs which require significant investment in staff, technology, and network building.

In contrast to German and to a somewhat lesser extent UK practice, domestic sourcing for short runs and replenishment is quite frequent among US coordinating firms, particularly in the NY and LA garment districts (US-C-12), and some domestic fabric sourcing is also more common among US than German and UK firms interviewed. This is due to two reasons: the strong presence of quick turn, flexible, and relatively low-cost firms in the NY and LA garment districts, often run by immigrants with immigrant employees; and because a relatively high proportion of sourcing from the Far East needs to be complemented by some quick-turn sourcing to satisfy retailers' 'lean retailing' strategy (Kessler 2002; Palpacuer 2002; Interview Notes 2003–04; Doeringer 2005). This continued reliance on domestic suppliers also has to be seen in the context of the widely perceived inability of Mexican firms to master the quick turn/small runs strategy (Birnbaum 2004). The use of smaller firms in the informal sector raises the same social issues we have discussed in the UK case.

Strategy (b), manufacturing in fully owned or joint venture manufacturing facilities in lower-wage countries, has largely been avoided by US firms as it entails more risks than contracting (Bonacich and Applebaum 2000: 56; Collins 2003: 49). The low choice of production in foreign subsidiaries is also confirmed by a study of firms in Mexico's Torreon district. Of the 10 largest firms making jeans in Mexico's Torreon district, only 3 were US owned (Gereffi and Memodovic 2003). Manufacturing in foreign subsidiaries was not popular among our sample of US firms and, according to one large UK retailer's comment on the US industry, is becoming less popular as supplier firms are reaching maturity (UK-R-1). Despite their huge power, US retailers cannot influence firms on this aspect, as at least one large retailer does in the UK, since 'private label' manufacturing, among our interviewees, was in no case an exclusive strategy. (For a discussion of retailer power, see Chapter 4.) Some of the branded marketers had never been in manufacturing and thus did not have affiliates devoted to it. Two of the branded marketers without a manufacturing tradition (US-C-1 and US-C-6), explicitly rejected strategy (b). but had some remnants of ownership through recent acquisitions.

Nevertheless, our own further research has shown that manufacturing in fully owned subsidiaries was still practised by a significant number of large firms with a manufacturing legacy. Some had had a long and sometimes strong commitment to it, but, for various reasons, had started to pull out of 'own manufacturing' in foreign subsidiaries during the 1990s and 2000s. Firms such as Levi Strauss and Jones Apparel have abandoned foreign ownership reluctantly as an economic necessity. Levi Strauss, due to declining sales, had closed all but five of its foreign subsidiaries and was outsourcing 90 per cent of production volume in 2005 (Datamonitor 2005). VF, too, still made 38 per cent of its American sales in its own subsidiaries in Mexico and the Caribbean Basin (Company web site 2006). Only one of the eight firms interviewed (US-C-7), which has a manufacturing tradition and has a high-end/high-skill segment among its products, maintained a significant fully owned production facility in Mexico and engaged in systematic technical training. This was said to be cheaper than sourcing garments from China. Its other fully owned factories, however, both in the USA and in Latin America, had been closed recently. Once again, knowledge of the institutional environment of firms' countries of origin and the market orientation it is said to foster was a reliable predictor where 'own manufacturing' was concerned.

Strategy (c), use of third-party suppliers, is by far the most frequently used by US firms. Branded marketers view the management of GPNs as their main skill and the basis of their competitiveness (e.g. US-C-1). Although few interviewees revealed details of their motivations for adoption of this strategy, it is clear that a preoccupation with cost saving is uppermost (US-C-1; US-C-9 [an industry consultancy]). Indeed, the latter respondent speaks of 'competition for the lowest prices, which initiates a race to the bottom' (see also Appelbaum et al. 2005). Additionally, it is evident from sourcing trends that flexibility, that is, the ability to move strategically between suppliers in different countries, is viewed as a strong plus factor for third-party contracting. The relatively high proportion of listed companies makes reduction of capital investment a likely motivator for this strategy. Moreover, the comparatively (relative to European firms) very high order volume of US firms gives them the high degree of control over suppliers normally only realized by ownership. Their volume is indicated by the very high turnover of giant companies like VF and Levi Strauss, with the first having achieved revenues of US$6.5 billion (Hoover's, 28 October 2005) and the second US$4.1 billion in 2004 (Company web site). (See also size ranges on turnover in Chapter 3, Table 3.2.) The number of suppliers for the large firms in the sample ranged between 250 suppliers in 35 countries (US-C-1) and 852 suppliers (including those for material and trim) in 52 countries (Levi Strauss). But a significant reduction of vendors and countries has been planned by many of the larger firms post-2005 (Appelbaum et al. 2005: 5). This reduction was, indeed, confirmed by one of the US firms in our sample (US-C-1), as well as by some Turkish suppliers we interviewed (see Chapter 8).

Concerning the mode of third-party sourcing by US firms, production-sharing has been popular in the past to qualify for the 'reduced tariffs' arrangement, but since NAFTA and a similar Caribbean Basin arrangement in the mid-1990s, this is no longer the main motivation. Nevertheless, according to Gereffi and Memedovic (2003: 29), production sharing endures for the more standardized garments made in the large factories of Mexico, Central America, and the Caribbean Basin— regions where full-package skills are not yet highly developed. But a marked shift towards full-package seems to have occurred, particularly among branded marketers such as Liz Claiborne, Donna Karan, Ralph Lauren, Tommy Hilfiger, and Nautica (Bair and Gereffi 2002). Additionally it is common among providers of retailers' 'own label' garments, although this strategy is less popular among firms with a recent manufacturing tradition (Gereffi and Memedovic 2003: 21). This change in mode of sourcing overlaps with the recent geographical shift in sourcing to China and the utilization, by the large and giant firms, of middleman firms, to strip out extra cost from the value chain (Appelbaum 2008). (See also Chapter 6.) Reducing investment costs is one important motivation for the listed companies, as acknowledged by Liz Claiborne for whom 'full package' had already risen to 93 per cent in 1999 (Collins 2003: 119). Whether these companies nevertheless maintain indirect control over fabric selection is not clear but given the big emphasis on speed of sourcing, it seems unlikely. One large firm informant (US-C-1) stated that, for full package, they could only choose the broad fabric count, not the thread count or the specific mill, except for some high-end products. In contrast, the smaller firms in the sample were not beholden to full package buying (e.g. US-C-2). Two interviewees pointed out the necessity to maintain relationships with mills and other suppliers, and noted that suppliers are more responsive to direct clients (US-C-2; US-C-5)—an attitude more in concert with those found among our German *Mittelstand* firms. We have no information about the importance of 'direct buying', but, given the hands-off stance of branded marketers, it seems highly likely that US firms will have moved in this direction. (Indeed the rise of the network orchestrators and transnational contractors discussed in Chapter 6 substantiates this view.)

More generally the large/giant US firms—in contrast to UK and especially German firms–have since the late 1990s retained in-house merely the functions of design and marketing and sometimes distribution. (An exception to this trend was a maker of garments sewn in-house in Mexico [US-C-7], but even this firm outsourced many functions including fabric converting, printing, and testing.) They no longer retain in-house pre-assembly functions, such as marker making, pattern grading, and sample making, and sometimes they even externalize quality control (US-C-1; US-C-4; US-C-6; Gereffi and Memedovic 2003: 7). 'Pattern making already has been separated out of the apparel design process. It's an art, but a "manufacturing art", and sample making is following' (US-C-11). This extension of outsourcing has been connected with huge cost savings (US-C-1). The process has in part been hastened by advances in CAD technology and the appearance of firms specializing in providing these pre-production functions. Moreover, several informants predicted an intensification of outsourcing of pre-assembly functions in the near future, including even design. 'I told Henry Tang [a big Chinese agent], all I want to do is send him a sketch, and then send him a cheque' (US-C-1). Indeed, the setting up in China of a 'one stop' Supply Chain City, which will lower inventory costs and increase margins, is under discussion (ibid).

A generally more hands-off stance to suppliers, particularly the use of agents, is notable (US-C-6; US-C-1 2003; US-C-6 2003; Gereffi and Memedovic 2003: 20; Appelbaum 2008). While the disadvantages of using agents—a more distant relationship with suppliers and the payment to agents of 7 per cent commission—is inducing some firms such as The Gap to set up their own in-house sourcing bureaux, the trend described above points in a rather different direction.

In conclusion, despite extensive outsourcing comparable to the UK volume and slightly lower than that of German firms, the many SMEs in the Los Angeles and New York clothing districts still remain important in replenishment and 'quick turn' manufacturing. The number of functions externalized by the large US firms is greater than in the other two countries, leaving firms close to becoming mere wholesalers primarily focused on marketing. The influence of powerful retailers and the pressures for shareholder value from investors make cost-saving a prime strategic target of large US firms, and the generally large volume of clothes sourced from any one supplier supports firms in realizing this strategic objective. A comparatively more distant relationship with suppliers completes US firms' more market-oriented sourcing practices which is consonant with Hall and Soskice's LME type. However, the medium-sized firms interviewed differed from the large quoted firms on several aspects of sourcing and were less prone to engage in practices consonant with a LME institutional environment.

7.5. GEOGRAPHICAL LOCATIONS OF PRODUCTION NETWORKS

Locational decisions of firms are influenced by a range of considerations which, furthermore, have altered over time in concert with changing geopolitical and global and regional regulatory influences. While some commentators, for example, Dicken (2007), regard GPNs in this industry as primarily regionally, rather than globally based, we found that this is no longer generally applicable. It is true that there remains a strong regional orientation among firms practising primarily CMT sourcing, such as most German and some British and US firms. Firms based in the two European countries have many suppliers in the countries of CEE and Turkey. But, at the same time, British firms also had a strong focus on South East Asia and North Africa. US firms, while formerly oriented towards Mexico and Caribbean Basin countries for production sharing, in recent years have turned to a significant degree to China and other Asian countries. Thus regionalization may be said to gradually be giving way to more global locational choices. This is particularly true for full-package sourcing, where China has acknowledged strengths, and both Mexico and CEE countries are still lacking. Furthermore, a growing amount of triangle manufacturing also spans continents, as when a Korean supplier company invests in Central America or a Taiwanese company in Africa. (For details, see Chapter 6.)

German firms have a long historical tradition of sourcing in the countries of CEE which well pre-dates the end of communism (Froebel et al. 1980: 100f). In the 1960s and 1970s, Yugoslavia was a very popular location. In the 1980s and 1990s, Poland and Hungary became attractive, whereas currently Romania has become the most popular location. According to surveys of German coordinating firms' locational choices at the start of the twenty-first century, four-fifths of outwardly processed clothes came from central and east European states, plus Turkey (Groemling and Matthes 2003: 80). Poland and Romania were by far the two most important sources. According to the industry association BBI (2002: 24), in 2001 only 8 countries among the 23 largest German suppliers were not from CEE. Among Asian countries, China is the most popular, with about 4.1 per cent of clothing imports having come from Chinese firms during the decade 1990–2000 (Groemling and Matthes 2003: 49, figure 13b). Our own data broadly support this distribution of supplier locations. Most firms in our sample source exclusively or predominantly from CEE, and all have some suppliers in CEE. This choice is mostly influenced by the search for geographical proximity but is additionally due to the fact that these countries have well-motivated and well-trained people (GER-C-14). (Two large MNCs in our sample, not in ladies' outer wear, were notable exceptions.) Yet some interviewees see the under-development of a native textile industry in CEE as a locational disadvantage. Turkey, in contrast, scores highly for the presence of a well developed fabric industry, together with good manufacturing; the absence of customs duties; and the short lead time its proximity to Europe makes possible. But for a few of our respondents China has become or is becoming one of the most important locations, having most of Turkey's advantages but much lower costs. China is widely considered to have very skilled, flexible, and efficient suppliers which, combined with the easy availability of fabric for FP production, makes it the favourite supplier country in Asia. Because of longer lead times, however, no firm relied exclusively on Asia. One very high-end designer firm even stated that it would not consider Asia, 'because of the quality and brand risk', and this firm alone had many of its suppliers in another western European country, Italy.

The development of GPNs in Asia, despite its cost advantages and the command of 'full package' expertise, was also regarded to hold disadvantages. One German firm, which sourced a relatively high proportion of clothes from China, nevertheless emphasized that the relationship with suppliers in Asia was less collaborative. Chinese suppliers, it was held, are less inclined to provide feedback and advice on the making of individual products. 'In Asia, what we would like to have—but which is a problem in Asia—is the creative side of our suppliers, which we find easier here in Europe, even Eastern Europe. The creative side and the kind of giving us tips and feedback and maybe suggestions for improvement, this is something that in Asia is very hard to find because they have their specifications and they do it like this.... We have better flow of information and exchange of information with the companies in eastern Europe' (GER-C-5). This firm also acknowledged that Asian suppliers were no good for 'flash programs' and hence it was attracted to China mainly by the lower costs.

Thus, to sum up, German 'manufacturers', consonant with their strong emphasis on CMT, based their production networks predominantly in CEE and Turkey. But most of them had some diversification of locations, sourcing also from Asia, and the move towards China had become more prominent for a few firms. The orientation to Asia came earliest and is most pronounced among Germany's large export-oriented sportswear and underwear-producing companies, for whom constantly changing fashion cycles are a less pressing issue. The resulting geographical complexity of German production networks, increased by the comparatively (with the UK) large number of suppliers, is shown in Table 7.1 below.

Information about UK firms' locational choices comes mainly from our interviews. Although the UK firms are said to have a geographically balanced sourcing strategy, our own interview results show a relatively strong focus on countries in Asia Pacific, particularly Hong Kong and China, as well as Bangladesh, together with some Mediterranean rim countries. The greater choice of more distant suppliers is consonant with the greater use of full package rather than CMT sourcing. However, CEE locations were not negligible. A few small firms (in terms of turnover) used only CEE locations for either third-party contracting or overseas in-house manufacturing, whereas for many other firms CEE countries supplemented far-flung locations. CEE suppliers are said to provide both a quick-response capacity and supply the more structured tailored clothes previously made in the UK (UK-C-1; Oxborrow 2005: 8). Turkey is a popular location among UK firms for the same reasons as among German firms. Italy was highly praised by the one large high-end British designer firm in our sample, as was the case with the German designer firm. As in Germany, many favourable comments were made about China, and several firms intended to increase their presence there. Some of the countries where UK firms invested and/or used third-party contracting, such as Bangladesh, Mauritius, and Cambodia, had no evident locational advantages beyond low production and/or tariff costs and were rarely, if at all, mentioned by our German respondents.

To sum up, several UK firms had geographically highly dispersed networks, with a stronger concentration than German firms on geographically more remote

Table 7.1. Supplier networks and relationships

	Mode of sourcing	No. of third-party suppliers	Importance of firm to supplier(s)' business	Production locations	Length of relationship
UK-C-1	100% CMT	1	Takes 90% of output	Turkey	7 years
UK-C-2	Some FDI, some FP, some buying in	7–8	Takes around 20%, definitely would not want 100%	China, Turkey, Morocco, S. Europe	Mix of long and more transient relationships
UK-C-3	60% foreign JVs, 35% FP, small remaining domestic in-house mfg after recent closures	3	Aims for 20–25% of output, be biggest single customer	Turkey, Sri Lanka, Bangladesh, UK	Long term, not 'factory-hopping' or 'country-hopping'
UK-C-4	60% FDI, rest FP/CMT	8	Wants at least 50% of output	China, S.E. Asia, Morocco, CEE	Longest is 12 years, but also regards own factory closures as 'core skill'
UK-C-5	100% CMT	4	Takes 100% of output	CEE	10 years
UK-C-6	100% FP	14	Wants to be sole UK customer; US firms are usually bigger customers	China, some India	About 10 years
UK-C-7	Mostly FDI; some FP; direct buying of one product. Domestic in-house mfg recently closed	Few		CEE; Far East for direct buying	A few years; haven't been mfg outside UK very long
UK-C-8	100% domestic in-house mfg	n/a	n/a	UK	n/a
UK-C-9	Mostly FP, some CMT, tiny residual domestic mfg (recent closures of rest)	Many	Wants to take 30–40% of output	CEE, China, Egypt	Prefers long term
UK-C-10	80% FDI, some CMT	10	Aim not to be sole customer	China, Sri Lanka, S.E. Asia, Morocco	Longest is 20 years
UK-C-11	100% CMT	10 key suppliers, plus >50 others	Exclusive customer in many cases	Italy, China, Morocco	Longest is 15 years
GER-C-1	One JV, rest CMT			Mostly CEE, 10% Germany (but declining), tiny part from Asia	Long term

GER-C-2	100% FP	>100	No particular policy	China, S.E. Asia, Turkey, S. Europe	20–35 years
GER-C-3	100% CMT		Seeks mutual dependence	S.E. Asia, Turkey, S. Europe, CEE, but strong shift towards China	15–20 years
GER-C-4	FDI, CMT, small amount of direct buying, small residual domestic mfg	30–40 key suppliers, plus many others	Sometimes 100%		10–30 years (depends on garment)
GER-C-5	CMT in CEE, FP in Asia	reducing (prev. high) number	Exclusivity in CEE	60% Asia (esp. China); CEE, S. Europe, Turkey	10 years
GER-C-6	100% of one process is domestic in-house mfg, but garment assembly is 100% outsourced	19	100% with many	CEE	6–8 years
GER-C-7	100% CMT	8 in Asia, unspecified in CEE	Normally the biggest customer	China, S.E. Asia, CEE, Russia	Long term
GER-C-8	Mostly CMT, some JV mfg, 5% domestic in-house mfg		Never 100%	Mostly CEE; Turkey, Tunisia	7–8 years
GER-C-9	50% CMT (all in CEE), 50% FP	16	Exclusive in one case, takes small share of others' output	CEE, Turkey, S. Europe; Asia (via agents)	Aim for long term
GER-C-10	Mostly CMT, 25% FDI, FP in Turkey only, closing residual domestic mfg			40% CEE; Turkey, S.E. Asia, China (increasing)	Long term
GER-C-11	Mostly CMT, small FDI, some remaining domestic in-house mfg	20	Rarely seek exclusivity	Mostly CEE, some Turkey, a little HK	10 years
GER-C-12	100% domestic in-house mfg	n/a	n/a	Germany	n/a
GER-C-13	100% CMT but moving towards FP		Sometimes demands exclusive use	China, S.E. Asia, Turkey, CEE	Some evidence of moving countries
US-C-1	Mostly FP	250 in 35 countries; 75% from 30 facts.	25–40%	China, S.E. Asia, India, Korea, C. America, Jordan, Turkey	Medium
US-C-2	Mostly CMT	~7	100% in US locations	90% USA (LA), 10% Hong Kong	Long
US-C-3	—	Few		30–40% USA	Long
US-C-4	Mostly CMT	~500 in 32 different countries	20–50% wants no more than 50%	One USA; Far East 66%; Europe 11%; CB/S. America 23%	—

(cont.)

Table 7.1. (*Continued*)

	Mode of sourcing	No. of third-party suppliers	Importance of firm to supplier(s)' business	Production locations	Length of relationship
US-C-5	30% FP, CMT 70%	—	High in Chinese factory	20% USA; 60% Mexico; 20% China, rest Mauritius	—
US-C-6	—	—	60–70%	China 64%; Asia 17%; 807/CB 13%; Europe 6%	Some long ones in Asia
US-C-7	—	5	—	Mostly in-house Mexico, 2 in Israel, 3 in China	15 years
US-C-8	None	None	—	Solely USA	—
Levi Strauss	Mostly FP, 'small' CMT, some remaining overseas in-house mfg	Over 800 in 52 countries	5–50%	Many in China, also India, other Asia, Mexico, C. & S. America	Major start 1997; active supplier base 'changes constantly'
VF	~ 68% FP, rest CMT and in own factories in Mexico and Turkey	>1,000 mainly in Asia	Not important in Asia	Many countries in Asia, incl. China; Mexico, CB countries; Turkey, Poland and Malta for European countries; small in Middle East and N. Africa	Not known. Recently moved from US locations to Asia Pacific
Jones Apparel	Mainly FP; some CMT; own facilities in Mexico and USA	Not known	Not known	Asia 89%; USA and Mexico ~11%; some in C. & S. America	No long term relationship with fabric suppliers, but good, long relationships with many contractors

Note: CMT, cut-make-trim, FP, full package, FDI, foreign direct investment, JV, joint venture.

locations. But a significant proportion, particularly the relatively small firms, concentrated more on CEE and Turkey. But, on average, the significantly smaller number of UK suppliers than of German ones, considerably reduced the over-all organizational challenge of coordinating their GPNs. For greater detail, see Table 7.1.

General statistics for US sourcing locations are provided only in the form of apparel import data, which therefore also include direct imports by retailers (AAFA 2004: 24, table 2). In 2003, US apparel imports came predominantly— 24 per cent—from the Caribbean Basin area (Costa Rica, Dominican Republic, El Salvador, Guatemala, Honduras, and Nicaragua), followed by China (14%) and Mexico (11%), with China overtaking Mexico for the first time (ibid, own calculations). The next location in the hierarchy of importance, according to 2002 figures cited by Gereffi and Memodovic 2003, was Hong Kong, while a number of South and Southeast Asian countries—India, Taiwan, Korea, and individual Central American/CB countries—provide a very small proportion of supplies. Italy and Turkey are the only western/southern European sourcing countries. Because of their relatively high cost, they supply only a very small proportion of garments, while CEE countries do not figure at all (ibid). Turkey was selected mainly by companies with a significant level of European sales, such as Levi Strauss and VF (Company web sites 2006).

Individual profiles of the large and giant US companies in our sample illustrate two features of their GPNs. First, these networks are geographically highly dis-persed, often spanning several continents. This is primarily a result of the quota system and consolidation now is in process (e.g. US-C-1). Second, most of the big companies source the majority of their goods from Asia, particularly from China. Thus, Levi Strauss in 2005 had suppliers in 52 countries and three continents, with 213 of its 852 suppliers in China (Company web site 2005). VF also sources a majority—59 per cent—of its clothes in Asia (Company web site 2005), as does Jones Apparel (Company Annual Report 2005). The four giant firms interviewed also had a majority of production in China. China's popularity is due not only to its low price but also to the fact that Chinese firms are able to provide 'full package' supply. The latter has become an increasingly important mode of supply because it reduces both cost of investment in fabric and, crucially, lead time. The other two large firms and a medium-sized jeans producer among our interviewees had a strong presence in 807 territory, but at least one firm (US-C-5) was seeking to reduce it and move to China. Thus, during 2005, US imports of apparel from China grew to 26.7 per cent, whereas those from Mexico showed further marked decline (AAFA 2006: 3).

US interviewees made many comments shedding light on the recent shift in production from Mexico to China. One large firm respondent (US-C-1) pro-nounced Mexico 'a disaster'. Suppliers, in his view, had been unable to manage the shift towards shorter runs since 2001 due to poor middle management, even in the biggest and best factories. This firm was therefore seeking to expand and con-solidate its suppliers in China after 2005, placing 50 per cent of its business there. 'The Chinese make the best product, at the best price, with the greatest flexibility' and, despite tariffs, will remain competitive. China's distance from the USA was not seen as a prohibitive disadvantage. Another large firm respondent (US-C-4) was 'not optimistic for apparel makers in the Americas', due to problems with local fabric, and saw the main post-2005 gains arising in East and South East Asia. Two smaller firms complained in strong terms about the quality of the fabric available in Mexico (US-C-2 and US-C-5) and the 'terrible needlework' and rising prices (US-C-5). Jones Apparel pulled out of Mexico mainly because of rising costs (Company Annual Report 2005). Bair and Dussel Peters (2006) point out that efforts to achieve 'full-package' production in Mexico mostly have been unsuccessful, constituting another barrier to attracting large US firms now (since 2001) wedded to the full-package mode of sourcing. The only defender of Mexico as a location, particularly for long runs, was the firm maintaining a very large subsidiary there (US-C-7). Levi Strauss, and, more so, VF, also maintain a significant proportion of their supply base in Mexico and the CB countries (Company web sites), mostly for large volume jeans production. The ascendancy of CB suppliers has been due to both geographic proximity and the efficiency of supplier firms—which are mostly in East Asian ownership.

The large US firms, unsurprisingly, had the most complex GPNs, being both geographically highly dispersed over several continents and consisting of a large number of suppliers. The above account has additionally shown that, despite some clear country patterns in choice of sourcing locations, there also is some within-country diversity in firms' locational strategies, most prominently resulting from firm size and also product strategy.

Table 7.1 summarizes some of the divergences in sourcing strategies between the firms in the three countries discussed so far.

At the end of the 1990s, in response to pressure from retailers, a strong preoccupation arose with 'quick response' production of fashion garments, particularly in the USA (e.g. Abernathy et al. 1999; Bonacich and Applebaum 2000). (For greater detail, see Chapter 4, on retail.) Although this concern has not disappeared and remains a pressing demand particularly from fashion-oriented retailers, resigned acceptance that the reality falls far short of the ideal seems to rule. While new technology facilitates speedier reaction to consumer demand, the globalization of production networks often impedes it. The associated demise of the model of vertical integration, that is, keeping all functions under one roof, constitutes a further powerful impediment to just-in-time delivery.

Everybody wants short-cycle speed to market, but wholesalers [coordinating firms] don't have that level of control yet. The *whole* industry needs to change to operate like [the Zara model] ... Retailers are pushing for more replenishment and want wholesalers to invest in fabric and finished goods, but I don't have a lot of faith that that is going to happen. Unless you control your mills like Zara does, quick turn is nearly impossible. No one is copying Zara, it would require too big an investment [in fabric mills]. (US-C-6)

Although US textile mills that relocated to Mexico tried forward integration into sewing in order to increase speed to market, hardly any were successful in this endeavour (US Interview Notes). With the locational swing back to China, speed to market in any case is compromised. In Germany and the UK, too, although the success of the Zara model was widely acknowledged, no firm had the intention or capability to copy it (Interview Notes). Thus, an increase in fashion cycles is evident in all three countries and 'flash' or 'season express' programmes are inserted to introduce new items within seasons. Although the greater turn to 'full package' has facilitated a shortening of lead times, quick-cycle or JIT production remains a challenge for the industry.

7.6. THE GOVERNANCE OF GLOBAL PRODUCTION NETWORKS

The governance of production networks is shaped by the product paradigms of firms and the mode of sourcing (CMT vs. full package), and the locational choices associated with it. These, we have pointed out earlier, are partly influenced in turn by the institutional framework in firms' country of origin. This section analyses how managers of coordinating firms view relationships with their third-party contractors, starting with an exploration of their attempts to mix a purely transactional relationship with elements of relational contracting. In a second step, the main differences in the ways in which UK, German, and US firms manage the relationship are highlighted, with a strong focus on the differing degree of control they are able to exert and the mechanisms used to this end. While this section focuses only on inter-firm relations, relationships with employees in contractor firms are examined in some detail in Chapter 10.

7.6.1. Transactional Versus Relational Contracting

A notable paradox in establishing relationships in supplier countries is the widely expressed wish to build longer term relationships of around 10–20 years' duration while simultaneously expressing the need to retain freedom of movement to escape feared wage increases. The actual length of relationships showed that footloose behaviour was not rampant in any of our sample firms, although it is seen by industry observers (e.g. UK-R-1; UK-R-2; US-C-9) to be significantly more prevalent in the USA. But moving between suppliers was nevertheless a strategy that firms in all three countries envisaged. 'Every season, we have to work on their quality and on their price level, otherwise we are not married' (GER-C-7), or 'I'd just move again ... we only ever plan for seven years in any country, anyway' (UK-C-10). 'Our active factory base changes constantly' (Levi Strauss, company web site, 2006), or 'we do not have long-term relationships with any of our suppliers' (Jones Apparel, Annual Report 2005). Several US firms were actively planning to pull out of certain locations and to expand or consolidate in others. 'Fewer countries, fewer vendors, greater buying power—that's what 2005 means to us' (US-C-4). Some of our interviewees in Turkey did, indeed, confirm the withdrawal of American, but not British or German, firms from the country, following the abolition of quotas in January of 2005.

More UK and US firms seemed intent on chasing price reductions. 'My constant challenge is to make it cheaper and manage the overheads' (US-C-5). The preoccupation with price-cutting, according to a UK respondent (UK-C-6), may be attributed to financial pressures associated with the high levels of gearing that have accompanied management buy-outs in the late 1990s. Both a garment industry consultancy firm (US-C-9) and a UK retailer (UK-R-2) contended that US firms shift from one supplier to another almost every year, because they source competitively based on price. Collins (2003), too, points out that US firms have no long-term commitment to the places where they produce and have been vocal about their willingness to relocate if wage levels rise. This must be due to the extremely strong pressure experienced from both large retailers and investors.

Different time horizons in supplier relations manifest themselves in differing degrees of connection to foreign production sites. German firms and associations seemed relatively deeply embedded in Romania and Turkey. This is indicated not merely by their training activities in individual firms but also by the accompaniment of firms in a given country/region by an industry-focused development agency and program, GTZ (Society for Technical Cooperation), which is sponsored by the German government. In contrast, 'deterritorialised [USA] production regimes', it is suggested by Collins (2003), 'develop few connections to regions and workers' (ibid: 61), and US firms develop only 'thinly constituted, singularly focused and more ephemeral relations' (ibid: 152). The growing custom by large American firms to hire mainly Asian middleman firms (Appelbaum 2008) in any case usually cuts the direct connection between buyer firms and actual producers. We have no comparable information regarding British firms, but it seems likely that their degree of social embeddedness is closer to that of their USA than their German counterparts.

A glance at historical shifts in sourcing locations since the early 1960s by firms from all three countries confirms a move from countries where labour costs have risen over time. This was particularly prevalent when geopolitical transformations had opened up or closed off industrial spaces, such as the disintegration of Yugoslavia in 1991, the fall of communism in CEE in 1990, and the introduction of trade agreements such as NAFTA in 1994–95. The end of the Agreement on Textiles and Clothing and of the quota system it entailed in January 2005 has constituted a particularly significant transformation, introducing a violent new shake of the kaleidoscope of supplier countries and initiating a consolidation of GPNs (for details, see Chapter 6). In addition to cost saving, firms also expect a reduction in lead times from a consolidated and smaller GPN—crucial to satisfying retailers' demands for 'fast fashion'.

At the same time there were several firms in both European countries, as well as a few in the USA, that had a credible commitment to a longer term partnership. 'It's a long, very good relationship, we definitely do not move about' (GER-C-7) or 'We do give people the opportunity to put things right…we would not give up a supplier lightly' (UK-C-3). One US company had long-term relationships of 'around 15 years—you are not scrabbling around to find new factories every year' (US-C-7), and one of the smaller US firms (US-C-2) explicitly declared a commitment to longer tem relations. A giant US firm expressed wariness of constant location-hopping.

There has been a march, from Japan to Taiwan to Korea to Hong Kong to China to Singapore to South Asia to Jordan, a constant march, ... with lots of investment from big agents like Li & Fung and Newtimes, but nobody has ever found a gold mine ... Performance is excellent everywhere. Everywhere there are quality [factories] and everywhere there are weak [ones]. (US-C-6)

On average, German firms had the longest sourcing partnerships (see also Schuessler 2008: 200). This may be explained partly by their early start in building GPNs and partly by their greater investment in training their partners. The large US firms, on average, have the shortest relations, being accused by many industry and academic commentators of an extreme market-type orientation and of footlooseness. An arm's length orientation has found its ultimate development in the use of Asian middleman firms, such as Li & Fung, obviating the need for any contact with actual producers. This strategy crucially depends on volume buying and thus is open only to the large American firms.

The reasons provided for cultivating longer term relations were varied. Firms in both European countries, but no US firms, stressed that it can take three or four years to train a supplier to fully understand his western customers' requirements, and two managers with foreign subsidiaries claimed that profit is made only in year five (UK-C-10 and UK-C-4). An entirely different reason for a longer term association was given by two UK managers, who deemed it is easier to achieve price reductions once trust has been built. 'If you have trust, you get the reduction in price points' (UK-C-2, but also UK-C-9).

Many firms in both European countries and one US firm (US-C-2) talked of partnership, give-and-take, trust and gentlemen's agreements. 'They're usually very helpful ... I think we have a very good working relationship ... it's two-way ... they always say this is a partnership' (UK-C-1). Indeed, many small services were provided by the western firms, and time was granted to suppliers 'to improve and adapt' (GER-C-11). But, at the same time, most suppliers were given no contract guaranteeing a certain volume of business during a season. Usually they had only promises regarding capacity utilization. According to several UK firms, suppliers did not even expect that customer firms kept these promises. 'There is no guarantee, but there is desire and hope, so often they [suppliers] take the risk that they believe us' (UK-C-4). 'They will, you know, reserve production happily for us, but if we don't take it up, it's not a big deal, they'll find someone else' (UK-C-6). Coordinating firms receive no guarantees from their retailer customers and hence see themselves as simply passing on the insecurity they are exposed to. A US firm (US-C-6) justified the absence of contracts in the following terms:

Highly specified contracts don't work well in the garment industry ... With the big boys, like Ralph Lauren and Raymond Fung, both are kind of hooked—put in a win/win or lose/lose situation. The bets are too big for both sides [to default on an agreement] ... Small wholesalers [coordinating firms], without a lot of bargaining power, get screwed...The letter of the law is immaterial in these cases.

Only three (German) firms concluded contractual agreements with firms in CEE, reflecting perhaps the greater juridification of business relationships in Germany (Lane and Bachmann 1997).

Interviewees sometimes spoke of a trusting relationship but shortly afterwards mentioned practices completely incompatible with such a relationship. This led us to suspect that trust was fairly superficial. Thus one British manager assured us that 'everybody, the whole world, works on trust' not long after he had confided that 'So, by being a little brighter, a little more intelligent with everything we can share the risk [of stock holding] ... amongst our supply chain so we can effectively keep our level of risk lower while spreading it to other people' (UK-C-5).

7.6.2. Leverage and Control: Determining Price, Quality, and Speed of Delivery

It is clear that, owing to the oversupply of suppliers, coordinating firms generally, though not invariably, hold the power in their relationships with suppliers. However, one UK firm pointed out to us that the power imbalance in relation to retailers is much greater than any power imbalance with their suppliers (UK-C-6). A German retailer remarked that, particularly in China, there now exist some giant supplier firms which, moreover, take care not to become dependent on any one coordinating firm (GER-R-3). (See also the section on China in Chapter 9.) This is also confirmed by Appelbaum et al. (2005: 7) who point to the emergence of Asian, particularly Chinese, TNCs, which have set up subsidiaries in many countries and have a huge sales volume (as discussed in Chapter 6). In Central America (Guatemala), there is Koramsa, with 14,300 employees (Just-style.com 12 July 2004). Moreover, size (in employment terms) will further increase in the consolidation process, and is predicted to reach 30,000 workers (*Wall Street Journal* 28 December 2004). Such giant global companies will not tolerate being pushed around by western buyers in the future. However, during the time of our research, the power still lay mainly with western companies, particularly with retailers. (For variation in degree of retailer power, see Chapter 4.)

The degree of leverage possessed over suppliers was widely seen as strongly connected with order volume, and many smaller European companies were painfully aware of the fact that, particularly in comparison with US firms, they did not enjoy the status of a 'preferred' customer. The large US firms were, indeed, very conscious of the power to dictate terms that a large order volume bestowed. 'Size brings leverage'. Large firms like US-C-6 control production by 'dominating' a factory. 'A Jones, a Liz Claiborne, a Kellwood—if they find an excellent factory, they want to control it' (US-C-6). Volume sourcing enables the large US firms to employ Asian middleman firms whose coordination services shorten the buying cycle and strip out costs. (For further details, see Chapter 6.) Conversely, small buyer firms have no leverage and often get 'screwed' by their suppliers (US-C-6).

Several firms in all three countries attempted to address the issue of volume sourcing by rationalizing what had sometimes become an unwieldy supplier base and by buying a sufficiently high proportion of a supplier's production. 'Large firms can do it by placing a large enough order to consume a factory's production—do the lion's share of the manufacturing in that plant'. Someone like Raymond Fung (a large owner of textile and clothing firms and an agent for western firms) may own the factory, but 'to all intents and purposes it is your plant' (US-C-6). In several German firms (but less among UK firms and not at all among large US firms), volume buying amounted to taking 100 per cent of a supplier's production. This use of exclusive suppliers signals quasi-integration. It makes it worthwhile to invest in training suppliers and serves to guarantee a high degree of control. But such exclusivity also seriously restricts buyer firms' flexibility, posing the conundrum of commitment versus flexibility. As US firms and, to a lesser degree, German firms on average have a significantly larger turnover than UK coordinating firms (as is indicated in Chapter 3, Table 3.2), their ability to achieve control over terms through volume buying is also superior. Although the supplier firms of the US large/giant companies are also very large, there is no fear of becoming captive to any one supplier, even after the move to full package buying (US-C-1).

However, several larger German firms made it clear that they would not exploit their power advantage. 'We do have the leverage, but we tend not to use it to pursue transactional issues' (GER-C-3). In contrast one UK manager of a medium-sized firm vividly illustrated the degree of power his firm enjoyed. 'When I tell them to jump, they only ask "how high"?' (UK-C-9). A second UK manager recommended to 'go for the jugular on price' during months of a lull in production (UK-C-2). US firms, in addition to using volume buying to bring down costs, stood out in the use of another cost reduction strategy: the stripping out of most pre-production and of some training and control functions and their transfer to suppliers (e.g. US-C-1). British and to a greater extent German firms were still intent on retaining these functions, in the interest of preserving product quality.

In addition to price, other aspects of supplier selection and network management merit attention. When asked for selection (and retention) criteria, the fairly uniform answer in both European countries was 'price, quality and reliability of delivery'. A prominent and somewhat exceptional UK retailer, however, made it clear that quality was the company's uppermost concern and that they aimed for lower, rather than lowest cost (UK-R-1). Nevertheless, the UK managers more often mentioned price first and subsequently frequently re-emphasized the absolute priority of getting a low price/getting down a few price points. This again reflects the high degree of dependence on, and pressure from, large retailers that UK firms are exposed to— 'every year the opening conversations [with retailers] are always about price, always...Quality comes free' (UK-C-6). In contrast, several German firms, but only one large high-end UK firm, either did not mention price or emphasized that quality was more important than price. 'Well the most important thing is quality' (GER-C-5). 'We do not put cost uppermost, usually we go to countries other suppliers have left, where there is accumulated experience. I do not want them to build experience with our high-end products' (GER-C-6). One German firm turned away orders if it could not execute them at the customary high level of quality (GER-C-3). This again illustrates the retention among German firms of a high competency in production, even if production itself now no longer occurs in Germany. Among US firms, quality was not especially singled out as a prime concern in sourcing, and price control seemed uppermost. The pressure against the use of high-quality fabric was emphasized by one textile supplier to the industry: 'Twenty years ago, the quality of fabric mattered. Today, you have to meet price points to be even in the game' (US-T-5). But an up-market branded marketer—Jones Apparel—had a system of quality control similar to that of many German firms (Company Annual Report 2005).

An important issue is how and to what degree vertically disintegrated firms manage to retain control over the quality of the garments provided by their nominally independent third-party suppliers. At first sight, it seemed to us that there was no discernible difference between German and UK firms in this respect. Both uniformly expressed themselves highly concerned to safeguard the quality of their supplies and mentioned several similar measures to ensure a high level of control, such as various checking procedures by specially appointed QC departments (in large firms) or by individual technical employees. Quality control was particularly stringent among the several suppliers to Marks & Spencer. It also was deemed to be stringent in the case of a Mexican supplier of Liz Claiborne, where it took the impersonal form of statistical process control in production (Collins 2003). But a closer analysis revealed several important differences, indicating a more thorough quality control by German firms. This was manifested in the following actions: (a) only CMT sourcing—more prevalent among German firms—gives full control over fabric selection, a very important factor in the appearance and quality of garments; (b) more German firms mentioned an iterative process of control before the start of production. This required the supplier to return a sample garment which would then be checked and adjusted before being sent back to the supplier. 'So it is basically a quite constant check and feedback with our manufacturers' (GER-C-5); (c) more German firms executed double quality checks of garments, both on the supplier's premises and on return to their own warehouses; and (d) probably most important, most German firms have permanent technical employees stationed with all their suppliers, whereas UK and US firms more frequently use either roving inspectors or appoint agents to execute QC. Last but not least, German firms invest considerable effort in training their suppliers, render technical support and supply know-how to improve the product. This emerged not only from our interviews in supplier countries but is emphasized also in the secondary literature (Heidenreich 1990; Bloecker 2005; Faust 2005; Wortmann 2005; Schuessler 2008). In contrast, supplier training was not reported by either UK or US firms and their suppliers. Thus, the remark by Wrona (1999: 161) that production of outsourced garments in reality remains under the influence of the German coordinating firm, ensuring virtual vertical integration, is largely confirmed by our research in German firms. 'With our quality control system with production, I think we influence our suppliers heavily, so sometimes they are treated as our own factories' (GER-C-1).

However, integration of suppliers was not, as it would have been in domestic supplier relationships, accompanied by authority sharing (Whitley 2005: 236). The largely *Mittelstand* firms in the German industry jealously guard their expertise and brand, fearing that suppliers may turn into competitors and thus limit authority sharing. This was perceived negatively by at least a few suppliers. It is well illustrated by the following quotes from Romanian contractors supplied by Berger (2005: 191): 'Our German clients... continually watch over our shoulders and tell us how to do everything. The Germans have their own technicians who are in the plant every day... mostly they are unwilling to send us patterns by e-mail... because they're afraid we'll be able to get their secrets and know-how' and 'even with long-standing German customers, we have endless negotiations about every conceivable problem that could possibly come up' (Berger 2005: 191). For the UK firms, in contrast, such virtual vertical integration of suppliers did not seem assured. This well illustrates that the elusive concept of quality may mean different things to different people and that claims of quality assurance should not be accepted at face value. It is on this aspect that the influence of the domestic institutional environment is most pronounced.

US firms did not explicitly refer to the issue of quality control or the means of accomplishing it, other than referring to the existence of tough general certification systems. But several indirect clues lead us to conclude that quality control was less important than price control. Of the large firms, only one (US-C-7) engaged in systematic training, but in its subsidiary rather than of suppliers. Several firms used agents and hence maintained a more remote relationship to suppliers. One giant firm mainly assigned quality control to its suppliers, 'so [we] wouldn't have to control lots of quality control personnel' and quality-checked only 10 per cent of incoming goods for fit, sew and fabric (US-C-1). One of the medium-sized firms, in contrast, maintained a QC manager on site, checking 20 per cent of garments (US-C-2).

This overview of the nature of relationships between coordinating firms and suppliers vividly illustrates the different imprint of the three varieties of capitalism and of the production paradigm connected with each. Although firms from all three countries demonstrated some arm's length market-type behaviour, supplier integration, we have shown, is significantly more pronounced for the German than for the UK and US firms. Whereas in the US case lack of integration is to some degree counterbalanced by control through volume-buying, this was not the case for UK firms. However, the German approach also required greater commitment of investment and expenditure, obliging firms to recreate in an individualistic manner the levels of skill that had been supported by institutional structures in their domestic setting.

7.7. CONCLUSIONS

This chapter has mapped out the complex factors which shape the organization and governance of GPNs, as well as showing the diversity in sourcing patterns and network structures between the three countries. The divergence is most marked between Germany's CME firms and the LME firms of the USA. Reciprocity was best achieved by German firms which, despite a lack of ownership control, achieved a close vertical integration of supplier firms. US firms managed to impose control over suppliers through volume buying but do not favour close involvement with or foster commitment from suppliers. UK firms present a more complex picture. Although UK firms display a liberal-market stance, their generally smaller size and low market power prevents them from achieving control, based on volume buying. Also the historically grown dependence on one giant retailer obliges several of them to maintain ownership control much longer than is the case in the other two countries.

Our analysis of the coordination and governance of GPNs indicated that, despite the detachment from the home country institutional context that foreign sourcing inherently entails, firms in all three countries still showed the imprint of the variety of capitalism of their country of origin. This was evident in the fact that arm's length relations with suppliers and lack of commitment to them were considerably more pronounced among firms from the two LMEs, and particularly US firms. In both countries pressure for low prices exerted both by very large retailers and, in the American case, by investors led to a more exclusive preoccupation with costs. In the US case, domestic institutional constellations had created many very large and mostly listed firms which, despite distant and detached relationships with suppliers, nevertheless achieved cost control because sheer size enabled volume buying. Furthermore, full-package buying and use of Asian middleman firms enabled them to strip out further costs because of time-saving. In the UK context, such a strategy was precluded by the much lower average size of 'manufacturing' firms, and the adoption of FDI and ownership control was often an alternative strategy. German firms, in contrast, integrated their suppliers more closely, particularly through training efforts. However, even in the case of German firms, institutional incompleteness meant that some of the supports for the training effort had fallen away. Firms had to internalize the function, previously shared between unions, employers, and the state. Moreover, as training was no longer accompanied by the same degree of authority sharing as present in the German domestic context, 'integration through training' sometimes was perceived negatively as mere control. The contradictory mixture of institutional pressures and voluntarism present in all three cases often led to the adoption of hybrid forms of network governance where firms tried to square the circle of lack of mutual commitment with aspirations for reciprocity.

Institutions in the sphere of employment and industrial relations mainly influenced the time when outsourcing was first embraced. German firms had negotiated an early adoption of the foreign sourcing route with unions, whereas in the USA, and particularly in the UK, the exodus of 'manufacturing' firms was both more rushed and accomplished in a more adversarial manner. The influence of the state on GPNs was mostly through the exertion of political influence in both regional and international institutions, particularly of the US and German states. This had secured favourable access for firms to labour in developing countries— the competitive strategy that Palan and Abbott (1996) term 'banding together in regional blocks'. In the USA, the state had kept down the price of raw materials, such as cotton. It also had secured an agreement in the NAFTA which strongly favoured American textiles producers, to the detriment of Mexican clothing firms—a competitive strategy more akin to that of 'hierarchy' (Palan and Abbott 1996). In the German case the facilitating role of the state was also evident. There was no specific support for the clothing industry but general industry policies, such as development aid flanking firms' foreign operations through activation of domestic associations, benefited also the clothing industry.

The above institutional shaping of GPNs by domestic institutions was overlaid by and interacted with the influence of international institutions. The latter shaped both the size and geographical dispersion of networks and, since 2005, their consolidation and greater geographical focus. Locations are not socially neutral, in that the greater turn towards sourcing in Asia and particularly China since the early 2000s has further loosened relationships and introduced more intermediaries (agents) between buyer firms (particularly branded marketers and 'private label' 'manufacturers') and their geographically remote suppliers. Also firms, finding themselves in new contexts or faced by new challenges, sometimes exercised strategic choice. They adopted practices at odds with their domestic institutional environment. Thus German firms gave up ownership control, were prepared to give up suppliers if wages rose, and began to embrace FP sourcing.

We additionally found variation in sourcing practices within countries. Some of these related mainly to differences between larger and smaller firms and to the lack of investor pressure on the latter. Other divergences within economies were connected with varying production paradigms or value orientations. The latter were related to family ownership and attachment to a given traditional geographical location. However, these latter differences within countries were exceptions which did not overrule the imprint of the national variety of capitalism.

8

The Clothing Industries in Supplier Countries: Buyer–Supplier Relations (1)

The analysis in Chapter 7 focused on how western buyer firms coordinated and governed their GPNs and on how their strategies had been shaped by their domestic and international regulatory environment. Our recognition that GPNs are situated at multiple geographical and social institutional levels and that globally active firms 'touch down' in specific geopolitical and social spaces, requires a study also of supplier countries and firms. Chapters 8 and 9 therefore present detailed analyses of some important supplier firms situated in their specific social and geopolitical environments. These chapters enquire how national contexts have shaped firms' capabilities and their competitiveness as suppliers. They additionally explore how supplier firms view the relationships with their buyers, with a particular focus on the distinctions they make between trading partners from different national origins. By again adopting a relational analysis of GPNs, we are able to provide a valuable check on the understandings of network relationships communicated to us by firms from the three western countries and to confirm, by and large, the interpretations offered in Chapter 7.

Suppliers in the global clothing industry now exist in a large number of developing and transition countries around the globe, and high selectivity in studying them was necessary. Our coverage in this chapter of Turkey and Romania focuses on the two most important suppliers in terms of import volume to European buyer firms, situated in geographically close Eastern European and Mediterranean Rim locations. Turkish firms additionally have supplied clothing to American buyers, albeit in much smaller volume. In Chapter 9, we analyse supplier firms in Mexico, still the most important geographically contiguous supplier country for US firms, and China, now the most important supplier country for both US and European buyers. The leading trading relationships for the USA and EU are indicated in Table 8.1.

8.1. TURKEY

8.1.1. Geopolitical Position, Industrial Development, and Institutional Structure

Turkey is a very large country, with 72.98 million inhabitants in 2006 (World Bank 2006a). It bridges Asia and Europe, Islamic religion/culture and secularization

Table 8.1. EU-25 and US imports of textiles and clothing by country and region

EU-25 imports (Jan–Oct 2005)[a]			US imports (2005)[b]		
Source	Value (US$ bn)	Growth (%)	Source	Value (US$ bn)	Growth (%)
1. China	24.2	+44	1. China	27.2	+43
2. Turkey	11.5	+6	2. CAFTA[c]	9.6	−4
3. India	5.9	+19	3. East Asia[d]	9.4	−17
4. Romania	4.2	−4	4. Mexico	8.1	−6
5. Bangladesh	3.8	−6	5. EU-25	5.8	−3
6. East Asia[d]	3.5	−28	6. India	5.4	25
7. Tunisia	2.8	−3	16. Turkey	1.7	−9
World (excl. intra-trade)	77.8	7	World	102.6	6

[a] *Source*: Eurostat, as cited in WTO (2005).
[b] *Source*: US Department of Commerce, Bureau of the Census, International Trade Statistics, as cited in WTO (2005).
[c] Costa Rica, Dominican Republic, El Salvador, Guatemala, Honduras, and Nicaragua.
[d] Hong Kong, China; Republic of Korea; Macao, China; and Chinese Taipei.

in the public sphere, a highly educated elite in the west and a large, relatively poor and backward population in the largely rural east of the country. After a volatile history with a fairly recent attainment of genuinely democratic politics, an open economy and a stabilized currency, Turkey now is developing rapidly. Industrialization proceeded unevenly and slowly due to a state monopoly in many sectors from the 1930s to 1980. But state ownership and promotion during the 1930s and 1940s nevertheless laid a solid foundation for the contemporary textile industry, ensuring the establishment of a number of very large and often vertically integrated enterprises (Phillips 2005: 150). Export-led economic take-off began only from the 1980s onwards and was highly subsidized by the state (Tokatli 2007: 79–80). In contrast to CEE countries, Turkey has been unable to attract extensive FDI. Its comparatively long-standing low rate of FDI is attributed to problems in the areas of macroeconomic and political stability, corruption, and high energy costs and poor transport infrastructure (Tusiad and Yased 2004). FDI into Turkey, given its legally problematic status until 1986 (Cepni 2003: 105) and the country's volatile business environment, has remained relatively low both in the economy as a whole (net inflows as a proportion of GDP stood at 4.98% in 2006 [Data and Statistics 2006]) and in the textile and clothing industries in particular. In 2005, textiles and clothing attracted around US$105 million or about 1.85% of all foreign direct investment into Turkey (fDi 2005: 2). Consequently, the development of the clothing industry was, in the main, the result of an internal, government-supported effort by indigenous firms and their associations. As one experienced entrepreneur has commented: 'there has been an extraordinary, incredible development...Think of the last crisis.... Turkey did this and that, gave itself to export and pulled through....we tend and try to get out of the quagmire by our own efforts',[1] albeit with a little help from the state.

Its geographic closeness to the European Union, its political importance as a bridge between Asia and Europe, and its relatively well-educated urban population place Turkey on the politico-economic semi-periphery, with aspirations for further economic and political integration into Europe. Germans first persuaded Turkish firms to enter into contract manufacturing in the 1980s, and generous development help from the Paris Club helped Turkish firms to modernize their textile machinery (Schuessler 2008: 156). The Customs Union with the EU, achieved in 1996, greatly increased trade with Europe, while the clothing industry's trade relations with the USA remained governed by the MFA and (from 1995 to 2005) MFA/ATC import restrictions and the use of quota arrangements.

Prospects of European integration were encouraged by Turkey's impressive export-fuelled rate of economic growth from the 1980s onwards, following the structural adjustment program of 1980. The latter ushered in the replacement of an inward-looking import substitution strategy with an export-oriented strategy, as well as privatization (Cepni 2003: 39). Turkey's GDP per capita grew from US$2,987 in 2002 to US$5,008 in 2005 (TEA [Turkish Exporters' Assembly] 2006), but levels of inequality remain very high (Cepni 2003: 178). The Customs Union with the EU has brought strong advantages in the shorter term, such as total elimination of quotas and tariffs in Turkey's main market. It has exerted greater pressure on Turkish firms to modernize. Additionally, joining has generated many EU-sponsored development projects, targeted especially towards the SME sector, in the areas of technology transfer in textiles, training towards higher labour standards, and the establishment of two textile quality control laboratories. In the longer term, however, the adoption of the EU's liberal stance on trade and hence relatively low tariffs on imports from non-EU countries—Turkey is unable to make independent bi-lateral trade agreements—has made Turkey vulnerable to flooding with cheap imports from developing countries with lower wages (Phillips 2005; Turkish Business World, Internet Edition, 13 March 2006: 2).

But growth did not bring stability. Until quite recently, the Turkish economy has been dogged by a very low level of monetary and therefore economic stability, manifested in high and wildly oscillating levels of inflation and high interest rates (Cepni 2003; TEA 2006). Turkish firms not only learnt to live with it but even devised strategies to manipulate this environment for extensive rent-seeking (Tokatli 2007: 80). Only following IMF intervention in 2004 did inflation come down to single-digit figures (TEA 2006). Turkey has therefore provided an unpredictable and risky business environment for both domestic firms and foreign investors (Tokatli and Eldener 2004: 177), though much less so than in the past.

Tokatli and Eldener (2004) and Tokatli (2007: 80f) refer to a weakly institutionalized, particularistic business environment, hinting at continuing corruption, particularly in state–business relationships (see also Tusiad and Yased 2004: 5). But Turkey's problems need to be placed in perspective. Many of them are shared with other developing countries, but in comparison to other prominent supplier countries in the clothing industry (cf. Evgeniev 2006 on Bulgaria, Hungary, and

Poland) it enjoys a number of institutional advantages: a high degree of ownership integration; a uniform national banking system; a reasonably developed social infrastructure (particularly in the western part of the country); efficiently organized and active industry associations; and a higher level of state support for economic development.

The state has been supportive of outward-looking industrial development since 1980, but support has been inconstant and is considered insufficient by the industry. It is fair to say that the state's stance to the textiles and clothing industry has been mixed, but positive measures seem to outweigh negative ones. On the one hand, the state has encouraged exports (through massive tax rebates, subsidization of foreign trade shows, and establishment of foreign sales offices, as well as the foundation of an effective industry-financed association to promote export, ITKIB). Additionally, the state has stimulated R&D and regional industrial development through soft loans, grants and tax exemptions (Phillips 2005), and has provided high-quality specialized and higher educational institutions (e.g. 13 universities have degrees in textile engineering and in fashion design and marketing [Interview with TCMA, May 2006]). On the other hand, the textile and clothing industry does not receive the recognition its size warrants, with attention having been diverted to the financial sector in recent years.[2] Unlike the Chinese industry, it receives no government subsidies. Energy prices and employment taxes have been kept comparatively high (Tusiad and Yased 2004: 6), and the high and unpredictable interest rates have made borrowing for investment hazardous.

In addition to state support for the industry, industry associations have been well developed, active, and influential. The most important are the Turkish Clothing Manufacturers Association (TCMA) and the Istanbul Textile and Clothing Exporters Association (ITKIB). These associations have not only represented members' interests vis-à-vis the Turkish state, but, since 1996, have also formed a very active 'anti-trade liberalization' group within Euratex to lobby the European Commission in favour of the imposition of China safeguards (Interview with TCMA 2006). They have also provided valuable practical support and strategic advice to member firms. The TCMA has facilitated participation in foreign trade fairs and has encouraged foreign marketing (Neidik and Gereffi 2006: 2297). More recently, the Association has encouraged the transfer to/expansion of manufacturing plants in Anatolia to keep the industry competitive in the face of rising wage costs (Interview with TCMA 2006). Whereas membership of the TCMA is voluntary, the ITKIB is financed by a compulsory levy from all exporting firms and effectively promotes firms' exporting interests (Interview with ITKIB 2006).

Turkey has a very large labour force (23 million out of a population of 73 million) which is considered comparatively highly skilled, but the high tax burden on wages has fostered the development of a large informal sector (Tusiad and Yased 2004: 6). Concerning the institutions coordinating labour, unions have been legal since 1947 (Cepni 2003: 27). But the dualistic industrial structure has made union recognition very uneven and left the majority of employees unrepresented.

Employees working in the formal economy have experienced rising wages, receive adequate social payments, and enjoy rudimentary union representation. (For further details, see the following section.) Because of inadequate information on the large, informal sector of the clothing industry, what follows refers mostly to the formal sector.

8.1.2. Structure and Performance of the Turkish Textile and Clothing Industries

The textiles and clothing industries constitute an exceedingly important part of the Turkish economy, in 2006 representing 18.4 per cent of industrial manufacturing production, 23.9 per cent of manufacturing employment, 13.6 per cent of total employment, and 28 per cent of total export earnings (ITKIB 2006). Exports in clothing and textiles of US$18.9 billion far exceed imports of US$6.7 billion (ibid). Exports, particularly of clothing, have been expanding vigorously between 2000 and 2005 (TEA 2006: 12). Turkey's importance in the global economy is indicated by the fact that, in terms of exports, textiles ranked about ninth and clothing ranked fourth in 2005 (after China, Hong Kong, and Mexico) (ITKIB February 2006: 4). Regarding production volume, in 2006 Turkey was in third place, after China and Italy (*Turkish Business World* 2006). Turkey is not only a regional supplier of textiles and clothing but also sells to North America. The importance of the Turkish industry in the European and global T/C industry has been recognized by the fact that, in 2006, the President of the Turkish Clothing Manufacturers Association sat on the Board of Euratex and held the office of Senior Vice President of the International Apparel Federation.

The textiles industry was one of the priority industries in the government's 1934 five-year plan (Cepni 2003: 26; Phillips 2005: 150) and thus is relatively well established in Turkey. During the years of state planning and import substitution policies it developed only gradually, but a number of very large state-controlled as well as private enterprises nevertheless became established. They were able to control the industry and to enjoy oligopolistic profits throughout the industrialization period (Voyvoda and Yeldan 2001). But growth accelerated after limited liberalization in the early 1950s (Cepni 2003: 28) and following government incentive measures introduced in 1967, such as import tax exemptions, tariff, and tax deductions on capital goods and low-cost credit (Turkey Sectorial Report for Fashion-Net Project 2004; Neidik and Gereffi 2006: 2293). A further developmental spurt occurred in the early 1980s with market liberalization. Buoyed up by the developing clothing industry, the textiles industry experienced a second development spurt from the mid-1990s onwards.

The clothing industry began to manufacture for export markets only from the late 1970s/early 1980s—as enterprises were privatized and manufacturing in western countries began to be phased out. During the 1980s but less so since then (Phillips 2005), the industry engaged in the very lucrative so-called suitcase exporting[3] to Russia and countries in CEE. This has enabled enterprises to accumulate the necessary investment capital for expansion (Interview Notes 2006). The industry expanded very rapidly from the mid-1990s onwards and, after a brief downturn in the early 2000s, more steeply since 2002. The clothing industry now is by far the larger exporter of the two industries (TCMA 2005a: 4; TEA 2006: 14). In 2005, the Turkish clothing industry was the second largest provider of clothing—after China—to the EU, with 65 per cent of its exports going to EU-25 nations (ITKIB 2006: 4–5). Many large firms have sales offices in Europe, and most regularly attend European fashion fairs. Only 8.1 per cent of Turkish exports went to the USA (ibid). Although this makes Turkey only one of the smaller US suppliers (9th largest in textiles and 19th in clothing), US business nevertheless is very important to Turkish firms. The industry's biggest rival now is China which also was by far the largest exporter of clothing to Turkey in 2005 (TCMA 2005a: 9).

One of the problems of the Turkish clothing industry is its large informal sector of unregistered firms. This makes acquisition of precise industry statistics highly problematic. According to Phillips (2005: 151), there are around 45,000 textile and clothing firms, employing around 2 million people. Concerning its size composition, the Turkish clothing industry, in common with many developing and developed countries, has a large component of small- and medium-sized enterprises (SME), that is, firms with fewer than 250 employees. SMEs amount to 99 per cent of all firms in the industry, providing 77 per cent of employment and 27 per cent of value-added. Among SMEs micro-firms, which employ fewer than 50 persons, accounted for 56.5 per cent of employment in 2001. (All statistics have been taken from various Reports by the Turkish Clothing Manufacturers Association.) Reliable figures on employment in the large informal sector of unregistered firms are hard to obtain. Unions have estimated the number of unregistered workers to be between 2 and 2.5 million and point to an additional cheap reservoir of foreign labour of between 1 and 1.5 million (CEPS/WIIW 2005: 9).

However, the industry also has about 105 very large and efficient firms, many of which are part of conglomerates (Phillips 2005: 151). Only a small proportion of clothing firms—3.5 per cent—employ more than 500 persons. But many of these larger firms employ more than 1,000 workers (Interview Notes 2006). The textiles industry has a similar size distribution but the proportion of firms employing more than 500 was larger at 5.2 per cent (own calculations, based on figures of the Turkish Statistical Office, cited by CEPS/WIIW 2005: 17, table). (These figures exclude unregistered firms.)

As already noted, there are relatively few foreign direct investors in the T/C industry. Even firms which entered into joint ventures with reputable Turkish firms in the late 1980s (e.g. Benetton and Levi Strauss with Boyner) pulled out again when the economic situation deteriorated badly in 1993–94 (Tokatli and Eldener 2004: 182). Their numbers increased somewhat after 1997, particularly in the clothing industry (Foreign Capital Association, Yased, cited by CEPS/WIIW 2005: 57), and in 2005 there were 67 firms in textiles and 224 in ready-made garments (fDi 2005: 2). Investors are mainly west European, particularly German (Republic of Turkey Undersecretariat of Treasury[4]). At least two US firms have invested: Cone Mills formed a joint venture with denim company Isco, and VF, the largest US clothing company, also has a plant. This comparatively low volume of inward investment has meant that Turkish firms themselves had to act as engines of growth. However, low representation of foreign firms also has deprived Turkish firms of opportunities for social learning and of stimuli to innovate.

The industry is regionally highly concentrated, with 75 per cent of T/C located in the western towns of Istanbul and Izmir. Bursa, Ankara, Denizli, Gaziantep, Kayseri, Tekirdag, and Adana in the inner provinces also have sizeable concentrations (TCMA 2005c). While Istanbul, as the creative and commercial centre, will remain important, regional wage disparities and high regional inequality have prompted an industry policy of de-centralization into rural Anatolia, which is supported by both the state—through subsidization of firms settling in these underprivileged areas—and the TCMA, the clothing industry association. There exist, however, some misgivings that 'minor Chinas' will be established, hampering the move towards upgrading to higher-quality products (Interview Notes 2006).

Concerning contracting relations with western buyer firms, Turkey may be placed in the first supply ring, together with China/Hong Kong. The Turkish industry has relatively high costs compared with its main competitors, not only in labour but also in energy and loan capital (high interest rates). However, communication and transport costs, as well as corporate income tax, are relatively low (TCMA 2003). In 2001 wages in the formal sector of the T/C industry stood at 20 per cent of the EU-15 level. Wages in the clothing industry are somewhat higher than in Bulgaria and Romania and considerably higher than in China. Recent comparative figures on production expenses per minute put Turkish costs at between €0.14 (Istanbul/Izmir areas) and €0.10 (rest of Turkey), above those for Mexico (€0.6–0.8) and Romania (€0.08), and well above the €0.03 for China (GTZ 2006). Indirect wage costs are particularly high, mainly in textiles (CEPS/WIIW 2005: 33f). Compared with China, its strongest competitor, Turkey's disadvantage in wage levels is partially off-set, according to industry estimation, by slight to considerable advantages in the following areas: cooperation with the textile industry and producers of trim and accessories; yarn quality; technological level; flexibility to produce smaller batches; reliability of delivery and delivery lead time (delivery to Europe by truck takes four days); and efficiency (TCMA 2003). In relation to European markets, Turkey's greater geographical proximity is of huge importance, with delivery time a mere four weeks from receiving the order (Interview with TCMA May 2006). Productivity in the clothing industry, as in most countries, is well below that of manufacturing as a whole, at 36 per cent of total industry productivity, due to the high concentration of SMEs and particularly of micro-firms. A comparative view of productivity puts it at a higher level than in Romania, but slightly lower than in Poland (CEPS/WIIW 2005: 31).

There are eight unions active in the T/C industry. The largest union, TEK-SIF, organizes almost 75 per cent of the largely blue-collar workers who tend to be male in textiles and female in clothing (CEPS/WIIW 2005: 19). But only very few unionized workers are in clothing. Hence only a handful of clothing firms, according to Ascoly, Dent, and de Haan (2004), have union representation. Although wages are low in comparison with those in highly developed countries, they have been rising, as have social payments. However, the very many employees in unregistered firms, particularly in the clothing industry, have to accept inferior pay and conditions and are not in a position to protest. These firms use a whole range of illegal practices, and wage levels are only about one sixth of those in the formal sector. (For greater detail on labour standards, see Chapter 10.) Unions have struggled to recruit these workers but meet strong employer resistance (CEPS/WIIW 2005: 19). Firms in the formal sector resent the lack of registration and non-payment of taxes it entails but, given the high pressure on prices in the global economy since 2005, these unregistered firms remain part of the subcontracting system (FairWear Foundation 2003, cited by Ascoly et al. 2004: 39; Bulut and Lane 2008).

8.1.3. Supplier Firms: Structure, Strategy, and Performance

The 45,000 firms in the T/C industry cover a very wide spectrum, both in terms of size and degree of vertical integration. The largest firms have internalized all steps of the value chain whereas many of the smaller firms specialize in only one or two steps of the T/C process. In 2005 about 1,000 enterprises accounted for 50–60 per cent of the market (TCMA 2005c), indicating a high degree of polarization. This section relies on interview material collected from seven firms, supplemented by published information on them and thus is biased towards the larger and more efficient firms in the industry. Three of our firms are among the 10 largest firms in the Turkish T/C industry, each enjoying an annual turnover of up to US$400 million and employing several thousand people.

Family ownership predominates in both textiles and clothing (Phillips 2005). A holding structure also prevails in several of the largest firms (Interview Notes 2006)—a historical legacy of the highly restrictive and inefficient financial system prevalent until very recently (Cepni 2003: 46f.). A few of the biggest firms now have a proportion of shares listed, to finance expansion (e.g. T-TC-2). 337 firms are foreign-owned, accounting for 5.2 per cent of all foreign-owned firms in Turkey (TCMA 2005c).

Every firm interviewed was predominantly family-owned, sometimes already in the second generation. Family ownership colours both the management philosophy and the expansion strategy. For example, the President of T-C-2, one of three brothers owning the firm, started to help out in the firm from the age of 12. His own daughter has just been entrusted with the task to move the company into women's wear and runs her own profit centre. The founder of Altinyildiz, when looking back on his career at the age of 80, expresses the view that a clothing company can flourish only with the constant close attention and dedication accorded by an owner.[5] Although professional managers were employed in most of our firms, owners continued to take an active part in management. Qualifications of interviewed owners and managers generally were high, with degrees in relevant disciplines, such as textile engineering and economics.

Extensive vertical integration was common in all seven firms. It constituted part of a strategy to strengthen their market position and was accomplished in a step-by-step fashion, due to the high expense involved and the reliance on mainly internal capital. Integration occurred within the textile value chain and comprised forward integration into manufacturing of clothing and, in a few cases, into retailing. Vertical integration in textiles usually meant combining all the steps from spinning to finishing. Backward integration into cotton growing existed in one case (T-T-1). Several of the big textile firms we interviewed had forward integrated into clothing production, deriving equal shares of turnover from both activities, but two textile firms (Arsin and T-T-2) reported that such forward integration efforts had failed.

Concerning product strategy, the textiles industry specializes in cotton but also produces synthetic and woollen materials. Turkey now has the sixth-largest capacity for synthetics in the world (SOMO 2003: 4). Of exported fabrics, knitted fabrics constitute the most important product group, followed by woven apparel (TCMA 2005c). The clothing industry, which relies on both domestically produced and imported fabric, produces a full range of men's and women's clothing from underwear via T-shirts to tailored outer wear, with blue jeans having become a very important export item. It also contains the whole spectrum of market strategies. Cheap and simple mass-produced garments still predominate (65 per cent of all products), and customized, luxury and technically sophisticated products amount to only 15 per cent, while fashion-oriented middle market, small-batch products take up the remaining 20 per cent (TCMA 2003). Given the above figures, Phillips' (2005) claim that the CMT mode of manufacturing still predominates is plausible. The statement by Neidik and Gereffi (2006: 2286) that 90 per cent of direct exports are full package is slightly misleading, given that direct sourcing by retailers (as opposed to sourcing by branded 'manufacturers' and marketers) is, by its very nature, predominantly 'full package'. Nevertheless, even Phillips (2005) points out that 'full package' contracting by western buyer firms has increased strongly in recent years. Hence retailers' private label products and 'manufacturers'/'marketers' brands are dominant, and own brands are still a very small proportion of output.

Nevertheless, prompted by increased competition following first the Customs Union and then the abolition of quotas post January 2005, several Turkish clothing firms (one interviewee [T-TC-3] put the number at around 15) have upgraded to become 'original brand manufacturers' (OBM) who have also developed their own retail outlets. While most are serving only the Turkish market, several have made inroads also into western markets. Boyner now is the largest non-food retailer in Turkey, serving almost all segments of the market (Tokatli and Eldener 2004: 175). (For details on brand names, see Tokatli and

Kizilgun 2004.) Contradicting Hassler (2003), who comments that it is uncommon to combine CMT for western brands with OBM, several Turkish firms have successfully implemented this strategy. One company even claims that familiarity with 'own brand' production gives the company a special advantage when dealing with foreign brands (Mavi Jeans website), but a second big producer following the dual strategy admits that it has become harder to maintain in recent years (T-TC-3).

Among OBM companies, Mavi Jeans has been the most successful and merits closer description, based on an interview with the company in May 2006. The parent company, Erak, 100 per cent family-owned and founded in 1984 as a contract manufacturer, created the Mavi Jeans brand in 1991. It became a separate division within the company—Mavi Jeans—in 1994 and, by 1997, had become leader in the Turkish market for jeans. Exporting started around 1996, first taking the form of 'suitcase exporting' to the Balkan countries and Russia. It soon expanded to western Europe, particularly Germany, where Turkish middlemen were used to achieve market entry. Of total jeans production, 60 per cent now is for other major up-market brands and 40 per cent is for the Mavi brand, of which two-thirds still sell in the Turkish market. Showrooms were opened in North America (Vancouver and Los Angeles) in 1997, and by 1998 sales of jeans in the USA, the citadel of jeans manufacturing, began to take off with product adoption by Nordstrom and Bloomingdale. The brand is now successful in several American speciality and department stores. Mavi's first flagship stores were opened in 2002 and 2003 in Germany, Canada, and the USA. Altogether, the company operates 170 retail outlets, most of which are still in Turkey. Mavi now has foreign sales offices, a design team in the USA and merchandizing people in Germany and Canada. It follows US accounting standards and is currently looking for a foreign JV partner.

Mavi's success rests on thorough prior market exploration by a younger, western-educated member of the founding family and a strong advertising campaign, as well as on the merit of the product itself, described to us as a sub-premium brand. Mavi Jeans combines high quality with a more moderate price than is commanded by the US-made premium brands. The company uses mainly Turkish fabric and applies all the latest finishing techniques, such as enzymes and laser treatment (Interview with Mavi Jeans May 2006).

Turkish supplier firms are, by and large, relatively stable core suppliers to western firms. As pointed out in Chapter 7, a large proportion of German and British buyer firms regularly sourced from Turkey and expressed themselves as highly satisfied with their Turkish suppliers on all counts. Only the relatively high wage costs prevented these firms from placing higher orders with Turkish suppliers. Among our US firms, in contrast, Turkey was rarely mentioned as a supplier country, due in some part to the fact that large retailers and designer firms did not figure in the sample. As one Turkish interviewee commented: 'Only high-level producers can afford Turkish fabric', which also carries high import duties in the USA (T-C-1). By far the biggest volume of Turkish T/C exports, in 2005, went to Germany (20.7%), followed by the UK (12.8%), with the US occupying a distant third place (8.1%)—a much reduced proportion in comparison with earlier years when the US was a bigger customer than the UK (ITKIB 2006: 6).

Interviewed firms were large exporters of both fabric and clothing to all three countries. They did business with all the major retailers in several European countries, as well as supplying fabric to 'manufacturers' of retailers' 'own label' garments, such as Steilmann (Germany) and Dewhirst (UK). Branded 'manufacturers', such as Betty Barclay, Hugo Boss, Marco Polo, Calvin Klein, Esprit, and Escada, constituted another large group of customers. Being among the largest manufacturers, several of our interviewees did major business with US firms, such as The Gap (fabric only), Banana Republic, Ann Taylor, Liz Claiborne, Calvin Klein, and Tommy Hilfiger. Many firms are highly dependent on exports to a few US firms—for T-C-2, for example, 70 per cent of exports went to the USA—and therefore are vulnerable to significant post-quota withdrawal of US firms. One firm among our interviewees (T-TC-3) had lost most of its US business during 2005, and several others were complaining about the footlooseness of US buyers.

Turkish firms, in turn, maintain their own production networks both within and beyond Turkey, utilizing both outsourcing and FDI. Thus, although triangle manufacturing (Gereffi and Memedovic 2003) is not as high as it is among some Asian companies, it has nevertheless existed for two decades and has increased since the 2000s. FDI in the early 1990s occurred in culturally and geographically close Central Asian republics, such as Turkmenistan and Uzbekistan, which exported to the USA (Neidik and Gereffi 2006: 2295), and from the late 1990s onwards, following the Customs Union with the EU, in CEE countries, particularly Bulgaria. More recently, several interviewed firms were about to invest in Egypt, attracted by the tax free industrial zones, the low labour costs (about one-tenth of Turkey's), the availability of good local cotton and the relatively low geographical distance to Turkey (Interview Notes 2006). Outsourcing by Turkish firms is said to be very high—accounting for 65 per cent in 2005 (TCMA 2003).

Whether large firms make use of the large domestic unregistered sector could not be ascertained during interviews but, given the high profile of their buyers and their monitoring practices, it seems unlikely that this is a prominent strategy. Large-scale outsourcing is associated with mass production of standard clothes, and the TCMA's sectoral strategy recommends a drastic reduction to 20 per cent by 2010 (ibid). Among our big firms, for example, one (T-TC-2) has 30 clothing subcontractors but always does its own cutting. A second firm (T-C-2) has exclusive suppliers in Turkey and others in Romania and Morocco. Turkish suppliers were regarded as problematic by one interviewee because of their comparatively high level of social payments (T-C-2). Not all interviewed companies were major users of subcontracting—one (T-TC-2) sought to keep the bulk of production in-house, and a textile firm (T-T-1) said that, in its line of business, labour costs are not the important factor. Among small- and medium-sized firms, sub-contracting to even smaller firms and engaging home workers is said to be very common (Phillips 2005).

8.1.4. Relations of Supplier Firms with British, German, and US Buyer Firms

We pointed out in Chapter 7 that significant national differences exist in how western firms govern their global production networks and relate to their foreign suppliers. It is therefore interesting to explore how Turkish suppliers of both textiles and clothing themselves view the relationships with their various foreign buyers. Most of our respondents readily told us about the very different contracting styles by firms from the UK, Germany, and the USA, and only one believed that there were no differences between German and British buyer firms. Their comments related mainly to four themes: first, the closeness and directness of the relation, indicative also of its durability; second, the product and labour standards expected and the nature of control exerted by buyers; third, business morals, such as the degree of honesty of western buyers and the trust extended to them. Trust was exemplified particularly by responses to payment methods used by western buyers and accepted more or less grudgingly by their Turkish suppliers. Fourth, the perceived upgrading experienced through teaching by western buyers is of interest. Last, a few comments were also made about the divergent fashion understanding of European and American firms.

8.1.4.1. Closeness and Durability of Buyer–Supplier Relations

Here we found parallels with Hassler's (2003) observation on the Indonesian clothing industry. Close and direct relations with suppliers afford buyers a central role in the quality control process, whereas the use of agents as intermediaries shows a loose form of buyer engagement, prone to easy dissolution of ties if prices elsewhere become more enticing (Hassler 2003: 523). Closeness and the control this affords were gained through maintaining local buying offices, but close contact also took the form of frequent visiting. Last, the use of other intermediaries in the process of quality control—particularly certification of fabric by testing laboratories—was seen by suppliers to give buyers effective control.

Several supplier firms saw German buyers as maintaining closer and more direct relations with their Turkish suppliers than either UK or US firms. 'They visit us and expect to be visited. They invest more in business, find best possible sources' (T-T-1). This was confirmed by a second firm which further elaborated that Germans visit once per season to view the products and that Americans come least of all to visit and inspect merchandise (T-TC-2). This latter firm also pointed out that their German retailer buyer had opened a local office already 20 years ago, whereas British Marks & Spencer had opened an office only 3 years before. Another firm pointed out that, with the exception of Next, UK retailer buyers did not have buying offices and mainly relied on agents (T-TC-1). Two respondents (T-TC-2 and T-T-1) spontaneously attributed to German buyers a high degree of loyalty to their suppliers. 'Germans would be loyal, but sometimes circumstances dictate change' (T-T-1). Comments on UK firms' loyalty were more negative: 'No loyalty, even Marks & Spencer are leaving Turkey for Sri Lanka' (T-T-2).

The low frequency of personal visits from US clients was also connected with a low level of loyalty both to American middle-men and Turkish suppliers: 'Americans change their "commission makers" almost every season...Europeans have longer-term relations' (T-TC-3). This company was the only one to regard German and British firms' behaviour as the same, which—given the comparatively short period of British presence in Turkey—is not highly credible.

8.1.4.2. *Buyer Control and Enforcement of Standards*

The above divergences in the directness and longevity of buyer–supplier relations may to a significant extent be mapped onto the degree of control over product standards demanded, as well as being related also to the priorities set between quality and price. At the same time, indirect quality control in the choice of fabrics, through the use of local laboratories by British buyers, seemed to be considered highly effective. (German customers were more interested in the ecological soundness and required an ÖkoTex 1000 certificate.) Several firms contrasted the direct and personal control of German buyers with the indirect control of British buyers, particularly of Marks & Spencer. Quality standards of Marks & Spencer were considered the highest of all buyers, sometimes exceeding what is considered justified. 'Concerning standards, the UK is the most difficult in Europe, particularly Marks & Spencer. Standards are overly high' (T-T-2). 'British buyers want labs to approve the fabrics and ask to see the test results. Marks & Spencer has the highest standards in fabric, higher than German and US buyers' (T-TC-2). This led one company to suggest that 'German customers are a lot easier than British ones' (T-T-2), whereas others commented on the different, more personal control of German buyers. 'British buyers do not visit as much as German firms to inspect products' (T-TC-2), or 'German customers take care of quality of workmanship—they are more fastidious' and exert direct control (T-C-2). 'UK buyers do not inspect fabric directly, they go through testing labs' (T-T-1). Another firm pointed out that 'Germans check the final product more than other nationalities' (T-TC-2). 'American buyers are mainly 'full package' store buyers. They say where to buy the fabric, but we make the first and last relation with the fabric mill' (T-C-2). Other comments referred mainly to the American preoccupation with cost control and the hard bargain they drove in this respect. 'US buyers are hard negotiators on price' (T-TC-2). 'US buyers are always very tough, they prefer the Far East for lower prices' (T-T-1). 'For Americans figures always come first. It forces you to control your figures yourself' (T-C-1). One firm attributed similar behaviour to UK buyers on price: 'UK firms push down prices more than other European countries' (T-TC-1), a view corroborated by comments from other firms cited below. There were few very large German retailers among buyers of fabric, and it was observed that 'German buyers generally buy in lower volume than their British (mostly retailer) counterparts and hence at a higher price' (T-T-2).

8.1.4.3. Business Morals and Trust

The business morality of their western buyers and the ability to trust them is, for Turkish suppliers, strongly related to their behaviour regarding price negotiation and to their payment methods. Germans were generally trusted the most, and no unethical business practices were attributed to them. British large retailers, in contrast, were more often lumped together with American buyers in these respects.

It was revealing to the first author, who has conducted a previous study of supplier relations within Germany and the UK (Lane and Bachmann 1997), that many of the domestic practices concerning payment methods were replicated in firms' relations with Turkish firms. German customers were said to pay mainly according to the principle of 'cash against (customs) documents'—the safest and most advantageous method for Turkish suppliers. 'Germans pay on time and pay by 'cash against documents—best method. We trust Karstadt. They will pay' (T-TC-2). They also are lauded for being very punctual with payment. 'German buyers promise to pay on the 30th or 60th day net. They are more trustworthy buyers [than UK and US buyers]. They have been longer with us in Turkey...they would even be welcome to buy on open terms—we trust them to pay' (T-T-1).

British buyers paid more often on 'open terms' or used the similar method of 'factoring' which is not underwritten by a bank guarantee. 'The British pay by factoring—equals open terms or cash against goods' (T-T-1), particularly for textiles. 'We sell to UK buyers on open terms. Their reason is that, if delivery is more than 10 days late, T-T-1 has to take a 10 per cent reduction in price' (T-T-1). US customers adhere to the payment method of 'cash on delivery'—which means slightly later payment for their Turkish suppliers. 'US companies use letters of credit' (T-TC-1) which entails a bank guarantee but costs more for Turkish firms.

Our respondents also pointed towards other business practices in relation to costs, designed to tip the balance in favour of Anglo-American buyers, some of them distinctly unethical. 'Clothing is a cut-throat market. Americans have discount, charge-back (for small mistakes made, say in labelling) and mark-downs (for garments not sold)' (T-C-1). In contrast, German retailers were viewed as more straight: 'German department stores have a lot of discussions beforehand and then they accept' (T-TC-1).

It is difficult to work with [British retailers] Arcadia and BHS—too much squeezing of price. They make suppliers pay a lot for shortages and damage. Turkish companies take steps to play the game on their terms, take steps to secure their own position. Standards of behaviour, particularly in Arcadia, are distressing...It is better to deal with brands than retailers (T-T-2).

Although a particular British retailer usually is singled out for criticism, one respondent even reproached Marks & Spencer. 'M&S announced a 10 per cent cut of profit, with a month's notice. If we cannot do it they will move to the Far East' (T-TC-1). Another kind of disloyalty attributed to British buyers was: 'British buyers are not at all loyal—they take Turkish fabric to have it copied in the Far East (T-T-2)'.

8.1.4.4. Training of Suppliers

We did not systematically probe what kind of assistance had been given by western buyers but received two interesting spontaneous observations on this topic, both relating to German firms. One Turkish firm acknowledged the training received from their German buyers over the years: 'Germans brought a lot of conditions which educated Turkish sub-contractors. They brought us up to compliance standards, made it easier for Turkish producers' (T-C-1). However, another Turkish supplier bemoaned the recent deterioration in the behaviour of German firms, connected with generational change. 'The old generation of Germans is going, there is less teaching now. Germans are becoming more opportunist, more like Americans' (T-C-2). This firm may have referred to the fact that some German branded 'manufacturers' no longer have first-hand manufacturing experience, and/or to the change in generation currently under way in several companies (German Interview Notes 2003).

8.1.4.5. Fashion Understanding of Europeans and Americans

One company [T-TC-1] observed that European companies were more observant of fashion trends than their American counterparts—they now have more models and smaller batches. A second firm [T-C-1] confirmed this and pointed out that this different fashion understanding between Europe and USA made selling more complicated.

8.1.5. Future Prospects of the Turkish Clothing Industry

The above account has demonstrated that the Turkish textiles and clothing industry is efficiently organized, with high levels of competence and adaptability. This makes it very competitive compared with Central and Eastern European and Mediterranean suppliers. This is due in part to competent organization of both the two industries and the efforts of their large firms, assisted by past and present government policy. However, an insufficient level of industry regulation, particularly in the informal sector and concerning labour, continues to place serious constraints on the extensive small-firm sector.

In the short run, quota abolition has not yet had a serious impact, but the expiry of China safeguards in 2008 may worsen the situation. A document compiled by the OECD, WTO, and the US National Council of Textiles Organizations reported Turkey as suffering least market loss after January 2005 (TEA 2006: 17). Yet Turkish suppliers are justifiably concerned about how the end of the quota system, together with Turkey's open market, will affect the industries over the following decade. The shadow of China falls here as everywhere else, and many concerns about the impact of China were being expressed during our interviews.

According to Ascoly et al. (2004: 35), 'experts suggest that Turkey is poised to consolidate its positions as a producer and sourcing hub that serves the European market and beyond'. While this estimation may be correct with reference to the European market, its place in the US market now is much less secure. Following quota abolition, the Turkish industry is expected to experience a significant decline (of between 20% and 25%) in global market share. The General Secretary of the TCMA, in an interview with the authors in May 2006, reported a 25 per cent loss of market share in the US clothing market in 2005 which, given the above figures, might have been compensated for by gains in other markets. It appears that, post-January 2005, there has been a sudden rush into China but that more up-market and fashion-conscious branded 'manufacturers'/marketers have come to realize the drawbacks of this move. Some of our interviewees remarked that buyers who had deserted them were returning.

The industry organizations, TCMA and ITKIB, as well as individual firms, certainly are very conscious of the 'China Challenge' and have devised strategies to address it, within existing institutional constraints. Two adjustment strategies are being put into place. The first, which seeks escape from comparatively high labour costs (wages and social payments), involves relocating production facilities to Anatolia (for lower wages only) and to countries like Egypt and Turkmenistan, which can compete with China on both wage levels and social payments. At the same time, there is a realization that competing solely on costs/price would be futile. The second and more urgent strategy is upgrading. Thus, the Industry's Strategy Horizon 2010 envisages that, through continuous upgrading, it will move into the global market band of 'quality-price' competition. The ultimate aim is to join 'market maker' countries like Italy and Germany, and, by using creativity and innovation, sell more expensive products and branded fashion. This will not only require upgrading by individual companies. The Association calls additionally for more targeted government subsidies in the areas of R&D, design and brand development, marketing, and finance, as well as fostering more inter-company co-operation, both in Turkey and with foreign companies (TCMA 2005*b*). More concretely, the foundation of an Apparel Institute is contemplated. Firms have been issued detailed instructions on how to improve in all business functions. Thus, for example, for production, the recommendation is not only technological upgrading, through CAD–CAM technology. Additionally, improved relations with subcontractors are highlighted, which entail consolidation of the network, more durable relations, and more training of contractors to required standards (ibid). The biggest weaknesses of the industry, hampering upgrading, are said to be the financial structure and the large SME sector (TCMA 2005*c*). Although some progress already has been made in upgrading, recent figures on the composition of exports in value terms reveal that there is still a way to go in this direction (Phillips 2005).

Moving to the level of firms, it is recognized that raising general standards of quality and, more so, movement into OBM will be very difficult. One firm (T-C-1) pointed out that, even if producers go up-market and compete mainly on quality, there is the danger that foreign branded marketers begin to source in China and thus render Turkey-oriented OBM producers uncompetitive. But the large firms nevertheless are committed to upgrading, and several firms told us of their efforts to gradually raise the quality of products and to move up the value chain from CMT operations to 'full package' and even OD and OB manufacturing. Forward integration into retail is part of the latter strategy. Those already at the OBM stage were intent on consolidating their position by improving their marketing through greater physical presence in their main markets. To these ends, firms have made huge investments in new machinery, particularly in the textiles industry (40% of investment is not taxable [T-T-2]). Certification with ISO 9001 and ISO 9002 is widespread in the industry (Interview material 2006). Some of the large textile firms (e.g. T-TC-2 and Arsin) have small R&D departments and engage in constant innovation of process technology. Such efforts already yield some results. Thus, the unit value on a scale of 1–5 (for quality) of exported clothing has risen in recent years from 5 to 3, and Turkey is moving close to Italy's standard of 2 (CEPS/WIIW 2005: 53). In sum, although Chinese competition should not be underestimated, it is likely that, for all the reasons rehearsed above, the Turkish industry will retain a high rank in the international hierarchy of exporters.

In conclusion, the comparatively strong, even if not flawless, competitive position of the Turkish T/C industry in the global industry cannot simply be ascribed to the efforts of the Turkish state and its competitive strategies (Palan and Abbott 1996). Although there is a long history of state support for this industry, there has been no clear state competitive strategy. On the one hand the state supports upgrading to more full-package and own-brand manufacturing and the use of a relatively well paid and secure labour force in the formal economy. On the other hand, the Turkish state has not yet tackled one of the greatest obstacles to reaching the goal of product upgrading, namely, the continued existence of a large informal sector of largely small firms with low labour standards and wages. Instead the industry's large vertically integrated firms and their well-educated owner-managers, which have grown and upgraded their performance over a long period of time, have been left to do so relatively independently. By the time they became integrated in the European Customs Union they were already sufficiently advanced to cope with the intensifying competition in the run-up to and since 2005. They have been supported in this endeavour by well-organized industry associations. Referring to the typology of competitive strategies developed by Palan and Abbott (1996), one cannot ascribe any clear industry strategy to the Turkish state, but more a 'muddling through', trying to please different industry constituencies.

8.2. ROMANIA

In this section we turn to another country on the eastern edge of Europe which, like Turkey, is strongly oriented to European markets. But the Romanian clothing industry is generally at an earlier stage of development than Turkey's and faces a number of additional problems.

8.2.1. Geopolitical Position, Industrial Development, and Institutional Structure

Romania is one of the newest members of the European Union, which it finally joined in January 2007 after 12 years of negotiation. Geographically situated on the Black Sea in south-eastern Europe, and having borders with Bulgaria, Hungary, Moldova, Serbia, and Ukraine, it is the only European former communist-bloc country not to share a common border with any of the 15 EU members of the 1990s. This lack of a common border with richer industrialized nations is seen as one reason for Romania's comparatively difficult transition to a market economy (Smith 2001). Its population of 22.3 million is relatively young in European terms, with an average age of 37 years, but the country is also one of the poorest in the EU. Per capita GDP was just €3,440 in 2005. Poverty remains widespread. Many Romanians have migrated to Spain and other southern European countries in search of better-paid work,[6] which is causing labour shortages in the textile and clothing industry (Interview Notes 2006). An average unemployment rate of 5.8 per cent in 2005 masks wide variations geographically and structurally, with joblessness in farming regions of around 20 per cent (in the north-east and south-west of the country) contrasting with tight employment conditions in the capital city, Bucharest, where only 3.8 per cent of people are without work.

Reforms since the 'bloody' revolution of December 1989 that overthrew Ceauşescu's regime have been concentrated on several fronts: the political, with the attempt to create a liberal, democratic society in place of the restricted freedoms of the former one-party state; the economic, where the Soviet-era command economy is gradually being replaced with functioning, competitive market conditions; and the social, with the shift towards meritocratic processes, equal opportunities, and respect for 'western' norms of human rights (Phinnemore and Light 2001: 2). But the former communist elite within the security services, the military and business, including banks, held a tenacious grip on power and influence in the early 1990s, and the rent-seeking behaviour of these networks is seen to lie at the root of Romania's continuing problems with corruption (Mungiu-Pippidi 2006: 21).

The 1990s has been a decade of stop-start recovery from the impoverishment and financial crises of the previous decades that were rooted in Ceauşescu's Stalinist economic policy. Another severe financial crisis in 1998–99 necessitated the negotiation of an IMF standby facility. Hesitant privatization of loss-making large and medium-sized industrial enterprises (Smith 2001) and the continuation of government subsidies to loss-making industries lay behind Romania's slow progress on structural reforms relative to other transition economies in CEE. Greater financial discipline has been evident since 2001, but GDP in 2003 was still lower than it had been in 1989.

The slow pace of macroeconomic and structural change delayed Romania's entry to the EU, which had become a major policy goal in 1996. It was not until October 2004 that at last the European Commission awarded it the status of 'functioning market economy' (Smith 2006) that opened the way to full membership

27 months later. But Romania's relationship with the EU is a long one compared with other CEE countries. Pursuing a determinedly independent line from the USSR, Romania had become a party to the European Community's GSP as early as 1974, and it gained Most Favoured Nation status with the USA in 1975. The resulting lower tariffs on its exports enabled the start of relationships with various European clothing producers, although under quite restrictive trade arrangements. No other CEE country entered such a relationship until 1986, when MFA-style agreements came into force between the EU and Romania, Poland, Hungary, Czechoslovakia, and Bulgaria (Yoruk 2001). Having joined the World Trade Organization in 1995, Romania in 1997 signed the Central European Free Trade Agreement (CEFTA) as a stepping-stone towards EU membership through trade and economic integration. Each of these steps was important in reinforcing the opportunities for Romania's clothing exports.

Per capita exports in 1997 to the industrial West, the EU-15, the former Soviet Union and CEE, and to other developing countries were all below the levels achieved by other European transition economies (Smith 2001: table 6.2). Since 2000 the EU has been both the largest export destination and the largest provider of imports to Romania. Total bilateral trade with the EU reached €37.1 billion in 2005, three times the level of 1995 and equivalent to nearly 70 per cent of total foreign trade. Turkey (5.4%) is also a significant bilateral trade partner. Overall, compared with Bulgaria (which was also to join the EU in 2007), Romania has relied to a far greater extent on labour-intensive industries for its export base and has generated very few exports that depend on high level human-capital intensive activity (ibid).

The Ceauşescu-era emphasis on heavy industrial development reduced the share of light industry (including textiles and clothing) in total output from over 60 per cent before the Second World War to less than 25 per cent in the early 1980s. Textiles and clothing production—most of which was exported—contributed around half of this (Bachman 1989). Publication of production statistics for the textile and clothing industry ceased during the 1980s (ibid.), but the sector once again became crucial to the economy after the revolution. Exports destined for the EU-15 in 1996 were heavily weighted to the textiles and clothing sectors, accounting for nearly 35 per cent of the total; the next-largest export sector was footwear with 10.5 per cent (Smith 2001). The following trade figures demonstrate the extent of the geographic shift in apparel export markets: exports of clothing to the former Soviet Union plunged from US$96 million in 1991 (representing 32% of the total) to just US$7 million (0.4%) in 2004; meanwhile exports to Italy and Germany expanded by 54 times and 14 times, respectively, over the same period (Crestanello and Tattara 2006, Table 3).

Romania attracted only US$9 billion in foreign direct investment between 1989 and 2002, compared with the US$22.5 billion invested in Hungary in the same period, due to the volatility of the economy and significant levels of corruption. Investment inflows rose sharply from 2004 as EU membership approached, reaching US$11.4 billion in 2006 alone. Approximately half of FDI has gone into the privatization of large state-owned industrial enterprises. The textiles, clothing, and footwear sector accounts for only 2.6 per cent of the total FDI stock (*Business Eastern Europe* 2007), with Italian firms particularly prominent (CDC 2003) and to a lesser extent German firms (Interview Notes 2006). The intermediate inputs sector, supplying items such as thread, buttons, and zippers, has also attracted some foreign investment.

Estimates of union density in the T/C sector vary between 25 per cent of workers (Ghinararu and Mocanu 2006) and 35 per cent (*Dialog Textil* 2007), and participation rates are particularly low in companies established since 1989 (ibid.). The influence of labour representatives has changed since the pre-Revolution years, when trade unions were part of the Party apparatus and only nominally represented workers' interests. Since 1989 the Labour Code has allowed freedom of association and collective bargaining, although regulations are better observed in unionized firms than in the generally non-unionized small and medium enterprises that make up the majority of the clothing and textile sector. Doubts also remain among workers about the independence of unions from management (Trif 2005). A collective bargaining agreement is negotiated at the national level for the industry, but is poorly respected and implemented at factory level, especially in those that are privately owned (Clean Clothes Campaign 2001). Work schedules are reported to be changed frequently in order to meet contractual obligations, with tight deadlines often used as a means of cutting (labour) costs via non-payment of overtime. Particularly in the clothing industry, where in 2002 82 per cent of workers were women, mechanisms to implement legal provisions around equal opportunities and pay, maternity leave, etc., are not well developed (Ghinararu and Mocanu 2006).

Although Romania has a skilled labour force, there remains a shortage of managers trained in western business practices. This is as true of the T/C industry as it is of other manufacturing activity. Commercial skills in industry have been slow to develop as pre-revolution trade relations, including all contacts with foreign buyers, were handled by industry-specific departments in the trade ministry (CONFEX for the clothing industry). These special departments also made management decisions on production planning, and on which orders would be filled by which factories (Clean Clothes Campaign 2001). Since the design demands of a fast-moving European or American fashion industry had little effect on the centrally planned Romanian T/C industry, as in other CEE countries, a widespread practice of home tailoring contributed to the pool of relatively skilled workers able to move into the industry (Pickles et al. 2006). In contrast to the paucity of management-level training, the education system for decades focused on apprenticeships and the training of technically competent workers. Hence the quality of output is generally regarded as good, although productivity and efficient working practices have taken time to develop.

A number of specialized schools and universities serve the textile and clothing industry, of which the best-known for textile engineering is the Technical University in Iaşi, in the north-east of the country where many of the country's synthetic fibre and yarn production plants were concentrated. Its dedicated faculty offers specialized 4-year undergraduate degrees and a variety of graduate programmes in various aspects of the textile and textile engineering industry. It also organizes seminars and offers technical advice to firms (Yoruk 2002). Many firms' chief line managers and specialist engineers are graduates of this university (Interview Notes 2006). Other institutions, such as the University of Art and Design in Cluj-Napoca, Transylvania, focus more on the creative design element, graduating 20–25 students each year (Interview Notes 2006). Business support for the sector is provided by various local chambers of commerce, and by FEPAIUS, the federation of employers associations for the light industry, as well as its constituent members including Romconf (ready-made clothes), Tricontex (textile and knitwear goods), and OCIMM (SME garment producers) (FEPAIUS 2006). In addition the German agency GTZ has been active in Romania since 1994 providing technical cooperation for SMEs in the T/C industry (and others) to prepare for EU membership.

8.2.2. Structure and Performance of the Industry

The economic importance of the textile and clothing industries is clear from the following data: in 2005–06 they accounted for 10.5 per cent of national industrial production, 19 per cent of exports, and 10 per cent of imports (GTZ 2006). T/C turnover as a percentage of GDP grew from 5.2 per cent in 1995 to 7.1 per cent in 2001, an extremely high level of dependence compared with, for example, Poland, which has a much more diversified economy (IFM 2004). Exports of textiles and clothing increased by 220 per cent between 1993 and 1997, with ready-made clothing produced under cut-make OPT contracts accounting for 89 per cent of the total in 1996 (Clean Clothes Campaign 2001). T/C has been one of the country's most dynamic sectors since the end of the Ceaușescu regime, in particular the clothing manufacturing segment, which achieved an average annual growth rate of 11.4 per cent in the period 1995–2001 (IFM 2004). In contrast textile output declined throughout the 1990s and is now far from satisfying the needs of local clothing manufacturers.

International trade in the industry is strongly oriented towards Europe: in 2002, even before membership of the EU, 94 per cent of Romania's T/C exports and 86 per cent of its T/C imports were with EU-27 partners (including accession candidates) (Commission of the European Communities 2003). Our analysis of the Romanian T/C industry therefore concentrates on the relationship with EU markets. The largest individual trade partners are Italy, Germany, France, the UK, and Turkey; together these five countries accounted for 50 per cent of T/C exports in 2003, compared with 39 per cent in 1992 (FEPAIUS 2006). Its exports are far more heavily concentrated on only a few countries than, for example, Turkey's (ROM-2). Romania is the third largest supplier to the EU-25, following China and Turkey, of ready-made clothing, worth €3.7 billion in 2005 for a share of 6.7 per cent figures from (Eurostat database). Its exports to Germany and the UK that year amounted to €811 million and €551 million, respectively. But exports to the EU in 2005 fell 9.4 per cent from the previous year and fell again in 2006, as

EU buyers sourced more from Asian suppliers following the end of trade quotas. Leu appreciation against the Euro also pushed up Romanian selling prices. T/C trade with the USA has been limited by US tariffs on textiles ranging from 12 to 32 per cent, despite its Most Favoured Nation status (CDC 2003).

At the same time as being a major ready-made clothing exporter, Romania is the second largest consumer, behind the USA, of EU-produced textile fabrics, taking 10.2 per cent of EU-25 exports in 2005. Its share of fabric exported from the EU-15 countries nearly doubled between 1995 and 2002 (IFM 2004: table 3), reflecting the rapid growth during this period of simple garment assembly for EU markets. Whereas the greatest part of T/C imports in 1999 was accounted for by fabric, more recently imports of ready-made clothing have been increasing dramatically as the consumer market develops (Interview Notes 2006). Following entry to the EU in 2007, Romania's remaining textile producers have faced greater competition from non-EU fabric suppliers, principally China and India, as import tariffs fell from 18 per cent to the EU level of 8 per cent.

Before 1990 the T/C industry was Romania's second largest employer, organized in large state-owned units of production. Employment plunged to about 80,000 in 1995 (WBF/GTZ 2006) with the collapse of central planning and the loss of traditional export markets in other socialist countries (Clean Clothes Campaign 2001) but began to recover in 1997 as the investment climate became more favourable. By 2005 the 347,000 T/C workers slightly exceeded pre-revolution levels and represented 10.5 per cent of total manufacturing employment (WBF/GTZ 2006). But the difference now lies in the balance between textiles and clothing employment: the clothing sector employed 262,400 in the year 2001 versus 94,500 employees in textiles, whereas in 1989 the clothing sector had employed only three-fifths as many people as the textile producers (CDC 2003). Of the 60,000 textile workers who lost their jobs in 1997–2002, roughly 80 per cent were female (Evgeniev 2006). The clothing sector experienced another downturn when the exchange rate deteriorated in 2005, leading first to the collapse of many subcontractors and later to that of financially weak CM producers (*Dialog Textil* 2006). More importantly, labour shortages in the industry began to emerge as a serious issue in 2003, and this problem continues unabated owing to migration to EU countries (Interview Notes 2006). It has been reported that one Romanian company began bringing Chinese workers into the country in 2006 in order to resolve its labour shortages.

Despite labour problems, salary levels in the T/C industry remain the second-lowest of all branches in industry. For operatives (e.g. sewing machinists) gross pay ranges from RON 440 to RON 650 per month (€125 to €185), while more highly skilled employees such as managers, engineers, and technical specialists earn RON 3,500 or more (*Dialog Textil* 2007). The minimum monthly wage, which many machinists earn, increased from about €86 in 2004 to €100 and again to €125 in 2007. Per minute production costs of €0.08 compare favourably with the rest of Eastern Europe, Turkey, and North Africa, as well as Shanghai and Hong Kong, although not the rest of China or Vietnam (GTZ 2006). However, wages and labour-related costs are expected to rise sharply following EU membership. Productivity remains an issue for Romania, with only Bulgaria among the EU-27 nations achieving lower annual turnover per employee, although this is associated with dependence on low value-added CM/CMT production.

According to GTZ (2006), the industry comprises some 170 textile firms and around 5,040 clothing producers. Private firms account for 97 per cent of production and 98 per cent of exports (FEPAIUS 2006). Large numbers of new clothing firms emerged during the 1990s, with up to 85 per cent estimated to have been established since 1989 (CDC 2003), some of them by managers of the former CONFEX trade department who took their clients with them (Clean Clothes Campaign 2001). As in most countries there is a polarization between a relatively small number of large firms and a long tail of SME and micro-enterprises. Although IFM (2004) found that only around 300 firms producing textiles and clothing employ more than 250 workers, GTZ (2006) suggests that the largest enterprises in the industry have over 3,000 employees—possibly because several production units have been grouped under a holding company. Nearly 70 per cent of firms are small and medium enterprises with fewer than 10 employees and another 10 per cent have 11–100 employees (GTZ 2006). The medium to longer term outlook for many companies is not promising: a FEPAIUS representative has forecast that up to 40 per cent of smaller firms in the sector might be forced to close in and after 2007 due to non-compliance with EU regulations on social, environmental, and security standards.

Ownership patterns and business models in the industry have changed dramatically in the last two decades: pre-1989, all textile and clothing enterprises were state-owned and were highly vertically integrated, addressing every stage of the value chain from natural or synthetic fibre production through to the finished consumer goods (CDC 2003). Each enterprise employed a large workforce, ranging from 2 to 3,000 employees upwards: the biggest, located in Bucharest, boasted a 16,000-strong workforce (Clean Clothes Campaign 2001). Being purely production units, however, these state enterprises handled neither financial nor commercial aspects of the business and often had no knowledge of the customers or markets they were manufacturing for. Exports were handled entirely by the foreign trade companies. Romania's status as an important locus of clothing production within the Soviet Union combined with, since the early 1980s, experience of export production for non-Soviet markets (Interview Notes 2004, 2006; Pickles et al. 2006), aided some firms to make the transition from state ownership. German buyers in particular played an important role in sustaining the industry. In the 1990s a rapid shift from state into private hands took place, often accompanied by the fragmentation of large-scale enterprises—the largest factory in Bucharest, for example, was split into 8 separate units (Interview Notes 2006). Clothing manufacturing units tended to move fairly early into private ownership, as those taken over by former CONFEX managers in particular were able to maintain contact with foreign customers. Nevertheless, all former state-owned units were forced to shed large numbers of employees and improve their efficiency in order to survive. From the mid-1990s, when demand for CM/CMT production began increasing dramatically, a new wave of completely private small business formation occurred. Fabric production, on the other hand, remained longer in state-ownership (*Dialog Textil* Interview Notes) owing to its greater capital intensity and the obsolescent condition of much of the machinery. As of 2001 only 52 companies in the T/C industry were still in the hands of the state (IFM 2004), practically none of which were manufacturing clothing.

Building on a relatively firm technical base, Romanian ready-made clothing firms benefited during the 1990s from the steady shift eastwards, from Poland, the Czech Republic, and the western provinces of Hungary, of EU customer-driven OPT demand. Romania became the EU's largest OPT supplier with a 19 per cent share in 2002, having captured the lead position from Poland, which in 1995 had 27 per cent of the EU's OPT production compared with Romania's 10 per cent (IFM 2004). Dependence on simple garment assembly for foreign customers is thought to be around 80 per cent (Ghinararu and Mocanu 2006) compared with the 'nearly 100 per cent' found in 2003 by IFM (2004: 262). Not only High Street retailers but also high fashion and top-end brands consign production to Romania.

Geographically, clothing firms are concentrated in four main areas of Romania, some of which cater to a particular client base (CDC 2003; Interview Notes 2006). In the western region around Timisoara, in close proximity to the Italian border, are many firms serving the Italian garment industry. German buyers source primarily from the central area of Transylvania, which has strong historical and cultural connections with Germany; it is also the home of the Romanian garment industry and geographical diversification from there first occurred only in the 1970s (Clean Clothes Campaign 2001), hence Transylvanian clothing manufacturers can perhaps lay greatest claim to longstanding traditions of quality clothing production. Activity in the north-east of the country is clustered around the town of Iaşi, home to the specialist textile institute. Finally, there is a strong presence in and around Bucharest, which has a mixed customer base (Interview Notes 2006).

State-owned fabric producers suffer both from under-utilization of capacity and severe financial constraints, the latter preventing investment in modern technology. According to IFM (2004), only 17 per cent of fibre and fabric producers have modernized their equipment, compared with four-fifths of garment producers. This is despite the fact that most textile machinery was already 20 years old in 1990. The decline in local yarn and fabric production and employment since 1989 can also be attributed to the failure of fabric producers to adapt manufacturing practices to serve the needs of the now much smaller privatized garment producers. These latter had no need for the huge bolts of fabric that were typically produced and used in state-owned factories (CDC 2003). One of our interviewees blamed the poor quality of fabrics made for domestic use and state-owned factories' neglect of foreign orders for the loss of the textile industry in the 1990s (ROM-1). Five 'very good' worsted and carded wool factories disappeared, along with cotton, silk, synthetics (for linings), and accessories (ibid.). Instead, private clothing firms increasingly bought fabric from abroad or else used materials supplied to them by the foreign (mostly European) firms for CM production. Meanwhile remaining domestic fabric producers have sought niche export markets in order to earn working capital to fund much-needed investment. One of the larger foreign investments in the industry, Akrom Akal Textile, which set up in 1999 as a subsidiary of Ak-Al Tekstil Sanayii of Turkey to produce knitwear-related acrylic yarn for export markets, declared bankruptcy in summer 2007 citing the strength of the leu against the euro and the dollar, a lack of skilled workers, and heightened competition since 2005 from Chinese producers (various press reports, 2005–07).

State support for the textile and clothing industry (CDC 2003; Evgeniev 2006) prior to EU accession took the form of a higher effective import tariff of 12–32 per cent (vs. 4–13 per cent for the EU average), which provided some protection for the local industry, but this disappeared on EU entry. A government-sponsored attempt, via a public–private partnership with a German company, to stimulate the indigenous textile industry by reviving cultivation of locally available natural inputs such as hemp and wool has not been particularly successful (IFM 2004; Interview Notes 2006). Local farmers are unwilling to grow such crops unless there are local mills to process them. The government has recently sought to encourage Romanian firms to develop their own collections for both domestic and export markets in order to reduce dependence on contract manufacturing (IFM 2004). Our own interviews, conducted in and around Bucharest in late 2006, confirmed this policy intent especially with FEPAIUS and other related associations. The government will give financial assistance to brand-owners wanting to attend trade fairs, but not to pure producers (ROM-6). Overall there seems to be little funding available for industry support: non-sector specific grants are available from the Ministry of Trade and Commerce and the National Agency for SMEs, but only for 'good projects' and if firms 'apply early' (Interview Notes 2006). Learning (and marketing) opportunities for firms occur through the government-supported Romania Fabric Days exhibitions, which occur twice yearly, and via the German agency GTZ. The latter provides technical cooperation to SMEs, regularly bringing German consultants and technical staff to Romania for conferences as well as providing support to firms attending German trade fairs (Interview Notes 2006). Firms themselves (e.g. ROM-4) feel there is little government support for the industry, with greater emphasis placed on encouraging consumption rather than developing production and related capabilities. At a general level, although corporation tax has been reduced from 25 to 16 per cent, social costs remain unchanged. For clothing firms, a reduction in labour taxes—among the highest in Europe—would be of far more benefit (ROM-6).

Overall, the Romanian ready-made clothing sector can claim a number of advantages over competitor countries, in particular: (1) its well-qualified operational workforce based on strong technical education (although some managerial skills are lacking); (2) wages—at around €100–150 per month, translating into costs per minute of €0.06–0.09—are low, particularly in comparison with competing North African countries; and (3) proximity to EU markets allows fast delivery times (2–3 days to Germany and the UK, according to interviewees), enabling Romania to play a key role in 'quick response' supply. EU firms were able to make use of these advantages prior to the end of MFA/ATC quotas in

2005 because Romanian products have since the mid-1990s enjoyed duty-free access to the European Union. On the other hand Romania is at a disadvantage to countries like Turkey owing to the lack of a strong domestic industry providing raw materials on the one hand and machinery and equipment on the other; and to the low level of modernization in the fabric and fibre sector (IFM 2004). It is also at risk of losing OPT orders to countries on the fringes of Europe with lower labour rates, such as Moldavia, Belarus, and the Ukraine, highlighting the need for firms to develop greater technological and marketing capabilities (CDC 2003) and financial strength in order to move up the value chain.

8.2.3. Supplier Firms: Strategy and Performance

The vast majority of Romania's export-oriented clothing firms—themselves a subset of the industry—currently operate in the cut-make segment of the value chain, although some European customers now require their clothing suppliers to work closer to the 'full package' model of activity. Many are trying to operate a combination of the two business models and a few are developing their own brands for the domestic market. A tiny minority of firms has established a branded presence in international markets. The strategies and performance of these different producer types will be discussed in this section, which draws on published material to supplement data gathered during 10 interviews with firms and government agencies/business associations in the Bucharest area. The sample of firms is heavily skewed towards the more advanced businesses and hence is not representative of the industry as a whole, but it does illustrate some of the capabilities and business models used in Romania. We visited too few firms to distinguish clearly between different attitudes of British and German firms to their Romanian suppliers (and none was producing for American buyers); however, various comments about production preferences will be made where available.

Given the recent history of Romania, firm ownership patterns cannot yet be described as predominantly family-oriented: many firms newly established by entrepreneurs are less than 10 years old, while a number of those that emerged from the ruins of state ownership are managed by entrepreneurial former bureaucrats. Under the privatization process state-owned company employees became partial shareholders, which in some firms (such as Braiconf) helped to encourage more positive attitudes to quality production and productivity (Yoruk 2002). The ownership picture is thus fairly typical of transition economies and stands in sharp contrast to the strong family business orientation of, for example, the Turkish industry. In recent years some regrouping of production units has taken place as stronger firms reorganize into holding companies and bring weaker sites under their umbrella (e.g. ROM-1; ROM-6). Other firms that have failed to make the transition, or have been unable to hold onto their employees, have simply disappeared.

The problem of labour migration is a source of serious concern for all firms. Labour shortages tend to be greater in the big towns as there are generally alternative job opportunities (ROM-2; ROM-4), and Bucharest in particular suffers from a tight employment market. In Transylvania, where living standards are relatively high because of western influences (from Italy, Austria, Hungary), labour problems were especially acute in 2006 (ROM-2). Thus ROM-1, which is one of Romania's largest clothing firms and a major exporter, has seen employment dwindle from over 8,000 employees in 2002 to around 6,300 by the end of 2006, resulting in a reduction in the number of shifts and the loss of production capacity. Customers who cut their orders in the last two to three years to experiment with Chinese production have not necessarily been able to get back capacity in ROM-1's factories. In part this is because ROM-1's need to focus on productivity has led it to turn away the less profitable orders, that is, those for complicated styles in difficult fabrics in small quantities. Bucharest-based ROM-6 experienced 10–20 per cent labour turnover in 2006, but felt that the situation was worse in 2004–05 when visa-free travel in the Schengen countries became possible. While factories continuing to operate under an old 'communist-style' mentality are unlikely to survive this shake-out, firms whose management provides reasonable conditions and training opportunities for employees can survive (ROM-4).

The principal area of expertise is in production of tailored clothing: men's jackets and trousers; ladies' coats and dresses, and formal jackets, skirts and trousers; and shirts for men and women. Indeed UK-C-5 relied entirely on firms in Romania for its tailored clothing. In the opinion of ROM-4, production quality of tailored ladies' wear is better in Romania than in Turkey which, it claimed, has relatively few factories producing such items and charges relatively high prices. But this was not entirely the impression we gained from either our interviews in Turkey or interviews in the UK (e.g. UK-C-1, which had trialled a Romanian factory but reverted to its Turkish producers). Large runs of dresses and blouses are also more easily produced in Romania than in Turkey, since the average size of each factory in Romania is greater. On the other hand Romania cannot compete with Turkey on items requiring specialized washing finishes, or on denim clothing given the large volumes of denim fabric Turkey produces. Equally, orders for fairly standardized products not requiring tight delivery schedules, such as men's suits— which are made in similar fabrics, colours, and styles, from year to year—have largely been lost to China (ROM-4).

Domestic suppliers of trim did not survive the early 1990s transition period (ROM-1), but foreign trim and accessories firms—Kufner (interlinings), Textil Gruppe Hof (interlinings), Knopf-Schäfer (buttons), all from Germany; Coats (sewing thread) and Labelon (labels) from the UK; and YKK (zips and fastenings) from Japan, among others—have been investing in Romania since the mid-1990s, and in some cases they use Romania as a base to supply other CEE countries. The arrival of trim companies marks a crucial step in establishing Romania's presence in the fast fashion business, although the range of suppliers is nowhere near as great as in Turkey (ROM-2). Trim orders can be filled in two days now, instead of the week it takes an order to arrive from Turkey (ROM-4). Trim suppliers invested in Romania for two reasons: rising labour costs made their own products manufactured in western Europe too expensive; and they followed customers who were increasingly closing their UK, German, and other clothing manufacturing facilities and sourcing production elsewhere. (Reconfiguring production networks can cause internal problems: the Romanian factory of one trim supplier reportedly found itself competing for business in Romania against its own longer established Turkish factory.)

The possibility of sourcing export-grade inputs locally represents an important factor in enabling domestic firms to begin the shift from CM towards CMT production. It is a simpler first step than having to seek out and import such items and, crucially, it accelerates the turnaround time of orders, enabling clothing producers to provide a better service to buyers. The next step is for local firms to source specified fabrics themselves, but only the larger firms are able to take on the much greater financial and organizational burdens this entails: working capital is required to finance investments in materials before the garments can be produced. While many firms have ambitions to do so, in practice only a small percentage of Romanian firms will succeed in this next step. Where Romanian clothing firms are particularly disadvantaged, especially in comparison with Turkey, is in the lack of access to a strong domestic fabric industry. All companies complain at the absence of good textile mills (ROM-2). Their lack has been felt more keenly as a problem in recent years, because of the delays entailed in shipping fabrics from overseas suppliers: 'if we still had textiles, we would be better placed now' (ROM-1). As noted earlier, there has been some foreign investment in the textile sector—UCO of Belgium recently established a denim plant—but the range of fabrics available in the country will never match that of Turkey. All export-oriented Romanian firms regard Turkey as a far more threatening competitor than China, because it similarly targets quick response demand from EU markets. Productivity is said to be higher in Turkey too, which is an issue of 'mentality' (ROM-6).

Production turnaround times for orders are 3–5 weeks, and with trucking times all over Europe only 2–3 days factory owners are confident that they justify their 20 per cent premium on price over China (e.g. ROM-6). (One source suggests that because Romanian road infrastructure remains poor, the ideal truck size is sufficiently small to avoid the Sunday travel restrictions in some European countries.) ROM-6 claims that production quality is better in Romania than in China, yet acknowledges that China has many different suppliers offering different levels of quality.

The long-established practice of OPT manufacturing for EU customers undoubtedly assured the survival of a meaningful garment production activity in Romania after the loss of Soviet Union markets and stimulated the radical transformation of the sector from very large, fully integrated producers to the current mass of small- and medium-sized firms. However, more recently CM/CMT production has been recognized as a double-edged sword for the industry. On the one hand it is appreciated by clothing producers for its relatively fast cash flow and low risk. It has enabled them to learn from their foreign customers and to enter new foreign markets. On the other hand firms' competitive position is limited to the supply of cheap labour, and they suffer from constant pressure on margins, especially when inflation is high and the exchange rate moves against them as has been the case in 2005–07. As Pickles et al. (2006: 2313) discovered in the cases of Bulgaria and Slovakia, rising cost pressures place firms relying on CM production in highly precarious positions. The subsequent near-collapse of the local textile industry and the financial fragility of many clothing producers have exacerbated the situation—the financial underpinning, for example, through export subsidies and various rent-seeking activities, for Turkish firms in their formative years (Tokatli 2007) is absent in the Romanian case. Whereas Romanian production skills may be strong, its firms have no tradition of commercial activity—again unlike the Turkish industry. And yet firms that are able to assimilate from their customers an understanding of product development as well as commercial and organizational know-how may be able to evolve towards other forms of cooperation.

Our interviews indicate that UK buyers are far more likely to work on a CMT or full package basis with Romanian factories than are the more conservative German buyers, who continue to place CM-only orders. German firms came early to Romania and simply wanted labour (and fewer are still working in Romania than in the mid-1990s), but UK firms arrived only in the late 1990s and wanted much more (Interview Notes 2006). In some cases they even demand sample-making and the presentation of collections for private labels. ROM-6, which works a little for UK buyers and none at all for German firms—its major customer base is in France, because the owner had previously worked for a trading company dealing with France—operates on a roughly 50/50 CM and CMT basis. One of his UK customers imposes the lining supplier, but leaves it to him to negotiate prices and delivery dates. He earns slightly better margins on CMT, depending on his ability to negotiate trim prices—but adds the proviso that customers placing CMT orders must be reliable. He sends his in-house procurement staff to accessory fairs in order to be able to personalize the trim, and higher quality customers want this.

In contrast, according to one informant (ROM-2), a trousers factory in Transylvania that is fully equipped with CAD systems continues to receive all the inputs from its German clients, on the basis that proximity to Germany makes it logistically easy to do so. ROM-1, which has been producing trousers for German brands such as Gardeur, Baumler, Leineweber, and Gerry Weber since the early 1990s, built its reputation on CM production and acknowledges that it has been slow to try switching to full package. There has been 'some interest' from other customers, however, in having it provide additional services. And yet ROM-1 has a technical school in each of its factories, where potential recruits are tested, new employees are trained in simple and later more complicated tasks, and longer-standing employees receive ongoing training. This investment in training, giving the firm a basis of well-qualified staff, has proved to be cost effective. Even so, ROM-1 lost a very important customer (a major retailer) in the late 1990s 'because they always wanted lower prices', so departed for Bulgaria and Moldova. He bemoaned the unwillingness of buyers to pay higher prices for more complicated orders and wanted to escape the constant pressure on margins. A number of

German firms (e.g. GER-C-11 and GER-C-13) are now doing their CM/CMT production in Ukraine, which is said to be at a similar stage of economic development as Romania 15 years ago: much of Ukrainian industry having collapsed, there is a plentiful workforce to employ in clothing factories (Pickles et al. 2006, Interview Notes 2006).

Attitudes towards the use of subcontracting orders also vary. ROM-6 uses around 20 smallish subcontractors in the south and east of the country to supplement capacity at his two factories (one of which, established in 1989, is in a building in the shell of an otherwise nearly abandoned SOE). Since his customers demand flexibility, he uses subcontracting to achieve capacity and delivery schedules. Complicated pieces and silk garments are made in his own factories; either specialized (e.g. dyeing, washing, embroidery) or very simple work is put out. His technical department arranges all the technical details, ranging from the sketch through to pre-production, for the subcontract firms, and his quality control and technical control visit them. ROM-6 claims his customers are happy to have this network available, and that they visit the subcontractors as well as his factories. ROM-3 also uses a range of subcontractors to supplement in-house capacity—which accounts for only 25 per cent of output—and provides constant technical support to ensure quality. The sourcing firm ROM-4, on the other hand, strictly forbids its factories to subcontract work to others: it closely controls the work being done, and receives daily reports on which lines (and how many) are being used.

Fabric used in the making-up of garments is mostly foreign sourced, usually from Turkey, France, Italy, and other European countries. A truckload of fabric leaving Turkey on a Friday will be at Romanian Customs the following Monday and in ROM-4's factories by Wednesday. Since the European buyers choose the fabrics, unless Romanian textile producers exhibit at the foreign trade fairs their product range will not be seen (ROM-6). ROM-6 is slightly more optimistic about Romanian knitwear yarn production since the Italian Radici group bought one of the state-owned producers. However he comments that whereas lower quality customers never ask questions about where the yarn is sourced from, his medium and higher quality customers require him to use yarn from Italy.

European retailers with strong commitments to sourcing in Romania, including mail order specialists like Otto Versand and Quelle of Germany, and High Street retailers such as Next and C&A, have established local sourcing offices to oversee their supplier factories (Interview Notes 2006). US firm The Gap is reported to have considered a Romanian buying office through which to supply its European stores. Such offices employ experts to prepare collections and technicians to manage quality control at the various factories to which production is consigned. One major British retailer operates entirely on a CM basis in Romania, using its sourcing office there to organize fabrics, trim, patterns, and technical documentation, negotiate prices and arrange garment assembly among a network of production facilities throughout the country, manage quality inspections, and despatch finished garments. Developing Romanian suppliers to the required level has been 'a long learning curve' since the retailer prides itself on its exacting quality standards, but once the factory shows during trial production runs its capability to learn and acceptance of the technical advice given, ROM-4 prefers to stay with it rather than moving on in search of others on the basis of price alone. After poor trial experiences with some foreign-owned facilities, the company now chooses to work with Romanian-owned supplier factories. From 2007 it expects to begin gradually shifting towards CMT, though 'it will take a while'. The arrival of western trims and accessories suppliers in Romania facilitates this process. Approximately one-fifth of its supplier factories already attempt to develop their own brand presence in the domestic market, which it approves of and is ready to support.

Some upgrading of capabilities—and productivity—has taken place as garment producers try to lure back buyers who had gone to try out China after quotas were lifted in 2005: 2006 was a good year for machinery firms such as Brother and Juki, who sold new sewing machine attachments that allow firms to make in one shift what had previously taken three (ROM-2). Clearly this is also a potential solution to the labour problem, and firms that are less interested in CM activity therefore also have incentives to invest. But some firms have upgraded other equipment also. ROM-1 has fully equipped all its four factories with modern specialized machinery for cutting, sewing, and finishing and is in the process of installing sub-systems to control workflows. In the first factory to have the new control systems, productivity has risen 10 per cent and management can easily monitor progress and bottlenecks along the production line. It has brought technical consultants from overseas to train managers and employees, and regularly meets suppliers at fairs to discuss new equipment that holds the 'secrets' of better performance (ROM-1). ROM-6 has installed a Lectra cutting machine and is planning to invest in CAD–CAM.

8.2.3.1. Own-Product and Brand Development

Greater integration of steps in the value chain occurs among firms producing purely for the domestic market, sometimes with own brands, and there is a small number of relatively recently established companies that have targeted the upper market internationally. The degree of vertical integration by clothing firms does not, however, extend either to yarn and fabric production or in a significant way (yet) to retail activity. The near total absence until recently of an organized distribution system did not encourage the early emergence of domestic clothing brands and that picture is changing only slowly, with heavy emphasis on the largest cities. As is common in developing countries, consumers who can afford to purchase branded clothes prefer foreign names, initially at least (Interview Notes 2006). Low consumer purchasing power and unsophisticated demand throughout the 1990s kept domestic clothing prices low and the many micro-enterprises manufacturing exclusively for this market produced garments of low quality. Hence clothing made for local consumption was very different from that produced for international markets. High tariffs on imported apparel (averaging 30% in 2004) helped to protect the domestic market. More recently low-end producers have faced tough competition from cheap imports from India and China (Crestanello and Tattara 2006) as Romania prepared for EU entry. However some small and medium firms are beginning to try to develop their own medium-level brands, usually for distribution inside Romania (IFM 2004, Interview Notes 2006). While the producers of essentially unbranded products for the domestic market are not discussed here, the following paragraphs discuss examples of firms that have either developed a domestic brand in parallel to their ongoing CM business and have subsequently expanded (or intended to expand) into nearby countries, or else have from the outset aimed to establish themselves as high quality brands in international markets. Neither category represents a large group within the total population of Romanian clothing firms.

Both ROM-1 and ROM-6 have made the first steps into domestic brand development. The former began tentatively as long ago as 1998, testing out its men's wear designs, later experimenting with—and dropping, then trying again with—women's clothing. Its own brand, sold through its own two stores, now accounts for 2–3 per cent of group sales. Some effort is also going into developing export sales in Russia and other nearby countries, both with the ROM-1 brand and with a couple of foreign mass market brands for which it holds the licence. ROM-1 very much sees its future as split between full package production for others and the development of its own brand. ROM-6 has moved into brand activity by acquiring a majority stake in a local children's wear company that had run into financial difficulties. It developed its first small collection in 2006 and sells through supermarkets in Romania such as Carrefour and Cora. Sales represent only a fraction of group turnover. The brand is expected to develop in the future, and the collection will be expanded by buying in ready-made items from Turkey and China. On the other hand there are no immediate plans to attempt to develop the ROM-6 name as a brand. Nor are there ambitions—unlike ROM-1—to forward integrate into retailing.

In addition to these two small players there are perhaps 10–12 Romanian firms making a concerted effort to invest in brand development and technology, coupled with development of their own retail chains specifically to overcome the lack of proper distribution channels (Interview Notes 2006). Few are likely to be strong enough to survive the arrival of the big European High Street retailers now beginning to invest in Romania. Since many of these large retailers already source in Romania—H&M and Zara are well established—they understand the Romanian market place. Steilmann, present as a manufacturer since the early 1990s and with four factories producing for export markets around Europe, has also been steadily opening retail outlets in the major cities.

One of the leading domestic firms with aspirations towards its own brand is former state-owned company Braiconf. Privatized in 1996, it is one of Romania's leading men's shirt and women's blouse manufacturers. Its investments in design capabilities began as early as 1993 with the employment of a University of Iaşi graduate and a young assistant, and it developed an understanding of contemporary fashion trends through its work for foreign (especially Italian) brands (Yoruk 2002). The company also financially supported the training of technicians in prototype development. An early joint venture with an Italian firm, lasting for 10 years until 2001, helped to provide financial stability during the difficult early years after the revolution as well as providing crucial know-how about quality manufacturing and efficient production organization (ibid). As Romania became a more attractive CM/CMT production location from the mid-1990s, the share of Braiconf's output destined for export markets expanded, reaching approximately 90 per cent. Half goes to Italy and most of the rest to Britain, Germany, and France (press reports, various). Pricing pressure progressively reduced the profitability of production for foreign buyers despite a wide spectrum of production relationships, ranging from simple CM, through CMT to full package including the purchase of foreign fabrics (Yoruk 2002). This reinforced the management's wish to develop Braiconf's own brand presence in the domestic market. Regular machinery upgrades (e.g. the installation of CAD systems and an automatic cutting machine) to improve quality and productivity, coupled with further expansion of in-house design capabilities, positioned the company in 2003 to develop this strategy. Commercialization takes place through wholesale channels (retailers and hypermarkets) and the company has also forward integrated into retailing, owning 18 stores in 2007. Braiconf is thus able to draw on the professional skills, design capabilities, brand creation, and marketing abilities developed over the last decade in order to distance itself from the profitability problems caused by the depreciation of the euro since 2005. It has further ambitions to develop new export markets in Russia and other nearby non-EU markets, independently of its ongoing contract manufacturing work.

ROM-5 is one of the tiny number of firms to target international markets from the outset. It is a small company, with €10 million turnover in 2005, of which 80 per cent came from exports. Operating in a niche segment, it has invested heavily in image and quality production in order to establish a presence in leading European and American department stores. North America is its biggest market, but France is the best market because customers are so demanding. Competition is defined entirely in terms of foreign designers in the same niche, and ROM-5 regularly participates in foreign trade fairs. Early collaboration with a French company, which has subsequently left Romania, provided the necessary learning experience. Of its 300 employees, around 20 are involved in design and in quality control. Only imported fabrics—primarily silks, microfibres, lace, and Italian embroidered materials, of the type used for haute couture—are used and all production is done on-site (within a former state-owned company). A very basic range is sold in Romania, through Carrefour. It is interesting to observe the emergence of such firms, though ROM-5 is by no means a typical case.

Among British-based firms, a major supplier to the Arcadia Group and Debenhams relocated its entire production of women's wear from Cyprus to Romania in 1997, having established a manufacturing base near Bucharest as early as 1994. In addition to opening a second factory in 2000, bringing employment in its directly owned production facilities to some 1,200 people, the company uses more than a dozen local subcontractors. A new distribution centre opened in 2006, and the steady shifting of further activities such as quality control and finished goods handling from London to Romania allows garments now to be shipped directly to UK customers. Whereas the London office had been purchasing 50 per cent of the fabric required by its Romanian operations, from 2007 the Romanian subsidiary will take entire charge of fabric acquisition. Only around one-fifth of the fabric used is sourced domestically, with the remainder imported mainly from Turkey and China.

8.2.4. Future Prospects for the Romanian Clothing Industry

EU customs agreements and trade policies have undoubtedly shaped the Romanian (and other CEE countries') T/C industries: they have encouraged the expansion of EU buyers' networks into the region using OPT as a means of aiding EU T/C industries' adjustment to liberalization. These trade advantages have been withdrawn from CEE and extended further east, to countries such as Ukraine (Pickles et al. 2006). But their legacy in Romania is clear.

The Romanian industry has thrived for the last decade or more as an efficient assembler of ready-made clothing for EU markets. Yet it clearly faces major challenges in the years following entry to the EU. The decline in exports to the EU since 2005 is a result not only of greater competition from China and other Asian countries for EU markets following the end of quota regimes but also of the effect of rising Romanian labour and associated costs in the run-up towards EU membership. While a strategy of focusing on good quality CM production of tailored outerwear was undoubtedly highly successful in providing much-needed employment for thousands during the transition years, the development of better-paid jobs in other industries and rising costs overall have, with the passage of time, made this type of activity increasingly unprofitable. Firms that have failed to learn the skills and management practices necessary to upgrade to higher value-added production activity are collapsing in increasing numbers as CM/CMT processing work shifts to cheaper locations—Moldavia, Ukraine, and Russia—that are nevertheless close enough to serve the EU fast fashion market. Industry association representatives and other observers suggest that CM will have disappeared from Romania by 2010 (Interview Notes 2006). Better commercially oriented management skills, more investment in modern technology, and stronger human resource management skills are needed, but these require financial commitments that many CM-dependent firms are not able to undertake. Transition to full package or even own brand development cannot take place without the addition of technical developers and, for the latter, design capability.

While the opportunities for sourcing local inputs—a necessary first step towards production upgrading—are improving with the investment of foreign trim suppliers, Romania suffers from the collapse of its once-thriving textile industry. Competition in the region from Turkey, and more geographically distantly from China, is much strengthened by their strong and varied fabric producers. Production in China will, however, displace only the small part of the industry remaining in Romania that focuses on standard men's suits and other segments where fast fashion is not important. For fast fashion, European buyers will still look to Romania (and Turkey). Indeed, a good proportion of the order volume lost to China in 2005 as customers tried out production there is reported to have returned to Romania. The greater flexibility of Romanian producers and the variety of styles and fabrics that they can work with—in contrast to the long runs demanded by Chinese manufacturers—is a clear advantage.

Finally, industry associations such as FEPAIUS and other agencies such as GTZ are actively promoting the need for upgrading. Yet the former body lacks the resources enjoyed by, for example, its Turkish counterparts to help firms do this in a material way. Indeed, membership of FEPAUIS may actually be declining as the number of members going out of business exceeds those joining the organization (Interview Notes 2006). The terms of engagement for GTZ, which was to accompany Romania into the EU, have now expired, thereby removing an important source of technical aid to the industry.

NOTES

1. *Turkishtime* interview with Osman Boyner, www.turkishtime.org downloaded 8 March 2006.
2. *Turkishtime*, interview with Umut Oran, www.turkishtime.org downloaded 8 March 2006.
3. Suitcase exporting refers to the (now discontinued) practice of selling directly to Russian purchasers who take the garments into Russia without paying the necessary customs duties or middleman fees.
4. See www.treasury.gov.tr
5. *Turkishtime* interview with Osman Boyner, www.turkishtime.org downloaded 8 March 2006.
6. According to Smith (2006), the remittances of more than 2 million workers abroad now represent one of the major sources of Romania's external income.

9

The Clothing Industries in Supplier Countries: Buyer–Supplier Relations (2)

In the previous chapter the supplier countries we examined were largely (although not exclusively in the case of Turkey) oriented towards Europe. In this chapter our attention turns first to the giant of the textile and clothing industry, China, which exerts strong competitive pressure on all the other supplier countries as well as on the industries of the developed countries. In the second part of the chapter we examine the case of Mexico, whose proximity to the USA nominally at least places it in a similar position to that of Romania in relation to the EU.

9.1. CHINA

9.1.1. Geopolitical Position, Industrial Development and Institutional Structure

The dramatic growth of the People's Republic of China during its 30-year transformation from Maoist communism into a 'socialist market economy'—the combination of a market economy with a socialist political system—has turned it into a major player in the world economy and in the global textile and clothing industry. Annual per capita GDP increases averaging 8.1 per cent between 1978 and 2003, in parallel to population growth of more than 310 million (Dussel Peters 2005), is a remarkable feat. Real GDP since 2003 has risen by around 10 per cent per year. GDP per capita (PPP) reached an estimated US$6,760 in 2006, compared with US$1,330 in 1990. Average data in a country the size of China mask wide regional variations and, despite significant progress on poverty reduction, nearly 300 million people out of a total population of 1.3 billion still live on less than US$1 per day. Nevertheless the OECD (2005a: 16) describes China's record as 'one of the most sustained and rapid economic transformations seen in the world economy in the last 50 years'.

China took its first tentative steps towards integration into the modern world economic system when Deng Xiaoping launched his 'Open Door Policy' in 1978. Laws permitting foreign direct investment were passed in 1980. Reform of the agricultural sector in the early 1980s rolled back collectivized farming, generating production increases and raising incomes which created the social and political conditions to enable reforms in the industrial sector. During the 1990s progressive abolition of price controls, the introduction of laws permitting private company ownership and the abolition of the state's monopoly over export trading[1] all contributed towards the development of an economy driven by market forces. The opening process proceeded cautiously, often on an experimental basis, and frequently subject to conflicting priorities between central and provincial or municipal governments—which contributed to bureaucratic arbitrariness and to the potential for corruption. Government coordination remains a key factor on all political, economic, and social levels. Throughout this period of change the Communist Party has retained its firm grip over all political activity. Pragmatic leadership has allowed economic experimentation, while at the same time ruthlessly quashing moves towards a more democratic exercise of power. Competent economic management at the highest levels has created a political legitimacy for the Communist Party lacking in other countries making the transition from central planning to a market orientation.

Entry to the WTO in December 2001 represents a significant landmark in the economic transformation process, signalling a degree of consistency with the rules of world trade as well as protection against an unpredictable bureaucracy for foreign trade and investment partners (IFM 2004). Compliance with WTO obligations necessitated important changes to China's legal and economic framework, including the reduction or abolition of tariffs and quotas, the lifting of many restrictions on foreign investments and imports, the removal of requirements on technology transfers by foreign investors, and the elimination of discriminatory standards as well as aid to state-owned firms (Nolan 2001). All had important implications both for the nature of competition within the domestic Chinese market and for the WTO's ability to hold China to account over its international trade activity. Regulatory transparency, levels of government corruption, intellectual property rights protection, and high levels of brand name counterfeiting are continuing areas of concern for WTO members. As a WTO member China is now exposed to threats of anti-dumping actions. More positively, the effects on China of integration into the WTO are seen to include deepening regional integration in Asia, increased participation of foreign firms in China's domestic economy, and further stimulation of Chinese income and international trade in the clothing sector (Dussel Peters 2005).

The industrial structure of China has changed dramatically since 1978. State owned enterprises (SOEs) generated three quarters of industrial output in 1980 and, by virtue of a monopoly over foreign trade, all export activity. As other forms of economic activity developed and the export licensing system was relaxed their share declined, until by 2000 SOEs accounted for just one quarter of exports (Dussel Peters 2005). Central government gave increasing autonomy in the 1980s to local and municipal government to create town and village enterprises (TVEs), which became an important mechanism to provide both employment and income for populations outside the major cities (Nolan 2001).[2] The first tentative steps towards private industrial activity occurred in 1984, although a full legal framework for private ownership did not emerge until 1994 and only in 2001 could private business owners join the Chinese Communist Party (Dussel Peters 2005)—still a key mechanism for getting ahead in life. Despite the discrimination they faced versus state-owned enterprises with respect to access to finance, property rights, and markets, a number of strong domestic private firms emerged in relatively low technology sectors (Nolan 2001) to develop both brand names and in some cases an international presence.[3] By the end of the 1990s the government had acknowledged the contribution of the private sector to rising living standards, amending the constitution in 1999 and 2004 to give explicit recognition of private property rights and remove the risk of expropriation. By 2003 the private sector accounted for more than three quarters of value-added in 11 industries, including textiles and clothing (OECD 2005).

In the clothing industry the decline of state-owned enterprise activity since 1978 has been swift, though rather slower for textiles. Following the expropriation of all private firms in 1949, the textiles and clothing industry was regarded as a pillar industry of the state. State-sponsored plans established the expansion of all types of textile production as an essential aspect of economic development, a focus on volume at the expense of quality which continued well beyond 1978 (Williams, Kong, and Yan 2002). The 'iron rice bowl', which guaranteed workers' job security and provided through their work units accommodation, healthcare, pensions, and children's education, brought over-manning and inefficiency as well as heavy financial losses. Deregulation and the withdrawal of the state commenced in the early 1990s when the Ministry of Textile Industry was broken up, but the process of SOE modernization, restructuring, and re-investment only began in earnest between 1997 and 2000 as preparations for WTO membership accelerated (WTO 2006). Loss-making textile factories were made bankrupt or forced to merge, 1.2 million workers were 'displaced' and millions of obsolete cotton, wool, and silk spindles were scrapped (Williams et al. 2002, WTO 2006).[4] Thousands of TVEs in the textile dyeing sector (and other highly polluting industries) were ordered to close on environmental grounds (Nolan 2001). At the same time over US$30 million of advanced textiles machinery was imported as part of a new drive towards increased quality, variety, and output performance (WTO 2006). Even so, in 2001 around 90 per cent of installed equipment in the cotton spinning sector was over 10 years old.

During 1997 and 1998 the central government provided substantial subsidies or forgave taxes to aid the process of restructuring—Dussel Peter's (2005) analysis suggests that the state-owned textiles and clothing industry was one of the biggest recipients of Chinese subsidies during the late 1990s. Since then the industry has received no special government aid (WTO 2006), although municipal governments have been important providers of infrastructure to facilitate the development of specialized industrial districts (Li & Fung Research Centre 2006). Firms (not only in the textile and clothing industry) have also benefited from tax relief on investments in domestic equipment used for technological upgrading.[5] As for industry oversight, the State Textile Industry Bureau, which had regulated the industry in the 1990s, was dismantled in 2000 and since then no specific government agency has administered textiles and clothing business. Former textile ministry officials remain, however, involved with various associations related to the industry. The China National Textile & Apparel Council (CNTAC) was formed in 1998 as a federation of the many different industry associations to 'protect the interests of the industry'[6] and to promote its rationalization and modernization. The China National Technical Import and Export Corporation (CNTIC), meanwhile, has been active in encouraging the modernization of the textile industry and is said to want to play an intermediary role between fabric mills and foreign buyers (USITC 2004). The China National Garment Association (CNGA) currently focuses on efforts to incubate and promote original clothing brands and conducts industry analyses to help with government decision-making and enterprise market positioning.[7] CNTAC also issues guidelines for enterprises to help them cut or stop exports of textile or clothing products that are subject to restrictions by certain countries (WTO 2006). The state's recent 5-year plans have tended to emphasize textile industry sensitivity to market demands in addition to the continued modernization of equipment and consolidation of production (IFM 2004).

As a source of low cost production, China became the primary developing country destination for multinationals' foreign direct investment (FDI) in the early 1990s. Asian investors—Hong Kong,[8] Japan, Taiwan, and Korea—dominate, with the USA accounting for a further 10 per cent of investments and Germany the largest European investor. In 2000 seventy per cent of investment flowing into textiles and clothing manufacturing came from Hong Kong, with Taiwan adding a further 10 per cent (USITC 2004). China was by far the largest recipient worldwide of foreign-invested T/C projects in 2002–04, receiving 48 investments compared with 18 projects in Bulgaria, the second largest host (UNCTAD 2005). Much of this investment occurred in anticipation of the benefits arising from abolition of MFA/ATC quotas.

The territory of Hong Kong has played a significant role in the social and economic development of China since 1978. Its clothing, footwear, toy, and electronics enterprises were early investors in the Special Economic Zones (SEZs) of the Pearl River delta, eventually becoming extensively vertically integrated into the Chinese economy; property developers and infrastructure builders brought their expertise to the mainland; shipping firms facilitated the export of Chinese-made goods via its efficient container ports; its well-developed capital market acted as a bridge between Chinese firms and foreign investors; and its professional services supplied legal, managerial, and other expertise. Many European and American firms chose to set up subsidiaries or agency arrangements on the island to handle dealings with the mainland. Western-educated Hong Kong business people were popular choices among western firms as China subsidiary managers, in the expectation that a common ethnic background would ease the problems of language and of dealing with administrative corruption as well as confusing and often conflicting regulations.

Rather than displacing domestic investment, the combination of foreign companies' management skills and technology with local labour has improved both the overall productivity of the economy and export performance. Even apparently low tech Hong Kong garment firms acted as effective technology transfer conduits for the Chinese clothing industry, particularly with respect to soft managerial practices and organizational skills, including the discipline of meeting sophisticated buyers' demands (Thompson 2003). Domestic firms have been found to increase their R&D intensity more rapidly in sectors where foreign competition is strong (OECD 2005). Foreign-invested firms dominate exports in some industries—although not textiles and clothing, where domestic companies now play the major role—and account for 55 per cent of exports overall; in the domestic market, by contrast, foreign firms have captured a 13 per cent share.

The strong export orientation and geographic distribution of foreign investments has been shaped by Chinese government restrictions and incentives. FDI was initially contained within Special Economic Zones—only later was it permitted throughout the coastal provinces and finally in the major cities of inland provinces—and until WTO accession foreign invested firms were required to export at least 50 per cent of production (Williams, Kong, and Yan 2002). For these reasons clothing factories have been concentrated in particular regions, notably across the strait from Hong Kong in the Pearl River delta and in the provinces around Shanghai. Liberalization of access to domestic distribution channels, the gradual opening of service industries, the lifting of restrictions on wholly owned foreign enterprises and the rising cost of labour in the coastal provinces have broadened the spatial, sectoral, and ownership pattern of FDI during the last decade.

According to the OECD (2005: 30) China has made a marked impact on world trade only since 1999. Exports accounted for 36 per cent and imports 34 per cent of GDP in 2004, when it overtook Japan as the world's third largest exporter, behind the USA and Germany (Amiti and Freund 2007). Examining the composition of exports, important structural shifts in China's trade occurred over the last three decades: from a concentration on commodities in the early 1980s to labour-intensive industries including clothing, footwear and toys in the late 1980s to early 1990s, and to more advanced products such as electrical goods and electronics such as office machines, electrical machinery, and telecommunications from the late 1990s onwards. Although both apparel and textiles continue to figure among the five largest export sectors and labour intensive exports such as clothing and footwear have increased in absolute value terms, the dynamism of their growth is lower than that of Chinese exports as a whole (Dussel Peters 2005). Data on skill intensities indicate that the export share of mid- to high-skill products has risen over this period, but that the increase is due almost entirely to more sophisticated imported inputs for China's export processing (Amiti and Freund 2007).

Taiwan, South Korea, and Japan all run healthy trade surpluses with China based on component inputs for processing and subsequent re-export, in contrast to the heavy orientation towards exported finished goods that underlies China's substantial trade surpluses with the EU and (especially) the USA. Cotton and non-cotton clothing accounted for US$24.5 billion (8.5% of the total) of China's US$287.8 billion exports to the USA in 2006 (although auto parts and electronics trade is growing more quickly). Rapid growth in exports to the USA and Europe finally forced Beijing into partially floating the currency in July 2005, and by February 2008 the renminbi had risen more than 13 per cent against the dollar. This has had a noticeable effect on clothing exporters' margins, encouraging some producers to switch their attention to the domestic market and others to quote prices in euros (which are little changed against the renminbi) or introduce exchange rate adjustments for dollar-denominated orders (Kwong 2008). According to the Guotai Junan Securities Research Institute, a 1 per cent appreciation in the currency reduces profit margins in the textiles and clothing industry by 2 per cent (Xinhua Net 2008).

9.1.2. Structure and Performance of China's Textile and Clothing Industry

The textile and clothing industry has been central to the transformation of China from a centrally organized state-run economy to a market economy. Its performance has been based on the one hand on the dynamic rise since the mid-1980s of TVEs and on the other hand on the outward processing arrangements of (primarily) Hong Kong-owned firms.[9] It has been at the forefront of China's economic development for 25 years, and the most rapidly growing of the world's major clothing producers (Appelbaum et al. 2005: 5). Its contribution to GDP peaked at 10 per cent and its growth rate has been 8 per cent for over a decade. Until the mid-1990s it was the principal export category (with a share of 30% in 1995), and between 1996 and 2002 accounted for 87 per cent of the country's entire export surplus (Dussel Peters 2005). The industry is both far more vertically integrated and far more diversified than that found in most other developing economies, boasting a presence across the value chain from raw material production (e.g. cotton and silk), yarns and fibres, textiles, and accessories, through to garment production. A seemingly unending flow of migrant workers has helped to keep wage costs low and the industry highly competitive in world markets. As incomes have risen the domestic market, which accounted for approximately 70 per cent of total industry output in 2004, has actually begun to grow slightly faster than exports (China Daily 2005).

In terms of industry structure, the WTO (2006) refers to some 1,274 state-owned enterprises and over 3,500 foreign invested enterprises that were engaged in the manufacture of textiles in 2004, and a further 332 SOEs and 4,450 foreign firms producing 'wearing apparel, footwear, and caps'. Dussel Peters (2005), citing data from the National Reform and Development Commission of China, refers to 18,900 enterprises, either state-owned or with other forms of ownership, with revenues over RMB5 million. According to the USITC (1999) 42 per cent of clothing companies were town and village enterprises, a similar proportion were foreign-invested, 7 per cent were private and 6 per cent were state-owned.[10] Five years later the same source notes that Zhejiang province alone boasted some 250,000 small firms (i.e. family-based producers with annual revenues below RMB 5 million) operating in the industry (USITC 2004). By 2008, CNTAC was said to be tracking 44,200 textile and apparel companies (Mitchell 2008*b*). UNCTAD (2005), meanwhile, claims nearly 6,000 textile and clothing enterprises with foreign ownership had invested in 2003 alone, apparently in anticipation of the elimination of export quotas at the end of 2004. From the plethora of figures available from a wide range of agencies it is clear that the Chinese textiles and clothing industry is populated by significant numbers of firms of all sizes and ownership bases and operating in many different segments.

As with the number of firms, employment data vary widely depending on the source and its coverage. Nordås (2004: 11) notes a substantial decline in employment in the textile sector, from 6.7 million in 1995 to 4.8 million in 2001 as a result of enterprise restructuring, while in the clothing sector employment levelled off to around 2 million (from a 1997 peak of 2.4 million) despite substantial export growth over the same period. Clothing makers are mostly small and privately owned, with an average of 300 employees (USITC 2004). IFM (2004) suggests that, adjusting official statistics to include firms with sales of less than RMB 5 million, the T/C industry provides employment and subsistence for some 15 million people, and a further 13 million are engaged in natural fibre processing. Meanwhile the WTO (2006) finds total employment in the textile and clothing industry of 19 million in 2004 (including large numbers of rural households involved in the textile sector), representing 22 per cent of the country's manufacturing workforce.

State-owned enterprises contributed only 9.5 per cent of industry output, predominantly in textiles, in 2004. This represented a smaller share than the 11.7 per cent produced by foreign invested enterprises, with non-state domestic firms accounting for the remaining nearly four-fifths of output (CNTAC data, cited by WTO 2006). Rural enterprises (TVEs) were particularly dynamic, increasing clothing output at 2.5 times the rate of the state sector in 1986–92 and rapidly gaining export share (Yang and Zhong 1998). Despite higher overheads because of the (usually) Hong Kong-based fixed costs that must be factored in, the profitability of foreign-invested firms is significantly greater than that of the state enterprises (which, indeed, were generally loss-making when producing textiles) (WTO 2006). Broadly speaking, profitability is slightly greater in clothing firms than in textile firms, many of which are producing commodities and semi-finished goods. In terms of exports, the private sector (Chinese and foreign-invested) accounted for nearly 95 per cent of the industry total (Li & Fung Research Centre 2006). A different source suggests that private domestic and foreign-owned firms are together responsible for 80 per cent of textile exports and 90 per cent of garment exports (OECD 2005).

Geographically the export-oriented segment of the T/C industry is clustered in the coastal regions. Zhejiang, Jiangsu, and Guangdong provinces are the top T/C export-producing provinces (Table 9.1), providing not only the best infrastructure for information, communication, and transportation but also proximity to the major cities of Shanghai and Hong Kong (Zhang, To, and Cao 2004). Five provinces plus the city of Shanghai account for over 80 per cent of the country's

Table 9.1. Geographic distribution of Chinese textile and apparel export production, 2004

Province	Value (US$ bn)	Share (%)
Zhejiang	20.38	20.9
Guangdong	18.01	18.5
Jiangsu	15.32	15.7
Shanghai	12.09	12.4
Shandong	9.12	9.4
Fujian	4.47	4.6
Other provinces	18.01	18.5
Total	97.38	100.0

Source: Li & Fung Research Centre (2006).

export output. Guangdong and Fujian provinces are strongly oriented to clothing production, and each has attracted substantial investment by Hong Kong and Taiwanese investors, respectively. In contrast production in Zhejiang and Jiangsu provinces, which border Shanghai to the north and south, is more evenly balanced between textiles and clothing. According to CNTAC, these two provinces are home to two-thirds of China's textile clusters (Li & Fung Research Centre 2006). Datung in Zhejiang province has developed from a rural village in the late 1980s into a specialized township of some 2,200 firms and 10,000 households working at various stages of the value chain to produce one-third of the world's sock output (Applebaum 2008). The city of Ningbo, also in Zhejiang, has been described as one of the largest garment manufacturing and marketing locations in Asia (Li & Fung Research Centre 2006), with some 2,000 enterprises accounting for 12 per cent of China's total clothing production capacity. Municipal and provincial governments have played a key role in providing land for industrial parks, wholesale markets, and other infrastructure for these industrial districts (Applebaum 2008; Li & Fung Research Centre 2006).

Textiles represent a slightly greater share of the Chinese industry's total output than clothing (53% vs. 47% in 2004), but clothing production is the more export-oriented, accounting for around two-thirds of total T/C exports. China has held the position of the world's largest apparel exporter since 1993 (Rivoli 2005), overtaking Hong Kong, Taiwan, and Korea in part due to the transfer to China of their lower value-added activity in the industry. Exports increased nearly five-fold between 1980 and 2002, to reach US$ 41 billion or approximately one-fifth of the world's total (Appelbaum et al. 2005). They rose a further 80 per cent over the following three years, to US$74 billion. Output remains positioned largely at the low to middle-end product range and prices are some 20–50 per cent below world average (Li & Fung Research Centre 2006). This has allowed Chinese producers to make substantial inroads the markets of lower income countries than the EU or North America—a source of growing concern for local producers in Central American, African and some Asian countries. Nevertheless, the greater part (by value) of apparel exports is destined for developed countries.

Textile exports tend to be of low value, and are a relatively recent phenomenon, having contributed a negligible amount to exports prior to 2000. The average export price in 2001 of just US$0.72 per metre compares with an average price 43 per cent higher (at US$1.03 per metre) for imported fabrics used in garment export processing (IFM 2004). The quality of locally woven fabric is generally rather low, as is the variety and design (USITC 2004), but is improving sufficiently for increasing numbers of foreign buyers to accept its use (Interview Notes), and indeed is said to account for 40 per cent of the fabric used by Guangdong apparel producers (USITC 2004). Textile exports include semi-finished products as well as greige goods shipped to a diversified customer base across Southeast Asia and Africa (IFM 2004). Since the Chinese dyeing and printing sector lags in investments in technology and expertise, some unfinished textiles are shipped to Hong Kong for finishing and are re-imported for use in the apparel manufacturing sector (USITC 2004).

As a share of China's exports both yarns/textiles and apparel/accessories have declined in importance though remain significant, especially in the case of clothing. Meanwhile their share of the world market has increased (Table 9.2). A 21 per cent surge in the value of textile and clothing exports in 2004 was still a slower rate of growth than the 35 per cent increase in China's overall merchandise exports (WTO 2006). A further 20 per cent growth in clothing exports during 2005, the first year without MFA/ATC quotas, pushed China's share of world exports to 27 per cent. Textile exports, meanwhile, grew by an even faster 23 per cent to give China a one-fifth share of the world textile market (Adhikari and Yamamoto 2007).[11]

In 1999–2001 only 22 per cent of China's textile and apparel exports were destined for the quota-constrained markets of North America and the EU. By 2004 the largest export destinations were Hong Kong (19%), the EU-15 (12.2%), the USA (10.2%), and Japan (8.3%). Evidently, China exports to a highly diversified range of countries unlike other supplier countries we discuss, such as Romania and Mexico, whose exports are dependent on a single country or region. Indeed, as noted in Chapter 5, China displaced Mexico as the largest clothing supplier to the USA in 2003 despite the discriminatory tariffs it faced. The high share of exports going to Hong Kong is explained by the very high proportion—as much as 90 per cent according to some sources (USITC 2004)—of clothing production conducted under outward processing arrangements between Hong Kong and China, indicating how closely intertwined are the industries of these two economies. In developed markets other than the USA and EU such as Australia, which eliminated import quotas in the mid-1990s, China has become the dominant supplier—an important indicator of its ability to deliver products in the higher as well as lower quality market segments(Abernathy et al. 2006).

China's share of textile imports (including home textiles) to the USA remained relatively stable in the period 1995–2002, at around 14 per cent (although the market size expanded), and it retained its position as the top supplier; in clothing, on the other hand, it had by 2002 regained the leading position it lost to Mexico in 1999, with a share of the US market that had increased from 15 per cent in 1995

Table 9.2. Evolution in China's share of US and EU markets

	Value (US$million)									Annual change (%)			Share (%)	
	1990	1995	2000	2001	2002	2003	2004	2005	2006	1995/1996	2004/1995	2006/2004	1995	2006
US imports														
Textiles	816	1,812	2,029	1,934	3,150	4,351	5,630	7,262	8,549	9.5	17.9	23.2	13.8	39.5
Clothing	2,739	3,518	4,499	4,602	5,594	7,258	8,928	15,143	18,518	5.1	10.9	44.0	10.2	25.9
Total T/C	3,555	4,800	6,528	6,536	8,744	11,609	14,558	22,405	27,067	6.2	13.1	36.4	10.9	29.0
EU-25 imports														
Textiles		1,325	1,948	1,970	2,318	3,051	3,949	4,938	5,942		12.9	22.7	8.3	24.0
Clothing		4,633	7,144	7,460	8,806	11,532	14,251	20,919	23,390		13.3	28.1	14.5	31.3
Total T/C		5,959	9,093	9,430	11,124	14,584	18,201	25,857	29,331		13.2	26.9	12.4	29.5

Source: International Textile and Clothing Bureau, Geneva (www.itcb.org).

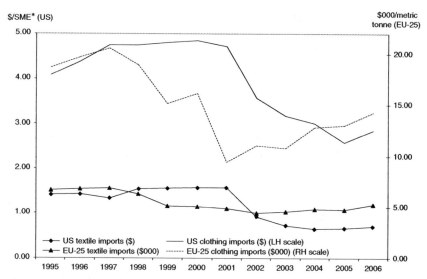

Figure 9.1. Trends in unit prices of textile and clothing imported from China into the US and EU-25, 1995–2006

Source: calculated from ICTB data.

to 16 per cent (of a bigger market) in 2005. Turning to the EU, China's market share in textiles increased from 9 to 11 per cent during the period 1995–2002, but leading supplier Turkey increased its share from 10 to 16 per cent; the picture was reversed for clothing, in which China expanded its share of the EU market from 14 per cent to 20 per cent between 1995 and 2002, whereas second-placed Turkey only retained a stable 10 per cent share (Nordås 2004). By 2006, however, China had expanded its share of the (enlarged) EU clothing market to 31 per cent while Turkey's share as the second-largest supplier had increased at a much slower pace to 14 per cent (Brocklehurst and Anson 2007). But both in the US market and in EU markets Chinese (and other developing country) imports of textiles and clothing faced heavy deflationary pressure: average clothing import prices fell 35 per cent in the USA between 1996 and 2006, and by 28 per cent in the EU (see Figure 9.1), demonstrating the power of the giant retailers to exert pressure on prices (Ahmad 2007; see also Chapter 4 on retailing).

MFA/ATC quotas undoubtedly restrained China's exports of clothing to the USA and EU before 2005.[12] Unable to participate in the MFA/ATC quota phase-out programme that began in 1995 until it became a member of the WTO, China's quota growth rates for exports to the EU and USA remained unchanged and no products were removed from quotas. Following accession in December 2001, the industry benefited overnight from the liberalization effects accumulated by other countries over the seven years since January 1995 (*Textile Outlook International* 2006). The lifting of quotas on categories of product already made quota-free for other countries, combined with accelerated increases in quota for remaining products, led to an immediate surge in shipments to the EU and the USA. The US trade deficit on textiles and clothing from China surged to US$26.6 billion in 2006, and jumped by nearly one-fifth the following year to US$31.8 billion, despite the safeguard quotas on key product lines. The US National Council of Textile Organizations claimed that for non-quota restrained items China had already captured on average 60 per cent of the market (*Just-Style* 2008). Within the EU, a one-third decline in the average price of Chinese T/C imports between 2001 and 2004 had a significant displacement effect on other suppliers (*Textile Outlook International* 2006). Safeguard agreements imposed in mid-2005 slowed the overall rate of increase in Chinese clothing exports to the EU, but it remained the largest supplier, in value terms, of pullovers, men's shirts, women's overcoats, and dresses. Imports in non-quota categories were strong, while the effect of restraint on clothing categories covered by quota was a marked increase in average price (as can be seen in Figure 9.1). EU buyers were said to be competing with each other for limited supplies of quota, allowing Chinese manufacturers to demand higher prices (Brocklehurst and Anson 2007).

A primary source of China's long-running competitiveness in the T/C industry has been the low cost of its labour. Disparity in wages between China, including the Pearl River delta, and Hong Kong accounts for the importance of outward processing arrangements in Hong Kong firms' production strategies: in 2002 the cost per operator hour, including social benefits, was US$0.69 in China's coastal areas compared with US$6.15 in Hong Kong.[13] Particularly in the coastal provinces, where in 2002 labour costs were nearly 70 per cent higher than in the inland rural areas, average wage data suggest it is no longer cheaper to produce in China than in alternative locations such as India, Indonesia, or Bangladesh (IFM 2004). Demand for skilled labour—the result both of domestic demand and even greater export demand—drove up T/C wage levels in China by 20 per cent on average in 2005, although with great variation across provinces (Brettschneider 2006). In Guangdong province, basic monthly salaries in the footwear industry (which pays similar wages to the clothing industry) doubled to US$200 between 2006 and 2007 (Mitchell 2008*a*). Just as problematic is the high rate of labour turnover in clothing factories, said to range from 20 to 50 per cent across China for entry-level production workers (Li 2007). Despite the increase in labour and other input costs, notably of cotton and energy since 2003, China remains highly competitive on a unit cost basis. The diversity of China's production capabilities is such that even in the more expensive coastal areas factories are able to compete in the medium-priced garment segment, while inland areas are competitive in the lower price brackets. Hence, as long as production can move inland or more labour can migrate to the coastal regions, the industry's exports are likely to remain competitive for the foreseeable future.

A high degree of vertical integration also contributes to industry competitiveness. As the world's largest producer of raw materials such as cotton and silk, and of man-made fibres such as flax and ramie, the Chinese textile and clothing industry sources most of its inputs domestically (UNCTAD 2005). Nordås (2004) calculates that the share of imported intermediate inputs is just 5.7 per cent. The main raw material import has traditionally been wool, primarily sourced from Australia and New Zealand, but in 2004 it was also the world's largest importer of raw cotton, with 1.1 million tonnes of its 1.9 million tonne imports sourced from the USA (WTO 2006). Imports of cotton escalated to 2.6 million tonnes in 2005 as domestic production failed to keep up with booming demand. A sharp rise in cotton prices since 2003 pushed many smaller and less efficient cotton spinners out of the market, leading to greater consolidation of the cotton-producing sector. Over-capacity and declining margins in certain segments of the textile industry remain a problem, notably in man-made fibres where China been responsible for 70 per cent of the increase in worldwide output since 1995 (IFM 2004). Structurally much of this production occurs at factories up to 30 times smaller than in competing countries (ibid.), whereas foreign-invested man-made fibre production sites, for example, by Japanese, Korean, and Taiwanese firms, tend to be international in scale (Interview Notes 2004) and hence enjoy lower production costs. Although the export-oriented clothing sector has always contained a high imported fabric content—four-fifths of that fabric is bought from regional sources, notably from Japan, Korea, and Taiwan, and 10 per cent from Italy—the potential is increasing for greater vertical integration between the domestic textile industry and the export-oriented clothing sector, in line with technological upgrading and foreign investment in textile plant (Nordås 2004). Trim and accessories (such as buttons) are also widely available locally (USITC 2004): Zhang et al. (2004), for example, describe the industrial cluster in Shengze (Jiangsu province), which specializes in manufacturing light-weight lining fabrics, while Makou Town (Hebei Province) focuses on thread production (Li & Fung Research Centre 2006).

Buoyant demand for Chinese-made clothing has stimulated massive over-expansion in production capacity at various stages of the value chain, leading to significant price deflation over the last decade in both the domestic and export markets. The government determined that as much as 87 per cent of textile goods were in oversupply, and has reportedly imposed strict limits on further industry expansion amid calls for further modernization and quality improvements (*China Economic Review* 2006). Beijing has been keen to encourage a shift in the focus of Chinese T/C exports from quantity to quality, to avoid the worst effects of continuing protectionism by the USA and the EU. And yet price pressure in the domestic clothing market continues: in January 2008 clothing prices fell 1.9 per cent year-on-year (against an unprecedented overall inflation rate of 7.1 per cent due to commodity price increases), in part reflecting a switch by exporting companies to production for the domestic market to offset the effects of currency appreciation. Around four-fifths of China's exports are said to be denominated in dollars.

9.1.3. Supplier Firms: Strategy and Performance

The sources for this section are both published materials and information gathered from 8 interviews conducted in Hong Kong, Guangdong province and Jiangsu province (near Shanghai) in 2004. These enterprises ranged from middleman agency and buying office operations through textile mills and garment factories. All the manufacturing firms we visited were Hong Kong or Japanese owned and were export-oriented (in the case of clothing producers) or producing fabric for use in garments for foreign buyers.[14] We gathered relatively little first-hand information about interactions with US customers since these firms either supplied only European (or Japanese) customers or we were meeting merchandis-ers in charge of European rather than American clients. Our interviews provide no more than a flavour of the situation, given the small size of our sample and the absence from it of any mainland Chinese-owned enterprises, but they did reveal interesting differences in the attitudes of the customers they served. Interviews with the agency and buying offices based in Hong Kong gave us an insight into the way that western buyers and retailers work through knowledgeable intermediaries to source garments in China. Our manufacturing firms generally focused on particular segments of the value chain, although one was vertically integrated from fabric production through to retail (and has developed a bigger retail presence in the years since our visit). Two firms owned manufacturing facilities in other parts of Asia as well as in China. In contrast to our firms, many successful Chinese private/joint stock firms appear to have diversified into a wide variety of activities, ranging across the textile and clothing spectrum as well as into other unrelated industries.

In terms of ownership the vast majority of indigenous Chinese firms serving the textile and apparel market are less than 30 years old, having been established from the early 1980s onwards, although a few trace their origins to the 1950s or earlier. While those set up as private enterprises from the start tend to have remained family owned and are probably still in their first generation (though perhaps with the next generation already involved in management), firms emerg-ing from state ownership or established in the early 1980s as TVEs have gone through various styles of ownership. Over time many local TVEs have merged into enterprise groups, some of which are substantial in size and may even have group members listed on the Shanghai or Hong Kong stock exchanges. Examples include Shandong-based Weiqiao Textile Co., now China's largest cotton textile producer, which listed on the Hong Kong stock exchange in 2003 but whose controlling shareholder is majority owned by a collective enterprise in Zouping County; and Youngor Group, which was established in December 1979 as a TVE in Ningbo, Zhejiang province, was listed on the Shanghai stock exchange in 1998, and is China's largest men's suit and shirt manufacturer. Zhang et al. (2004) describe the development of the Shengze lining fabric cluster, comprising around 1,100 factories and 4,000 buying and selling offices in a town of 200,000 inhabitants (vs. 30,000 two decades previously), most of them migrant workers from other parts of the country. The first factories started as TVEs, and the entrepreneurs who ran them were previously peasant farmers who began with outdated machinery from former state-owned plants. Over time they invested in the most advanced water-jet and air-jet looms and now export to international markets. The original entrepreneurs have in many cases turned over their firms to university-educated professional managers.

Broadly speaking, SOEs produce for the domestic market and privatized SOEs or TVEs mainly do so, while private firms are often oriented towards the export market (and foreign invested firms almost entirely so) (USITC 2004). Firms of all ownership types in the coastal provinces are more likely to be directing at least part of their output towards export markets. As noted above, the relatively few remaining state-owned enterprises are textile producers. Privatized state-owned firms have converted into joint stock enterprise groups, and some have partial stock exchange listings. Shanghai Silk Group grew out of the China Silk Corporation, which was founded in 1949, and underwent a management buyout in 2003 that took it out of state ownership. According to CNTAC data, it is now China's largest garment exporting company with exports of US$ 443 million in 2006. Nanjing Textiles Import & Export Corp., founded in 1978 as the textile import-export arm of Nanjing province, converted into a stock company as early as 1994 and was listed on the Shanghai stock market in 2001. Like Shanghai Silk Group it is one of the country's largest textiles and clothing exporters. Both Shanghai Silk and Nanjing Textiles are enterprise groups embracing a large number of factories and subsidiaries engaged not only in textiles and clothing but also in such diverse industries as chemicals, machinery and light industry.

Foreign-invested clothing firms and knitted fabric producers are mostly Hong Kong owned. Korean, Taiwanese, and Japanese firms, in contrast, have made big investments in man-made fibre production. Clothing firms vary in size from single sites with a couple of hundred sewing operatives to enormous groups with multiple factories on the mainland and in other countries. The factories we visited employed between 1,000 and 2,000 workers each, although the sister factory of CH-1 reportedly had nearly 6,000 employees. A combination of proximity and formal Outward Processing Arrangements between Hong Kong and China has been of immense importance not only in the development of China's clothing industry but also in the continued existence of Hong Kong's. High speed ferries and trains link Hong Kong island to Guangdong province's highly industrialized Pearl River delta (encompassing the cities of Shenzhen, Dongguan, Guangzhou, Foshan, Zhongshan, and Zhuhai) in only an hour.[15] OPA began in the 1970s—when transport links were considerably less developed—as a means of sidestepping Hong Kong quota constraints, and accelerated as Hong Kong wage levels rose. But such OPA activity in the clothing industry may have emerged irrespective of the quota situation, given its prevalence in other industries such as consumer electronics (Nordås 2004). Starting initially with subcontracting to mainland factories in the 1970s and 1980s, Hong Kong firms eventually relocated some of their own production facilities to the Pearl River delta, although more sophisticated and higher priced products, including knitted fabrics and complex dyed and printed fabrics which China's firms are unable to make, remained in Hong Kong (USITC 2004). Firms with large amounts of Hong Kong quota—including three of our interviewees—did a lot of OPA between the mainland, Hong Kong and sometimes Macau (Interview Notes 2004).

Nordås (2004) describes two different OPA patterns. In the first, the Hong Kong-based lead firm produces, dyes, and prints the fabric and contracts out the

sewing and other operations to a partner or directly owned factory on the mainland. The second pattern involves greige fabric from a Chinese textile mill being
sent to Hong Kong (or Korea or Taiwan) for dyeing and printing and then re-
export to the mainland for cutting and sewing. Our interviewees were all following
the former pattern. OPA requires firms to plan their production carefully so that
just enough operations take place in Hong Kong for a garment to qualify as 'made
in Hong Kong'. In the case of a long-sleeved shirt, for example, only the sewing
of the shoulder seams, the side seams, and the sleeve seams had to be done in
Hong Kong, while the rest of the assembly as well as non-assembly operations
(fabric inspection, washing, packaging) could take place in China (USITC 2004).
CH-4 described how the same garment could cross the border several times: most
cutting was done in Hong Kong and the bundles sent to China for making up
(e.g. inserting pockets, cuffs, and zips); then the garment, still in pieces, returned
to Hong Kong for final sewing into pairs of trousers, at which point it was sent
again to China for washing and packing, before finally returning for onward
shipment under the Hong Kong quota. The same factory owner sometimes also
bought quota in China, through the market, in which case the entire production
process could take place on the one site—indicating how much simpler manufacturing would become once quota restraints were removed. CH-2 took decisions
(in discussion with the client) on which of its factories in China to use for a
particular order based on current quota prices: in 2004 its site in Guangdong was
90 per cent dedicated to producing garments with high quota costs, so that Hong
Kong OPA could be utilized. This interviewee described OPA as 'troublesome' and
'not easy', especially for merchandisers whose job it was to keep track of work bundles moving between factories. With or without quotas, however, Hong Kong itself
remains an important element in China's textile and clothing industry because of
the value-added headquarters activities of its many production and trading firms
and because of its capital markets, even though rather little production now takes
place in the territory.

The breadth and diversity of China's export-oriented industry—and over
25 years of experience since the country opened up—means that western buyers
are able to source on a CMT or FP basis, according to their preference. Few other
developing countries are able to offer anything close to this range of capabilities. Whereas until the late 1990s European buyers expressed scepticism over the
quality, reliability, and timeliness of production in China, those concerns have
now been put aside. Sewing operatives are regarded as hard-working and skilful,
and some US importers are reported to have claimed they would be prepared to
have any garment made in China (USITC 2004). Our UK buyer firms, on the
other hand, tended to distinguish between orders requiring rapid delivery (when
supplier countries closer to Europe were more likely to be used) and those with
a longer time scale for which China manufacturing could be used. According
to one of our interviewees, 'We can do the manufacturing on whatever basis
a customer requests: OPA, full package, whatever. Sometimes customers don't
specify anything other than the price and the quality of garment they want,
they just leave it to [us] to decide' (CH-1). Whereas one of its British customers

was very 'hands on' and had a manual to control every step of the production process, another more fashion-oriented British customer handed over orders and simply expected the goods to be delivered on time—which afforded CH-1 greater flexibility in the organization of its production schedules. A German customer of CH-2 is sometimes involved in product development but pays the FP price. For the majority of its styles the customer sends patterns directly and CH-2 makes adjustments as required, but sometimes, for a few styles, the customer sends a sketch and has them develop the pattern and sample from scratch. Samples are always made and couriered to Germany for final approval before production can start.

The *raison d'être* of CH-5, the middleman operation, is to provide a full service to its European clients: designing a collection from which the customers choose styles (or, alternatively, taking a customer's designs and interpreting them into a product), sourcing the fabrics and trims, making samples, placing orders with the factories in China it works with, controlling the flow of production, doing quality control checks, and arranging the shipments. Although the numbers of such Hong Kong-based middlemen may be shrinking as more customers begin to buy directly from factories in China (Interview Notes, USITC 2004), quality conscious customers in the higher unit price segment of the market still use such agents. (And the major supply chain firms such as Li & Fung, discussed in Chapter 6, provide these services on a much greater scale.) One small UK customer (UK-C-2), for example, appreciates CH-5's local knowledge and understanding of what can be achieved with the Japanese fabrics it sources: fabrics that UK-C-2 might reject out of hand appear more interesting when CH-5 has interpreted them into styles, with suitable embellishments.

Many Hong Kong-owned firms are large enough to serve a variety of geographic markets, which offers them protection against downturns in one region or another, as well as different market segments. The largest market for CH-1 is the USA, followed by continental Europe (although individual European markets are small) and third is the UK. CH-2 also serves the US and European (including UK) markets, with business split roughly 50–50. CH-4, which owned only European quota, exported to the UK, German and French markets but was looking forward to the elimination of the quota system in order to be able to break into the US market. 'We don't put all our eggs in one basket', says one firm, which limits individual customers to a maximum 4 per cent of its business—while nevertheless admitting that if the market situation required, managers would seek to fill up production with extra orders. In total it had around 35–40 customers worldwide. Another firm thought that it was the largest though not the exclusive supplier of jeans to a German customer, which accounted for perhaps 40 per cent of its output—'we each have to spread our risk'. Clearly, however, each factory produced for a range of customers whose price points were very different, which meant that high priced garments could be produced on one line next to another manufacturing for a much lower price segment. Having a mix of department store, mail order, wholesale importer, and branded clothing customers was an important hedge against peaks and troughs in annual order flows (CH-3): mail order houses tended to place their orders first, followed by the department stores, while the branded marketers delayed their orders as long as possible.

As for the source of fabric used to fulfil customer orders, CH-2 buys from mills designated by the customer but sources most of the trim itself except for specialist items (e.g. buckles) where again the supplier is designated. One UK high street customer specifies fabric from Korea, Taiwan, and China, whereas a German mid-price customer uses Korean, Taiwanese, Japanese, and sometimes German fabrics; for a US customer that has a lot of wool garments fabrics are imported from Italy. This adds considerably to production times, since the finest woolen fabrics can take 75 days to manufacture and dye, to which must be added a further one month for shipping between Italy and China. Our interviewees generally agreed that only one or two Chinese woolen mills were capable of making good quality fabrics. CH-4 also buys all the heavy woven fabrics needed for its production and works on a FP basis. It sources fabric mainly from China (and sometimes Pakistan) but the better quality or stretch fabrics come from Taiwan and Korea. CH-1 also uses fabrics sourced mainly from China—especially its pure cotton or cotton blend shirting fabrics—but additionally imports from Taiwan, Korea, Malaysia, Thailand, and Indonesia. In particular it buys synthetic branded materials such as tencel and viscose from Taiwan and Korea, although these are expensive compared with Chinese-produced man-made fibres. As for the textile factories we visited, CH-7 sold approximately half its output made from domestic inputs into the domestic market and the rest to apparel makers in Europe and the USA; but around 10 per cent of production required raw materials from Japan and the finished fabrics were re-exported to Japan; CH-6, meanwhile, worked mostly with US customers but also with Japan, the UK, and Germany, and had a global account with a multinational German garment producer. For CH-6 it was important to attend the big European fabric fairs, sometimes with customers, because designers from the USA and Europe also attended.

The ability to hire labour varies according to the (fashion) season: during slack times—usually January–March—it is relatively easy to recruit, but factories compete with each other for new workers in the peak periods. Much investment poured into the Pearl River delta area from 2003 in expectation of quota abolition, and this pushed up wages making it more difficult to retain workers. Employees often defected if they thought they could earn more money elsewhere. CH-1 claimed that customer compliance required it to restrict overtime work, limiting how much its sewing operatives could earn. During slack periods it paid only the minimum wage (RMB 450 per month at the time), so unless there was regular work—in which case machinists could earn more at piece rates—workers would quit. CH-2 was paying new recruits without experience RMB 500 per month, although an experienced machinist working hard could earn double the amount. CH-4, however, was having to pay up to RMB 1300 per month (depending on the work and skill of the employee) versus RMB 800–900 three years earlier and yet still found it difficult to take on as many workers as were needed. In the textile factories wages averaged RMB 1,000, but new recruits with high school education earned RMB 800 at CH-7 compared with RMB 600 at CH-6. CH-7 compared the motivation, willingness to learn and diligence of Chinese workers favourably to the attitude of workers in other Asian countries: 'the ones who are clever recognize it's not just the money that counts'. It had been able to capitalize on the restructuring of SOEs to employ redundant technicians. Firms generally relied for recruitment on a government contractor who advertised in the different regions of China, or local agencies, or by simply putting up a 'Situations Vacant' banner outside the factory gate. Employing workers from different provinces could prove a challenge for management: CH-4 housed groups from different region in separate quarters[16] and provided meals based on their own cuisine in order to prevent unrest.

Training for raw recruits to the production line generally takes place on a special line where skills are brought to the required standard over a period of up to three weeks. For merchandisers, 'on the job training' appears to be the normal route, requiring a basic knowledge of garment making including how to read a pattern as well as a basic knowledge of English. In the Hong Kong-owned firms factory managers were all from Hong Kong (and this was the case at CH-1's non-Chinese factories too), though supervisory grade staff were local Chinese. The Japanese firms also filled the management levels in their Chinese factories with their own nationals. As for training or financial help provided by western customers to the clothing factories, this seemed unusual. Occasionally a buying office (e.g. CH-3) would give a seminar on quality standards or new technology, but in general 'buyers want to buy products, not give training' (CH-4). It was not unknown for importers to use seminars to impose their standards or working methods, with the implicit threat that otherwise no orders would be forthcoming (CH-3). In contrast, a German firm with its own manufacturing sites in China (GER-C-4) regularly provided technical advice to the third-party factories they were involved with. In Chinese firms factory middle-level managers are generally regarded as business-savvy and focused on the need to meet western buyers' needs, and increasing numbers of experienced production specialists are available to oversee operations (USITC 2004). Many of these will have learned their skills in Hong Kong-owned operations (Thompson 2003).[17]

As labour costs in coastal provinces have risen, business volumes with some customers have fallen. CH-1 noted that orders from a UK client to one of its Guangdong factories had dropped to one-third of previous levels (although the Hong Kong HQ may have diverted that client's business to another production site in a cheaper location). Despite the rising costs CH-1 remained deeply committed to its Guangdong factories, not least because its sites further north were not yet able to meet customer compliance standards. But in terms of shipping finished product, the factories further north were at no disadvantage since the port facilities of Shanghai were only a couple of hours away. Although in the past CH-1 had sourced supplies from Mongolia, neither the communication nor the transport links were good enough for it to consider locating a factory that far north for at least another 10 years—nor, indeed, was it yet possible to obtain all the necessary trim and accessories there, and to ship them north from Hong Kong or Guangdong would be prohibitively expensive. And yet some companies such as Esquel, the Hong Kong-owned shirt maker, have continued to invest heavily in Guangdong province despite rising costs, focusing on improved productivity and quality to achieve higher prices from customers (Mitchell 2008c). Luen Thai, another major garment producer, has built a 'supply chain city' in Dongguan that acts as a vertically integrated one-stop-shop for its customers: it brings together on a single campus over 12,000 staff engaged in 'design to store' services for visiting foreign buying teams (Applebaum 2008).[18] By improving human resource management practices, investments such as these aim to reduce chronic labour turnover (Li 2007). In some cases (e.g. CH-4) major investments are financed through the sale of valuable land in Hong Kong.

When it comes to identifying differences in the quality and durability of relationships with US, UK and German customers, CH-2 saw no clear-cut distinction: the emphasis given to price negotiation depended more on the company than its nationality. But the styles required by one of its UK customers were much simpler than those of a German customer, and that was naturally reflected in the prices CH-2 could charge. It was possible to get the pricing wrong, however: on one particularly complicated style for the German client, involving detailed quilting, CH-2 had actually lost money as it had been unable to find a specialist quilting subcontractor capable of doing the work and had had to do the quilting in-house by hand. CH-1 also found that no single customer consistently gave a good price: some styles earned better margins and it also depended on whether the fabric it located for the customer was exclusive or easily found in the market. Nevertheless, one of its UK customers might be prepared to pay a slightly better price for better quality and there were often compromise negotiations whereby a higher margin might be allowed on one style in exchange for a lower margin on another—but this accommodation was built on the trust developed over a relationship lasting many years.

As for loyalty per se, each factory could point to long relationships with German and/or UK customers. CH-4 could point to 30-year relationships with both a German customer and a UK customer: they followed as the factory moved first to larger premises in Hong Kong and then to China, and as ownership passed from father to son. In other instances we found partnerships—as they were referred to—lasting over 10 years or 20 years. Only one interviewee (CH-1) commented on its US customers, indicating that they were more focused on price and hence tended to be less loyal than European buyers, that is, they were more likely to shift their supply base each year. And yet it also complained about one UK high street retailer notorious in the industry for squeezing supplier margins, which pressed the price down in one season and the following season placed orders at an even lower price, 'but we accept'. Meanwhile CH-4, which was building up connections in the USA in preparation for the post-quota era, expressed anxiety over the potentially greater risk involved in dealing with much larger US order volumes. In his father's day the factory had faced problems with US customers being 'tricky' on price over minor manufacturing or delivery faults. The buying office, CH-3, observed that US importers tended to have lower quality standards and were less precise about the fit of garments than were European buyers, but had other preoccupations such as insisting that all fabrics should be washable.

From the customer perspective, there was concern among UK and German buyers that they could be squeezed out of their chosen factories by the large volumes ordered by US firms: 'if you go to China, and the factories are making for Reebok or whoever, you know you are going to be very, very small' (UK-C-11). With very short runs—perhaps only 200–300 pieces for one of CH-2's German customers—sewing operatives barely had time to learn how to make the style before the order was complete; with longer runs, on the other hand, it was easier to control the quality of work and for the sewers to make their money. Small quantity runs require the same amount of management and preparatory work as large orders. China is said to be losing some EU customers because clothing producers will accept only large orders (e.g. a minimum order level of 5,000 pairs of trousers), whereas producers closer to home in CEE, Turkey, and North Africa routinely take minimum orders of 500 or 1,000 pairs.

Differences were observable in the approach to quality control, for medium to upper price buyers a crucial issue. QC could be managed either by the customer's agent (which could be a buying agent or a specialist inspection and verification company such as SGS) or by the customer's own staff based in the region. In the case of one of CH-2's major UK clients, its own locally based inspection team came to the factory every day to check product before shipment to Europe, while an important German client relied on its Hong Kong-based buying agent who would come to inspect a product both on the line and before shipment. A major UK customer for CH-1, in contrast, sent monthly inspection teams from its own factory based elsewhere in Asia as well as supplying a QC manual. CH-4 received QC inspection visits 2–3 times per week from the Hong Kong office of its biggest German customer—which also provided a QC manual—whereas its two largest UK high street fashion customers relied on a third party inspection specialist. CH-5 visited regularly the factories it had chosen to produce for its main UK customer. Broadly speaking, with respect to quality control there seemed to be less of a distinction between German and UK client attitudes than between the market segment served (high fashion vs. middle market). As CH-1 noted, 'people come quite often to educate our employees to their standards, but every customer has its own standards so it's quite hard.' The same interviewee observed that it had much greater flexibility to handle the orders of customers which took a rather 'hands-off' attitude, and that it would be 'impossible' if all its customers were as demanding as one particular client. Completely separately from quality control, most buyer firms would send audit teams to check the factories they were using for social, health, and safety compliance.

Hong Kong clothing firms are also increasingly actively engaged in manufacturing for Chinese customers in the domestic market, where increasing affluence means that high rates of growth are anticipated over the next decade.[19] CH-1 was making for at least 10 Chinese brands, but had a different relationship with them compared to that with its western customers. On the one hand Chinese customers were far less interested in compliance 'because they know how Chinese factories work', but on the other they were seen to be far less trustworthy, especially if they were unknown names: 'if you don't know them, they could disappear without paying' (CH-1). As a result, whereas the western customers paid by letters of credit, Chinese customers were required to put down a 20 per cent deposit and pay the balance before delivery. In other words, whereas western buyers could impose their payment terms on Hong Kong producer firms, the latter were more able to impose their own terms on the Chinese buyers.

Rather few Chinese firms can yet boast internationally recognized brand names, but increasing numbers over the past five years have been directing their efforts to building a brand presence in the domestic market. The better-known brand names were just as concerned about product quality as western clients. A few Chinese companies have begun to invest overseas: Dussel Peters (2005) notes that Sinatex invested US$96 million in a fibres and textiles mill in Mexico in 2001. The largest foreign investment by the industry to date is a US$120 million acquisition finalized in January 2008 by Youngor Group. Youngor bought XinMa Apparel International, a Hong Kong-based firm, from Kellwood of the USA, which had used it to develop its Smart Shirts wholesale manufacturing and marketing business. The acquisition gives Youngor Group manufacturing bases in Sri Lanka and the Philippines as well as additional sites on the Chinese mainland that currently produce for international brands sold mainly in North America (China Daily 2007).

9.1.4. Future Prospects for the Chinese Clothing Industry

China was widely predicted to be a major beneficiary of the elimination of quotas, with the US International Trade Commission concluding that it would become the 'supplier of choice' for most US importers in light of its ability to produce many different types of textile and clothing at many quality levels and at a competitive price. Similar conclusions were voiced within Europe (USITC 2004). China's capacity to serve developed country markets is demonstrated by average annual growth of 13 per cent in textile and clothing imports to both the US and EU-25 over the period 1995–2004, and by 36 and 27 per cent, respectively in 2004–06, giving it a 29–30 per cent share of both markets by the end of 2006, substantially higher than the share achieved by the second largest supplier (Mexico and Turkey, respectively).[20]

Initial expectations in the run-up to 2005 generally held that EU and American buyers would heavily consolidate the number of countries in their sourcing network following quota-elimination, and that China would be a major beneficiary of this trend. But other factors point to limitations on the extent to which China will be able to increase further its global market share. Buyers are unlikely to want to depend too greatly on a single sourcing country (concern over the impact on sourcing strategies of events such as the SARS epidemic in 2004 militates against over-dependence), and are hence likely to turn to other potential major suppliers such as India and Vietnam. A second factor limiting further market share growth is the importance in the western clothing retail industry of high value garments and fashion items, for which labour cost considerations are comparatively small when set against the need for reliable delivery and short lead times. Although considerable improvements in Chinese infrastructure and factory efficiency have cut shipping times to the east coast of the USA to 12–18 days (USITC 2004) or 21 days to Europe, countries neighbouring the USA and EU still have the competitive edge in this regard. Third is the desire of the government to promote higher value-added export activity, both within the textiles and clothing industry and in the manufacturing sector more generally. Coupled to the evolution in the Chinese economy that this implies is growing interest among producers in brand development for the domestic clothing market. Some manufacturers have begun to divert attention away from export contracts to counteract rapidly shrinking margins brought about by currency appreciation, which itself is exacerbating the already steep declines experienced in export unit prices over the last 10 years. But even in the domestic market the trend in prices has been deflationary since the late 1990s, indicating a heavy over-supply situation. Currency appreciation may help the consolidation of the industry by allowing only the more competitive firms to survive.

The attractions of China as a manufacturing base for western buyers are nonetheless manifold. Both central and provincial governments have, in different ways, contributed to the successful transformation of the textile and clothing industry from a bloated and inefficient state sector into a vibrant industry predominantly though not exclusively in private hands; and municipal authorities have invested heavily in developing wholesale markets and other infrastructure to facilitate the development of specialized industrial districts (Li & Fung Research Centre 2006). The intertwining of the Hong Kong industry with China's has produced firms that offer value-added services, are responsive to changes in retailer and buyer demands, and are readily able to meet production standards; they tend to be flexible in making samples and small runs, and boast high productivity levels coupled with (relatively) low wages; and shipping times to the USA and Europe are favourable compared with those offered by other Southeast Asian countries (USITC 2004). There remains scope to generate further significant productivity improvement since value-added per employee continues to lag other nations (Nordås 2004).

But IFM (2004) argues that China lacks marketing experience and advanced technology in value-added areas, and that it will make no major inputs into either design or product engineering for years to come. Unless domestic Chinese clothing firms can develop the design, branding, management, and marketing skills necessary to compete fully with developed country counterparts, the majority will remain contractors to western retail giants. One of the reasons for the rapid decline in unit prices of Chinese (and other developing country) exports over the last decade is that competition has been focused on price. Yet brand and marketing skills may be learned over time, by drawing directly on the expertise of ethnic Chinese business people from Hong Kong and elsewhere, and by ripple effects from employees trained in foreign-invested firms (Thompson 2003). A small proportion of Chinese firms, encouraged by domestic retail market development, are developing local brands; a smaller proportion still is attempting to create a brand presence in external markets; and a very few (such as Youngor) are using their financial muscle to buy recognized foreign brands. The ability to assimilate the expertise thus acquired may determine the success of these manoeuvres.

At a broader level China faces several socio-economic challenges, not least the polarization of incomes between urban and rural areas, and between inland and coastal provinces; the need to constantly generate millions of jobs; the inflationary pressures on commodity inputs caused by China's economic growth; and the very serious problems arising from environmental degradation and water shortages. Labour unrest due to dissatisfaction with wages and/or working conditions is rising, particularly in the southern provinces. Higher employer costs associated with new labour laws (see Chapter 10), combined with the expense of installing proper pollution control equipment in clothing firms' laundries, will almost certainly drive the less efficient producers from the industry.

9.2. MEXICO

9.2.1. Geopolitical Position, Institutional Structure, and Industrial Development

Mexico—a country of around 103 million inhabitants in 2005—forms the bridge between Latin America and the USA. However, for many decades it had insulated itself from the USA, pursuing an independent and distinctive political and economic course. Since its revolutionary transformation during the 1910–20 period, the country effectively had a one party state, run along populist and authoritarian lines by a self-perpetuating political elite. Labour and the unions were the party's ideological centre and provided party and government political support. However, the Mexican corporatist system only granted the unions a subordinate role and incorporated union leaders through a mixed policy of clientelist reward and suppression.

Economically Mexico followed a strategy of import substitution, developing its economy behind high tariff walls. During the 1980s, there were repeated peso crises and subsequent hyper-inflation. The state actively intervened in economic development, and large-scale public ownership prevailed in many sectors of the economy. (For further details see Middlebrook 1995 and Dussel Peters, Duran, and Piore 2002.) During the period from ∼1940 to 1980, the state directed the industrialization process and picked the winners, that is, sectors and firms which would benefit from state policy (Carillo, Hualde, and Almaraz 2002: 196, fn 1).

From the early 1980s onwards, this regime began very gradually to transform. Politically, democratic tendencies achieved a breakthrough in 2000, with the election of Vincente Fox and the establishment of multi-party competition. Although the democratization process is by no means complete, change at the national political level came to have multiple consequences at other levels, particularly at the level of labour representation (Middlebrook 2004). Economically, change first came through a partial opening of the economy to inward investment from North America and then, following entry to the GATT in 1986, a more radical transformation ensued. Under the Salinas presidency of 1988–94 the economic strategy fully changed towards market liberalization, culminating in the joining of NAFTA in 1994. Large-scale privatization and the withdrawal of the state from active economic intervention followed, including the surrender of any sectoral policy (Dussel Peters 2004: 2). The active pursuit of inward FDI fundamentally changed the economic terrain. Mexico transformed itself within a decade or so from one of the world's most closed to one of the most open economies (Spener, Gereffi, and Bair 2002).

The joining of NAFTA and the concurrent peso devaluation ushered in a rapid and thorough-going economic integration of Mexico with the USA, through both FDI and trans-border outsourcing by US MNCs, predominantly in the auto, electronics, and textiles and clothing industries. To encourage and attract North American companies, labour markets were partially de-regulated, wages kept low and any independent labour protests suppressed (Spener et al. 2002: 11; Dussel Peters 2005).

Although the authoritarian legacy of the one-party state was hard to dislodge (Middlebrook 1995), there now are signs, following the defeat of the one-party system, of modest change towards a more pluralist system and some democratization also in civil society (Middlebrook 2004). The political elite has loosened ties with the PRI (the ruling Institutional Revolutionary Party) and the unions. Independent and more critical unions, supported by US unions such as UNITE, and by anti-sweatshop NGOs such as the Workers' Rights Consortium, are cautiously challenging official unions and trying to displace them (Chan and Ross 2003: 1022; Bensusan 2004). Additionally, wages were made subject to inflation control (Dussel Peters 2004: 3).

The economic consequences of incorporation into NAFTA remain disputed. On the one hand NAFTA brought a more stable currency, modest inflation, plentiful FDI, and the generation of industrial employment. On the other hand the economic benefits have remained unequally distributed, with wages kept low and labour benefiting only marginally. Moreover, rather than stimulating independent economic growth, the Mexican economy became highly dependent on the USA. Critics of NAFTA saw it as consolidating Mexico's position as the 'low-wage periphery' of the USA, turning the whole country into a *maquiladora* (Bair and Dussel Peters 2006: 209). (*Maquiladoras* are defined as firms that produce 100 per cent for export and have no local linkages for inputs [Carillo, Hualde, and Almaraz 2002: 192].) This involved not only full exposure to the economic cycles of the US economy but, much worse, high vulnerability to the changes in locational choices of US companies following the integration into the world economy of China in 2001 and the end of the MFA/ATC quota system in January 2005.

In contrast to Turkey, Mexico does not have active industry associations, nor has its textile industry benefited from strong state support during the period of import substitution. This has prevented the development of a strong textile sector which would have been able to support the upgrading of the clothing industry at the current time. Despite the government's 2001–06 National Plan for Development, which regards the fibre, textile, and clothing industries as strategic priority sectors and major generators of employment(USITC 2004: H10), the government has few major programmes to assist its T/C industries. Hence, in contrast to the situation in the Chinese T/C industry, there now is neither sustained state nor bank support for industrial upgrading. Shortage of investment capital, particularly among the many weak SMEs, was further exacerbated by the rise in interest rates following the economy's opening to trade. The banking system has undergone nationalization and then re-privatization. It is now highly centralized in Mexico City and lacks the local knowledge to undertake screening of firms for credit-worthiness and hence does not extend credit (Dussel Peters et al. 2002: 238). Although the National Bank of Foreign Trade has some programmes to champion Mexican firms (Bair and Gereffi 2002: 43), they fall short of significant investment to support upgrading.

9.2.2. Structure and Performance of T/C Industry and its Firms

Mexico has had domestic textile and clothing industries since the beginning of the twentieth century (Carillo et al. 2002: 184). But the number of firms, the volume of production and employment only became highly significant after joining NAFTA.

Until 1987–88, the Mexican T/C industry was highly protected by import licences and tariffs. Following liberalization, the US government introduced a gradual reduction of quota restrictions on re-imports from Mexico. Prior to 1994 a bi-lateral agreement permitted production-sharing arrangements with US firms. This entailed the exporting of cut-garment parts to Mexico and the re-import of assembled garments—in other words the CMT mode of sourcing. NAFTA was the culmination of these developments. Since the 1980s, the Mexican T/C industry's development trajectory has been shaped by US investors, suppliers, and buyers not only in quantitative but also in qualitative terms.

NAFTA provided Mexican apparel producers with exclusive duty- and quota-free benefits (USITC 2004: H11). Although there is equality of NAFTA partners regarding duties and quotas, this equality does not extend to rules of origin. In contrast to most international rules, country of origin is not defined at the product, but at the yarn level (Birnbaum 2000: 38; see also Chapter 5). NAFTA preferences apply to products (fabrics and trim) made in North America from the yarn stage forward ('yarn forward' rule). NAFTA thereby introduced new opportunities for American textile firms which, following the start of foreign sourcing from the late 1970s, gradually saw their customer base in the US clothing industry whittled away. Hence the 'yarn forward' rule that tied Mexican trade privileges to making clothes with fabrics made from US yarn both stunted the development of an indigenous Mexican textile industry and restricts the access of Mexican T/C firms to globally competitive yarn and fabric (Bair and Dussel Peters 2006: 216; Dussel Peters 2008: 16–17).

The implementation of NAFTA in 1994 and the devaluation of the peso in 1995 gave a tremendous boost to the expansion of the *maquiladora* sector. *Maquiladora* employment rose from 64,000 in 1993 to 285,600 in 2001 (Carillo et al. 2002: 182). It assisted Mexico to become the largest foreign supplier of textiles and clothing to the USA during the 1990s (USITC 2004: H3). But it also tied the Mexican industry to the US market, creating a dangerously high level of dependence. In 2002, around 93 per cent of Mexican T/C exports went to the USA (Dussel 2005: 78). In 2001, the T/C sector accounted for 1.2 per cent of Mexico's GDP, 7.1 per cent of manufacturing GDP, and about 18 per cent of manufacturing employment (USITC 2004: H3). Its importance thus lies primarily in its contribution to employment and rather less in that to GDP. Although the sector has boosted export revenue and employment, the T/C industries have failed to stimulate the rest of the economy because they work mainly with imported inputs. While Mexican textile firms export to the USA, such exports are relatively low, and the trade balance has remained highly negative.

Mexican apparel exports to the USA peaked in 2000, constituting 13.2 per cent of the export value among the world's top seven apparel exporters. By 2001, it had dropped to 12.7 per cent, and Mexico had been overtaken by China as the largest supplier of apparel. By 2004, Mexico's share of the US market stood at 11 per cent, with Mexico coming third after China's 20 per cent (including Hong Kong and Macau) and the Caribbean Basin countries (16%) (Birnbaum 2004: 13). In 2005, Mexico reached a new low, and now accounts for only 7.7 per cent of total US apparel imports (AAFA 2006: 3). China's entry into the WTO and accelerated market liberalization made Chinese firms more attractive suppliers, and the 2005 abolition of quotas further accelerated the rush of US firms to China. Job loss has engulfed even the most developed T/C cluster, Torreon, where employment declined by 35,000 between 2000 and 2004 (Rosenberg 2005: 47). This large-scale desertion of their Mexican suppliers by US clothing firms had a number of reasons. They were connected both with China's advantages and with the deterioration of the Mexican industry's cost structure (appreciation of the peso and rises in wage levels), as well as with its comparatively lower quality standards and efficiency, particularly on delivery time (Interview Notes of US firms 2003–04; Birnbaum 2004: 19f). Membership of NAFTA and the relatively greater proximity to the USA, compared with China, did not compensate for the perceived weaknesses—both costs and speed to market—of Mexican firms in the eyes of American buyers. For some categories of clothing, such as knit shirts and cotton trousers, lead time in Mexico is longer than in China (Birnbaum 2004: 2). Shipments of garments to the USA declined by 20 per cent between 2000 and 2004 (Dussel Peters 2005), and employment between 2001 and 2005 fell by 41 per cent to 174,000 (Gruben 2006: 1; Dussel Peters 2008).

The industry can be divided into three distinct segments: (domestically oriented) clothing firms, *maquila* establishments and textile producers. Domestically oriented clothing firms constitute the largest proportion of firms (79%), *maquila* establishments account for a mere 6 per cent and textile firms for 15 per cent (USITC 2004: H4). *Maquila* employment as a share of industry employment was

19.1 per cent in 2001 (Carillo et al. 2002: 182), indicating that *maquila* firms, on average, are much larger than domestically oriented ones. Domestically oriented firms, in contrast to *maquila* firms, did not benefit from NAFTA. The peso devaluation in 1994 destroyed consumers' purchasing power (Bair and Dussel Peters 2006: 209), and, more recently, cheap imports from China have been further undermining them.

Between 1995 and 2000, total investment by US firms into Mexico doubled from US$176 million to US$343 million, of which 40 per cent went into the apparel industry (USITC 2004: H9). In 2001, US firms were the predominant investors (62%) in T/C firms, followed by Korean (13%) and Spanish and Chinese investors, each with 3 per cent (USITC 2004: H9). US wholly owned subsidiaries of clothing firms disappeared as US firms moved towards contract assembly (USITC 2004: H6). The big US textile mills, in anticipation of more full-package buying but also pressurized by the large clothing firms (Collins 2003), re-located to Mexico from the late 1990s, either through FDI or joint ventures with Mexican clothing firms. They made major investments and tried to achieve more integrated production and quicker turnaround. These investments largely failed. (For further details, see below.) By 2003, the sector accounted for only 2.4 per cent of FDI in the manufacturing sector (USITC 2004: H3).

The Mexican industry covers the entire production chain from fibre and yarn to clothing, but the clothing industry is the largest segment in the chain, accounting for 86 per cent of exports to the USA in 2002 (USITC 2004: H4). Although the clothing industry has some competitive advantages compared to those of other countries, its weaknesses, due to its institutional environment, are beginning to outweigh the strengths. Spener et al. (2002: 9) somewhat optimistically single out as advantages the industry's relatively low cost; the existence of an indigenous entrepreneurial class capable of undertaking assembly and, in some cases, also 'full package'; the comparatively reasonable quality of its transportation and communication infrastructure; its proximity to the USA; and the NAFTA preferential quota and tariff regulations. Others are, however, much less sanguine about the industry's advantages. The cost structure, if a 'full value' cost analysis (taking into account macro, direct, and indirect costs) is undertaken (Birnbaum 2000), is no longer so advantageous: wage costs have risen with the peso revaluation, and in 2004 wages per hour of US$2.35 contrasted with only US$0.4 per hour in China (Dussel Peters 2005: 73, chart 1). Wages are also higher than those of competitors in neighbouring Central American countries. Other costs, such as bank interest charges, raw materials, energy, and construction also are considerably higher than in China (ibid). Mexico's geographical proximity to the USA looks less of a plus factor when the country's poor transport network is taken into consideration, with lorry transport to Los Angeles often being more expensive than sea transport from Taiwan (ICFTU 1996: 4). Finally, the capabilities of the entrepreneurial class are no longer rated very highly by (former) US buyers and are considered, at best, uneven (Interviews of US companies 2003–04). A particularly serious failing of Mexican firms is their inability to upgrade to full package suppliers (Bair and

Dussel Peters 2006) and to master fast delivery of smaller orders (Birnbaum 2004). Because of the lack of upgrading of the Mexican T/C industry and the continued dependence on imports of fabric and trim from the USA, domestic value-added, as well as learning processes and spin-off effects for the rest of the economy, have been minimal (Dussel Peters 2008: 19).

A deeper understanding of the weaknesses of the Mexican T/C complex relative to that of its Chinese competitor has to focus both on the shortcomings of the textile industry, with its vital up-stream position in the supply chain, and on the structure and strategy of *maquila* clothing firms. Vertical integration in the textile/clothing value chain is important for the quick-turnaround strategy which became essential after large US retailers turned to just-in-time delivery during the 1990s (Abernathy et al. 1999). Easy access to good-quality textiles, either through vertical integration or close geographical proximity in T/C clusters, became an important requirement when many US buyers, and particularly the large retailers, turned towards full package supply. Substantial vertical integration has eluded most Mexican firms (USITC 2004) as well as the US textile inward investors who thought they could compensate for the weaknesses of Mexican firms. US textile firms, in our interviews, explained this negative outcome in the following ways. In the face of currency devaluations by East Asian economies following the 1997 Asian crisis, and confronted with competition from Mexican textile mills, they found themselves overstretched (US-T-2) and began to go bankrupt in large numbers. 'Investments in Mexico have been a disaster', because of an unreliable infrastructure and the high expense of substituting American for Mexican staff (US-T-1).

Mexican clothing firms are highly dependent on US and Mexican textile firms. Because of NAFTA trade rules, particularly the yarn-forward rule, they do not have access to globally competitive fabric, nor are they able to shop around for a particular quality of fabric. Although there is a reasonably sized Mexican textile industry, many firms (around 40%) are very small, under-capitalized family businesses (USITC 2004: H5). Nor does the industry produce the whole range of fabrics. The Mexican industry is by no means self-sufficient but imports 80 per cent of its cotton, yarn, and fabric requirements from the USA (USITC 2004: H6). The industry produces mainly denim, denim-lycra blends and fabric of speciality man-made fibres (USITC 2004: H5). These fabrics traditionally have been sold to domestic firms but three large firms—Kaltex SA, Lear Mexican Trim, and Eagle Trading Company—export to the USA and, to a lesser degree, to Central American clothing firms. Mexican fabric is said to be less expensive and available in greater supply than American fabric, but also often deficient in quality, particularly in the finishing process (Interview Notes on US firms 2003–04). Mexico is considered competitive in the production of denim and certain wool fabrics but not in other fabrics, particularly man-made fabrics (USITC 2004: H6). Mexico's special strength in denim supports the high-volume jeans production in Torreon, the new Jeans Capital (Gereffi et al. 2002). Recently, the Mexican market has been impaired by trans-shipped textiles and clothes from Asian countries 'that make use of western US ports of entry' (USITC 2004: H6). The number of firms dropped steadily during the 1990s, but overall employment growth signalled growth of the largest firms (Bair and Gereffi 2002: 45–6).

In common with clothing industries in many developed countries, the Mexican industry has both a large informal sector and, overlapping with it, a very large and financially weak SME sector. Nearly 98 per cent of firms are SMEs, that is, they have less than 50 employees (USITC 2004: H4). As Carillo et al. (2002: 182) point out, it is very hard to distinguish between formal, informal, and clandestine plants. The large segment of relatively weak SME firms, in the absence of significant financial support from either the state or the banks, partly accounts for the fact that transition to the full package strategy has remained very patchy. SMEs are family-owned firms which lack modern technology and manufacturing methods. They are described as 'a large group of smaller producers, that have been unable to meet international quality standards and are floundering even in their own national market place' (Dussel Peters et al. 2002: 243).

The bulk of the clothing firms have never advanced beyond simple assembly operations, and upgrading to full package production has been hampered through lack of access to affordable credit (USITC 2004: H6; Bair and Dussel 2006: 211, 217). Firms have not invested sufficiently in production technology as compared with, for example, their Chinese competitors (USITC 2004: H8). But in recent years, a small number of full-package producers nevertheless has emerged. According to Bair and Dussel Peters (2006: 210), the development of full-package capabilities 'is highly uneven across the industrial landscape of Mexico's textile and apparel sector'. They appear to be concentrated particularly in Torreon, the centre of jeans production, where many firms also developed cutting, laundering/stone washing, hand-sanding, and other finishing operations, as well as some pattern-making (Rosenberg 2005: 53). In Torreon, by 2005, full package accounted for between 60 and 100 per cent, on average, of the volume of the largest firms in the area, and full-service was provided by around 20–30 per cent of these firms (Rosenberg 2006: 11). Additionally, there are several firms doing 'full package' production for large retailers, such as The Gap and JC Penney (ibid). Strategies involving further upgrading, such as going into own brand manufacturing and forward integration into retailing do not seem at all common, although instances exist (e.g. Rosenberg 2005: 73, on jeans manufacturing in Laguna). This lack of upgrading across the industry is a very serious shortcoming, in view of the fact that Mexico's Chinese competitors have no problem in fulfilling their US customers' demand in this respect. Equally serious is the fact that Mexican firms, as suppliers mainly of fashion, rather than commodity products, cannot achieve the short delivery time demanded by US customers (Birnbaum 2004: 19f). The latter therefore speaks of the 'strategic failure' of the Mexican industry and, moreover, detects no attempts to overcome it (ibid: 25).

The clothing industry produces basic fashion garments, mainly five-pocket jeans and T-shirts, destined for export to the USA. Spener et al. (2002: 6) confirm that exports to the USA are dominated by mass produced standardized garments, with men's and women's trousers, men's shirts, and brassieres predominant. An excessive degree of concentration on only a few products is singled out as a weakness of the industry by Birnbaum (2004: 16f) and Bair and Dussel Peters (2006: 210). Other problems of the industry, identified by their US clients, are inability to meet quality standards, to produce in sufficient volume and to deliver on time (Birnbaum 2000: 260; Dussel Peters et al. 2002: 231; Interviews of US companies in 2003–04). While Dussel Peters et al. (2002: 231) view these shortcomings as a legacy of sheltered markets the more enduring characteristics of small size, insufficient financial resources, and managerial capabilities must also be strongly implicated.

There is only general information in the literature on the degree to which the large Mexican suppliers to US customers rely on further subcontracting in cheaper neighbouring countries or domestic regions. According to Bair and Gereffi (2002: 47) and Collins (2003), large full-package suppliers often rely on tiers of smaller sub-contractors. The former point out that, at the lowest levels of the network, risks are highest, wages lowest, and the work conditions poorest (Bair and Gereffi 2002: 47). Most of the SME apparel firms mainly act as subcontractors, doing cut-and-sew operations (USITC 2004: H4). Rosenberg (2005: 48) additionally points out that the heightened competition with China and the intensified cost pressure accompanying it has induced some firms to shift their production to lower-wage regions in southern Mexico and in Central America.

9.2.2.1. Regional Distribution

The industry is geographically highly fragmented. It is located mainly in the industrial states of the South-Centre—Mexico, Puebla, Tlaxala, Morelos, Hidalgo, and Jalisco. But significant clusters also may be found along the US–Mexican border, in the states of Coahuila, Chihuahua, and Sonora. The latter are mainly *maquiladora* establishments (USITC 2004: H4). Northern border regions have been losing ground to those in the interior from the late 1980s, due to stiff competition for real estate and workers from other industries (Spener et al. 2002: 9). Collins (2003: 142) points out that such re-location also enabled firms to gain access to more disciplined or pliant workers. By 1996, growth mainly occurred in non-border areas. Among the inland regions, the La Laguna region and especially Torreon has achieved particular prominence (Bair and Gereffi 2002; Gereffi et al. 2002; Rosenberg 2005, 2006), due to its ability to develop a successful jeans cluster and transition to full-package supply, based on partial upgrading of functions. The cluster, developed out of a long-established local T/C industry, is centred on a number of very large, mainly Mexican firms which produce jeans in very large volumes, surpassing that of the former Jeans Capital in El Paso, Texas (Gereffi et al. 2002: 207).

Mexican *maquiladora* firms employ a large proportion of young and female workers without union experience, and the industry has a long history of collaboration between state labour officials and company managers. These features have made the industry notoriously hostile to effective union action. Unions rarely have any presence on the shop floor. With a few exceptions, unionization rates in the *maquiladora* industry are very low (Collins 2003; Fox 2004). (For further details on labour, see Chapter 10.)

9.2.3. Relations of Supplier Firms with US Buyer Firms

The relationships of Mexican supplier firms with their buyers cannot be covered in the same degree of depth as were those of Turkish, Romanian, and Chinese firms. First, because Mexican firms are highly dependent on only one foreign buyer—US firms—no comparisons are possible to highlight distinctive national practices. (It is notable though that the relations of US firms with their Mexican suppliers share much in common with those with their Turkish suppliers.) Second, in the case of Mexican suppliers we were unable to conduct interviews. By relying instead on comments of US firms made during interviews, as well as on the secondary literature on Mexican firms' perceptions of the relationship, we are unable to provide the same balanced and nuanced account.

In our interviews, several companies expressed the wish to establish longer-term relationships (e.g. US-C-7), and the few which had set up foreign subsidiaries or joint ventures in Mexico claimed to be there for the long haul. However, most industry observers identify a fairly loose relationship and emphasize the tendency among US firms in general to move frequently between suppliers (e.g. US-C-9). This tendency, already evident in the move from Northern border regions to lower-wage Mexican *maquilas* in the interior, intensified during the 2000s when it became evident that China presented a good alternative supplier country to Mexico. It is clearly expressed in the massive job losses in Mexico in recent years, indicated in Section 9.2.2. US firms do not fear becoming the captive of any one supplier (e.g. US-C-1) as they are never deeply committed in the first place. The widespread use of agents by US firms, too, shows the absence of close involvement with suppliers (e.g. Collins 2003). Such a brief and loose relationship is, of course, compatible with the fact that cost saving is uppermost for most buyer firms and drives their restless search for new and lower-wage locations. How, in the face of shallow ties between buyer and supplier firms, do US buyers exert control over suppliers?

US buyer firms, whether manufacturers or retailers, are able to exert control over their suppliers by virtue of the fact that they are 'large volume' buyers. The following quote well expresses the awareness that large buyers can exert leverage: 'Size brings leverage. Large firms, like [US-C-6] control production, by dominating a factory. A Jones, a Liz Claiborne, a Kellwood—if they find an excellent factory, they want to control it' (US-C-6). Despite US firms' claims that competitive costs, quality, and prompt delivery count equally in their supplier selection, in fact cost considerations are usually at the forefront. A detailed analysis of Liz Claiborne's strategy in one contractor firm, however, established that, in addition to control through volume buying, direct control over the production process through statistical process control (SPC) was exercised, albeit by a Mexican agent of the firm (Collins 2003). During the 1990s quick turnaround also acquired importance (Abernathy et al. 1999; Rosenberg 2005), and Mexican firms have frequently been found wanting on this criterion (e.g. US-C-1; Birnbaum 2004).

Upgrading of suppliers' employees through training is fairly uncommon. This is compatible with the short duration of relationships and the dominance, within them, of cost considerations. 'Companies actively engaged in upgrading their suppliers in Mexico are relatively unusual' (Dussel Peters et al. 2002: 231). Of the large US firms interviewed only one engaged in any training—US-C-7—and this was in a fully owned subsidiary, rather than in supplier firms. US companies complain about poor middle management in Mexican companies (US-C-1) but do not usually put in the effort to raise levels of competence.

In general, the relationship between US buyers and *maquila* firms is one of no obligation on either side, beyond a given short contract. But some clients, particularly in the somewhat exceptional La Laguna region, have sought longer-term relations from the larger *maquilas*, urging them to update to acquire 'full package' capabilities (Rosenberg 2005: 58–9).

9.2.4. Future Prospects of the Mexican Clothing Industry

Whereas the work of Bair and Gereffi (2002) was still full of optimism about the future of the Mexican clothing industry, more recent studies express considerable pessimism. The work by Rosenberg (2005) on the same region comes to the conclusion that the Mexican industry is viable only for rapid replenishment orders, not stock orders. USITC (2004), too, holds that Mexico is now considered only useful for quick turnaround, mid-season delivery or replenishment of certain basic garments (ibid: 2). It relegates Mexico to the position of a second tier supplier (ibid). Birnbaum's (2004) pessimism about the industry's future ability to improve on 'quick turnaround' delivery puts even this advantage in question. The high level of import of US fabric, a poor transport infrastructure and the inability of many firms to do smaller runs all stand in the way of being highly effective in executing rapid replenishment.

The loss of US customers, of course, is not only due to failings of the Mexican state and firms but also to the stronger lure exerted by competitors, above all by China, but also by Central American countries. The latter offer both lower labour costs and the advantage of close geographical proximity to the USA. The chances that Mexican firms, like their Turkish counterparts, develop a strong indigenous textile industry and move into higher quality market segments are currently slim. Membership of NAFTA and the absence of an interventionist state to promote investment for upgrading rule out the adoption of this strategic path. Many of the larger firms in the industry themselves rule out a promising future for the Mexican T/C industry (Birnbaum 2004) and instead are beginning to shift their resource into other higher-value industries (Rosenberg 2006).

Thus the strategy of the Mexican state to improve the country's competitive position by joining a trade block (Palan and Abbott 1996) has not served the T/C industry well. This is primarily due to the fact that the joining of NAFTA was accompanied by extensive economic liberalization, including a loss of state control over the banking system. This obviated the state's capacity and willingness to invest in the T/C industry and the economic infrastructure more generally. The entrenched habits on the part of firms, formed during the long economic regime of import substitution, additionally meant that firms' capabilities to compete were poorly developed. Last, the political legacy of the 'revolutionary' period vis-à-vis labour rendered it impossible to champion a competitive strategy based on lowering labour and social costs. The Mexican competition state (Palan and Abbott 1996) thus was left with few viable competitive strategies to save the T/C industry.

NOTES

1. Throughout the early years of economic reform the government rigorously controlled which firms could gain access to foreign currency.
2. Although TVEs were controlled by local governments, they were run independently of central state planning and workers were not state employees (hence did not receive state welfare entitlement and could be fired). This made TVEs both more productive and more market oriented than SOEs. Since villagers and township people were shareholders, they reaped part of the profits and the taxes generated by TVEs were invested locally. Although TVEs benefited from political connections and faced softer budget constraints than private firms, they had less access to bank finance than SOEs (Jin and Qian 1998). Until the mid-1990s TVEs played a more important role than private enterprises in rural industrialization.
3. Examples include Huawei (IT and communications hardware), Haier (consumer electronics), and Lenovo (formerly Legend, producing personal computers).
4. Over the 5 years, 1998–2003, the number of state-controlled industrial firms fell by 57% and 22 million employees in the state-controlled business sector lost their jobs (OECD 2005). In contrast private sector employment soared by 18 million over the same period, yet one survey suggests that only 7% of privately registered companies are the direct result of state-owned enterprise restructuring. Despite years of preferential access to financing, 35% of remaining SOEs are still loss-making and very few achieve healthy profit margins—the median rate of return on capital is just 1.5% (ibid).
5. According to the US's NCTO, the Chinese government makes at least 63 subsidies available to the textile industry. These may be subject to attack by US firms filing subsidy cases against China (*Just-Style* 2008).
6. See http://www.ctei.gov.cn/cntac/e_xhjj.asp for details.
7. See http://www.cnga,org.cn for details.
8. Substantial 'round-tripping' of investments by Chinese firms via Hong Kong in order to qualify for foreign investor tax privileges is hard to quantify but does distort overall FDI data.
9. Japanese clothing firms also engage in OPA, but primarily to serve their own domestic market.
10. Cited by Dussel Peters (2005).

11. In comparison exports from India—another expected beneficiary of the ending of the quota regime—grew by a faster 25% in 2005, but it was still the origin of only 3% of internationally traded garments.

12. Originally administered solely by the Ministry of Foreign Trade and Economic Cooperation (MOFTEC), Chinese quota allocation was given only to firms who had permission to export; in later years administration was shared with the Chinese Chamber of Commerce for the Import and Export of Textiles (USITC 2004). Quota assignment took place through a mixture of auctions (for 'high fill' quota categories), 'first come, first served' allocation (for categories with lower fill rates the year before) and MOFTEC assignment (whereby for some categories free quota was given to a select list of firms). The secondary market in quotas was illegal but apparently widely used, with prices—sometimes considerably higher than those on the official market—available on the Internet (USITC 2004).

13. Data from Werner International Management Consultants, cited in USITC (2004).

14. We do not refer in this section to the interviews with the Japanese-owned manufacturers, which were producing mainly for the Japanese market.

15. Macau, which is also just a one-hour journey from Hong Kong and Guangdong, is also used for OPA production since Hong Kong firms opened factories there to avoid safeguard quotas on China-made goods. CH-2, for example, established a Macau production facility in 2004 to assemble the garment panels made in the Guangdong factory so that they qualified as 'Made in Macau'.

16. Every factory required its workers to live in company dormitories which had kitchens and/or canteens attached. Some also provided recreational facilities.

17. One interviewee (CH-7) noted that, although Chinese-owned factories could increasingly afford to import the same sophisticated production machinery used in foreign-invested factories, they still lacked the soft technology skills and experience to make the best use of it.

18. See also http://www2.luenthai.com

19. Hypermarkets such as Carrefour have a well-established presence in China, and fashion retailers have followed more recently. Uniqlo (Japan), Esprit (Hong Kong), Zara, and H&M all have retail networks under development, C&A opened its first outlet in Shanghai in April 2007, and both Topshop and Marks & Spencer announced plans to open branches during 2008.

20. All data from the International Textile and Clothing Bureau, Geneva (http://www.itcb.org).

10

The Regulation of Labour Standards/Rights in Supplier Countries: The Role of Firms, Nation States, and International Organizations

10.1. INTRODUCTION

A central consequence of globalization, in the terms established by Polanyi, has been 'to disembed the economy from society', that is, to relieve lead firms in GPNs of the responsibility for the workers who vitally contribute towards final profits. In the globalized clothing industry price competition constitutes the central dynamic and hence shapes the way western lead firms utilize third-party contractors and their employees in low-wage countries. Firms outsource the manufacturing process to remain competitive, thereby shedding the responsibility and cost of maintaining regular employment and the accompanying wage and social costs. This problem has become more acute after the abolition by the WTO in 2005 of restrictive quotas on exports. Ensuing greater ease of corporate movement between countries has led to much intensified global competition and, worse, the abandonment of some less cost-effective countries and their workers. The industry has become emblematic of the excesses of the new global system.

Escaping national institutional constraint in particular functional areas is an inherent feature of globally networked firms. Market-shaping institutions and regulatory systems in newly industrialized supplier countries, particularly those pertaining to the utilization of labour, are often still underdeveloped (Chan and Ross 2003; Czaban et al. 2003: 18; Faust et al. 2004: 72; Sum and Ngai 2005). Where such institutions have emerged governments do not necessarily enforce their regulations, for fear of deterring western firms that seek local contractors.

Drawing on the discussion of the concept of the competition state introduced in Chapter 2, the governments of many developing countries have been constrained to adopt a competitive strategy of 'downward mobility' (Gritsch 2005). Palan and Abbott (1996: 141) further concretize this state position by pointing to two strategies employed either separately or in combination: (1) to exploit the

country's abundant labour to attract foreign capital and (2) to develop special economic zones. In the words of Evans (1985), 'both state officials and transnational
managers know that their survival depends on their ability to achieve mutually
acceptable accommodations'. In other words, states are complicit in the oppressive
labour regime of MNCs' local contractors. Palan and Abbott (1996) recognize that
the trade policy of western hegemonic states, in attempting to protect its own
firms, is equally complicit in this disregard of labour standards and rights.

Hence the management of global production networks has raised dilemmas of
governance. National governments are unwilling and unions powerless to solve
them, and international institutions have not yet acquired the legitimacy and
power to take up the slack. Companies therefore are able to operate in global
spaces whose non-existent web of regulation constitutes one of the incentives for
building such networks. The regulatory gap permits them to engage in 'regime
shopping'. Additionally, emphasis is put on the 'gender' aspect of labour regimes,
that is, on the fact that 'competition states' facilitate and condone the practice of
firms to seek out the cheapest and most pliable elements of labour—young, poorly
educated women.

This situation has given rise to a globalization backlash, creating social movements whose members contest the current forms of economic globalization and
their social consequences in developing countries. This protest has been articulated and converted into active intervention by so-called transnational advocacy
networks (Keck and Sikkink 1998), that is, networks which plead the cause of others [ibid: 8–9]. They are usually organized and dominated by non-governmental
organizations (NGOs) which initiate action and put pressure on more powerful
actors to take positions (ibid). By mobilizing domestic consumers in developed
countries, NGOs have been able first to form national anti-sweatshop movements
and, more recently, to build coalitions at both regional and global levels with other
actors, both in the public and in the private sphere. The global regulatory vacuum
has encouraged transnational advocacy networks (TANs) to take up the mandate
of regulators, that is, to assume the role of devising and monitoring the implementation of labour standards and rights. Keck and Sikkink's model of intervention
by TANs—described as initiating the boomerang pattern (12f)—envisages that
NGOs stir up protest and intervention by intergovernmental organizations and
western states, which, in turn, put pressure on competition states in developing
countries. Our account, in contrast, will show that such political intervention has
been rare in the economic sphere. Western states are competition states themselves
and do not call buyer firms in GPNs to account. Inter-governmental organizations
consequently lack the requisite power to intervene. For TANs, trying to abolish
sweatshops in developing countries, the main addressees are western lead firms in
GPNs. But the involvement of the latter in TANs put them in a very ambiguous
position—they may be both members of the TAN and a target of NGO action.
Consequently, the intervention by TANs (and their member firms) has been
viewed by many as problematic, and, we will show, has enjoyed only limited
success. Although TANs have attempted to call trans-national capital to account,

the disruption of the 'race to the bottom' in the field of employment conditions has been only very partial.

Following Sum and Ngai (2005), we uncover the paradoxes entailed in establishing such a bottom-up private regulatory regime, in the face of continuing intense price- and time-based competition. We take into account the continuous struggle over the extraction of value by various participants in the GVC, forcing TANs to confront and balance the conflicting interests and incentives of the many actors engaged in establishing a regulatory regime. This chapter tries to maintain a balance between, on the one hand, voicing profound scepticism about the possibility of ethical sourcing and socially responsible firms and, on the other, recognizing the partial progress some TANs and firms have nevertheless achieved in this area.

We start by examining the labour standards and rights which exist in low-wage supplier countries and the role played by national institutions—particularly the state and unions, but also firms—in either strengthening or, more often, undermining them. Our analysis focuses on the shortcomings of existing regulatory regimes in three of the four sourcing countries, examined in Chapters 8 and 9. The three cases we survey—China, Mexico, and Turkey—are not representative of low-wage countries with a strong concentration on the clothing industry, but neither are they 'worst scenario' countries. They were chosen because they are very large (in terms of export volume) supplier countries which are of great importance to either European (the case of Turkey) or US buyers (the case of Mexico) or are the largest suppliers to both regions (China). We additionally review the regulatory regimes adopted under initiatives by inter-governmental organizations, firms, industry associations, unions, and NGOs, singly or in TANs, to improve labour rights and standards in supplier countries and firms. Implementing and monitoring the observance of labour standards and rights are shown to be problematic. Ethical sourcing in a globalized capitalist economy raises a number of paradoxes when we consider the impact of privatized regulation on both firms and their workers.

Our data come from a wide range of reports by NGOs, unions, governments, and inter-governmental organizations, ensuring a balanced coverage of the topics.[1]

10.2. LABOUR RIGHTS AND STANDARDS IN SUPPLIER COUNTRIES

To appreciate the problems of implementing labour codes in newly industrializing countries, one must take into account the economic, political, and social contexts in which firms are situated and which affect labour relations. Taking such differences into consideration helps to define the scale of the problem faced by reformers, as well as providing an idea of how far supplier firms can realistically be pushed to improve.

10.2.1. The Situation in China

China is the world's largest producer and exporter of textiles and clothing, accounting for one-fifth of the world's total production. Exports in 2004 amounted to US$35.8 billion (Li & Fung Research Centre 2006: 1, 2), of which clothing constituted 60 per cent. As indicated in Table 8.1, the USA and the EU are the biggest importers of China's textiles and clothing, which is mainly oriented towards low- to middle-end products at prices well below the world average (Li & Fung Research Centre 2006: 4). (For greater detail on the Chinese clothing industry, see Chapter 9.)

China began to open itself to foreign investment during the late 1970s and initiated more systematic re-structuring towards a market economy from the mid-1980s onwards. This effort greatly accelerated during the 1990s and early 2000s, following Deng Xiao Ping's visit to South China in 1992 (Gallagher 2005: 30, 72), the 15th Party Congress in 1997 (Pringle 2002) and China's accession to the WTO in 2001. To cite a Chinese slogan, 'setting China on the track of globalization' (Ngai 2005: 4)—through both FDI and contract manufacturing—brought not only fast economic growth and reduction of poverty but also faced the state with a set of intractable problems, mostly around labour utilization and employment. To generate taxes and create employment for both the surplus rural population and the large number of urban unemployed, the state decided to adopt the competitive strategy of 'downward mobility' in designating special economic zones and lowering labour standards (Palan and Abbott 1996; Gritsch 2005), in order to attract and retain foreign capital. It had to guarantee labour standards and levels of pay which render China competitive with the many other low-wage countries in this industry, particularly in Asia. Moreover, following economic de-centralization of the Chinese economy to municipal level, competition to attract a high volume of foreign business had the effect of pitting one municipality against another. Not only is performance of local government officials assessed on their ability to attract and retain FDI (Gallagher 2005: 2) but, in the face of the reduction of central subventions (O'Rourke and Brown 2003: 379), they also depend on the tax income and the employment that foreign-invested enterprises generate. Whereas in the past workers enjoyed guaranteed employment even during periods of slack demand—the so-called iron rice bowl—such protection no longer exists in private enterprises.

The central state has made efforts to protect labour through new legislation, setting comparatively high minimum labour and safety standards. But the incentive structures set for both local politicians and firms force them to ignore legal regulation. The lack of resources invested to secure implementation of laws and the locally engendered free-market mentalities have induced widespread and consistent violation of labour law and of guidelines for setting minimum wages. The accommodation of foreign capital has invested management with overwhelming power to determine labour practices and standards. Together, these circumstances have turned China into a neo-liberal haven for western companies.

10.2.1.1. *Chinese Labour Standards and Rights: The Legal Situation*

In the face of the increasingly one-sided exercise of management power, the Chinese government sought to stem the tide of labour market liberalization by legal means. It introduced a series of labour and trade union laws, resulting in the national Labour Law of 1994 (Guthrie 1999: 58f; Gallagher 2005: 110f.; Chan 2006), as well as the more recent law of 2008. The 1994 laws enshrined the basic rights of all Chinese workers, regardless of enterprise type, as well as setting minimum standards for them. These laws stipulate the maximum working hours, vacation time, mandatory provision of social insurance, and health and safety standards (O'Rourke and Brown 2003; Lee 2007).

Individual labour contracts, introduced gradually from the 1980s onward and made mandatory in 1995 (Lee 2007), detail the length of employment, of the work day and vacation, wages, and welfare benefits, insurance and disciplinary procedures, as well as renewal and cancellation of contracts. But adoption of such contracts has been only very partial, with 40 per cent of employees having no contract. Even when they are adopted, contracts have been widely ignored (Divjak 2008: 1; Morris 2008: 2).

The Labour law of 1994 also created local labour arbitration committees (LAC), made up of representatives from the local organizations of labour (labour and trade union bureaus) and of enterprise managers, as well as so-called Letters and Visits Offices (Thireau and Linshan 2003). Workers can appeal to these committees if they feel their legally guaranteed rights have been violated. Judgments by the LAC can be contested by workers in the civil courts (Gallagher 2005: 115f). Additionally, the government has provided a framework for the determination of minimum wages, decreeing that they should be pegged at between 40 and 60 per cent of the average wage in the region, as well as being linked to levels of inflation and the local cost of living (Chan 2003: 42, 43; Chan and Ross 2003: 1017).

The new Labour Contract Law of January 2008, introduced in the face of growing labour unrest (Divjak 2008: 2), has received a huge amount of publicity. It is trying to increase the employment security of workers, as well as regularizing their pay. The key provision is that all workers must have a labour contract that stipulates their wage rates and under what conditions they can be fired. Employers must contribute to funds for both social insurance and unemployment pay (Divjak 2008; Morris 2008). Furthermore, employers are bound to seek the guidance of the AFCTU (official state union) on the formulation of contracts (ibid). But independent unions remain illegal. Also penalties for offenders against the Law have been significantly increased (Harris & Moure 2007). It is still unclear whether the new Law will be as widely flouted as the 1994 Law, or whether it will be observed more strictly. Commentators within China think it the most significant Law since the 1980s (Morris 2008) which will be more strictly enforced (Harris & Moure 2007). Some employers, who expect it to reduce employment flexibility and raise wage costs, have been very worried by it. Others remain more sceptical. They expect the Law to benefit only parts of the labour force, particularly those at middle and upper levels on longer-term employment contracts (Divjak 2008; Morris 2008), or are sceptical that the new Law will be better enforced than the 1994 Law.

This relatively high level of legal regulation of the labour market (Asian Focus Group 2005: 2), however, has been completely undermined by three sets of circumstances characterizing the clothing industry: the absence of enforcement of legal standards at local level; the non-existence of free collective organization of labour; and the *hukou* system of population control which turns migrant labour into a reserve army of labour. Although the 2008 Law is likely to be more influential, it is doubtful, because of these three sets of circumstances, whether it will benefit workers in this industry to a significant degree (Morris 2008: 3).

Due to strong countervailing pressures exerted by competition for contracts from western lead firms with other Asian countries, between Chinese municipalities and between individual firms, together with the absence of independent unions, it remains to be seen whether this new law can be implemented more effectively than its precursor in 1994.

Given the incentives for municipal functionaries to preserve a flexible local labour market to attract investors and buyers, implementation of legally existing labour standards and wage regulation depends on strong enforcement capacity. But the completely inadequate level of factory inspection—there roughly is only one government inspector per 35,000 workers (O'Rourke and Brown 2003: 380; see also Gallagher 2005: 77)—and the absence until very recently of political sanctions by higher-level state organs for gross and constant violation of standards have left the latter mostly unchecked from above. However, in June 2007 the Chinese legislature mandated strict punishment for public officials who are proven to be negligent or corrupt in tolerating abusive labour practices (Applebaum 2008). But it remains to be seen whether the Chinese state is able to re-impose control over the labour market.

10.2.1.2. The Role of Labour Unions and Other Channels of Representation

Chinese workers do not enjoy the basic labour rights of free association, collective bargaining, and the right to strike. Efforts to found independent unions have been blocked by the government, meeting with severe sanctions (Pringle 2002; Gallagher 2005: 82). Instead, all employed come under the All China Federation of Trade Unions (ACFTU), a branch of the state, which constantly faces a conflict of interests. According to law, all enterprises with more than 25 employees must establish a labour union under the auspices of the ACFTU (Gallagher 2005: 44). But the ACFTU now is unevenly represented in different types of enterprise and localities, having a particularly low presence in foreign-invested enterprises (particularly those owned by entrepreneurs from Hong Kong, Macao, Taiwan, and Korea) (Chen and Chan 2004: 1233; Gallagher 2005: 84f). Its effectiveness in protecting workers from excessive demands and bad conditions, despite some modest successes, is generally considered very low (O'Rourke and Brown 2003;

Gallagher 2005: 90f). Union representatives have effectively become a branch of management, akin to western HR managers (Chen and Chan 2004: 1233). Party cadres within enterprises also have been emasculated. The position of Party Secretary has now mostly merged either with that of trade union secretary or, worse, with that of general manager, and the position has become clearly subordinate to that of the top manager (Gallagher 2005: 70f). Additionally, there exist Workers' Representative Councils (WRC) at factory level which, although mandatory, are unevenly adopted, only meet sporadically and hence remain largely ineffective (Chan 2002; Guthrie 1999: 49–50). Consequently industrial workers, who are hired on individual labour contracts, are left atomized and poorly protected.

10.2.1.3. *Migrant Workers*

The level of defencelessness is particularly high among the large, mainly female labour force that has migrated from the inner rural provinces to special economic zones in the southern coastal areas (Chan 2003: 44; Ngai 2005: 5). China's rural population fell from four-fifths of the total population to 62 per cent between 1980 and 2003, implying a shift to the towns of around 290 million people. Guangdong province alone is reported to have attracted over 5 million workers from other provinces in 2002 (Dussel Peters 2005). The geographical movement of these rural workers is regulated by annual passes for residence outside their home area, administered by the *hukou* system of population control. Migrant workers are employed only as long as their employers' demand warrants it (Chan and Ross 2003: 1022). Although not introduced for the purpose of labour control, this system prevents the development of a free market in labour and serves to keep down wages (Chan 2003: 44). Workers live in dormitories in the factory grounds, and their coming and going is easily controlled by management. They have no employment security and are easily subjected to periodic demands for high and prolonged overtime. Managements and local functionaries are united in benefiting from exploiting this source of cheap and pliable labour—the local authority has no responsibility for them (Chan 2003: 44). In Ngai's words (2005: 48), the availability of 'this massive cheap and flexible labour force' has secured China's incorporation into the global economy.

10.2.1.4. *Labour Standards/Rights and Wage Levels in the Chinese Clothing Industry*

Uneven enforcement of labour standards and wage levels across types of enterprises and localities, it has already been pointed out, has been one mechanism which makes it possible to violate standards and rules. An analysis of conditions specific to the clothing industry will further amplify this point. Contract manufacturing for the western clothing industry is highly concentrated in the coastal provinces, notably in Guangdong, Zhejiang, Jiangsu, Fujian, and Shandong (Li & Fung Research Centre 2006: 4; see also Chapter 9, Table 9.1), which are designated as Special Economic Zones (SEZs). In Guangdong province alone, which has the most clothing clusters, there are around 30,000 clothing firms, employing around 5 million mainly migrant workers (Ferenschild and Wick 2004: 23; Dussel Peters 2005). In 2004, 95 per cent of the industry's exports came from privately owned enterprises, and just under half of the value of exports came from foreign-owned firms (Li & Fung Research Centre 2006: 3). A high proportion of these mainly small firms are under Asian (particularly expatriate Chinese, but also Korean) ownership (Chan 2006: 283). The latter is significant in that these multinational firms have escaped the pressures of rising wages and more democratized labour in their home countries and have not made concessions to labour in their new location (Gallagher 2005: 65). The Chinese press regards the managements of these enterprises as particularly exploitative and despotic, with coercive and even physically violent behaviour prevalent towards the mainly female workers (Ferenschild and Wick 2004; Ngai 2005; Chan 2006: 283f).

Such contract manufacturing started before the economic reforms, in the late 1970s, expanded after the creation in the coastal areas of SEZs in 1980 (Gallagher 2005: 38) and further accelerated its growth during the 1990s and in the 2000s (Ross and Chan 2002). From the beginning local authorities, concerned to attract and retain foreign investment and the ensuing tax benefits and employment creation, kept wages and conditions at low levels, and blatant violation of legal standards has been largely ignored (Ngai 2005: 94). The virtual absence of even the state-sponsored union in these foreign firms and the large, female migrant labour force—migrants constitute up to 80 per cent of shop floor labour in the Shenzhen SEZ (Ngai 2005: 36)—make it relatively easy to maintain labour market flexibility. Migrants have to be registered to receive temporary residence and work permits. Factories pay a fee for the registration certificates of each migrant worker (Ngai 2005: 43f) which, in turn, is deducted from workers' wages. Registration has to be renewed every year. If there is insufficient work, managers can refuse re-registration (ibid: 46). Over time, labour contracts have become increasingly informal, and one-sided violation of a contract by management is widespread (Gallagher 2005: 78f).

Consequently, labour standards and wages in this industry are exceedingly low, and the level of harassment and even violence is comparatively high (Ferenschild and Wick 2004: 24) in Chinese-owned as well as foreign-owned factories. A survey reported by Oxfam International (2004: 58) found that 60 per cent of women interviewed had no written contract and 90 per cent had no insurance. Gallagher (2005: 79, 109) reports hargh labour regimes in many of these factories, with 'horrific labour conditions, including lack of benefits and insurance, no job security, dangerous working conditions and non-payment of wages'. Non-payment of wages and long wage arrears are very common (Lee 2007: 4). Low wages and the *de facto* almost indentured status of migrant workers make it easy for employers to extract high levels of overtime in order to satisfy buyers' highly variable demand and frequent short-notice orders. Overtime is compulsory (Pringle 2002), and 12-hour days seem to be very common (Ngai 2005: 4), as is working on Saturdays and night-time work (Ferenschild and Wick 2004: 26). Long working hours, old machines, and generally low safety precautions have led to sharp increases in levels of industrial fatality and injury (Chen and Chan 2004: 1243). Given the predominantly female composition of the workforce, gender discrimination is not systematically reported, beyond references to abusive and invasive treatment of pregnant women. Forced labour and child labour receive no mention at all in the relevant literature.

Minimum wages, although high in comparative regional terms, have been kept well below the level stipulated by the centrally issued general guidelines, and wages now effectively are determined at enterprise level (Chan 2006: 278f.). The notion of a 'living wage' is not known in China. Although economic growth has far exceeded that of neighbouring late industrializing countries, like Vietnam and Cambodia, wages in the Chinese clothing industry have not kept pace with growth, for fear of their immediate Asian competitors (Chan 2003: 41–2). Wages for migrant workers in particular barely increased between the 1980s and 2004, even in economically developed Guangdong province. More recently, however, wage levels in the coastal areas have kept rising (China Textile and Clothing Trade 2003–04: 5; Applebaum 2008: 82; Quan 2008: 100). According to the National Bureau of Statistics, during the first 9 months of 2007, Chinese wages increased by 18.8 per cent (Divjak 2008: 4). In Guangdong province—where clothing firms are highly concentrated—minimum wages are set to rise between 17.6 and 20 per cent in 2008 (*China Daily* 2008).

10.2.1.5. *Workers' Responses to Poor Standards and Low Rights*

For a long time it has seemed as if this draconian factory regime could be imposed with impunity. In recent years, however, persistent and serious violation of laws has begun to be challenged. Labour protests at the enterprise level appear to be relatively uncommon, but attempts to obtain legal redress through formal complaints to the local labour arbitration committees have been growing steeply in number since the middle of the 1990s. (For details, see Chan 2003; and Gallagher 2005: 98f.) Complaints are directed mainly at the very worst practices, such as non-payment of wages and overtime and non-compensation for serious injury (ibid; Thireau and Linshan 2003). This development, initiated by the state, draws protest out of the enterprise and circumvents direct challenges to management power. Moreover, it also presents the state as the prime dispenser of justice to workers (Thireau and Linshan 2003). However, the fledgling legal system has proven only very partially effective in defending workers' rights (Lee 2007). Nevertheless, it has provided workers with a standard against which they can assess their actual situation and has encouraged them to protest if the gap becomes too wide.

In addition to seeking legal redress, workers are increasingly protesting against their conditions by voting with their feet. During the 2000s, growing numbers of migrant workers have not returned to work after their annual home leave. Chan (2006) speculates that both slight improvements in living standards in the countryside and migrant workers' disillusionment with their low rewards and harsh conditions explain the drying-up of this source of cheap labour. The resulting labour shortages, in turn, have encouraged remaining workers to demand better wages, frequently with success (Roberts and Engardio 2006: 53) or to change their place of employment in search of better conditions. During our interviews in Guangdong clothing factories in 2004, high labour turnover was judged one of the biggest problems by several of our managerial interviewees. In Guangdong province, for example, electronics assembly firms paid better wages than clothing firms causing factories to engage in continuous recruitment campaigns (Interview Notes 2004) and prompting some factory owners to invest further inland where competition for labour was less intense. One government survey found that one-third of vacancies (2.5 million jobs) advertised in Guangdong province went unfilled in 2006 (Applebaum 2008). In addition to individualized protest by labour, signs of collective unrest have begun to emerge. Despite the removal in 1982 of the right to strike, waves of protests against exploitative working conditions and demands for higher living standards have occurred across China: Guangzhou City alone reported close to 900 protests involving over 50,000 workers in 2004 (Applebaum 2008).

10.2.1.6. Conclusions

Labour standards and rights in the Chinese supplier firms of the clothing industry have been shaped by an amalgam of practices. Liberalization of markets has provided managements with ample opportunity to achieve labour flexibility, to control workers and to violate basic standards of decency in labour utilization. Political reaction by the central government has mainly taken the form of introducing relatively advanced labour law. But simultaneous pressures on firms for high economic performance and the resulting necessity to appease foreign capital, together with the absence of independent labour organization, have made attempts to curb the power of managements largely ineffective. Consequently, due to a lack of capacity on the part of the official trade union and a lack of will on the part of the local governments, firm managers, or owners overwhelmingly determine labour practices in a highly autonomous manner (Gallagher 2005: 64). Whereas under communism enterprises could win an award for being a 'civilised work unit' (Guthrie 1999: 200), under market liberalism factory despotism can freely rule.

The Chinese state, despite its huge resources and great power, has nevertheless been rendered powerless vis-à-vis transnational firms and, in its eagerness to become internationally competitive, has become complicit in the abuse of labour. It remains to be seen whether the new goals of the current 5-year plan (2006–10)—industrial upgrading, common prosperity, and sustainable development, rather than economic growth as the overriding objective—herald the adoption of a new state competitive strategy that will introduce significant improvements for labour under contract to western lead firms. The 2008 legislation is seen by some observers as a turning point but it remains uncertain whether it will be effective in this industry.

10.2.2. The Situation in Turkey

Since the 1980s, clothing has been a leading export sector in Turkey. More and more Turkish domestic firms have become connected to global networks by becoming manufacturers for western lead firms. (For details on the development of the Turkish T/C industry, see Chapter 8.) In 2006, according to the Ministry of Labour and Social Security, the total number of workers employed by the garment and textile sectors amounted to 588,903. However, associations of both employers and employees view this official figure as a gross underestimate of the real level of employment in this industry. Instead they estimate the total number of employed in this sector to be at least 3 million people (CCC 2005; JO-IN 2004). Of the employed, 31 per cent are women (Sugur and Sugur 2005). The proportion of women workers is believed to be much higher in the informal than in the formal sector, including many home workers. (The informal sector is defined as offering employment without secure contracts, worker benefits or social protection.) In sum, a huge informal sector, particularly in clothing, surpasses the formal sector in size. Informality in the clothing industry takes three different forms: (1) unregistered workplaces; (2) unregistered employees in registered workplaces—the most prevalent form; and (3) under-declaration of wages paid to registered workers, to save on social security and tax payments (Kaya 2004). Given the weight in the Turkish clothing industry of the informal sector, we distinguish, in the following account between the formal and informal sectors.

As in China, the Turkish state relies on this industry both for employment of the large, recently urbanized labour force, as well as for export earnings. Like the Chinese state, it has therefore adopted the competitive strategy of selective 'downward mobility' in the utilization of labour (Gritsch 2005). In contrast to China, however, Turkey's labour force commands significantly higher wages and the industry no longer tries to compete in the lowest market segment. Also the Turkish state has not developed special economic zones. The main ways in which the strategy of downward mobility has been pursued have been the toleration of an informal sector not subject to Turkish labour law, and the obstruction of union formation and growth.

The absence of economic decentralization has obviated the intense internal competition between regions and cities experienced in China although external competition, particularly from China, is perceived as a significant threat. The Turkish, unlike the Chinese industry, is largely domestically owned and adverse foreign influence on labour management practices has not been direct. The combined effect of these differences is that, although violation of labour standards is widespread, the same inexorable 'race to the bottom' has not occurred either in wages or in the conditions prevalent in China. At the same time the Turkish state, in order to attract and retain foreign buyers, has not actively intervened to protect labour standards and rights across the *whole* sector.

10.2.2.1. *Turkish Labour Standards and Rights: The Legal Situation*

The provisions of Turkish employment and labour law are relatively advanced. The government has reacted to the changed economic circumstances, and particularly to Turkey's inclusion in the European Customs Area, by passing a new Labour Act which became effective in 2003. Bringing labour legislation into line with the Community *acquis* has been a major and challenging step.

The new law contains clauses limiting discrimination and child labour, as well as regulating working hours/overtime, occupational health and safety, and various aspects relating to employment security. Overtime is regulated relatively tightly, setting a maximum of 45 hours per week and 270 hours per year, but permitting negotiation on the distribution of working hours over time (Sural 2005). Occupational health and safety provisions are comparatively good but apply only to firms with more than 50 employees (JO-IN 2004). Provisions on termination of employment limit employers' degree of discretion through costly compensation measures. Last, being a union activist does not constitute ground for dismissal (Interview Notes 2007).

10.2.2.2. *The Role of Labour Unions*

Unions have been legal since 1947 (Cepni 2003: 27). Although both freedom of association and the right to collective bargaining are guaranteed in the Trade Union Act it includes many restrictive and anti-democratic provisions which effectively prevent workers from making use of their rights (JO-IN 2004). Thus, individual registration is made very difficult and several provisions in practice prevent the occurrence of collective bargaining in lowly unionized industries. Turkish legal provisions in this area flout aspects of the ILO conventions (Sural 2005).

Consequently, out of the nine unions representing the textile and clothing industry, only three have the right to bargain collectively for their members, and most of these are in textiles. In the Turkish clothing sector as a whole, only a few workplaces have collective bargaining agreements, covering a mere 1 per cent of employees in the sector (CCC 2005).

Moreover, factory owners/managers are usually hostile towards trade unions and frequently act aggressively towards unionized workers. Despite a legal clause meant to protect union activists, they are often fired. A highly patriarchal attitude to workers in the many small owner-managed firms plays a part in this negative stance towards industrial organization. Workers themselves, valuing their comparatively good jobs in the registered sector, are not inclined to risk losing them because of unionization (JO-IN 2004).

Unregistered workers are not able to join existing trade unions or establish their own, leaving them entirely defenceless. Additionally, employees in small firms are protected to a lower degree, particularly in the area of health and safety. The majority of employers in the clothing sector consider labour legislation to be an obstacle in their way and prefer to conduct unregistered operations or to employ unregistered workers (JO-IN 2004).

Despite the fact that there are some restrictive and anti-democratic clauses, particularly in the Trade Union Act, the main cause of low labour standards in Turkey lies not in the laws, but in their non-implementation. Anxious about the international competitiveness of the Turkish clothing industry, public officials tolerate firms' practices of pushing down production costs and even encourage them to do so (Kamrava 2004). Such an un-inspected or uncontrolled environment, showing parallels with China's use of migrant labour in the SEZs, constitutes a perfect setting for employers to resort to all sorts of methods to lower labour costs.

10.2.2.3. *Labour Standards/Rights and Wages*

Making a distinction between the formal and the informal sector is difficult as it is common for the first tier of suppliers to make use of lower-tier sub-contractors. Hence the informal sector sustains the formal to a significant degree. Although against the rules of western lead firms, in practice such subcontracting is hard to police.

Gender discrimination is reported in both the formal and the informal sector. In the former it mainly takes the form of discrimination against women on pay, whereas in the latter it additionally entails sexual harassment and violence (SOMO 2003; CCC 2005). While there is no problem of child labour in the formal sector, in the informal sector a significant number of children under the age of 15 (180,000–200,000) are reported to work (JO-IN 2004). Practices such as forced labour, that is, use of bonded or prison labour are not observed in the Turkish garment industry.

In the area of occupational health and safety (OHS) the main problems are excessive dust and noise, as well as humidity in the ironing department. OHS committees tend not to exist, and medical attention is available only for those registered under the social security scheme (JO-IN 2004). Hence the working environment in this industry does not meet Turkey's health and safety regulations, but there are no reports of the high accident rates found in China.

Overtime working above the legal norm in the formal sector occurs at certain busy times of the year. However, in unregistered factories working days can be of 12–14 hours' duration. Illegal working on rest days and, for women and children, during the night is said to be common if order deadlines are pressing. It is, however, also the case that, due to low wages, workers actually value overtime.

Double bookkeeping is a standard practice in the sector. Even the registered companies frequently do not pay the statutory social security contributions on behalf of their employees or falsify records to pay less. At the end of each year, most production facilities fire all of their workers and rehire them again in the new year. Workers are commonly offered severance pay as well as a 'bonus' to discourage them from reporting this practice to the government. The savings come from avoiding higher severance payments later, as the amount owed increases exponentially with seniority (Interview Notes 2007).

While employment security is reasonably assured in registered workplaces where statutory severance pay exists, unregistered employees are considered a reservoir of flexible labour, hired and fired without penalty as the order book demands. Home-based workers—mainly women—are an integral part of the network of sub-contractors that produce for Turkey's clothing export sector.

Wages in the formal and particularly the unionized sector are said to be above the level of the minimum wage (since January 2007) of 562 YTL or £207 per month (before tax), and come to 403 YTL or £149 (after tax) per month for those over the age of 16. Workers are paid regularly and usually punctually (JO-IN 2004: 44). Overtime is paid according to the law. However, in many cases, real wages are not declared to the Social Security Department but are paid as cash-in-hand. Such wage levels, although high in comparison with other developing countries, cannot be considered 'living wages' as they are not sufficient to cover the minimum living expenses of a four-member family at a level considered adequate by Turkish standards. Such wage rates, however, are 7 to 8 times higher than those paid in the worst unregistered workplaces. Home workers are the ultimate reservoir of a flexible and cheap labour supply.

10.2.2.4. Conclusions

Conditions for labour in the Turkish clothing industry are due to historical legacies and to current pressures, similar to those faced by their Chinese counterparts. As in China, violations of legal stipulations and a lack of state sanctions for infringement are responses to intense global competition and to the particular demands of western lead firms for low prices and a 'quick response' turnaround of orders. In both countries labour is relatively defenceless against employers' demands. But, in contrast to the situation in China, in Turkey low labour standards do not characterize the whole industry but only the informal sector. Furthermore, independent unions in Turkey are legal, even if limited scope exists for representation of workers' interests. Whereas in China the large migrant labour force provides a reservoir of cheap and flexible labour, in Turkey it is the large informal sector, including home workers. Additional important differences exist between conditions in the two national industries. Turkey has a more mature industry, and its large enterprises became well established in the decades before liberalization. Also the country's partial integration into the EU market has benefited workers well beyond what Chinese workers can command. Hence, in contrast to the Chinese industry, there are few reports of labour unrest.

10.2.3. The Situation in Mexico

The situation of Mexican labour has been fundamentally shaped by the political and economic legacy of the corporatist post-revolutionary period from the

1920s to the late1980s. The post-revolutionary political regime, defined by its relationship to labour and the unions (see Chapter 9.2), had a mixed effect on labour rights and standards. One the one hand labour, represented by the 'official' unions, was always the subordinate partner in the corporatist state, with little autonomy to exercise labour rights independently and frequent violent suppression of labour protest. On the other hand the corporatist ideology obliged the state to symbolically reaffirm the national importance of the labour movement (Middlebrook 1995: 291). Hence the state acknowledged labour's special status in both constitutional and legal terms. It thereby created a system of labour standards which went far beyond that of most developing countries. Economically, the four decades (1940s to early1980s) of industrialization in the shelter of a policy of import substitution and extensive public ownership provided labour with security, albeit at a relatively low level of economic prosperity. The gradual opening of the economy during the 1980s and particularly the joining of NAFTA in 1994, followed by the drastic peso devaluation in 1995, fundamentally changed the economic and, eventually, also the political situation. The corporatist state, which had pursued a competitive strategy with at least elements of the social-democratic competition strategy, has turned into a competition state with a strategy of 'downward mobility' vis-à-vis labour facilitated by a suppression of unions (Palan and Abbott 1996; Gritsch 2005).

The *maquiladora* (assembly for export) sector had grown in tandem with Item 807 of the US Tariff Code, first established in 1963 and gradually expanded through the 1970s and 1980s (Collins 2003: 131–3). The implementation of NAFTA in 1994 and the devaluation of the peso in 1995 gave a tremendous boost to the expansion of the *maquiladora* sector. Employment in the sector rose from 64,000 in 1993 to 285,600 in 2001 (Carillo et al. 2002: 182). It assisted Mexico to become the largest foreign supplier of textiles and clothing to the USA during the 1990s (US ITC 2004: H3). But it also tied the Mexican industry to the US market, creating a dangerously high level of dependence. In 2002 around 93 per cent of Mexican T/C exports went to the USA (Dussel Peters 2005: 78).

Mexican apparel exports to the USA peaked in 2000. By 2001, Mexico had been overtaken by China as the largest supplier of apparel. Shipments of garments to the USA declined by 20 per cent between 2000 and 2004 (Dussel Peters 2005), and employment between 2001 and 2005 fell by 41 per cent to 174,000 (Gruben 2006: 1). This desertion of their Mexican suppliers by US clothing firms had a number of reasons already explained in Chapter 9.2.

Although NAFTA brought rapid economic development and a big expansion in industrial employment the economic benefits were not evenly distributed. In the new liberalized market environment, labour largely lost out. NAFTA brought both large amounts of American investment and extensive sourcing of manufactured components and products, but its success and that of Mexico depended on keeping Mexican labour pliant, flexible, and cheap. The understanding of this condition by both the Mexican state and by employers, as in China, created a competitive downward spiral among regions and firms. This has caused a deterioration in labour standards and little improvement in levels of reward

(Bair and Dussel Peters 2006). The withdrawal of the state from corporatist policy, the ensuing inability, and/or unwillingness of the old incorporated unions—CTM and CROC—to fight this development, together with only hesitant emergence of independent unions, particularly in the clothing industry (Collins 2003: 147), meant that Mexican labour was unable to oppose the pernicious consequences of NAFTA and the neo-liberalism it entailed.

In contrast to China, however, the legacy of the corporatist period was the existence of a culture which had nurtured expectations of levels of decency in conditions for labour below which employers could go only with difficulty. In Mexico, there is a culturally approved notion of a living wage (even if it is difficult to enforce), and this concept is used as justification for union bargaining (Chan and Ross 2003: 1021). Also, firms in the clothing industry are mainly Mexican-owned, although there exists some American and Korean ownership. Labour thus has not been exposed to the often despotic labour regimes of some of the Asian owners who are prominent in China's economy. Finally, the proximity of the USA and the out-migration of a significant proportion of workers able to earn wages several times as high as at home has put upward pressure on wages in the domestic economy (Hanson 2005). Consequently, for all the above reasons, the level of exploitation and abuse, though by no means negligible, has not reached nearly the same high levels as in China. The situation has been more akin to that in Turkey, including the recognition of unions and the existence of a significant informal sector.

10.2.3.1. Mexican Labour Standards and Rights: The Legal Situation

Until the 1990s, the quasi-corporatist incorporation of labour by the Mexican state protected labour, albeit at the price of strong manipulation of the 'official unions'. The state acted as an arbiter between employers and labour, exerting the power derived from Mexico's strongly presidentialist system (Middlebrook 1995). Hence, core labour standards and labour rights were incorporated relatively early—in the 1950s—into the Mexican Constitution and into a comparatively strong labour law (ICFTU 1996). Mexican labour laws require a universal insurance scheme (Rosenberg 2005), generous severance payments and holiday bonuses, and contain other regulations that restrict labour flexibility (US ITC 2004: H8). Levels of pay, although kept low by national corporatist pacts on wage restraint, nevertheless benefited from a legally mandated share of enterprise profits for labour (Middlebrook 1995: 289). Additionally, the Constitution affirms the freedom of association and trade unions' rights to bargain and strike. Moreover, the legal situation in the *maquiladora* industries does not differ from that in the rest of the economy, as the policy of Special Economic Zones has been eschewed by the government (ICFTU 1996: 3). A 'minimum wage' commission exists which should determine wage levels according to cost of living in a given region, but in reality levels established were the outcome of a political game (ICFTU 1996: 5–6). Any improvements gained by labour were largely the result of state intervention, rather than of collective bargaining (Middlebrook 1995: 288).

To understand the increased vulnerability of labour to violation of standards and rights since the late 1980s/early 1990s, it is necessary to consider the changed institutional and economic environment in which labour finds itself. Although there still exist a number of 'official' as well as independent unions, and collective bargaining is wide-spread, the influence of the unions now is low. Successful contestation of either the state or employers is relatively rare. Few strikes have been attempted. Any show of independence and militancy still meets with suppression, both from the official unions and from employers (ICFTU 1996: 2–3; Williams 1999: 140; Esbenshade 2004: 204). Hence unions have been powerless to stem the decline in labour's share of value (see figures below) and the deviation from core labour standards, as enshrined in the Constitution. However, in recent years independent unions are said to have gained a greater influence over public opinion and some isolated, high-profile successes (Collins 2003; Bensusan 2004).

Labour representation is particularly low in the *maquiladoras* (ICFTU 1996: 3) and is non-existent among the mainly female labour force of the clothing industry (Collins 2003). Obstructive restrictions of labour organization in the *maquiladoras* by state-instituted Conciliation and Arbitration Boards 'appears to be a deliberate strategy to prevent workers from bargaining for a reasonable share in the benefits of Mexico's rapid growth in manufacturing exports' (ICFTU 1996: 4). Employers have been particularly keen to keep out independent unions, such as the FAT (Bensusan 2004: 251).

Economic circumstances in the industry have further weakened labour's bargaining power. The combination of a large sector of economically weak SMEs and the intensification, following market opening, of internal and external competition made for massive employment cuts in the early 1990s (Middlebrook 1995: 297). Equally large job cuts since 2000–01 have further worsened the situation of labour (US ITC 2004: H7).

In addition to protection by national regulation, labour is supposed to benefit from so-called side agreements under NAFTA, the NAALC, which were introduced on the urgings of North American labour unions. The side agreements are meant to foster a commitment to upholding labour laws and deal with any violations notified to the NAALC but cannot issue sanctions against companies directly (Williams 1999: 150). This committee is widely held to 'have no teeth' (Collins 2003; Fox 2004). This is borne out by the fact that only seven submissions on violations had been reported by 1996 and no penalties had been decided on (ICFTU 1996: 3–4). Williams notes, however, that the Board's substantiation of complaints assures that they receive attention from the media and from the political authorities on both sides of the US/Mexican border (Williams 1999: 150).

10.2.3.2. Labour Standards/Rights and Wages

As in China and in Turkey's informal sector, there exists in Mexico a contrast between a strong commitment to core labour standards in the constitution and basic legislation and their widespread violation in practice. With liberalization of markets, this contrast has become all the more apparent (ICFTU 1996: 1).

An examination of the literature on actual labour standards finds relatively few detailed reports on the incidence and scale of violation, but the phenomenon of stagnant wages under NAFTA has received much wider coverage.

Maquiladora employers seek a special employee profile: women aged between 15 and 24, single, childless, with completed primary education (ICFTU 1996: 4); 53 per cent of workers are said to be female (CFO 2006: 2; Rosenberg 2006: 28, for the Torreon region). Many are also migrant workers. This employee profile indicates low levels of organization and ensures employers both of endurance power and pliancy (Collins 2003). At the same time, however, worker turnover in the industry is extremely high, coming up to 100 per cent per annum.

In contrast to the situation in China, migrant women workers neither have a legal restriction on their movement, nor do they live in factory dormitories. Many are married and/or have children (Collins 2003: 147). These facts prevent employers from exercising the tight control and imposing the super-exploitation (compulsory overtime working of very long hour and inadequate pay) known in China's SEZs (Chan and Ross 2003: 1021). Indeed, many of the women workers with children work only part-time.

At first sight, and particularly in comparative terms, the wage situation of Mexican workers does not appear to be too bad. Official wage rates in Mexico are significantly higher than in most other major supplying countries in Central America and more so in Asia (Birnbaum 2004; US ITC 2004: H7). Mexico's production costs per minute of €0.06–0.08 compare well with China's €0.03 and Bangladesh's €0.025 (WBF/GTZ 2006). Wages in *maquiladoras* appear to be slightly higher than in the rest of the economy, and wages in the clothing industry often follow those of other, higher-wage industries, such as the auto industry (US ITC 2004: H8). Largely based on piece work, remuneration is above the minimum wage. Rising wage costs have been cited as one of the main reasons for shifting production out of Mexico (Birnbaum 2004). Nevertheless, wages in the clothing industry fall well short of the notion of a 'living wage' (Collins 2003: 145).

But a glance at the development of wage levels since NAFTA shows a less positive situation. Wages in 2001 remained well below their 1994 pre-devaluation level (Bair, Spener, and Gereffi 2002: 332). Between 1990 and 2003, real wages in the *maquila* industry rose by barely 10 per cent while productivity increased by more than 115 per cent (Dussel Peters 2004: 4). Moreover, between 1975 and 2001, Mexico's wage gap has increased relative to the developed industrial countries (Dussel Peters 2004: 1–2). Poverty has greatly increased (Bair et al. 2002: 332).

There are several reasons for the stagnation of wage levels. First and foremost is the influence of market liberalization from 1988 onwards. US sourcing firms are constantly seeking to lower costs, and the competition between Mexican cities for American FDI and sourcing, offering cheap and pliant labour, plays into the hands of buyer firms. Second, and related to the first, is the serious decline in union influence (Spener et al. 2002: 11) and its virtual absence in clothing *maquilas*. Third, in more recent years, wage stagnation has been further sustained by drastic employment cuts in the industry, with huge job losses both in 2000 and again after

2005 (CFO 2006: 2). In addition to the downward pressure on wages effected by unemployment, a similar effect is exerted by the large informal sector.

Regarding the major forms of misuse of labour in developing countries—forced and child labour—both have been reported (Esbenshade 2004: 153), but there now is no major incidence of either in Mexico. Although child labour still is significant in the informal sector, it is believed that the state has instituted measures to bring the problem under control. We have not come across any mention of forced labour.

Workers' abuse in *maquiladoras*, claims Rosenberg (2005: 27), has been widely documented although we found it much less well documented than for China. It includes hazardous labour conditions, assault, and illegal dismissal of pregnant women and of labour organizers. CFO (2006: 2), too, speaks of over-exploitation and abuses in *maquilas* but provides no detail. Unpaid and forced overtime, verbal abuse and violations of the minimum wage are reported in Esbenshade (2004: 153). A 1997 survey established that 65 per cent of *maquila* workers received no benefits (ibid). Work organization, premised on piece work and tight specification of time norms for each piece, together with long hours, make for a relentless working pace (Collins 2003: 163).

The Mexican industry still supplies a sizeable proportion of US firms' demand, and its decline in share has only taken it back to its pre-NAFTA level (Gruben 2006). However, the prospects for workers in the Mexican T/C industry are not good. The industry's competitiveness is under pressure from both China and the Caribbean Basin countries. In this situation labour enjoys little leverage to either increase wages or improve conditions. With the state's transformation into a 'competition state', pursuing a strategy of 'downward mobility' (Palan and Abbott 1996; Gritsch 2005), it has withdrawn from the sphere of industrial relations and left the unions greatly weakened. Furthermore, in contrast to China and Turkey, the Mexican state, as a member of NAFTA, is strongly dependent on the USA and has little prospect of moving away from this strategy in times to come. Hence it is difficult to envisage who or what will save the industry and its workers.

10.2.4. Conclusions

As shown by this brief review of labour standards/rights in selected supplier countries, protective legislation alone cannot help improve labour standards. Despite the strong commitment to labour standards in legal documents of these countries, the non-implementation and non-enforcement of the regulations in practice by firms and states render the law irrelevant. Employers use two mechanisms to avoid their social responsibilities. They either conduct their operations in the informal sector or employ a high proportion of migrant workers with weak civil rights and high dependence on their employer. A third strategy used by employers in all three national industries is to exploit gender inequality and extract a particularly high degree of value from the labour of young women who are immobilized by family responsibilities or by residence in patriarchically run factory dormitories.

Employers are able to take the above approaches because states, for their part, do not want to conduct meticulous inspections to guarantee the implementation of labour regulations. They believe that companies' strict compliance with the legislation will decrease their competitive strength in the global market. To succeed with export-oriented growth strategies, it is believed, the developing countries need to attract and retain foreign capital. Low labour costs in this industry thus emerged as the key element for increasing international competitiveness. The much touted 'race to the bottom' in global labour standards unfortunately is no exaggeration in this industry.

10.3. INTERVENTION BY INTERNATIONAL ORGANIZATIONS, FIRMS, AND TANs

Given the entrenchment of the competition state and the resulting regulatory deficit at national level in relation to labour standards and rights in all three countries, it is pertinent to explore whether and to what extent public and private international organizations have taken up the slack. This section therefore distinguishes between four different sets of initiatives undertaken by different types of public and private bodies. After a review of the role of public inter-governmental organizations, we move to an examination of the private initiatives of companies, their industry associations, international unions, and of TANs. Among the last, NGOs have acquired particular prominence as both initiators and monitors of initiatives around labour codes.

10.3.1. International Institutions

At first sight it seems that nearly all significant public international governance organizations actively participate in the regulation of global labour markets. In addition to much increased interest in this field by the World Bank and the EU, the OECD, UN (Global Compact), WTO, and the ILO have been more or less actively involved. At closer inspection, however, it is evident that few have managed to intervene in a remotely effective way. Most have not moved beyond a merely consciousness-raising stage. Not only is it hard to receive a mandate for intervention from nation states, but even when such a mandate has been secured, as in the case of the ILO, commensurate monitoring and enforcement capacities have not been granted.

The ILO, a tri-partite inter-governmental organization established after WWI, functions as a clearing house to provide information on labour issues and as a facilitator to improve labour conditions. For the latter task, it may provide technical and financial assistance (Brown, Deardorff, and Stern 2002: 21). One of its principal functions is setting international labour standards through the adoption of conventions and recommendations on labour-related subjects. The ILO has been the most influential international organization in setting norms for the establishment of labour standards, and, somewhat less successfully, for laying down labour rights. It has gained a fair level of enactment of labour standards, but above all in individual developed countries. Its intervention is based on the realization, enshrined in its founding document, 'that the failure of any nation to adopt humane conditions of labour is an obstacle in the way of other nations which desire to improve conditions in their own country' (Cited by Murray 2002: 33). In other words, the ILO is founded on the realization that the attainment of decent labour standards and rights in the international economy is a 'collective action' problem which should be settled by international intervention.

The ILO has been active in this sphere since 1944. In 1977, a Tri-Partite Declaration of Principles concerning MNEs and Social Policy was negotiated between national governments. In 1998, the ILO issued the Declaration on Fundamental Principles and Rights at Work and obliged all ILO member countries to respect and promote these rights—in the form of five core conventions on labour standards. These are addressed to states, rather than NGOs or individual firms. The core conventions, which have become the model in the field of labour standards, cover the following codes: freedom of association; the right to collective bargaining; no forced labour; no child labour (variously defined); no discrimination; and equal remuneration. Its labour codes are procedural rather than substantive and thus leave uncovered many areas of labour abuse, such as high overtime and wages below a minimum standard. They have been ratified by between 119 (minimum age convention) and 161 countries (elimination of forced labour). The ILO expects all member nations to respect these core conventions, whether they have ratified them or not. But it has a low capacity to supervise and no enforcement capacity and has to rely on states' self-reporting and public shaming.

The ILO also participates in special programs of compliance with core conventions adopted by countries as part of bilateral trade agreements in order to be able to market themselves as observing labour standards. Such bilateral agreements have been concluded by the USA with, for example, Cambodia, Chile, and Vietnam, and the World Bank has helped these countries with capacity-building. The ILO monitors make regular visits and publish the results online (Appelbaum et al. 2005: 9). (For further details, see Chapter 5.)

In addition to member countries, the ILO has influenced public international organizations. Last, but not least, the core conventions also have provided the models adapted and extended by NGOs and individual companies (Jenkins 2002). Although, as Murray (2002) points out, they were not designed for this purpose it is among individual companies that labour codes have been adopted most widely. Hence ILO has succeeded in putting the issue of labour standards and rights firmly on the international agenda, although enactment of standards has been much slower to follow.

The World Trade Organization is one of the few international organizations with enforcement powers, and it is not surprising that western countries and labour activists have tried to press the WTO into service. The WTO's main purpose is to design and implement rules governing the conduct of trade among its member countries, and it can be argued that highly discrepant labour standards constitute a non-tariff barrier to fair competition in the field of trade. During the Uruguay Round of trade negotiations in 1994, discussion took place on incorporating the five core conventions—dubbed the social clause—into trade regulation. But, given the imbalance of power in the WTO and the lack of trust this has engendered among developing countries, the social clause was opposed by many of them on the grounds of disguised protectionism. The matter was raised again during successive ministerial meetings, but it has remained deeply divisive.

Some economists support developing countries' claim that a WTO social clause could be subject to capture by protectionist interests in developed countries (e.g. Brown et al. 2002: 22). Many NGOs also oppose it as they see the WTO as a neo-liberal institution that cannot be trusted (Wick 2005: 19). Other Western labour activists and trade unions, in contrast, regard non-adoption as a grave mistake (e.g. Chan and Ross 2003: 9f.; Oxfam International 2004: 10). They point out that rejection by developing countries was by no means universal. However, two of the most powerful developing countries, India and China, continue to oppose incorporation (Chan and Ross 2003: 9f.). Nevertheless, the transformation of the WTO into an organization guaranteeing labour standards and rights will remain on the agenda in the foreseeable future (Wick 2005: 19).

The World Bank has begun to lend support to the adoption of core labour standards only in recent years but this support, according to the ICFTU (1996), has not yet been followed up in projects at country level. In 2003, however, the World Bank's financial arm, the International Finance Corporation, committed to making support for trade union organizing and collective bargaining a part of its lending conditions (Oxfam International 2004: 42)—a promising move, given the relatively large loans the Bank dispenses in developing countries.

While globalization theorists almost unanimously talk about the increased importance of international organizations in a globalizing world (Held et al. 1999; and even Hirst and Thompson 1996; Scholte 2005), their role in guaranteeing labour standards and rights is primarily illustrative of their inaction/impotence in this field, rather than demonstrating any enhanced power. National competition states, particularly in developing countries, want to retain control over domestic labour as the basis of their only viable competitive strategy at the current stage of their industrialization process. In this situation, it will be shown, private regulatory bodies, particularly transnational advocacy networks and firms, have moved in to try and fill the regulatory gap by employing innovative enforcement mechanisms.

10.3.2. Initiatives of Western NGOs and their TANs

Versions of non-governmental regulation of labour standards and rights range from individual supplier factories paying to be certified, to multinational brands internally monitoring their contractor factories, to multi-stakeholder initiatives accrediting third-party organizations to inspect factories, to independent NGOs inspecting factories individually or in coordination with worker campaigns (O'Rourke 2003: 18).

10.3.2.1. Lead Firms in GPNs

Western companies set up GPNs in order to lower the cost of production, particularly the part constituted by wages and conditions of labour. Hence, during the 1980s, they resolutely refused to assume responsibility for labour employed by their suppliers, and no public governance body exists that can oblige them to do so. It was only from the early 1990s onwards that, after the mobilization of consumers by NGOs, some of the large branded companies reluctantly began to accept responsibility for labour standards in their supplier firms. In this they were primarily influenced by a concern to save or restore their reputation among consumers, as well as nurturing the hope that voluntary compliance at a relatively low level would stave off more onerous compulsory regulation. Companies most frequently developed and implemented their own labour codes, but they also joined collective initiatives introduced by industry associations. Last, some companies participate in so-called multi-stakeholder initiatives (MSIs) or TANs, consisting of NGOs, companies, associations, and sometimes unions. (The two terms will be used interchangeably in the following.) According to an OECD 2000 database on all initiatives, single firm initiatives were the most frequent, followed by association-led ones, and MSIs were the least common (Jenkins 2002).

This development first started and is most pronounced in the USA. With Levi Strauss and Nike the leaders in the early 1990s, 'hundreds of companies have followed suit' (Esbenshade 2004: 120). This is partly due to the fact that the prevalence in the USA of domestic sweatshops incited the protests of students whose corporate wear originated in some of them, and partly to the existence of many large prominent brands that were vulnerable to the destruction of their reputation. But the prevalence of code adoption by US companies may additionally be related to the fact that they exert exceptionally strong cost pressures on suppliers while simultaneously being prone to the development of 'minimum involvement' relationships with them (see Chapter 7). European companies, in contrast, have been targeted to a much lesser degree, although a few large international companies selling sportswear, such as Adidas and Puma, have not escaped the attention of NGOs. In Europe itself, code initiatives developed only after 1998 (Esbenshade 2004: 137). European MSIs have shamed some large companies, such as the German Otto Versand mail order firm and the sportswear company Puma, into the implementation of labour codes (Sum and Ngai 2005; Palpacuer 2006).

Firms greatly vary in how they choose to engage with labour codes. Variation is evident both in the range and kind of standards they expect their suppliers to adopt and in the degree of rigour with which they monitor code implementation. Whether companies regard the implementation of codes merely as a public relations exercise, or whether they are genuinely concerned to act in a socially responsible way, is shown by how much effort and cost they are willing to expend. Above all it is indicated by whether they are willing to open themselves to external monitoring with respect to the actual implementation of codes. The OECD 2000 database on code initiatives shows that, although companies have largely modelled their codes on the ILO core conventions, they are less likely than MSIs to go well beyond them. They rarely regulate working hours, wages, stability of employment, and use of casual labour. Few companies mention working hours (Jenkins 2002) or demand the payment of a 'living wage', and only a small proportion of companies (23.8% of those in the OECD database) call on suppliers to implement labour rights (ibid). Thus lead firms in GPNs are least likely to ask for the implementation of labour standards which would affect their ability to buy clothes cheaply and on time. For the same reason, they are not prone to demand the adoption of labour rights, particularly when they come from countries without a strong 'labour rights' tradition of their own, like the USA. Last, even when companies have built up the infrastructure to facilitate compliance with labour standards, Corporate Social Responsibility departments often do not communicate this to the firm's buyers, nor are the incentives for buyers set in such a way as to operate in accordance with the CSR commitment (Ascoly 2003: 3–4).

Some of the large companies, like Levi Strauss, Liz Claiborne, Adidas, and The Gap, have dedicated staff and elaborate internal procedures for monitoring supplier compliance. Other firms simply ask existing purchasing and quality control staff to take on the monitoring, without training them to execute this onerous task. Companies also differ on who is paying for the expense of implementing and monitoring better labour standards. Thus two of the biggest code initiatives in the USA, Social Accountability International and Worldwide Responsible Apparel Production (WRAP) require that supplier factories, rather than brands, be certified and pay for any improvements made.

The most important aspect of companies' code initiatives—which lends or takes away credibility from their intervention—is whether or not they appoint external or independent monitors of supplier compliance and whether they make the results public. To take seriously both implementation and monitoring of their often very large and far-flung supplier networks, as well as assist their suppliers to improve, is a very costly undertaking for a company. The Gap, for example, which sources from over 4,000 factories in 55 countries (Gap Inc. 2004), spent US$10,000 per year on monitoring just one controversial Taiwanese-owned factory in El Salvador. Individual inspections are said to cost from US$1,000 to US$6,000 (ibid: 60).

Esbenshade's (2004) analysis of a wide range of reports on company practices finds that most companies only monitor internally or simply demand contractual affirmation of compliance. Kolk, van Tulder, and Welters (1999) point out that in 41 per cent of codes they examined there was no mention of monitoring and in a further 44 per cent firms themselves did the monitoring. External monitoring thus was very rare in company code initiatives (ibid). Several commentators rightly point out that the most thorough monitoring occurs where the buyer deals directly with the supplier, rather than working through agents, and where there exists a longstanding relationship between buyer and supplier. Such relationships, we pointed out in Chapter 7, are much more frequently found in European (particularly German) than US buyer firms. More encouragingly, more companies have hired external monitors in recent years than in the past (Esbenshade 2004: 146).

Thus, whereas some big firms now act as if they are accountable for labour standards and rights, most merely go through the motions and regard it largely as a PR exercise. Despite the achievement of some marginal and occasionally a few substantial improvements, genuine accountability by trans-national capital proves irreconcilable with the way GPNs currently are organized and governed.

Some corporations have moved beyond in-house codes and have begun to collaborate with industry associations, trade unions, and NGOs. They have moved to the adoption of industry-wide codes or have joined multi-stakeholder initiatives. After a brief examination of industry-wide codes and union involvement, we will analyse MSIs/TANs in greater depth to examine whether they render private regulation of labour standards more credible.

10.3.2.2. Industry Associations

In both the USA and in Europe, the adoption of an industry-wide code is beginning to outpace company codes. Three explanations for this development may be advanced. First, industry-wide adoption takes the matter of labour codes out of market competition. Second, it alleviates the confusion created by a multitude of different codes and develops a general standard to which firms can orient their practices. Third, participating in voluntary certification initiatives may allow an industry to pre-empt the development of international labour law. A brief review of such collective initiatives in both the USA and Europe will show that, although they have acquired considerable appeal among their members, they have not succeeded in raising the credibility and legitimacy of private regulation of labour standards.

In the USA, the American Apparel Manufacturers Association established Worldwide Responsible Apparel Production (WRAP) as the industry's code initiative in the late 1990s. Neither NGOs nor unions are represented in WRAP. Not surprisingly, WRAP has been obliged to adopt the lowest common denominator in both code content and monitoring. Its labour standards are weaker than those of the best firms and MSIs in that, for example, it does not demand the payment of a 'living wage', and its endorsement of the right to collective bargaining is extremely weak. WRAP controls the implementation of codes but has recently accepted some NGO involvement. Monitoring is carried out by professional social auditing firms, and factories to be accredited receive warning before inspection visits. Suppliers in developing countries have to pay for the monitoring, and brands merely commit to using only factories certified by WRAP. This leaves US buyer companies to reap the rewards of this 'legitimation exercise' with little cost to themselves. Not surprisingly, WRAP is the most popular US programme in terms of the number of audits it has conducted.

The European (EU-wide) collective business initiative, the Business Social Compliance Initiative (BSCI), was launched in 2004 by an EU lobbying group, the Brussels Foreign Trade Association. It is, according to Wick (2005: 93), a copy of the CSR programme of the German Retail Association for External Trade and the Society for Technical Cooperation (GTZ), which is financially supported by the German government. BSCI is intended as a sector solution for European retail. Its code is similar to that of MSIs, but its practices and organization for monitoring closely resemble those of its US counterpart, in that the BSCI also eschews union and NGO involvement. In 2005, there were 30 company members from 7 European countries, so that BSCI has attracted more companies than the 2 main European MSIs, ETI, and CCC. (See Section 10.3.2.4 and Table 10.1 for these European MSIs.) There thus is a danger that these industry-based bodies, though useful for ending code confusion, will crowd out other initiatives, particularly the TANs with higher standards and more independent monitoring practices. (Accounts of both associations' initiatives are based on Jenkins 2000; Esbenshade 2004; and Wick 2005.)

10.3.2.3. *Unions*

International unions were among the first to be concerned with the power of international corporations. They worked with public international organizations such as the ILO and the UN to try and regulate TNCs from the 1970s onwards, but without enduring success. The issue of labour standards became alive again for unions from the 1990s onwards, when companies began to adopt them (Justice 2002: 42–3). The ICFTU (International Confederation of Free Trade Unions) has recruited many national union movements to its cause. It is trying to coordinate them to develop a coherent global strategy (Applebaum 2008: 83) but is working against tremendous odds. Trade unions are aware of the fact that some of the companies engaged in code initiatives are very anti-union in their home country, such as Walmart in the USA and Tesco in the UK. Justifiably suspicious, unions therefore believe that company-centred code initiatives are no alternative for good labour law and self-organization by adoption of industry-wide labour codes. However, the clothing industry is weakly unionized both in western countries and, even more so, in developing countries. Moreover, the ease of global mobility for lead firms not wanting to tolerate unions gives the unions little leverage in any conflict with employers. In the current circumstances, participation in multi-stakeholder code initiatives is often the only opportunity for intervention open to unions.

10.3.2.4. *NGOs and Multi-Stakeholder Initiatives/TANs*

In contrast to the commercial private regulatory actors just examined, NGOs and TANs may be described as independent civil society actors. The latter have been defined as self-generated associations of citizens with common concerns who seek, from outside political parties, to shape the rules that govern social life in a

Table 10.1. Important multi-stakeholder initiatives

Name of initiative	Country and year of origin	Membership	Aims and objectives	Methods/instruments	Monitoring/verification	Financing of MSI
Fair Labor Association (FLA)	USA in 1996 as AIP	Large US MNCs, universities, NGOs and Council of Churches	Improvement of labour conditions in world-wide industries producing under license for US universities. Deals with third party complaints	1. Work place code of conduct. 2. Special projects on important topics.	Internal and external monitoring. Participates in monitoring. Accredits brands.	Dues of member companies and universities or their licensees.
Workers' Rights Consortium	USA in 2000, on initiative of USAS	Representatives of universities, student organizations, 'labour rights' experts	Improvement of labour conditions in world-wide garment industry producing under license for US universities	1. Code of conduct. 2. Investigation and Remediation Reports in response to complaints. 3. Worker training	Licensee held responsible for monitoring, but independent verification. No certification.	40% from University licensing income, 60% from government grant
Social Accountability International (SAI)	US 1997, founded by Council on Economic Priorities	Convenes companies, unions, NGOs, government representatives, consumers, and investors	Improvement of labour conditions in all industries	SA 8000 implementation by means of certification. Training and assistance courses. Worker education programme.	External monitoring. Accredits independent monitors. Certifies factories.	Company membership fees and grants from independent agencies and US government.
Fair Wear Foundation (FWF)	The Netherlands in 1999, now extending into Europe. Set up by CCC.	Unions, NGOs, business associations, companies.	Improvement of labour conditions in world-wide garment factories, producing for Dutch market. Uses ICFTU standards. Trains suppliers.	Code of Conduct, based on ICFTU code. Auditing of management systems. Procedure for complaints from local organizations.	External audits, FWF verifies proportion of audits.	Social funds of industry associations, companies and Oxfam.
Ethical Trading Initiative (ETI)	UK in 1998, but now international. Received large grant from British government.	Companies, unions, and NGOs	Improvement of labour conditions in world-wide garments and food industry. Learning Initiative.	Member camps. committed to ETI base code experimental and research projects Building capacity and training in production countries	Different modes of monitoring and verification are being tested.	Mainly grant from UK government and payment from member companies. Some grants from NGOs and unions.
Clean Clothes Campaign (CCC)	The Netherlands 1988, but code only from 1998. In 1995, spread to 11 other European countries. Have global support network.	NGOs, unions, human rights orgs., researchers.	Pursues solidarity work and puts pressure on companies. Does pilot projects with companies. Lobbies with EU.		External audits by accredited agencies and by worker orgs.	D.K.

wide range of issue areas (Scholte 2005: 218), in this case labour standards and rights in GPNs. Unlike the business actors just reviewed, civil society actors are not motivated by generating and maintaining profits, but by aspirations to secure basic human rights at work for those not in a position to achieve it on their own.

Among such rule-making private actors NGOs have been particularly prominent. They have no political mandate, nor have they been appointed by private business. But, in contrast to the business initiatives, they are independent and willing to take a critical stance. However, global governance by such actors is often mediated, endorsed, and even copied by international and national public political organizations. Implementing codes in global networks is a very demanding task, requiring expertise and resources. Hence NGOs have joined forces with other interested parties, particularly unions and western buyer firms, thereby establishing multi-stakeholder initiatives (MSIs). This has not only increased their resources but also their legitimacy among firms.

As pointed out by Jenkins (2002), labour codes and implementation and monitoring practices of MSIs/TANs therefore should be viewed as the outcome of struggle between different stakeholders, and they entail conflict over whose interests will prevail. Where the union between NGOs and business has become close, Gereffi, Garcia-Johnson, and Sasser (2001) speak of an 'NGO-industrial complex', hinting that close collaboration with business may compromise NGO reputation and freedom of action.

Two further serious problems confronting NGOs are first, to establish a global reach and, second, to become socially embedded in the developing countries and the local communities they claim to represent. NGOs and their anti-sweatshop alliances originated in the USA in the mid- to late 1990s. They initially addressed themselves to widespread labour abuses in the domestic industry, with political mediation by the Clinton government. As production networks became more and more globally dispersed during the 1990s, the focus of code initiatives shifted to suppliers in developing countries. During the late 1990s comparable initiatives developed in Europe. Most recent developments show the reproduction of the global nature of production networks in the increasing global connectedness of and collaboration among NGOs. It is also evident in the issues they address, the way they communicate, and in the increased reach and density of their organizational infrastructures. (See also Palpacuer 2006 on the parallel structures and strategies of a MSI and the GPN of German Puma.) There also have been efforts by NGOs from the USA and Europe with similar projects and policies to join together at an international level, to avoid policy confusion and dysfunctional competition for funds. The result of the latter was the Joint Initiative on Corporate Accountability and Workers' Rights (JO-IN), inaugurated in London in 2004. It unites the most important US and European MSIs, but leaves out the two business code initiatives, WRAP and BSCI. JO-IN is conceived as a learning project that aims to develop a common code, with convergence towards the highest possible standards. JO-IN currently works in Turkish factories to systematically compare the strengths and weaknesses of different approaches towards code implementation, audits, and verification/certification.

It is now obvious to northern NGOs that their intervention in southern supplier firms would become more effective, as well as more legitimate, if local NGOs and workers' organizations were to be involved. In some countries of Latin America, for example, local NGOs are beginning to evolve, whereas in other countries they have to be slowly nurtured to become effective allies. As the relationships between North American NGOs and Mexican civil society groups, for example, in the Coalition for Justice in the Maquiladoras, show, such collaboration can be both fruitful and conflictual, as well as being mostly confined to a few high-profile campaigns. (See, for example, the accounts by Williams 1999: 151; Fox 2004: 480; Quan 2008) The lack of involvement in most initiatives of workers themselves is problematic. The latter either do not fully share the values and objectives of particular TANs or are concerned that involvement may cost them their jobs. It means that TANs have no mandate to act and may even be acting against the interests of local workers. As observed by Keck and Sikkink (1998: 33), the low level of involvement of local NGOs and workers themselves makes it questionable to perceive them as transnational 'civil society' actors.

What then are the objectives of MSIs or TANs? (While there are several dozens NGOs and MSIs in this area, only a few of the most prominent can be described here.) In very general terms, all MSIs are guided by ILO standards and/or by codes of international trade unions. However, most go beyond the core conventions and concern themselves with the following: wage levels; poor working conditions; frequent forced overtime; child labour; unsafe working conditions; gender discrimination; lack of labour rights. They differ from business codes in that most (with the exception of the Fair Labor Association [FLA] in the USA) demand a 'living wage' and all campaign for labour rights. MSIs differ among themselves in their objectives and in how they pursue them, as well as in their monitoring and implementation practices. These varying details depend on the coalition of interest groups pursuing the code initiative. They are summarized in Table 10.1.

10.3.2.5. *Monitoring/Verification*

One of the most intractable problems for both business and MS initiatives has been the monitoring or auditing of compliance with stipulated labour standards. A very common method has been to accredit and appoint an independent auditing organization. The latter carries out annual inspections and audits on a commercial basis and then provides certification of compliance. There now exists a proliferation of third-party certification initiatives, and observers speak of the rise of a new 'million dollar' industry in this area. While these auditors initially were the big international accounting firms, adding a 'social audit' to their business portfolio, most of them had abandoned social auditing by 2002 (Esbenshade 2004: 138). More recently, specialized 'social audit' firms, such as Veritas, Cal-Safety, and Global Social Compliance, have taken over. Profound scepticism has arisen over whether these commercial auditing enterprises are doing a worthwhile job. An exposure of Price Waterhouse Coopers by the labour activist Dara O'Rourke, who accompanied the PWC auditor on one inspection tour of firms in China and Korea, only provided the objective proof for the widely held suspicions of the inadequacy of audits (O'Rourke 2000). Another disillusioned inspector for a Californian social auditing firm recorded the following thought in his diary: 'I'm beginning to wonder just whose needs I am serving. Am I helping the industry to clean up its dirty laundry, or just to bury it a little further from the nose of American consumers?' (Brown 2001). As in any business undertaking, auditing firms have executed their task in a highly bureaucratic and routinized manner, trying to limit effort and expenditure. They are content to document practices and present a 'paper' record, without providing their auditors with more than very elementary training for this difficult job. As one local Chinese social compliance officer told Sum and Ngai 2005, 'the code monitors came for a few hours only for every inspection. They like tables, figures and data, don't they?' (ibid: 193). More recently, some of the MSIs have started to monitor the monitors or have moved into this field themselves, for example, the Fair Labour Association, and a new international standard, SA 8000, modelled on the ISO standards, also has been created.

Even where monitors are conscientious and have some local knowledge, the very nature of global production networks, as the section on supplier firms will make clear, frustrates genuine implementation of labour codes and rights by business enterprises themselves. Monitors only inspect the larger, first-tier contractors, while the predominantly small- and medium-sized firms in this industry, particularly the firms in the often sizeable informal sector, remain un-inspected. Hence there exists wide-spread scepticism over whether the exposure and correction of individual violations by supplier firms really leads to fundamental and lasting change in international labour standards and rights. There has been a tendency among many inspectors to record only blatant offences against health and safety regulations, as well as the use of child labour, which has probably declined (Esbenshade 2004: 147). Buyers' inspectors tend to overlook the more intractable problems around wages and overtime pay (Roberts and Engardio 2006: 54). Only in rare cases has implementation led to higher wages or the right to organize (Esbenshade 2004: 147). Even when serious violations of standards are detected and documented in specific supplier firms, remedial action is frequently not enforced (Brown 2001). Substantive achievements of NGOs and MSIs thus have been modest.

Most of the problems surrounding code implementation and the generally low rate of their success in improving workers' conditions and rights are due to the fact that NGOs have co-opted lead firms into their networks. They thereby have been prevented from offering diagnoses which turn lead firms into the very cause of existing problems, rather than presenting them as just occasional transgressors who can be persuaded to improve their standards. In other words, NGOs overlook that they are dealing with a structural problem, rather than ill will or negligence by firms. A closer examination of supplier factories and the orchestration of their production processes by western buyer firms will illustrate this claim.

10.3.3. Problems of Code Implementation in Supplier Factories

There is a widely accepted view in the literature that the low rate of success in improving labour standards and rights in a substantial and enduring manner should be attributed to the unwillingness of suppliers to comply, and that better monitoring might improve the situation. Commentators point to the guile of local factory managers/owners in deceiving the code monitors, particularly in China, India, and Bangladesh, and indict their widespread cheating. It is also contended that workers are often complicit in this deception, either because they are forced to cover for their employers or because they perceive a genuine threat to their jobs and their earning capacity if they alert auditors to violation of standards.

Many accounts of factory inspections relate incidents of 'lying and cheating' by local managers. Factory managers are accused of engaging in double book-keeping to hide the large amount of overtime worked and the inadequate pay for it. They are said to coach their workers to back up these false accounts when interrogated by inspectors (Asian Focus Group 2005: 2; Sum and Ngai 2005: 193f; Engardio and Roberts 2006: 50). There even exists a new type of Chinese consultancy firm that helps suppliers to evade auditors and pass the inspection (Roberts and Engardio 2006: 50). Another way to evade western inspection is to shift work to a lower tier supplier not approved by the buyer (ibid). A Veritas inspector of Chinese factories, checking for compliance with SA 8000, concluded: 'Right now, in labour-intensive industries in Southern China SA 8000 cannot be enforced effectively. The factories always find a way around the auditors' (cited by Esbenshade 2004: 136).

Factory managers, for their part, persuasively explain and justify both their poor record in upholding labour standards and their cheating by reference to the unreasonable demands of their western buyers. Because these demands are impossible to meet, they create powerful incentives to cheat (Brown 2001; Sum and Ngai 2005: 195; Roberts and Engardio 2006: 52). These unreasonable demands relate to constant pressures to both lower prices and cut delivery times. The constant demand for lower prices, suppliers suggest, makes it impossible for them to raise labour standards as all the cost for this has to be borne by them, rather than by their western buyers. As one factory manager told the western inspector, 'if I paid my workers more money, I'd have to raise the prices to my buyers, the people who are sending you here to inspect my factory. Do you think they would accept that?' (Brown 2001).

The constant price pressure, in the context of intense competition, has left Chinese suppliers with very slim profit margins of around 4 per cent in 2004 (Oxfam International 2004; Li & Fung Research Centre 2006: 4), forcing them to either run sweatshops or go out of business. Time pressures on delivery are attributed both to the increased number of fashion cycles and the associated 'quick response sourcing' and to 'bad habits' of lead firms, such as sending sample garments too late or changing orders at short notice. As suppliers are still expected to deliver on time and failure to deliver can result in costly penalties and loss of reputation, they are forced to deliver by hook or by crook. This includes utilization of extensive overtime and/or sub-contracting to a lower, unauthorized tier of suppliers (Oxfam International 2004: 51; Sum and Ngai 2005; Turkish Interview Notes 2007). As overtime payment is very expensive—under Chinese law time and a half is payable after 8 hours on week-days and triple pay at week-ends—providing for overtime pay presents the biggest challenge for suppliers (Roberts and Engardio 2006: 53). They are driven to 'cheat' their workers out of some of their payments, thus perpetuating the cycle of poor labour standards and the deceit of inspectors. Not surprisingly, the production manager of a factory visited by Sum and Ngai (2005) criticized the lead firm's labour code. She called it a 'paradoxical and hypocritical act', to 'assuage the inner sins' of the 'rich western countries' (ibid: 195). In sum, violations occur because of suppliers' inability to cover their overheads, pay their workers, and make modest profits, given the low prices manufacturers pay (Esbenshade 2004: 99). By focusing on problems at the point of production, factory inspections ignore the role of brands' and retailers' own purchasing practices in creating problems (Oxfam International 2004: 57).

Therefore the fundamental roots of enduring code violation lie much deeper, and must be sought in the very nature of GPNs and the discrepantly high degree of power western buyer firms are able to wield. The intense global competition in this industry and the footlooseness it encourages among western, and particularly American, lead firms does not predispose suppliers to accede to their costly demands for improving labour standards. In the apt words of Esbenshade (2004: 10), 'private monitoring accepts as given the industry's production practices—such as mobility and hidden chains of production—and its multi-layered structure. It does not effectively change working conditions, because it neither alters the structural practices under which sweatshops flourish, nor does it allow workers to address their own exploitation'.

10.4. CONCLUSIONS: THE PARADOXES OF PRIVATE MARKET REGULATION

This chapter has investigated labour standards and rights in the clothing industries of three supplier countries. It has revealed that the garment industry not only sources from countries with the lowest wages but further pushes down costs by utilizing workers with the lowest bargaining power—women and (im)migrants and other unregistered employees (Esbenshade 2004: 125).

Given the regulatory gap left by the inability/unwillingness of both national competition states and public international institutions to tame the market, we have focused in some detail on the efforts of various private market actors—firms, unions, and TANs convened by NGOs—to impose the implementation of labour codes. How far have the latter succeeded in alleviating the problems? If they have not succeeded, what alternative regulatory regimes are feasible?

Despite the many serious weaknesses in TANs, even many non-business commentators credit them with having achieved at least some success. Success, Keck and Sikkink (1998: 25) point out, can be achieved at several levels. Thus Roberts and Engardio (2006: 53) suggest that 'however compromised, pressure from multinationals has curbed some of the most egregious abuses by outside suppliers'. Quan (2008), too, introducing the case of the Korean plant Kukdong in Mexico, shows that TANs can be influential, at least in the short run. Gereffi and colleagues concur when they comment that '[code] initiatives have increased the extent to which large western corporations take responsibility for the employees of their contractors, and in several well publicized cases have achieved striking improvements in both standards and rights' (Gereffi et al. 2001: 62f.). Shaw and Hale (2002: 61) further contend that, 'codes, at the very least, represent a [new] corporate admission of liability for working conditions'. Only 10 years ago, companies routinely refused to accept responsibility for labour conditions in their production chains (ibid).

Others, however, point out that substantial improvements in standards have been rare occurrences and have not affected significant proportions of workers in a lasting manner (e.g. Fox 2004: 503, on Mexico; Sum and Ngai 2005, on China). If standards have improved marginally, labour rights have hardly benefited from private code initiatives. In the words of a Mexican commentator: 'Mexican organized labour continues to lose ground, and it has yet to win a significant foothold in the maquiladora industry' (Fox 2004: 503). Even Nike's Vice President for CSR recognizes the limits of the current system of private regulation when he comments that 'you can catch and fix a problem, but that doesn't change an industry' (Roberts and Engardio 2006: 58). NGO commentators, too, have serious reservations about solely private regulation of labour conditions. Some convincingly portray the geographical complexity (multiple layers of sub-contracting) and constant flux of GPNs as overtaxing the efforts of private regulators (O'Rourke 2003: 21).

But we should not expect the impossible from NGOs and the TANs they form. Wick (2005: 31) rightly suggests that NGOs can only function as 'catalysts to encourage the (better) enforcement of existing laws or the creation of new legislation—either nationally or internationally' (ibid). Keck and Sikkink (1998: 16) point out that NGOs are engaged in leverage politics and call on or shame more powerful actors to effect a change in law, policy, and/or practices. The main problem in the clothing industry is that both national competition states and firms have to be ruled out as powerful actors likely to attempt a transformation as they are complicit in the creation and maintenance of sweatshops. It does not make sense to expect lead firms in this industry to transform the labour conditions that sustain GPNs and the generation of value for such firms.

But rather than completely denigrating the tremendous efforts made by TANs of various sorts, it should be recognized that, first, they have put the issues of the global regulation of labour firmly on the public agenda; second, some have indicated that western buyer firms are as much implicated in labour abuse as their third-world suppliers (e.g. Oxfam International 2004); and, third, they have offered us a glimpse of a possible new system to regulate global production net-works.

Such a system, we contend, has to return to a reliance on public governance organizations. The task of taming fragmented global markets ineffectively reg-ulated by national competition states requires the intervention of international intergovernmental institutions, working in conjunction with national states, unions, and NGOs. Public power is necessary to enforce the adoption of broadly comparable labour standards and rights across nations. This, in turn, is the only way to curb the existing intense global competition in this industry. By creating a more level playing field, public intervention at the global level may prevent the regime shopping of mobile global corporations which drive down standards.

But which inter-governmental organization(s) should be nominated to take on this task? How, given their previous failure in this sphere, could the concern of developing countries that global enforcement of labour codes is a protectionist ploy of western countries be alleviated? To answer the first question, such an international organization has to have either regulatory competences or financial resources that are deemed valuable by developing and newly industrializing coun-tries, as well as possessing legitimate sanctioning and remediation powers. Such an organization should be able to complement sanctions with positive support, in terms of capacity building in developing countries.

A new EU scheme, the so-called General System of Preferences + trade policy (see Chapter 5) has also been accepted by the USA. It links trade preferences to good performance in the sphere of labour standards/rights via ratifications by the supplier country of international conventions. But this affects only a few of the smaller and weaker developing countries and does not create a level playing field. The ideal candidate to implement a scheme affecting all developing countries still remains the WTO. The WTO could link trade agreements to the legal and actual adoption of labour standards and rights, and use its existing remediation and enforcement mechanisms that are activated in trade disputes. The WTO would have to work in tandem with either the ILO or the World Bank to supplement sanctions with capacity building. The latter two, in turn, would involve NGOs. To counter opposition from countries such as China and India, such new regulation should not impose high western standards in a 'blanket' fashion on all members, but instead link standards, particularly in the area of wages, to existing economic capabilities. Fung, O'Rourke, and Sabel (2001), in their persuasive article on 'ratcheting' labour standards, demand the introduction of 'the most ambitious and *feasible* labour standards given their [countries'] economic development context'.

Another solution, which might prove as effective but easier to enforce, would be for the WTO to mandate only the adoption of labour rights, as defined by the ILO. This would have several advantages: it would put the achievement of decent labour standards into the hands of national trade unions which, because they would be oriented towards local economic conditions, would initiate a more gradual and sustainable improvement of conditions; simultaneously it could rely on unions to act as local enforcement agencies; and such mandatory adoption of effective labour rights would also affect those western countries where collective bargaining competencies of unions have been seriously undermined in recent decades. Such action would not constitute a non-tariff trade barrier as developing countries would still preserve an advantage in wage rates over developed ones. The highly fragmented and decentralized nature of the global clothing industry, and particularly its large informal sector, will make the enactment of any internationally mandatory standards and rights a very challenging task. But, given the highly unsatisfactory nature of the present situation in GPNs and the increase in competitiveness of countries like China, Brazil, India, and Turkey, it is one well worth attempting.

NOTE

1. For the case of Turkey, we gratefully acknowledge the work conducted by Tugce Bulut, a PhD student at the University of Cambridge.

11

Conclusions

In this book we have studied the role of firms, states, and international organizations in shaping global production networks (GPNs) in the clothing industry. Although such networks have been in existence for more than 30 years, at the turn to the twentieth century there occurred several new developments lending fresh interest to their analysis. Outsourcing and off-shoring of the manufacturing process by American and European clothing firms is almost complete. Sewing and assembly of clothes in western societies has become a rare occurrence. Furthermore, these functions have been dispersed across the whole globe, making this industry genuinely global in its reach. This has been facilitated by a second change towards the end of the last century, namely, the fundamental geopolitical transformation which turned former state socialist countries into capitalist market economies or, in the case of China and Vietnam, grafted marketization onto the old political structures. These transition economies immediately became places in which the GPNs of European and US firms touched down. Access was eased by historical economic or political ties—in the case of German firms with CEE countries and of UK firms with Hong Kong. The transition in several other countries (e.g. Mexico and Turkey) during the 1980s from trade regimes prioritizing import substitution to export-led growth further contributed to the global spread of the clothing industry. The accompanying phenomenal growth in the number of producers and potential contractors for western firms sharply increased competition between them and played further into the hands of western buyer firms. It also wrought fundamental social change, bringing large numbers of rural and mostly female workers into factories and wage labour. The third major international event, the abolition of import quotas by the WTO in January 2005, gave a more violent shake to the kaleidoscope of conditions that shape GPNs. This liberalizing reform of international trade regulation radically changed both the geographical profiles and size of GPNs, particularly for US firms, and thereby redistributed global employment from the less and least developed supplier countries to the more developed ones. (For details, see Chapter 6.) Our study thus may be used as a lens for understanding diverse global social and economic processes. But it poses the additional challenge of finding a better way to understand the interaction between GPNs and national capitalisms.

Influenced by the Varieties of Capitalism (VoC) approach, we started from the premise that GPNs are not a purely global or even international phenomenon but that, because they originate in and touch down in specific countries, networks are shaped by complex processes of social institutional interaction. Hence the main theoretical and empirical preoccupation of our book has been provided by answering the following three related questions:

1. To what extent and how are GPNs shaped by national capitalisms and to what degree are they influenced by global markets and by international/global organizations?

2. How do GPNs in the clothing industry impact on national capitalisms? Do they further strengthen a given economy's competitive advantage in a particular industry niche, or do they also undermine economic structures and disorganize or disrupt institutional arrangements?

3. How does a dual theoretical focus on the comparative capitalisms approach and the theory of global value chains/production networks improve our understanding of what drives network actors and the interrelationships within networks?

In answer to the first question our main finding, contrary to claims by Gereffi (2005) and Herrigel and Wittke (2005), is that GPNs remain substantially shaped by both national institutional ensembles and domestic markets. We further establish that differences between our three national industries largely, though not exclusively, follow the distinction between CMEs and LMEs introduced by Hall and Soskice (2001). Despite the radical social-institutional dis-embedding inherent in GPNs, firms' practices continue to bear the imprint of national institutions and, to a large extent, remain oriented to national markets. National institutions, particularly the system of vocational education and training, shape firms' capabilities and thereby their product and market strategy. While this institutional complex facilitates or impedes the adoption of a specific market strategy, other societal institutions/processes, such as the financial system and state regulation, influence the accumulation of resources necessary to adopt this strategy. Firm size, material resources, and a manufacturing orientation have been relevant in this respect. In the German case, for example, both production orientation and product strategy were moulded until 2004 by state regulation favouring market dominance by medium-sized firms, owned and managed by individuals with the qualification of a Master craftsman—the so-called *Mittelstand*. In the two liberal market economies, in contrast, the absence of such anti-competitive regulation and the presence of a developed market for M&A have prevented market domination by such firms and the pronounced production orientation they display. Although the UK economy has been dominated by the stock market as much as the USA, the strong downward spiral of competitiveness in its clothing industry has meant less stock market listing by clothing 'manufacturers', though not necessarily less dependence on the financial institutions shaped by the capital markets. In addition to institutional shaping, domestic markets and consumption styles have influenced the adoption of nationally distinctive product strategies. In all three societies, production volume is predominantly destined for domestic markets and for clothing retailers who cater for nationally distinctive demand. Internationalization of sales through both exporting and FDI remains relatively low for all three industries (see Chapter 4). This has resulted in the paradoxical outcome that firms predominantly engaged in global sourcing remain domestically oriented in their sales operations and hence, with a few notable exceptions among German and US firms, are not genuine multinational companies.

Nationally influenced product strategy, together with domestically developed modes of inter-firm contracting, then feed through into the way GPNs are coordinated and governed. We have shown in Chapter 7 that both geographical focus and size of networks differ between the three national industries, as did the onset of substantial foreign sourcing and the degree of conflict surrounding it. Regarding the latter, national systems of industrial relations and the degree of deliberation between employers and unions they facilitate were crucial for the early start in Germany. Distinctive product paradigms also influence the mode of contracting. Among UK and US firms, a more pronounced move to 'full package' sourcing implies a greater surrender of control over fabric selection and a number of pre-production functions.

In addition to these aspects of GPNs, our relational approach to contracting established that arm's length, market-type contracting was more prominent among firms from the two LMEs than among German firms. It was particularly marked among US companies, which were under the strongest pressure to lower prices/increase value from both retailers and investors. German firms' more relational style of contracting was distinguished by the practice of stationing German technicians in supplier firms and helping the latter to improve their production organization. This, in turn, involved longer-term retention of contractors than was common among British and, even more so, American firms. It was revealed to us by Turkish suppliers that even modes of payment of suppliers differ along national lines. In sum, ways of exerting control over suppliers differed according to national institutional imprinting. Whereas US firms gained control, despite their arm's length and inconstant relationships, through volume-buying, German firms aimed more often for virtual vertical integration. British firms were unable to use either strategy, and ownership control through setting up fully owned subsidiaries in supplier countries, rather than engaging in third-party contracting, was the preferred strategy among several 'private label' suppliers. In each case, national styles of contracting were neither purely relational nor purely arm's length but instead often showed marked tensions between the two basic orientations. This was due to the fact that the practices of and relationships between firms were not solely moulded by national institutions. They were also shaped by those in supplier countries, by global markets, and by both public and private international institutions.

We pointed out in Chapter 2 that the building of GPNs, which involves the jettisoning of owner control and a more pronounced externalization of functions than the MNC model suggests, leads to a more radical institutional dis-embedding. Outsourcing creates truncated firms, without a labour force of operators, and without institutions devoted to skill training, industrial relations or the creation of commitment that arises from both skill training and authority sharing (Whitley 1999). However, even hub firms in GPNs have to rely on reasonably efficient and committed operators and on suppliers who can deliver these qualities. Buyer firms can overcome this problem to some extent by selecting suppliers in culturally close countries, by internalizing skill training (as in the case of German firms), or by exerting strong pressures on suppliers through the constant threat of withdrawal of very large orders (as in the case of US firms). But, for a number of reasons, they cannot fully control the situation and solve the problem entirely. First, firms from all three economies were not fully committed to suppliers and, prompted by a volatile and highly competitive global market, would periodically change them, albeit to differing degrees. Second, supplier firms are operating in a global market concerning the price of the clothes they sell, and the high intensity of competition in this market makes it impossible for most to develop and retain committed labour (see Chapter 10). That western firms are aware of the problem of a partial loss of control is evident from the fact that many have detached themselves only hesitantly and gradually from their country of origin over a period of several decades. In some cases, companies try to recreate—in a voluntaristic manner— aspects of their domestic institutional environment in supplier firms (see Chapter 7).

Truncated western buyer companies additionally are influenced by their supplier firms and countries. Thus, seeking suppliers with commensurate capabilities to their own, as is common among German branded 'manufacturers', restricts their locational choices to a greater extent than is the case with firms serving the lower to middle market or that supply retailers with 'own label' garments, such as most British and US firms in our sample. Western buyers additionally rely on states in supplier countries to hold down labour costs by neglecting to police the implementation of basic labour standards and rights. Competitive advantage of firms is thus constituted by both their country of origin and by supplier countries, even if the former still predominates.

Finally, western buyer firms have been strongly constrained and enabled by both regional and international institutions' trade regulation. While both types of regulation were mostly devised by inter-governmental organizations and constituent states, trade rules have usually acquired their own momentum and have had unforeseen consequences that subsequently escaped the control of national states and firms (for details, see Chapter 6). Thus even the most interventionist state (the USA) had to accept that the system of trade regulation devised could not halt the competitive slide of either their textiles or their clothing industry. Less drastically, changing trade regulation, rather than managerial choice, has driven the periodic geographical reconfiguration of GPNs, with the recent shift of US firms from Mexico to China being only the latest illustration of this trend. Such geographical shifts are, of course, not socially neutral and require major adjustments by western firms. It is, however, worth emphasizing that the end of the Agreement on Textiles and Clothing in January 2005 did not signal the end of protective trade regulation. Some trade rules are still determined by national states/regional trade blocks—such as tariffs and preferential trade agreements, which involve national or regional rules of origin—and thus enable them to secure a 'trade rent' for their domestic firms. Comparing the trade policies of the EU and the USA/NAFTA in relation to this industry, the following contrasts emerge. US agreements generally are more restrictive and more complicated to navigate, due to extensive lobbying by different segments of the industry. EU trade policy appears more development-oriented, less restrictive, and preferential access to the EU is granted to more countries. (For further details, see Chapter 5.)

In this context, buyer firms often exercise strategic choice and make business decisions that evade or circumvent the influence of their domestic institutional environment yet ensure their survival in the domestic market. For example, German firms which have migrated ever further to the east in CEE in pursuit of lower labour costs are no longer acting in accordance with the principles of a CME. Similarly, the British retailer Marks & Spencer, which delayed off-shore sourcing until the late 1990s to support domestic industry, also exercised a strategic choice which proved to be dangerous in an LME environment.

The second major theoretical question we posed in this study has been how the processes of dis-embedding described above and the exertion of institutional influences on firms at multiple geopolitical levels have influenced national capitalisms. Firms in the clothing industry were the first to engage in the off-shoring of the whole production process, and initially little attention was paid to this process as it affected mainly lowly skilled and poorly remunerated work. But during the last 30 odd years the organizational template first developed by the clothing industry has been copied by other industries, and fragmentation of value chains and trans-border relocation of whole series of functions have proceeded apace. This wide-ranging process of dis-embedding has fundamentally and negatively affected the institution of industrial relations and has disrupted complementarity between various institutional domains, such as skill training and within-firm deliberation, particularly in CMEs such as Germany. Outsourcing of functions, particularly but not solely in the American industry, has been shown to be a progressive process, and more and more steps in the value chain have become externalized. While this may enhance the share of value captured by firms and their investors in the short term, in the longer term firms lose their industrial experience and expertise. This eventually undermines their competitive advantage. They lose the distinctiveness a given bundle of capabilities had given them and thus their niche in the market.

It is pertinent to ask how GPNs have enhanced the competitive advantage of national industries. The answer must be that global sourcing has mainly enabled firms to survive rather than strengthening them, and in the case of the UK industry decline has been more notable than even survival (see Chapter 3). In terms of export performance, German firms have retained and even advanced their superior position, whereas in the US industry high export performance remains confined to a much smaller proportion of firms. However, in overall performance terms all three industries are eclipsed by the Italian industry, the latest of the major European industries to start off-shoring.

We now turn to answer the third question posed above, namely, how analysis of GVC/GPN can benefit from taking on board insights from the comparative capitalism approach. We have already shown that the competitive advantage of lead firms and the way they organize their GPNs is strongly influenced by the social institutions of their country of origin. A more elaborate answer may be provided by concentrating on the issues of governance of GPNs, that is, the distribution of power within them and the resultant drivers of chains or networks. Gereffi (1994) was right to point out that the power in networks has passed from manufacturers to retailers and that, in the clothing industry, we see buyer-driven chains. However, his analysis, made in the American context, ignored the social foundations of power and thus was insufficiently nuanced. Gereffi adopted a structural concept of power and implied a zero sum approach to its distribution. We have favoured a more relational approach which distinguishes power relations in the network according to national origin of lead firms, as well as type of lead firm. Additionally, we allow for some power sharing between buyer and supplier firms or, at least, some holding in abeyance of power, in order to foster social learning and growth of supplier competence.

Thus our in-depth study of relations between retailers and 'manufacturers'/marketers in three divergent institutional contexts has shown that, although the imbalance of market power is even greater in the UK than in the USA, US retailers were the most inclined to use this power in an adversarial manner. In Germany we found both a much lesser imbalance of power between branded 'manufacturers' and traditional retailers and more evidence of cooperative relations. This appeared to be conditioned by a lesser degree of retailer concentration and a still confident sector of mainly branded 'manufacturers', but also by societal norms that govern inter-firm relations. These divergent retailer–'manufacturer' relations, we have shown, in turn influenced relations with global suppliers, leading to divergent styles of governing GPNs.

Last, it is notable that power relations in GPNs have been affected by the emergence of a new industry actor. Some mainly East Asian mega firms have evolved in recent decades to maintain large and sophisticated transnational networks and act both as 'network orchestrators' and as suppliers of western firms. Some western, mainly American, buyers who have outsourced most segments of the value chain have become dependent on the 'full service' these mega firms are able to supply. They may find that they are dealing with a newly powerful global actor, eclipsing the power even of large western retailers. (See the discussion in Chapter 6.)

One distinctive feature of our book has been that we have followed the value chain from buyer firms in developed countries to supplier firms in developing countries, viewing the latter also in their institutional, geopolitical, and global economic contexts. We enquired how supplier firms viewed their relations with different western buyers, enabling us to check the veracity of what we had learned in interviews with western firms or from accounts of industry experts. We further learnt that industry fortunes were, on the one hand, strongly raised or lowered by changing trade rules, such as when Turkey benefited from inclusion into the European Customs Union and Mexico suffered from the end of quota restriction and the shifting of many American customers to China (see Chapters 8 and 9). On the other hand, industrial competitiveness was enhanced by (mainly private) investment in the up-grading of processes and equipment and by the presence in the country of a strong textiles industry, which facilitates both mutual learning and the speeding up of the production process. Finally, social learning through long relationships with competitive western buyers also proved important. Taking all these influences into account, we found that Turkey and China, for slightly different reasons, have both significantly improved their comparative advantage in this industry. Romania's industry, after an initial boost from an EU customs agreement, has more recently encountered some problems and suffers particularly from the lack of a highly developed textiles industry. Last, the Mexican industry has experienced a marked decline, attributed by most commentators to its firms' lack of capability in full-package production and just-in-time delivery, exacerbated by poor social infrastructure.

There has been much talk about the inexorable rise of China and its eclipse of other 'developing country' producers in this industry. Although the Chinese industry has a towering and influential position at the current time, the most recent developments in the Chinese industry urge for greater caution regarding its future development. First, despite the industry's efficient organization, breadth, diversity, and close integration with a developed textiles industry, it will not become the sole supplier for most western, particularly European, branded 'manufacturers', who require more distinctiveness in both fabric and style. Second, costs for Chinese producers have risen, due to remimbi appreciation against the dollar, rising costs of inputs and, in recent years, of labour. Furthermore, the likely cost-increasing effects of the 2008 Labour Law and the Chinese government's plan to move the economy to higher level industries suggest a less important role for this industry in China's economy in future.

The impact of buyer firms on their suppliers in developing and emergent market societies also has a dark side, closely allied to the effects of GPNs. Due to the pressures for low prices and JIT delivery from western buyers, together with the complete lack of regulation of the global labour market and the impotence/unwillingness of developing country states to uphold labour standards and rights, there exists wide-spread violation of both labour standards and rights. The intervention by NGOs and the transnational advocacy networks they have formed (Keck and Sikkink 1998) to try to halt this 'race to the bottom' has only been very partially successful. A governance deficit of huge proportions remains. (For details, see Chapter 10.)

Following this presentation of our main empirical findings and theoretical insights, we offer some reflections on the advantages of the comparative method employed. The systematic comparison of the clothing industry in the context of one CME and two LMEs has afforded insights that enable us to amend a theory (global value chain [GVC] theory) based mainly on study of the US industry. But our comparison has also identified some weaknesses in the VoC approach, among others tendencies to ignore the impact of global markets and towards undue homogenization of cases. The book has focused mainly on the divergences between German firms' GPNs on the one hand, and US and UK firms' networks on the other. However, we have also highlighted divergences between the two LMEs, as well as some divergent cases within each industry. The differences between the two LMEs are difficult to explain in a fully satisfactory manner but the following factors appear to have played a role. First, the significantly smaller size of the UK home market has not facilitated the same high investment in managerial capabilities, particularly coordination capacities. Second, the long-time dominance of the UK retail sector by the retailer Marks & Spencer, together with lower managerial capability, has led firms to adopt a strategy of producing mainly for retailers' own labels, thus becoming highly dependent on them. The resulting weakness of the British clothing industry, in turn, has meant less access for firms to capital markets, less investment capital and less pressure to increase value from major investors. Third, the British state, which is more immune than the US state to pressures from industry lobbies and has long favoured market liberalization, has practised no intervention to halt the industry's decline, not even in the field of protectionist trade regulation.

The contrasts between firms *within* each industry can be ascribed mainly to differences in size, presence of family ownership and accompanying local embeddedness and, in a few cases, product strategy. Thus, high-end designer brands in each society departed in significant ways from other firms in the way they organized their GPN. But such firms were a small proportion of all firms and significantly less developed in the UK industry than in the other two.

Comparison alerts us not only to enduring divergence between varieties of capitalism but also to emerging trends towards convergence. One such trend is that outsourcing and off-shoring is roughly equally pronounced in the three national industries and did, indeed, start earlier in Germany's CME than the UK's LME. This market-type company strategy, designed to raise or preserve firm profits by saving on labour costs, has thus been embraced by firms from both types of capitalism alike. A second and more complex trend towards convergence comes from developments in the retail sector and parallel changes in consumer demand. In all three societies there now exists a discount sector which is capturing a growing proportion of the market and puts traditional 'full-price' retailers under pressure. The rise of the discount sector, although feared by traditional retailers in all three societies, is having the most pernicious impact in Germany where the mainly 'branded manufacturers' do not produce for either the lower middle market and/or the young casual fashion sold by discounters. The establishment and growth of the discount sector thrives on a change in consumer demand and a departure by German consumers from demanding solely well-made quality goods. The further expansion of the discount sector is favoured also by the recent liberalization of regulation of the retail sector and the negative consequences this has had on remaining independent retailers (see Chapter 4). Thus the viability of the German industry's focus on diversified quality goods—a hall mark of a CME—could paradoxically be undermined in the longer run by a new German retail actor, rather than by institutional change. It would constitute a significant shift towards the LME type.

What light do our findings throw on the process of global economic integration and its social and political consequences? Remaining globalization sceptics have been shown that the fragmentation of value chains and the dispersion of the various functions across the globe bring about deeper global economic integration than FDI. Further, the trend has attained an exceptionally wide global reach, encompassing all continents. Although some regionalization in location patterns still persists, this is now being superseded by more widely dispersed sourcing or, at least, a dual focus on the home region and on Asia. This integration also links the developed and the developing world ever more closely, as well as showing a distinct differentiation within the latter between the least developed countries, such as African Lesotho and fast developers, such as India and China.

This process of growing economic integration, although set in train by national states and intergovernmental organizations, seems to have largely escaped the control of any one national western state. Although a rearguard action has been fought by the USA and the EU since the abolition of quotas through the introduction of China safeguards, the weight in terms of the trade balance in this industry has now tilted irretrievably towards the countries of the developing world.

The last aspect of growing global economic integration to be considered concerns both its impact on labour and the dominance of pure market competition. Neither states of developing and developed countries, nor international organizations have succeeded in establishing labour standards and rights in supplier countries. This complete regulatory deficit is one of the factors that has contributed to the growth of a globalization backlash and the emergence in this area of transnational NGOs and their advocacy networks. Although these organizations have been able to curb the worst excesses and have induced branded lead firms reluctantly to accept responsibility for labour standards in supplier firms, their intervention has also demonstrated that private regulation alone cannot succeed in establishing a secure and decent labour regime. Concerning the impact of production relocation on labour in the three *developed* countries, the large losses of mainly unskilled and semi-skilled jobs in both the textile and the clothing industry of all three countries (see Chapter 3) have nevertheless had a varied impact. The negative effects on lower-skill workers seem to have been largest in the USA, where production had been highly concentrated in the less prosperous southern states—where, due to the back-loading of quota abolition, the impact on jobs was also more concentrated in temporal terms than in European societies. Last, politicization of such job losses is the most pronounced in the US political system.

At this point, readers may legitimately ask about the degree of typicality of the clothing industry for understanding both processes of economic globalization and the interaction of GPNs with national capitalisms. While the clothing industry is by no means representative of western industry it is also not entirely exceptional. There are many other light industries, including shoes, toys, and semiconductors as well as the agro-food industries and flower growing, which have undergone similar processes of outsourcing (Dicken 2007, part III). Although outsourcing in more advanced manufacturing and service sectors has not yet developed as far as in these low-skill industries and job loss have not yet been very great (Gereffi 2005), it is nevertheless a progressive process that is purely business led.

Concerning the interaction of global production networks and national capitalisms, there again appear to be some distinctive, though not entirely exceptional features in the clothing industry. The global market in clothing is exceptionally fragmented with countless small and inefficient firms in both the developed and the developing world. Hence there exists no global 'best practice' towards which lead firms in GPNs can orient their behaviour. Furthermore, firms in this industry have been more confined to national sales than most other consumer goods industries, due to impediments to cultural acceptance of foreign styles, and differences in sizing and climatic conditions. For both these reasons, the relatively strong shaping of firms' practices and structures by national capitalisms is probably more pronounced than would be the case in other industries where GPNs are common, such as in the car or in the electronics industry.

References

AAFA (American Apparel and Footwear Association) 2004, *Trends: A Compilation of Statistical Information on the U.S. Apparel & Footwear Industries*. Annual 2003 edition. Arlington, VA: AAFA.

—— 2006, *Trends: A Compilation of Statistical Information on the U.S. Apparel & Footwear Industries*. Annual 2005 edn. Arlington, VA: AAFA.

Abernathy, F. H., Dunlop, J. T., Hammond, J. H., and Weil, D. 1999, *A Stitch in Time: Lean Retailing and the Transformation of Manufacturing—Lessons from the Apparel and Textile Industry*. Oxford: Oxford University Press.

—— Volpe, A., and Weil, D. 2006, 'The future of the apparel and textile industries: prospects and choices for public and private actors', *Environment and Planning A*, 38, 12: 2207–32.

Adhikari, R. and Yamamoto, Y. 2007, 'The textile and clothing industry: adjusting to the post-quota world', United Nations (ed.), *Industrial Development for the 21st Century: Sustainable Development Perspectives*. Geneva: United Nations Department of Economic and Social Affairs, 183–234.

Adler, U. 2003, Suche nach Kernkompetenzen als Daueraufgabe—gibt es Grenzen der Produktionsverlagerung? Bekleidungsindustrie mit Zukunft, 65–78. IG Metall: Report on a conference organised by Textil- und Kleidungsverband Nordwest and IG Metall in Halle, Westphalia. 26 November, Frankfurt.

—— 2004, 'Structural change: the dominant feature in the economic development of the German textile and clothing industries'. Paper presented at the workshop on 'The European Clothing Industry: Meeting the Competitive Challenge, Centre for European Research in Employment and Human Resources', with the *Journal of Fashion Marketing and Management*, Ecole Superieure de Commerce, Toulouse, France, 26–27 February. Paper accessed at www.emeraldinsight.com/1361–2026.htm

Ahmad, M. 2007, 'Choices for developing countries in setting national brand strategies'. Presentation by the ITCB Executive Director to the 2nd China (Dalian) International Garment and Textile Fair, Dalian, 28 August. Accessed at http://www.itcb.org.

Aldridge, A. 2004, *Consumption*. Cambridge: Polity Press.

Amable, B. 2003, *The Diversity of Modern Capitalism*. Oxford: Oxford University Press.

Amiti, M. and Freund, C. 2007, 'China's export boom', *Finance & Development*, 44, 3 (September). Accessed at http://www.imf.org/external/pubs/ft/fandd/2007/09/amiti.htm

Appelbaum, R. 2008, 'Giant transnational contractors in East Asia: emergent trends in global supply chains', *Competition and Change*, 12, 1: 69–87.

—— Bonacich, E., and Quan, K. 2005, 'The end of apparel quotas: a faster race to the bottom?'. Unpublished paper, February, Global International Studies Program, University of California, Santa Barbara.

Arvidson, A. 2006, 'Brand management and the productivity of consumption', J. Brewer and F. Trentmann (eds.), *Consuming Culture, Global Perspectives: Historical Trajectories, Transnational Exchanges*. Oxford: Berg, 71–94.

Arvind Mills 2007, *Annual Report 2006–7*. Accessed at http://www.arvindmills.com/pdf/annaul_finacial_reporting/annual_report_06_07_unabridged.pdf

Ascoly, N. 2003, 'Prices in the global garment industry', Report of the International Seminar held by Clean Clothes Campaign and International Restructuring Education Network Europe, 20 February, Muehlheim, Germany.

—— Dent, K., and de Haan, E. 2004, *Critical Issues for the Garment Industry*. Amsterdam: SOMO (Centre for Research on Multinational Corporations).

Asian Focus Group 2005, 'China says no to developed countries' corporate social responsibility', *Asian Analysis*, February: 1–3.

Bachman, R. (ed.) 1989, *Romania: A Country Study*. Washington, DC: GPO for the Library of Congress. Accessed at http://countrystudies.us/romania

Baden, S. and Velia, M. 2002, *Trade Policy, Retail Markets and Value Chain Restructuring in the EU Clothing Sector*. Brighton: Poverty Research Unit, University of Sussex.

Bair, J. and Dussel Peters, E. 2006, 'Global commodity chains and endogenous growth: export dynamism and development in Mexico and Honduras', *World Development*, 34, 2: 203–21.

—— and Gereffi, G. 2002, 'NAFTA and the apparel commodity chain: corporate strategies, interfirm networks, and industrial upgrading', G. Gereffi, D. Spener and J. Bair (eds.), *Free Trade and Uneven Development: The North American Apparel Industry after NAFTA*. Philadelphia, PA: Temple University, 23–52.

—— —— 2003, 'Upgrading, uneven development and jobs in the North American apparel industry', *Global Networks*, 3, 2: 143–69.

—— Spener, D., and Gereffi, G. 2002, 'NAFTA and uneven development in the North American apparel industry', G. Gereffi, D. Spener and J. Bair (eds.), *Free Trade and Uneven Development: The North American Apparel Industry after NAFTA*. Philadelphia, PA: Temple University, 327–40.

Baldone, S., Sdogati, F., and Tajoli, L. 2000, 'International fragmentation of production and competitiveness in the textile and apparel industry'. Paper presented at the Second Annual Conference of the European Trade Study Group, Glasgow, 15–17 September.

Bargawi, O. 2005, 'Cambodia's garment industry—origins and future prospects', ESAU Working Paper 13, Overseas Development Institute, London, June.

Barth, K. and Hartmann, M. 2003, 'Germany', S. Howe (ed.), *Retailing in the European Union: Structures, Competition and Performance*. London: Routledge, 56–80

BATC 2003, *Trend Data 2002*. London: British Apparel and Textile Confederation.

Baudrillard, J. 1988, 'Consumer culture', *Selected Writings*. Cambridge: Polity Press.

BBI (Bundesverband Bekleidungsindustrie 2002) *Jahresbericht 2001/2002*. Cologne: BBI.

Bennett, M. 2006, 'Lesotho's export textiles & garment industry', H. Jauch and R. Traub-Merz (eds.), *The Future of the Textile and Clothing Industry in Sub-Saharan Africa*. Bonn: Friedrich-Ebert-Stiftung, 165–77.

Benson, J. 1994, *The Rise of Consumer Society in Britain*. London: Longman.

Bensusan, G. 2004, 'A new scenario for Mexican trade unions: changes in the structure of political and economic opportunities', K. Middlebrook (ed.), *Dilemmas of Political Change in Mexico*. London: Institute of Latin American Studies, 237–85.

Berger, S. 1989, 'The textile industry', M. L. Dertouzos, R. K. Lester and R. M. Solow (eds.), *Made in America: Regaining the Competitive Edge*. Cambridge, MA: MIT Press.

—— 2005, *How We Compete*. New York: Doubleday.

Bickerton, I. 1999, *Fashion Retailing in Europe*. London: FT Retailer Consumer., FT Business Ltd.

Birnbaum, D. 2000, *Birnbaum's Global Guide to Winning the Great Garment War*. Hong Kong: Third Horizon Press.

—— 2004, 'The rise and fall of the garment industries in Mexico and the Caribbean Basin', *Textile Outlook International*, July–August: 12–25.

Bloecker, A. 2005, 'Upgrading/downgrading and working conditions in global value chains'. Paper presented at the workshop on 'Governance of Value Chains by Retailers'. Wissenschaftszentrum, Berlin, 16–17 September.

—— and Wortmann, M. 2005, 'Strukturwandel und internationale Beschaffung im Einzelhandel mit Bekleidung', *Prokla, Zeitschrift für kritische Sozialwissenschft*, 138, 35, 1: 91–109.

Bonacich, E. and Applebaum, R. 2000, *Behind the Label: Inequality in the Los Angeles Garment Industry*. Berkeley, CA: University of California Press.

Bourdieu, P. 1984, *Distinction: A Social Critique of the Judgement of Taste*. London: Routledge and Kegan Paul.

Brettschneider, U. 2006, 'Challenges in global textile and apparel sourcing: focus on Li & Fung', *Textile Outlook International*, 124 (July–August): 10–28.

Brewer, J. and Trentmann, F. 2006, 'Introduction. Space, time and value in consuming societies', J. Brewer and F. Trentmann (eds.), *Consuming Culture, Global Perspectives: Historical Trajectories, Transnational Exchanges*. Oxford: Berg, 1–17.

Brocklehurst, G. and Anson, R. 2007, 'Trends in EU textile and clothing imports', *Textile Outlook International*, 130 (July–August): 60–116.

Brown, D., Deardorff, A. V., and Stern, R. 2002, 'The effects of multinational production on wages and working conditions in developing countries', Discussion Paper No. 483, Research Seminar in International Economics, School of Public Policy, University of Michigan, 30 August.

Brown, J. S. 2001, 'Confessions of a Sweatshop Inspector in China'. Accessed on 28 March 2007 at http://list.jca.apc.org/public/asia-apec/2001-December/001833.html

BTE (Bundesverband des Deutschen Textileinzelhandels) 2006, *Statistik-Report Textileinzelhandel 2006*. Cologne: BTE 1–193.

Bulut, T. and Lane, C. 2008, 'Who is going to civilise the market? Labour standards rights and the accountability of transnational capital'. Unpublished manuscript. Available from C. Lane, Department of Sociology, University of Cambridge.

Business Eastern Europe 2007, 'Looking to the future: Romania', *Business Eastern Europe* 10 September.

Cadot, O., Estevadeoral, A., Suwa-Eisenmann, A., and Verdier, T. 2006, *The Origin of Goods: Rules of Origin in Regional Trade Agreements*. Oxford: Oxford University Press.

CAPITB Trust 2001, *Sector Workforce Development Plan for the UK Clothing Industry 2001–2005*. Leeds: CAPITB Trust.

Carillo, J., Hualde, A., and Almaraz, A. 2002, 'Commodity chains and industrial organization in the apparel industry in Monterey and Ciudad Juarez', G. Gereffi, D. Spener, and J. Bair (eds.), *Free Trade and Uneven Development: The North American Apparel Industry after NAFTA*. Philadelphia, PA: Temple University, 181–99.

Carr, M. and Chen, M. 2004, 'Globalization, social exclusion and work: with special reference to informal employment and gender', Working Paper No. 20, Policy Integration Department, World Commission on the Social Dimension of Globalization. Geneva: ILO.

Cavanagh, J. 1981, 'The new wave of protectionism among western nations hurts third world producers, not multinationals', *The Multinational Monitor: Fibers and Textiles*, 2, 8.

CCC (Clean Clothes Campaign) 2005, *Workers' Voices: The Situation of Women in the Eastern European and Turkish Garment Industries*. Meissen: Evangelische Akademie and Clean Clothes Campaign.

CEC (Commission of the European Communities) 2003, 'The future of the textiles and clothing sector in the enlarged Europe', Commission Staff Working Paper, Brussels. Accessed at http://ec.europa.eu/enterprise/textile/documents/sec2003_1345en.pdf

Cepni, E. 2003, *The Economy of Turkey in Retrospect*. Istanbul: Beta Basim.

CEPS/WIIW 2005, *Final Report. The Textiles and Clothing Industry in an Enlarged Community and the Outlook of Candidate States. Part 1 Supplement: Turkey*. London: CEPS/WIIW, 113.

Cerny, P. 2000, 'Political globalization and the competition state', R. Stubbs and G. Underhill (eds.), *Political Economy and the Changing Global Order*, 2nd edn. New York: Oxford University Press, 300–09.

CFO (Comité Fronterizo de Obreras) 2006, 'A few facts about the maquiladora industry'. Based on INEGI statistics, published in November 2006. Accessed on 17 January 2007 at http://www.cfomaquiladoras.org/english%20site/numeralia.en.html

Chan, A. 2002, 'Labor in waiting: the international trade union movement and China', *New Labor Forum* Fall/Winter: 54–9.

—— 2003, 'A "race to the bottom": globalisation and China's labour standards', *China Perspectives*, 46 (March–April): 41–50.

—— 2006, 'Realities and possibilities for Chinese trade unionism', C. Phelan (ed.), *The Future of Organised Labour Global Perspectives*. Bern: Peter Lang, 275–304.

—— and Ross, R. J. S. 2003, 'Racing to the bottom: international trade without a social clause', *Third World Quarterly*, 24, 6: 1011–28.

Chen, M. and Chan, A. 2004, 'Employee and union inputs into occupational health and safety measures in Chinese factories', *Social Science and Medicine*, 58: 1231–45.

China Daily 2005, 'Local textile sales will offset export curbs', *China Daily* 23 May.

—— 2007, 'Youngor buys US shirt firm', *China Daily* 14 December.

—— 2008, 'Minimum wage hike planned to plug labour shortage', *China Daily*, 10 August. Accessed on 10. August 2008 at http://.www.chinadaily.comcn/china/2008–06–21/content_6784122.htm

China Economic Review 2006, 'Textiles: onward and upward', *China Economic Review* May.

China Textile and Clothing Trade 2003/04, Review and Outlook. Accessed on 1 November 2006 at http://64.233.183.104/search?q = cache:ZILt59ebs7MJ:www.unicom.com.cn/sparkiceApp/upload/new

Citizens Development Corp (CDC) 2003, *Assessment Report: Textile Sector*. Bucharest: Citizens Development Corp for the CHF Consortium in Romania. Accessed at www.chfro.org/pdf/textile%20sector%20Assessment.pdf

Clark, E. and Tucker, R. 2006, 'Changes sweeping global manufacturing', *Women's Wear Daily*, 14 March.

Clean Clothes Campaign 2001, *Romania—Factory Visits*. Accessed at www.cleanclothes.org/publications/easteuroma.htm

Cohen, L. 1998, 'The new deal and the making of citizen consumers', S. Strasser, C. McGovern and M. Judt (eds.), *Getting and Spending: European and American Consumer Societies in the Twentieth Century*. Cambridge: Cambridge University Press, 111–26.

Cohen, L. 2003, *A Consumers' Republic: The Politics of Mass Consumption in Postwar America*. New York, NY: Alfred Knopf.

Collins, J. 2003, *Threads. Gender, Labor and Power in the Global Apparel Industry*. Chicago, IL: Chicago University Press.

Corcoran, C. T. 2004, 'How star retailers turn fast', *Women's Wear Daily*, 14 November.

Crestanello, P. and Tattara, G. 2006, 'Connections and competences in the governance of the value chain: how industrial countries keep their competitive power', Working Paper in Technology Governance and Economic Dynamics No.7, Tallinn University of Technology, Tallinn.

Crewe, L. and Lowe, M. 1996, 'United colours? Globalization and localization in fashion retailing', N. Wrigley and M. Lowe (eds.), *Retailing, Consumption and Capital: Towards the New Retail Geography*. London: Longman Group.

Crouch, C. 2005, *Capitalist Diversity and Change: Recombinant Governance and Institutional Entrepreneurs*. Oxford: Oxford University Press.

Czaban, L., Hocevar, M., Jaclic, M., and Whitley, R. 2003, 'Path dependence and contractual relations in emergent capitalism: contrasting state socialist legacies and inter-firm cooperation in Hungary and Slovenia', *Organization Studies*, 24, 1: 7–28.

Datamonitor 2005a, 'The Gap, Inc.—Report'. Accessed via Factiva on 7 May 2005.

Datamonitor 2005b, 'The Gap, Inc.—SWOT Analysis', Datamonitor Company Profiles. Accessed via Factiva on 22 October 2005.

De Grazia, V. 1998, 'Changing consumption regimes in Europe, 1930–1970', S. Strasser, C. McGovern and M. Judt (eds.), *Getting and Spending: European and American Consumer Societies in the Twentieth Century*. Cambridge: Cambridge University Press, 59–84.

De Meyer, A., Mar, P., Richter, F.-J., and Williamson, P. 2005, *Global Future: The Next Challenge for Asian Business*. Singapore: John Wiley & Sons.

Deeg, R. and Jackson, G. 2007, 'Towards a more dynamic theory of capitalist variety', *Socio-Economic Review*, 5, 1: 149–80.

Der Spiegel 2008, 'Im Osten mehr Glitzer', *Der Spiegel*, 15 September: 92.

Dialog Textil 2006, 'Ups and downs for 10 years', *Dialog Textil*, October. Accessed at www.dialogtextil.ro

——2007, 'Only 35% of factories in the light industry have unions', *Dialog Textil*, July–August. Accessed at www.dialogtextil.ro

Dicken, P. 2003, *Global Shift: Reshaping the Global Economic Map in the 21st Century*. London: Sage.

——2007, *Global Shift: Mapping the Changing Contours of the Global Economy*, 5th edn. London: Sage.

——and Hassler, M. 2000, 'Organizing the Indonesian clothing industry in the global economy: the role of business networks', *Environment and Planning A*, 32: 263–80.

——Kelly, P. F., Olds, K., and Yeung, H. 2001, 'Chains and networks, territories and scales: towards a relational framework for analysing the global economy', *Global Network*, 1, 2: 89–112.

Divjak, C. 2008, 'China enacts new labour law amid rising discontent', World Socialist Web Site published by the International Committee of the Fourth International, 6 February 2008. Accessed on 7 August 2008 at http://www.wsws.org/articles/2008/feb2008/clab-f06.shtml

Djelic, M.-L. and Ainamo, A. 2005, 'The telecom industry as cultural industry? The transposition of fashion logics into the field of mobile telephony', C. Jones and P. H. Thornton (eds.), *Transformation in Cultural Industries. Research in the Sociology of Organizations*, Vol. 23. Amsterdam: Elsevier 45–80.

——and Quack, S. (eds.) 2003, *Globalization and Institutions*. Cheltenham: Edward Elgar.

Doeringer, P. 2005, 'Can the US apparel industry survive globalism?' Paper presented at the conference on Organisational Configurations and Locational Choices of Firms: Responses to Globalisation in Different Industry and Institutional Environments. Cambridge, UK, 14–15 April.

Doeringer, P. and Crean, S. 2006, 'Can fast fashion save the US apparel industry?' *Socio-Economic Review*, 4, 3: 353–78.

Donath, P. 2004, Personal Communication to C. Lane, IG Metall (Union), 7 January.

Dow Jones Newswires 2005, *Dow Jones Newswires* 26 October.

Dunford, M. 2001, 'The changing profile and map of the EU textile and clothing industry', typescript, School of European Studies, University of Sussex.

Dunford, M. and Greco, L. 2005, *After the Three Italies*. Oxford: Blackwell.

Dussel Peters, E. 2004, 'Conditions and evolution of employment and wages in Mexico', *Sustainable Economic Development*, April. Essay for the Jus Semper Global Alliance, The Living Wages North and South Initiative.

—— 2005, 'Economic opportunities and challenges posed by China for Mexico and Central America, German Development Institute (DIE) Studies 8. Bonn: DIE.

—— 2008, 'GCCs and development: a conceptual and empirical review', *Competition and Change*, 12, 1: 11–28.

—— Duran, C. R., and Piore, M. 2002, 'Learning and the limits of foreign partners as teachers', G. Gereffi, D. Spener and J. Bair (eds.), *Free Trade and Uneven Development; The North American Apparel Industry after NAFTA*. Philadelphia, PA: Temple University, 224–45.

Economist 2003, 'Reinventing the store', *Economist*, 22 November: 89–91

—— 2008, 'The sun sets on Cotonou', *Economist*, 5 January.

Edwards, T. and Ferner, A. 2004, 'Multinationals, reverse diffusion and national business systems', *Management International Review*, Special issue 1: 49–79.

EMDA (East Midlands Development Agency) 2001, *Developing the Clothing and Textile Cluster in the East Midlands*. Nottingham: EMDA, August.

Esbenshade, J. 2004, *Monitoring Sweatshops: Workers, Consumers and the Global Apparel Industry*. Philadelphia, PA: Temple University Press.

Estevadeoral, A. and Suominen, K. 2006, 'Mapping and measuring rules of origin around the world', O. Cadot, A. Estevadeoral, A. Suwa-Eisenmann and T. Verdier (eds.), *The Origin of Goods: Rules of Origin in Regional Trade Agreements*. Oxford: Oxford University Press, 69–113.

Euratex 2002, 'Evolution of the textile and clothing industry in the European Union between 1996 and 2000'. Bulletin No. 5, 18–159, Euratex, Brussels.

Euromonitor International 2007a, 'Clothing and Footwear Retailers—USA' 10 May.

—— 2007b, 'Retailing in the United Kingdom', *Euromonitor International*.

European Commission 2005, 'Generalised System of Preferences: EU "GSP + " granted to an additional 15 developing countries', Brussels, 21 December. Accessed at http://trade.ec.europa.eu/doclib/docs/2005/december/tradoc_126738.pdf

Evans, P. B. 1985, 'Transnational linkages and the role of the state', P. B. Evans, D. Rueschemeyer and T. Skocpol (eds.), *Bringing the State Back In*. Cambridge: Cambridge University Press, 192–227.

—— Rueschemeyer, D., and Skocpol, T. (eds.) 1985, *Bringing the State Back In*. Cambridge: Cambridge University Press.

Evgeniev, E. 2006, 'European core, semi-periphery and periphery in the context of the European Enlargement: the case of the textile and apparel industry'. Paper presented at the 18th Annual Conference of the Society for the Advancement of Socio-Economics, Trier, 30 June–2 July.

Faust, M. 2005, 'Reorganization and relocation in the German fashion industry'. Paper presented at the conference on 'Organisational Configurations and Locational Choices of Firms: Responses to Globalisation in Different Industry and Institutional

Environments', Cambridge, 14–15 April. Goettingen: Soziologisches Forschungsinstitut (SOFI) an der Georg-August-Universität.

——Voskamp, U., and Wittke, V. 2004, 'Globalization and the future of national systems: exploring patterns of industrial reorganization and relocation in an enlarged Europe', M. Faust, U. Voskamp and V. Wittke, V. (eds.), *European Industrial Restructuring in a Global Economy*. Goettingen: Soziologisches Forschungsinstitut (SOFI) an der Georg-August-Universität.

fDi (Foreign Direct Investment) 2005, 'Turkey changes tack', fDi, 1–3, 7 February. Accessed on 5 August 2008 at http://www.fdimagazine.com/news/fullstory.php/aid/1142/Turkey_changes_tack.html

Feenstra, R. 1998, 'Integration of trade and disintegration of production in the global economy', *Journal of Economic Perspectives*, 12, 4: 31–50.

FEPAIUS 2006, *Romania: Textile-Leather Industry*. Bucharest: Ministry of Economy and Commerce, FEPAIUS.

Ferenschild, S. and Wick, I. 2004, 'Global game of cuffs and collars', Südwindtexte 14. Published by Südwind Institut für Ökonomie und Ökumene and Ökumenisches Netz. Rhein Mosel Saar: Siegburg, Neuwied.

Ferner, A., Quintanilla, J., and Sánchez Runde, C. (eds.) 2006, *Multinationals, Institutions and the Construction of Transnational Practices*. Basingstoke: Palgrave MacMillan.

Fine, B. and Leopold, E. 1993, *The World of Consumption*. London: Routledge.

Fiscal Policy Institute 2003, *NYC's Garment Industry: A New Look?* New York, August.

Fox, J. 2004, 'Assessing bi-national civil society coalitions: lessons from the Mexico-US experience', K. Middlebrook (ed.), *Dilemmas of Political Change in Mexico*. London: Institute of Latin American Studies, 466–548.

François, J. F., McDonald, B., and Nordström, H. 1997, 'The Uruguay Round: a global general equilibrium assessment', D. Robertson (ed.), *East Asian Trade after the Uruguay Round*. Cambridge: Cambridge University Press, 101–30.

Froebel, F. J., Heinrichs, J., and Kreye, O. 1980, *The New International Division of Labour*. Cambridge: Cambridge University Press.

Fung, A., O'Rourke, D., and Sabel, C. 2001, 'Realising labour standards', *Boston Review*, February. Accessed at http://bostonreview.net/BR26.1/fung.html

Fung, V. K., Fung, W. K., and Wind, J. 2007, *Competing in a Flat World: Building Enterprises for a Borderless World*. Upper Saddle River, NJ: Wharton School Publishing.

Gallagher, M. E. 2005, *Contagious Capitalism: Globalization and the Politics of Labour in China*. Princeton: Princeton University Press.

Gambini, G. 2007, 'EU-25 trade in textiles 2005', *Statistics in Focus: External Trade, Eurostat*, Issue 63/2007.

Gap Inc. 2004, *Social Responsibility Report 2003*, 21 May. Accessed at http://www.gapinc.com/social_resp.htm

Gardner, C. and Sheppard, J. 1989, *Consuming Passion: The Rise of Retail Culture*. London: Unwin Hyman.

Gereffi, G. 1994, 'The organization of buyer-driven global commodity chains: how US retailers shape overseas production networks', G. Gereffi and M. Korzeniewicz (eds.), *Commodity Chains and Global Capitalism*. Westport, CT: Praeger, 95–122.

——1999, 'International trade and industrial upgrading in the apparel commodity chain', *Journal of International Economics*, 48, 1: 37–70.

——2005, 'The global economy: organization, governance and development', N. J. Smelser and R. Swedberg (eds.), *The Handbook of Economic Sociology*. Princeton, NJ: Princeton University Press, 160–82.

Gereffi, G. and Kaplinsky, R. (eds.) 2001, 'The value of value chains: spreading the gains from globalization', *IDS Bulletin* 32, 3, Special issue.

—— and Memedovic, O. 2003, 'The global apparel value chain: what prospects for upgrading by developing countries', Vienna: United Nations Development Organization, 1–36.

—— Korzeniewicz, M., and Korzeniewicz, R. P. 1994, 'Introduction: global commodity chains', G. Gereffi and M. Korzeniewicz (eds.), *Commodity Chains and Global Capitalism*. Westport, CT: Praeger, 3–14.

—— Garcia-Johnson, R., and Sasser, E. 2001, 'The NGO-industrial complex', *Foreign Policy*, 125: 56–65.

—— Martinez, M., and Bair, J. 2002, 'Torreon: the new blue jeans capital of the world', G. Gereffi, D. Spener and J. Bair (eds.), *Free Trade and Uneven Development: The North American Apparel Industry after NAFTA*. Philadelphia, PA: Temple University, 205–23.

—— Humphrey, J., and Sturgeon, T. 2005, 'The governance of global value chains', *Review of International Political Economy*, 12, 1: 78–104.

Gesamtverband Textil + Mode 2006, *Statistics for the Textile and Apparel Industry*. Eschborn: Gesamtverband der deutschen Textil- und Modeindustrie e.V., November.

Ghinararu, C. and Mocanu, C. 2006, 'Upgrading the textiles, clothing and footwear sector'. European Foundation for the Improvement of Living and Working Conditions. Accessed at http://www.eurofound.eu.int/ewco/2006/05/RO0605NU03.htm

Gibbon, P. 2002, 'South Africa and the global commodity chain for clothing: export performance and constraints', CDR Working Paper 02.7, Centre for Development Research, Copenhagen.

—— 2008, 'Governance, entry barriers, upgrading: a re-interpretation of some GVC concepts from the experience of African clothing exports', *Competition and Change*, 12, 1: 29–48.

Goodin, R. E. 2003, 'Choose your capitalism?', *Comparative European Politics*, 1: 203–13.

Grant, R. M. 1996, 'Prospering in dynamically-competitive environments: organizational capability as knowledge integration', *Organization Science*, 7, 4: 375–87.

Gritsch, M. 2005, 'The nation state and economic globalization: soft geopolitics and increased state autonomy', *Review of International Political Economy*, 12, 1: 1–25.

Groemling, M. and Matthes, J. 2003, *Globalisierung und Strukturwandel der deutschen Textil- und Bekleidungsindustrie*. Cologne: Deutscher Institutsverlag.

Gruben, W. C. 2006, 'NAFTA, trade diversion and Mexico's textiles and apparel boom and bust', *Southwest Economy*, 5 (September/October): 1–4. Federal Reserve Bank of Dallas.

GTZ 2006, *Textile and Clothing Industry, Romania 2006*. Commissioned by Bundesministerium für wirtschaftliche Zusammenarbeit und Entwicklung. Berlin: GTZ.

Guardian 2007, 'Boss quits as Asda's George loses its magic', 11 August: 41.

Guthrie, D. 1999, *Dragon in a Three-Piece Suit: The Emergence of Capitalism in China*. Princeton, NJ: Princeton University Press.

Hall, A. P. and Gingerich, D. W. 2004, 'Varieties of capitalism and institutional complementarities in the macroeconomy: an empirical analysis'. Max-Planck-Institut für Gesellschaftsforschung, Discussion Paper 04/5, Cologne.

Hall, P. 2007, 'The evolution of varieties of capitalism in Europe', B. Hancké, M. Rhodes and M. Thatcher (eds.), *Beyond Varieties of Capitalism: Conflict, Contradiction and Complementarities in the European Economy*. Oxford: Oxford University Press, 39–88.

—— and Soskice, D. 2001, 'An introduction to varieties of capitalism', P. Hall and D. Soskice (eds.), *Varieties of Capitalism: The Institutional Foundations of Comparative Advantage*. Oxford: Oxford University Press, 1–72.

Hamel, G. and Prahalad, C. K. 1994, *Competing for the Future*. Boston, MA: Harvard Business School Press.

Hancké, B., Rhodes, M., and Thatcher, M. 2007, 'Introduction: beyond varieties of capitalism', B. Hancké, M. Rhodes and M. Thatcher (eds.), *Beyond Varieties of Capitalism: Conflict, Contradiction and Complementarities in the European Economy*. Oxford: Oxford University Press, 3–38.

Hanson, G. H. 2005, 'Emigration, labor supply, and earnings in Mexico', National Bureau of Economic Research, Working Paper No. 11412. Accessed on 11 February 2007 at http://.www.nber.org/papers/w11412.pdf

Harris Infosource undated, *Apparel—Clothing Manufacturing Industry Report*. Twinsburg: Ohio, 1–13.

Harris & Moure 2007, 'China's new labor law: enforcement is the key', China Law Blog by Harris & Moure, 2 July 2007. Accessed on 7 August 2008 at http://www.chinalawblog.com/2007/07/chinas_new_labor_law_enforceme_1.html

Hassler, M. 2003, 'The global clothing production system', *Global Networks*, 3, 4: 513–53.

Haupt, H.-G. 2002, *Konsum und Handel: Europa im 19. und 20. Jahrhundert*. Goettingen: Vandenhoek und Ruprecht.

Hay, C. 2005, 'Two can play at that game... Or can they? Varieties of capitalism, varieties of institutionalism', D. Coates (ed.), *Varieties of Capitalism, Varieties of Approaches*. London: Palgrave, 106–21.

Heidenreich, M. 1990, *Nationale Muster betrieblichen Strukturwandels. Am Beispiel der französischen und bundesdeutschen Bekleidungsindustrie*. Frankfurt: Campus.

Held, D., McGrew, A., Goldblatt, D., and Perraton, J. 1999, *Global Transformations*. Cambridge: Polity Press.

Henderson, J., Dicken, P., Hess, M., Coe, N., and Yeung, H. 2002, 'Global production networks and the analysis of economic development', *Review of International Political Economy*, 9, 3: 436–64.

Herrigel, G. and Wittke, V. 2005, 'Varieties of vertical disintegration: the global trend towards heterogeneous supply relations and the reproduction of difference in US and German manufacturing', G. Morgan, R. Whitley and E. Moen (eds.), *Changing Capitalisms? Internationalization, Institutional Change, and Systems of Economic Organization*. Oxford: Oxford University Press, 312–51.

Hirst, P. and Thompson, G. 1996, *Globalization in Question*. Cambridge: Polity Press.

Ho, P. 2007, 'Small garment firms facing the chop', *The Standard*, 4 June.

Hoekman, B. and Kostecki, M. 1995, *The Political Economy of the World Trading System: From GATT to WTO*. Oxford: Oxford University Press.

Hollingsworth, J. R. and Boyer, R. 1997, 'Continuities and changes in social systems of production: the cases of Japan, Germany and the United States', J. R. Hollingsworth and R. Boyer (eds.), *Contemporary Capitalism: The Embeddedness of Institutions*. Cambridge: Cambridge University Press, 265–310.

Hoover's Company Records 2005, 'Jones Apparel Group'. Accessed on 12 September 2005 from Factiva.

Hopkins, T. K. and Wallerstein, I. 1977, 'Patterns of development of the modern world-system', *Review*, 1, 2: 111–45.

Howe, S. 2003, 'United Kingdom', S. Howe (ed.), *Retailing in the European Union: Structures, Competition and Performance*. London: Routledge, 155–87.

ICFTU (International Confederation of Free Trade Unions) 1996, 'Trade Union Campaign for a Social Clause'. Appendix on Mexico, 1–8. Accessed on 22 January 2007 at http://www.itcilo.it/english/actrav/telearn/global/ilo/frame/epzicftu.htm

References

IFM (Institut Français de la Mode) and partners 2004, *Study on the Implications of the 2005 Trade Liberalisation in the Textile and Clothing Sector, Consolidated Report*, Paris: European Commission.

ILO (International Labour Organization) 1996, 'Globalization of the footwear, textiles and clothing industries', TMFTCI/1996, Sectoral Activities Programme. Geneva: ILO.

—— 2005, 'Promoting fair globalization in textiles and clothing in a post-MFA environment', TMTC-PMFA/2005. Geneva: ILO.

INSAT (Inside Southern African Trade) 2005, 'Stripped of quotas', 1: 12–13, May. Accessed at http://www.satradehub.org/assets/images/newsletters/INSAT%201%20E-mail.pdf.

ITKIB (Istanbul Textile and Apparel Exporters' Association) 2006, 'Turkish textile and apparel industry', February. Powerpoint presentation received from ITKIB, May.

Jacoby, S. 2005, *The Embedded Corporation: Corporate Governance and Employment Relations in Japan and the United States*. Princeton, NJ: Princeton University Press.

Jefferys, J. B. 1954, *Retail Trading in Britain, 1850–1950*. Cambridge: Cambridge University Press.

Jenkins, R. 2002, 'The political economy of codes of conduct', R. Jenkins, R. Pearson and G. Seyfang (eds.), *Corporate Responsibility and Labour Rights: Codes of Conduct in the Global Economy*. London: Earthscan Publications, 13–30.

Jin, H. and Qian, Y. 1998, 'Public versus private ownership of firms: evidence from rural China', *The Quarterly Journal of Economics*, 113, 3: 773–808.

JO-IN 2004, *Background Study on Turkey: Basic Information on Labor Conditions and Social Auditing in the Turkish Garment Industry*. İstanbul: JO-IN.

Jones, C. and Thornton, P. H. 2005, 'Introduction', C. Jones and P. H. Thornton (eds.), *Transformation in Cultural Industries. Research in the Sociology of Organizations*, Vol. 23. Amsterdam/San Diego/London: Elsevier, xi–xix.

Justice, D. H. 2002, 'The international trade union movement and the new codes of conduct', R. Jenkins, R. Pearson and G. Seyfang (eds.), *Corporate Responsibility and Labour Rights: Codes of Conduct in the Global Economy*. London: Earthscan Publications, 90–100.

Just-Style 2007, 'China: Fewer exporters bid for US textile quotas', *Just-Style*, 18 September.

—— 2007a, 'Are new EU textile trade barriers likely next year?' *Just-Style*, 16 October.

—— 2007b, 'Analysis: Duty-free access to the US doesn't add up', *Just-Style*, 5 November.

—— 2007c, 'Price cuts fuel Vietnam's apparel exports to the EU', *Just-Style*, 13 November.

—— 2008, 'US textile industry to take aim at China in 2008', *Just-Style*, 28 February.

Kamrava, M. 2004, 'The semi-formal sector and the Turkish political economy', *British Journal of Middle Eastern Studies*, 31: 63–87.

KATAG web site, Accessed 24 May 2007 at on http.//www.katag.de/standard/page.sys/115.htm

Kaya, E. S. 2004, *Turkey's Position within the Global Garment Industry*. Amsterdam: Centre for Research on Multinational Corporations (SOMO).

Keck, M. E. and Sikkink, K. 1998, *Activists beyond Borders; Advocacy Networks in International Politics*. Ithaca, NY: Cornell University Press.

Kessler, J. A. 2002, 'The impact of North American economic integration on the Los Angeles apparel industry', G. Gereffi, D. Spener and J. Bair (eds.), *Free Trade and Uneven Development: The North American Apparel Industry after NAFTA*. Philadelphia, PA: Temple University, 74–99.

KFAT (Knitwear, Footwear and Apparel Trades) et al. 2000, *UK Garment Workers Report*, Leicester: KFAT National Group on Homeworking, Women Working Worldwide and Labour Behind the Label Network.

King, L. P. and Szelenyi, I. 2005, 'Post-Communist economic systems', N. J. Smelser and R. Swedberg (eds.), *The Handbook of Economic Sociology*. Princeton: Princeton University Press, 205–32.

Kitschelt, H. and Streeck, W. 2004, 'From stability to stagnation: Germany at the beginning of the twenty-first century', H. Kitschelt and W. Streeck (eds.), *Germany: Beyond the Stable State*. London: Frank Cass, 1–36.

Klein, N. 2001, *No Logo: Taking Aim at the Brand Bullies*. London: Harper Collins.

Kogut, B. 1984, 'Normative observations on the international value-added chain and strategic groups', *Journal of International Business Studies*, 15, 2: 151–67.

Kolk, A., van Tulder, R., and Welters, C. 1999, 'International codes of conduct and corporate social responsibility: can transnational corporations regulate themselves?', *Transnational Corporations*, 8, 1: 151–212.

Koudal, P. and Long, V. W. 2005, 'The power of synchronization: the case of TAL Apparel Group', Deloitte Research Case Study, June.

Krishna, K. 2006, 'Understanding the rules of origin', O. Cadot, A. Estevadeoral, A. Suwa-Eisenmann and T. Verdier (eds.), *The Origin of Goods: Rules of Origin in Regional Trade Agreements*. Oxford: Oxford University Press, 19–34.

—— and Tan, L. H. 1997, 'The Multifibre Arrangement in practice: challenging the competitive framework', D. Robertson (ed.), *East Asian Trade after the Uruguay Round*. Cambridge: Cambridge University Press, 59–77.

Kwong, R. 2008, 'Chinese exporters shun flagging US dollar in favour of stronger rivals', *Financial Times*, 28 March.

Laing, L. 2001, 'Delighting in denim—a wonder fabric', *Pursuit: Clothing and Textile Magazine On-Line (South Africa)*, August-September. Accessed at http://www.pursuit.co.za/archive/augsep_denim.htm

Lane, C. and Bachmann, R. 1997, 'Cooperation in inter-firm relations in Britain and Germany: the role of social institutions', *British Journal of Sociology*, 48: 226–54.

Lee, C. K. 2007, 'Mapping the terrain of Chinese labor ethnography', C. K. Lee (ed.), *Working in China*. London: Routledge, 15–38.

Li & Fung Research Centre 2006, 'Textile and apparel clusters in China', Li & Fung Research Centre Industrial Cluster Series, 5, May.

Li, A. 2007, 'Good parenting helps Luen Thai', *South China Morning Post*, 10 march.

Low Pay Commission 2008, *National Minimum Wage: Low Pay Commission Report*. Accessed at http://www.lowpay.gov.uk/lowpay/rep_a_p_index.shtml

Magretta, J. 1998, 'Fast, global and entrepreneurial: supply chain management Hong Kong style—an interview with Victor Fung', *Harvard Business Review*, September–October: 103–14.

Mann, M. 1993, *The Sources of Social Power, Vol. II*. Cambridge: Cambridge University Press.

Marks & Spencer 2004, *Annual Review and Summary of Financial Statements*. London: Marks & Spencer.

—— 2005, *Annual Review and Summary of Financial Statements*. London: Marks & Spencer.

—— 2007, *Annual Review and Summary of Financial Statements*. London: Marks & Spencer.

Mayer, J. 2004, 'Not totally naked: textiles and clothing trade in a quota free environment', Discussion Paper No.176, UNCTAD, Geneva.

McGovern, C. 1998, 'Consumption and citizenship', S. Strasser, C. McGovern and M. Judt (eds.), *Getting and Spending: European and American Consumer Societies in the Twentieth Century*. Cambridge: Cambridge University Press, 17–36.

Middlebrook, K. 1995, *The Paradox of Revolution: Labor, the State and Authoritarianism in Mexico*. Baltimore: John Hopkins Press.

—— 2004, 'Mexico's democratic transitions: dynamics and prospects', K. Middlebrook (ed.), *Dilemmas of Political Change in Mexico*. London: Centre for Latin American Studies, 1–56.

Mitchell, T. 2008*a*, 'Shoe industry under pressure amid rising costs', *Financial Times*, 26 February.

—— 2008*b*, 'Margins squeeze bites into China textiles sector', *Financial Times*, 10 March.

—— 2008*c*, 'China Inc. looks beyond low costs', *Financial Times*, 11 March.

Moon, B. E. 2000, 'The United States and globalization', R. Stubbs and G. R. D. Underhill (eds.), *Political Economy and the Changing Global Order*, 2nd edn. Oxford: Oxford University Press, 342–51.

Morgan, G. 2001, 'The multinational firm: organizing across institutional and national divides', G. Morgan, P. H. Kristensen and R. Whitley (eds.), *The Multinational Firm*. Oxford: Oxford University Press, 1–26.

—— 2005, 'Introduction: changing capitalisms? Internationalization, institutional change, and systems of economic organization', G. Morgan, R. Whitley and E. Moen (eds.), *Changing Capitalisms? Internationalization, Institutional Change, and Systems of Economic Organization*. Oxford: Oxford University Press, 1–20.

—— Whitley, R., and Moen, E. (eds.) 2005, *Changing Capitalisms? Internationalization, Institutional Change, and Systems of Economic Organization*. Oxford: Oxford University Press.

Morokvasic, M. 1993, 'Immigrants in garment production in Paris and in Berlin', I. Light and P. Bachu (eds.), *Immigration and Entrepreneurship, Culture, Capital and Ethnic Networks*. London: Transaction Publishers, 75–95.

Morokvasic, M. Phizacklea, A., and Rudolph, H. 1986, 'Small firms and minority groups: contradictory trends in the French, German and British clothing industries', *International Sociology*, 1, 4: 397–419.

Morris, L. 2008, 'An uncertain victory for China's workers', *Yale Global Online*, 24 June. Accessed on 6 June 2008 at http://yaleglobal.yale.edu/display.article?id = 10983&gclid = CK2-uc_Q-5QCFQznlAodhmQoBA

Mungiu-Pippidi, A. 2006, 'Europeanization without decommunization: a case of elite conversion', D. Phinnemore (ed.), *The EU and Romania: Accession and Beyond*. London: The Federal Trust, 17–28.

Murray, J. 2002, 'Labour rights/corporate responsibilities: the role of ILO labour standards', R. Jenkins, R. Pearson and G. Seyfang (eds.), *Corporate Responsibility and Labour Rights: Codes of Conduct in the Global Economy*. London: Earthscan Publications, 31–42.

Myers, H. 2006, 'Trends in European retailing', *European Retail Digest*, 47: 7–15.

Nathan Associates, Inc. 2002, 'Changes in the global trade rules for textiles and apparel: implications for developing countries' Nathan Associates Inc. Research Report, Arlington, VA, 20 November.

Neidik, B. and Gereffi, G. 2006, 'Explaining Turkey's emergence and sustained competitiveness as a full-package supplier of apparel', *Environment and Planning A*, 38: 2285–303.

Ngai, P. 2005, *Made in China: Women Factory Workers in a Global Workplace*. Durham, NC, and Hong Kong: Duke University Press and Hong Kong University Press.

Nolan, P. 2001, *China and the Global Economy*. Houndmills: Palgrave.

Nordås, H. K. 2004, 'The global textile and clothing industry post the Agreement on Textiles and Clothing', Discussion Paper No.5, World Trade Organization, Geneva.

O'Rourke, D. 2000, 'Monitoring the monitors: a critique of PriceWaterhouseCoopers labor monitoring', 28 September. Accessed on 17 February 2007 at http://nature.berkeley.edu/orourke/PDF/pwc.pdf

—— 2003, 'Outsourcing regulation: analyzing nongovernmental systems of labor standards and monitoring', *The Policy Studies Journal*, 31, 1: 1–29.

—— and Brown, G. D. 2003, 'Experiments in transforming the global workplace: incentives for and impediments to improving workplace conditions in China', *International Journal of Occupational and Environmental Health*, 9: 378–85.

O'Sullivan, M. 2000, *Contests for Corporate Control*. Oxford: Oxford University Press.

OECD 2005a, *China. Economic Surveys*, 13. Paris: OECD.

—— 2005b, *Trade and Structural Adjustment: Embracing Globalization*. Paris: OECD.

Office of National Statistics (ONS) 2005, *Labour Market Trends*. Accessed at www.statistics.gov.uk/statbase/product.asp?vlnk = 550

Owen, N. and Cannon Jones, A. 2003, A comparative study of the British and Italian textile and clothing industries, *Economics Paper No.2*. London: DTI.

Oxborrow, L. 2005, 'Global or global? Restructuring in the UK apparel industry'. Paper presented at the conference on 'Organisational Configurations and Locational Choices of Firms: Responses to Globalisation in Different Industry and Institutional Environments'. Cambridge, 14–15 April.

Oxfam International 2004, *Trading Away our Rights: Women Working in Global Supply Chains*. Oxford: Oxfam International, 2–100.

Palan, R. and Abbott, J. 1996, *State Strategies in the Global Political Economy*. London: Pinter.

Palpacuer, F. 2002, 'Subcontracting networks in the New York City garment industry: changing characteristics in a global era', G. Gereffi, D. Spener and J. Bair (eds.), *Free Trade and Uneven Development: The North American Apparel Industry after NAFTA*. Philadelphia, PA: Temple University, 53–73.

—— 2006, 'Global network firms and global NGO networks: towards a new mode of regulation?' Paper presented at EURAM, Oslo, Norway, 17–20 May.

—— 2008, 'Bringing the social context back in: governance and wealth distribution in global commodity chains', *Economy and Society*, 37, 3: 393–419.

—— Gibbon, P., and Thomsen, L. 2004, 'New challenges for developing country suppliers in global clothing chains: a comparative European perspective', *World Development*, 33, 3: 409–30.

Penrose, E. 1959, *The Theory of the Growth of the Firm*. Oxford: Blackwell.

Petrovic, M. and Hamilton, G. G. 2005, 'Making global markets: Wal-Mart and its suppliers', N. Lichtenstein (ed.), *Wal-Mart: The Face of 21st Century Capitalism*. New York, NY: The New Press.

Phillips, P. 2005, 'Profile of the textile and clothing Industry in Turkey', *Textile Outlook International*, September–October, 148–83.

Phinnemore, D. and Light, D. (eds.) 2001, *Post-Communist Romania: Coming to Terms with Transition*. Houndmills: Palgrave.

Pickles, J., Smith, A., Bucek, M., Roukova, P., and Begg, R. 2006, 'Upgrading, changing competitive pressures, and diverse practices in the East and Central European apparel industry', *Environment and Planning A*, 38: 2305–24.

Porter, M. 1990, *The Competitive Advantage of Nations*. New York, NY: Free Press.

Powell, W. W. 1990, 'Neither market nor hierarchy: network forms of organization', *Research in Organizational Behaviour*, 12: 295–336.

Pringle, T. 2002, 'Industrial unrest in China: a labour movement in the making', *China Labour Bulletin*, 31 January: 1–7.

Pye, M. 2002, 'A comprehensive summary of skills requirements in the clothing, textiles, footwear and leather and furniture, furnishings and interiors industries'. Research undertaken by Pye Tait Ltd., Harrogate, for the Department for Education and Skills.

Quan, K. 2008, 'Use of global value chains by labor organizers', *Competition and Change*, 12, 1: 89–104.

Quinn, J. B., Doorley, T. L., and Paquette, P. C. 1991, 'Beyond products: service-based strategy', C. A. Montgomery and M. E. Porter (eds.), *Strategy: Seeking and Securing Competitive Advantage*. Boston, MA: Harvard Business Review, 301–14.

Ram, M. Jerrard, B. and Husband, J. 2002, 'West Midlands: still managing to survive', J. Rath (ed.), *Unravelling the Rag Trade: Immigrant Entrepreneurship in Seven World Cites*. Oxford: Berg, 73–87.

Radocevic, S. 2004, 'Central and East European electronics industry between foreign- and domestic-led modernisation', M. Faust, U. Voskamp, and V. Wittke (eds.), *European Industrial Restructuring in a Global Economy*. Goettingen: Soziologisches Forschungsinstitut an der Georg-August-Universität, 267–94.

Rath, J. (ed.) 2002, *Unravelling the Rag Trade: Immigrant Entrepreneurship in Seven World Cities*. Oxford: Berg

Retail Intelligence 2000*a*, *Department Stores in Europe*. London: Retail Intelligence.

—— 2000*b*, *Retailing in Germany*. London: Retail Intelligence.

Richardson, J. 1996, 'Vertical integration and rapid response in fashion apparel', *Organization Science*, 7, 4: 400–12.

Rigby, D. 1996, 'The future of European textiles: mill or heritage centre?', The George Douglas Memorial Lecture, Manchester Business School, 22 November.

Ritter, G. and Kocka, J. (eds.) 1982, *Deutsche Sozialgeschichte 1870–1914: Dokumente und Skizzen*, 3rd edn. Munic: C. H. Beck.

Rivoli, P. 2005, *The Travels of a T-Shirt in the Global Economy: An Economist Examines the Markets, Power and Politics of World Trade*. Hoboken, NJ: John Wiley & Sons.

Rizvi, S. M. 2007, 'The Role of Trust in Ethnic Business Networks: A Study of the Indian, Pakistani and Bangladeshi Communities in Leicester'. PhD thesis, submitted to University of Cambridge, Judge Business School.

Roberts, D. and Engardio, P. 2006, 'Secrets, lies and sweatshops', *Business Week*, 27 November: 50–8.

Rosenberg, M. 2005, 'Dreams, denim, and destiny', MA. thesis, submitted to Harvard University, 24 March.

—— 2006, 'Losing the crown to save the kingdom: radical reorganization and renewed export dynamism in Mexico's Torreon apparel cluster'. Unpublished typescript.

Ross, J. R. S. 2004, *Slaves to Fashion: Poverty and Abuse in the New Sweatshops*. Ann Arbor, MI: University of Michigan Press.

Ross, R. and Chan, A. 2002, 'From North-South to South-South: the true face of global competition', *Foreign Affairs*, September/October: 8–13.

Rudolph, H., Potz, P., and Bahn, C. 2005, *Metropolen Handeln: Einzelhandel zwischen Internationalisierung und Lokaler Regulierung*. Wiesbaden: Verlag für Sozialwissenschaften.

Ryberg, P. 2008, 'Investigation Nos. AGOA-002/AGOA-003: Commercial Availability of Fabric and Yarns in AGOA Countries'. Statement submitted to USITC by P. Ryberg,

President, The African Coalition for Trade Inc. Accessed at http://www.acttrade. org/images/4–6ACT_ITCstatement.pdf

Sajhou, J. P. 2005, *Promoting Fair Globalization in Textiles and Clothing in a Post-MFA Environment.* Geneva: International Labour Organization.

Salmon, W. J. and Cmar, K. A. 1987, 'Private labels are back in fashion', *Harvard Business Review*, May–June: 99–106.

Scheffer, M. 2006, 'Study on the application of value criteria for textile products in preferential rules of origin, final report'. Tender 06-H13, 20 December, Brussels.

Schmidt, V. 2002, *The Future of European Capitalism.* Oxford: Oxford University Press.

Scholte, J. A. 2000, *Globalization: A Critical Introduction.* London: Palgrave.

—— 2005, *Globalization: A Critical Introduction*, 2nd edn. London: Palgrave McMillan.

Schuessler, E. 2008, 'Strategische Prozesse und Persistenzen. Pfadabhängige Organisation der Wertschöpfung in der deutschen Bekleidungsindustrie?' Dissertation submitted to the Faculty of Economic Sciences, Free University Berlin, Germany.

Shaw, G. 1983, 'Trends in consumer behaviour and retailing', T. Wild (ed.), *Urban and Rural Change in West Germany.* London and Totowa, NJ: Croom Helm and Barnes and Noble Books, 108–29.

Shaw, L. and Hale, A. 2002, 'The emperor's new clothes: what codes mean for workers in the garment industry', R. Jenkins, R. Pearson and G. Seyfang (eds.), *Corporate Responsibility and Labour Rights: Codes of Conduct in the Global Economy.* London: Earthscan Publications, 101–12.

Shurtleff, E. 2003, 'Still wanted: truly component technical designers', *Bobbin*, 1 February, www.bobbin.com

Simmel, G. 1997, 'The philosophy of fashion', D. Frisby and M. Featherstone (eds.), *Simmel on Culture: Selected Writings.* London: Sage, 187–205.

Singhal, A., Agarwal, P., and Singh, V. 2004, 'A new era for global textile and clothing supply chains', *Textile Outlook International*, November–December, 121–42.

SIPPO (Swiss Import Promotion Programme) 2006, *Outerwear: Overview and Marketing Guide. Germany* 50–87. Accessed on 24 May 2007 at http://www.sippo.ch

Skillfast-UK 2006, *Analysis of the Gaps and Weaknesses in Current Workforce Development Activity.* Leeds: Skillfast-UK, January.

—— 2006a, *Assessment of Current Education and Training Provision for Apparel, Footwear, Textiles and Related Business in England.* Leeds: Skillfast-UK, February.

—— 2008, 'Research warns: lack of technical skills threatens London Fashion Week'. Press release, 11 February. Accessed at http://www.skillfast-uk.org/news.cfm?newsid = 181

Skocpol, T. 1985, 'Introduction', P. B. Evans, D. Rueschemeyer and T. Skocpol (eds.), *Bringing the State Back In.* Cambridge: Cambridge University Press, 3–37.

Smith, A. 2001, 'The transition to a market economy', D. Phinnemore and D. Light (eds.), *Post-Communist Romania: Coming to Terms with Transition.* Houndmills: Palgrave, 127–49.

—— 2006, 'The Romanian economy since 1989', D. Phinnemore (ed.), *The EU and Romania: Accession and Beyond.* London: The Federal Trust, 29–37.

SOMO (Center for Research on Multinational Corporations) 2003, 'Garment and textile production: focus on Turkey', SOMO Bulletin, 3, November. Amsterdam: SOMO.

—— 2004, 'The phase-out of the Multifiber Agreement', SOMO Bulletin on Issues in Garments and Textiles No.5, April. Amsterdam: SOMO. Accessed at www.clean-clothes.org/publications/04–04-somo.htm

Sorge, A. 2005, *The Global and the Local: Understanding the Dialectics of Business Systems.* Oxford: Oxford University Press.

Spener, D. 2002, 'The unravelling seam: NAFTA and the decline of the apparel industry in El Paso, Texas', G. Gereffi, D. Spener and J. Bair (eds.), *Free Trade and Uneven Development: The North American Apparel Industry after NAFTA*. Philadelphia, PA: Temple University Press, 139–60.

—— Gereffi, G., and Bair, J. 2002, 'Introduction: the apparel industry and North American economic integration', G. Gereffi, D. Spener and J. Bair (eds.), *Free Trade and Uneven Development: The North American Apparel Industry after NAFTA*. Philadelphia, PA: Temple University, 3–22.

Stalk, G., Evans, P., and Shulman, L. E. 1992, 'Competing on capabilities: the new rules of corporate strategy', *Harvard Business Review*, March–April: 57–69.

Stamm, A. 2004, *Value Chains for Development Policy: Challenges for Trade Policy and Promotion of Economic Development'* Eschborn: GTZ GmbH, Eschborn: 1–38. Commissioned by BM für wirtschaftliche Zusammenarbeit und Entwicklung.

Statistisches Bundesamt 2007, *Statistisches Jahrbuch 2007*. Wiesbaden: Statistisches Bundesamt, September.

Steedman, H. and Wagner, K. 1989 'Productivity, machinery and skills: Clothing manufacture in Britain and Germany', *National Institute Economic Review*, 128: 40–57.

Stengg, W. 2001, *The Textile and Clothing Industry in the EU: A Survey*. Brussels; European Commission DG-Enterprise.

Streeck, W. 1992, *Social Institutions and Economic Performance*. London: Sage.

—— and Thelen, K. 2005, 'Introduction: institutional change in advanced political economies', W. Streeck and K. Thelen (eds.), *Beyond Continuity*. Oxford: Oxford University Press, 1–39.

—— and Yamamura, K. 2003, 'Introduction: convergence or diversity? Stability and change in German and Japanese capitalism', K. Yamamura and W. Streeck (eds.), *The End of Diversity?* Ithaca: Cornell University Press, 1–50..

Sugur, N. and Sugur, S. 2005, 'Gender and work in Turkey: case study on women workers in the textile industry in Bursa', *Middle Eastern Studies*, 41, 2: 269–79.

Sum, N.-L. and Ngai, P. 2005, 'Globalization and paradoxes of ethical transnational production: code of conduct in a Chinese workplace', *Competition and Change*, 9, 2: 181–200.

Sural, N. 2005, 'Reorganization of working time and modalities of employment under the new Turkish Labour Act', *Middle Eastern Studies*, 41, 2: 249–68.

TCMA (Textile and Clothing Manufacturers' Association) 2003, *Turkish Clothing Industry Horizon 2010 Road Map: Global Targets and Policies*. Istanbul: TCMA.

—— 2005a, 'Turkish textiles and clothing industry. Set of powerpoint slides, presented in Milan, 15, September, obtained directly from TCMA, Istanbul.

—— 2005b, *Horizon 2010. Global Repositioning in Turkish Clothing Industry*. Istanbul: TCMA.

—— 2005c, The Turkish Clothing Industry Horizon 2010 Roadmap. Accessed on 28 July 2006 at www.tgds.org.tr

TCSG 2000, *A National Strategy for the UK Textile and Clothing Industry*. London: British Apparel and Textile Confederation, Textile and Clothing Strategy Group.

TEA (Turkish Exporters Assembly) 2006, 'The overview of Turkish economy and exports'. Set of powerpoint slides, received from TEA 16 May.

Teece, D. J., Pisano, G., and Shuen, A. 1997, 'Dynamic capabilities and strategic management', *Strategic Management Journal*, 18, 7: 509–33.

Textile Outlook International 2005, 'Trends in consumer behaviour and the global clothing market', *Textile Outlook International* July–August.

—— 2006, 'Trends in EU textile and clothing imports', *Textile Outlook International*, 124 (July–August): 61–123.

Thireau, I. and Linshan, H. 2003, 'The moral universe of aggrieved Chinese workers: workers' appeals to arbitration committees and letters and visits offices', *The China Journal*, 50 (July): 83–103.

Thompson, E. R. 2003, 'Technology transfer to China by Hong Kong's cross-border garment firms', *The Developing Economies*, 41, 1: 88–111.

Tokatli, N. 2007, 'Asymmetrical power relations and upgrading among suppliers of global clothing brands: Hugo Boss in Turkey', *Journal of Economic Geography*, 7: 67–92.

—— and Eldener, Y. B. 2004, 'Upgrading in the global clothing industry: the transformation of Boyner Holding', *Competition and Change*, 8, 2: 173–93.

—— and Kizilgun, O. 2004, 'Upgrading in the global clothing industry: Mavi Jeans and the transformation of a Turkish firm from full-package to brand-name manufacturing', *Economic Geography*, 80, 3: 221–40.

Trentmann, F. 2006, 'The modern genealogy of the consumer: meanings, identities and political synapses', J. Brewer and F. Trentmann (eds.), *Consuming Culture, Global Perspectives: Historical Trajectories, Transnational Exchanges*. Oxford: Berg, 71–94.

Trif, A. 2005, 'Collective bargaining practices in Eastern Europe: case study evidence from Romania', Max-Planck-Institut für Gesellschaftsforschung (MPIfG) Working Paper No. 05/9, October.

Tsang, D. 2007, 'TAL Apparel adds value to supply chain management', *South China Morning Post*, 26 November.

Turkey Sectorial Report for Fashion-Net Project 2004, presented at the II OECD Conference on SMEs, Istanbul, 3–5 June. Accessed on 25 July 2006 at www.insme.org

Turkish Business World 2006, Internet Edition, 13 March.

Turkishtime 2006, Accessed on 13 March, www.turkishtime.org

TUSIAD and YASED 2004, 'FDI Attractiveness of Turkey: a comparative analysis': Report prepared by TUSIAD and YASED, 1–15. Istanbul', February.

UNCTAD (United Nations Conference on Trade and Development) 2005, *TNCs and the Removal of Textiles and Clothing Quotas*. New York GUNCTAD.

United Nations Comtrade data accessed at http://unstats.un.org/unsd/comtrade).

US ITC (US International Trade Commission) 2004, *Textiles and Apparel: Assessment of the Competitiveness of Certain Foreign Suppliers to the US Market*. Washington, DC: US International Trade Commision. Publication 3671. Downloaded on 25 November 2004 from hotdocs.usitc.gov/pub3671/main.html

Volksbanken, Raiffeisenbanken 2003, *Branchen Spezial*, July, 32.

Voyvoda and Yeldan 2001, 'Patterns of productivity growth and the wage cycle in Turkish manufacturing', *International Review of Applied Economics*, 15, 4: 375–96.

Wallerstein, I. 1979, *The Capitalist World Economy*. Cambridge: Cambridge University Press.

Warren, C. 2003, 'Garment industry subcontracting and workers' rights'. Report of Women Working Worldwide Action Research in Asia and Europe. Manchester: Manchester Metropolitan University, 231–54.

WBF/GTZ 2006, *Romania 2006: Textile and Clothing Industry, Programm für Wirtschafts- und Beschäftigungsförderung (WBF) in Rumänien, Bundesministerium für Wirtschaftliche Zusammenarbeit und Entwicklung/Deutsche Gesellschaft für Technische Zusammenarbeit (GTZ)*. Bucharest: WBF/GTZ.

Weiss, L. (ed.) 2003, *States in the Global Economy*. Cambridge: Cambridge University Press.

Whitley, R. 1996, 'Business systems and global commodity chains: competing or complementary forms of economic organization?', *Competition and Change*, 1, 411–25.

—— 1999, *Divergent Capitalisms*. Oxford: Oxford University Press.

—— 2001, 'How and why are international firms different?', G. Morgan, Kristensen R. and Whittey (eds.), *The Multinational Firm*. Oxford: Oxford University Press.

—— 2005, 'Developing transnational organizational capabilities in multinational companies: institutional constraints on authority sharing and careers in six types of MNC', G. Morgan, R. Whitley and E. Moen (eds.), *Changing Capitalisms? Internationalization, Institutional Change, and Systems of Economic Organization*. Oxford: Oxford University Press, 235–76.

Wick, I. 2005, *Workers' Tool or PR Ploy? A Guide to Codes of International Labour Practice*, 4th revised edn. Bonn: Friedrich Ebert Stiftung and Siegburg: Südwind.

Williams, F. 2008, 'Poorest nations stand to be big losers', *Financial Times*, 31 July.

Williams, H. 1999, 'Mobile capital and transborder labor rights mobilization', *Politics and Society*, 27, 1: 139–66.

Williams, M., Kong, Y.-C., and Yan, S. 2002, 'Bonanza or mirage? Textiles and China's accession to the WTO', *Journal of World Trade*, 36, 3: 577–91.

Williams, P. 2005, 'Leveraging change in the working conditions of UK homeworkers', *Development in Practice*, 15, 3 and 4: 546–58.

Wood, S. 2001, 'Business, government, and patterns of labor market policy in Britain and the Federal Republic of Germany', P. Hall and D. Soskice (eds.), *Varieties of Capitalism: The Institutional Foundations of Comparative Advantage*. Oxford: Oxford University Press, 247–74.

World Bank 2006a, 'Data and statistics: Turkey statistics'. Accessed on 4 August 2008 at http://go.worldbank.org?KMLVYJ93MO

—— 2006b, 'End of MFA quotas: key issues and strategic options for Bangladesh readymade garment industry', Report No. 34964-BD, Poverty Reduction and Economic Management Sector Unit, South Asia Region, World Bank.

Wortmann, M. 2003, 'Structural change and globalisation of the German retail industry'. Discussion Paper SPIII 2003–202b. Social Science Research Centre, Berlin.

—— 2005, 'Coordination of value chains: the sourcing country perspective: characteristics of retailing and global sourcing strategies in Germany'. Paper presented at the workshop on 'Governance of Value Chains by Retailers'. Wissenschaftszentrum Berlin, 16–17 September.

Wrigley, N. and Lowe, M. 2002, *Reading Retail: A Geographical Perspective on Retailing and Consumption Spaces*. London: Arnold.

—— —— (eds.) *Retailing, Consumption and Capital: Towards the New Retail Geography*. London: Longman Group.

Wrona, T. 1999, *Globalisierung und Strategien der vertikalen Integration*. Wiesbaden: Gabler Verlag.

WTO 2005, 'International trade statistics 2005'. Accessed at http://www.wto.org/english/res_e/statis_e/its2005_e/its05_toc_e.htm

—— 2006, 'China: trade policy review', WT/TPR/S/161, WTO, Geneva.

—— undated, 'Textiles Monitoring Body (TMB)—the agreement on textiles and clothing. Accessed at http://www.wto.org/english/tratop_e/texti_e/texintro_e.htm

Xinhua Net 2008, 'More businesses shift from exports to home market', 29 February. Accessed at http://www.cnga.org.cn

Yamamura, K. and Streeck, W. (eds.) 2003, *The End of Diversity?* Ithaca: Cornell University Press.

Yang, Y. and Zhong, C. 1998, 'China's textile and clothing exports in a changing world economy', *The Developing Economies*, 36, 1: 3–23.

Yoruk, D. E. 2001, 'Patterns of industrial upgrading in the clothing industry in Poland and Romania', Working Paper No.19, School of Slavonic and East European Studies, University College London.

—— 2002, 'Effective integration to global production networks: knowledge acquisition and assimilation: the case of Braiconf S.A. in Romania', Working Paper No. 26, School of Slavonic and East European Studies, University College London and Sussex University, Brighton.

Zhang, Z., To, C., and Cao, N. 2004, 'How do industry clusters success [sic]: A case study in China's textiles and apparel industries', *Journal of Textile and Apparel Technology and Management*, 4, 2: 1–10.

Index

Page numbers in bold indicate references to figures/tables